THE BODHISAṂB
COMMENTARY

The publication of this book has been enabled by
a generous donation from Freda Chen.

THE BODHISAṂBHĀRA TREATISE COMMENTARY

The Early Indian Exegesis on Ārya Nāgārjuna's

TREATISE ON
THE PROVISIONS FOR ENLIGHTENMENT
(*The Bodhisaṃbhāra Śāstra*)

Commentary by Bhikshu Vaśitva
(*circa* 300–500 CE)

Translation and Notes by Bhikshu Dharmamitra

KALAVINKA PRESS
Seattle, Washington
WWW.KALAVINKAPRESS.ORG

Kalavinka Press
8603 39th Ave SW
Seattle, WA 98136 USA

WWW.KALAVINKAPRESS.ORG / WWW.KALAVINKA.ORG

Kalavinka Press is the publishing arm of the Kalavinka Dharma Association, a non-profit organized exclusively for religious educational purposes as allowed within the meaning of section 501(c)3 of the Internal Revenue Code. KDA was founded in 1990 and gained formal approval in 2004 by the United States Internal Revenue Service as a 501(c)3 non-profit organization to which donations are tax deductible.

Donations to KDA are accepted by mail and on the Kalavinka website where numerous free Dharma translations and excerpts from Kalavinka publications are available in digital format.

Edition: BsamVas-SA-0308-1.0.

ISBN: 978-1-935413-03-5
Library of Congress Control Number: 2009920871

PUBLISHER'S CATALOGING-IN-PUBLICATION DATA

Vaśitva, Bhikshu, *ca* 300–500.
  [Puti ziliang lun shu/ The Bodhisaṃbhāra Shastra
  Commentary. English translation.]
  The Bodhisaṃbhāra Treatise Commentary. The Early Indian
  Exegesis on Nagarjuna's Bodhisaṃbhāra Shastra.
  Translation by Bhikshu Dharmamitra. – 1st ed. – Seattle,
  WA: Kalavinka Press, 2009.

    p. ; cm.
    ISBN: 978-1-935413-03-5
    Includes: text outline; stanza directory; facing-page
    Chinese source text in both traditional and simplified
    scripts; notes.
    Other author: Nagarjuna, 2nd c.

  1. Bodhisattvas. 2. Spiritual life—Mahayana Buddhism. I.
  Nagarjuna. II. Title.

2009920871
0902

Cover and interior designed and composed by Bhikshu Dharmamitra.

Dedicated to the memory of the selfless and marvelous life of the
Venerable Dhyāna Master Hsuan Hua, the Weiyang Ch'an Patriarch
and the very personification of the Bodhisattva Path.

Dhyāna Master Hsuan Hua

宣化禪師

1918–1995

Acknowledgments

The accuracy and readability of of these first ten books of translations have been significantly improved with the aid of extensive corrections, preview comments, and editorial suggestions generously contributed by Bhikkhu Bodhi, Jon Babcock, Timothy J. Lenz, Upasaka Feng Ling, Upāsaka Guo Ke, Upāsikā Min Li, and Richard Robinson. Additional valuable editorial suggestions and corrections were offered by Bhikshu Huifeng and Bruce Munson.

The publication of the initial set of ten translation volumes has been assisted by substantial donations to the Kalavinka Dharma Association by Bill and Peggy Brevoort, Freda Chen, David Fox, Upāsaka Guo Ke, Chenping and Luther Liu, Sunny Lou, Jimi Neal, and "Leo L." (*Camellia sinensis folium*). Additional donations were offered by Doug Adams, Diane Hodgman, Bhikshu Huifeng, Joel and Amy Lupro, Richard Robinson, Ching Smith, and Sally and Ian Timm.

Were it not for the ongoing material support provided by my late guru's Dharma Realm Buddhist Association and the serene translation studio provided by Seattle's Bodhi Dhamma Center, creation of this translation would have been immensely more difficult.

Most importantly, it would have been impossible for me to produce this translation without the Dharma teachings provided by my late guru, the Weiyang Ch'an Patriarch, Dharma teacher, and exegete, the Venerable Master Hsuan Hua.

Citation and Romanization Protocols

Kalavinka Press *Taisho* citation style adds text numbers after volume numbers and before page numbers to assist rapid CBETA digital searches.

Romanization, where used, is Pinyin with the exception of names and terms already well-recognized in Wade-Giles.

The Chinese Text

This translation is supplemented by inclusion of Chinese source text on verso pages in both traditional and simplified scripts. Taisho-supplied variant readings from other editions are presented as Chinese endnotes.

This Chinese text and its variant readings are from the April, 2004 version of the Chinese Buddhist Electronic Text Association's digital edition of the Taisho compilation of the Buddhist canon.

Those following the translation in the Chinese should be aware that Taisho scripture punctuation is not traceable to original editions, is often erroneous and misleading, and is probably best ignored altogether. (In any case, accurate reading of Classical Chinese does not require any punctuation at all.)

Contents

Directory by Verse to Commentary Discussions

(One-line verse synopses and section titles composed by the translator.)

INTRODUCTION

General Introductory Notes on This Text

Ārya Nāgārjuna's *Treatise on the Provisions for Enlightenment* (*Bodhi-saṃbhāra Śāstra*) together with its commentary by the Indian Bhikshu Vaśitva was translated into Chinese by the South Indian Tripiṭaka Master Dharmagupta in or around 609 CE in China's Sui Dynasty Capital. The two works are presented in interwoven format in the six-fascicle edition preserved in the Taisho edition of the Chinese Tripiṭaka (T32.1660.517b–41b). It is this sole surviving edition with its commentary that I have translated here in its entirety.

On the Distinctive Nature of the *Bodhisaṃbhāra Treatise*

The contents of this treatise are devoted to illuminating the most important motivations, principles, and practices essential to both lay and monastic practitioners of the Bodhisattva Path. Although these topics are treated elsewhere in Nāgārjuna's works, most notably in the *Ratnāvalī*, the *Daśabhūmika Vibhāṣā*, and the *Mahāprajñāpāramitā Upadeśa*, they are nowhere given such a closely-focused, potent, and essentially complete treatment as we find in this short treatise comprised of only 168 *ślokas*.

Although the special qualities of this work are numerous, I find that the most salient distinguishing features of the *Bodhisaṃbhāra Treatise* are Ārya Nāgārjuna's relatively brief but vividly clear depiction of the long-term multi-lifetime vision of the Bodhisattva Path, his delineation of the teaching stances and strategies essential to successful bodhisattva instruction of the various types of people, and his making of such powerful distinctions between the mind states cultivated by bodhisattvas as distinct from those considered most important in pursuing individual-liberation paths.

On the Commentary

The commentary by the early Indian Bhikshu Vaśitva (about whom nothing is known) is invaluable in unfolding the meaning of the treatise, this partly because the treatise verses are extremely terse, and partly because the ideas in the treatise require in-depth discussion to make their full meaning adequately apparent even to learned students of Buddhist doctrine and practice. Bhikshu Vaśitva's commentary is particularly skillful in demonstrating the deeper meaning of the more abstruse concepts and phrasings in Nāgārjuna's treatise. An especially fine contribution provided by the commentary is the extensive discussion of the ten pāramitās.

On Authorship

Ārya Nāgārjuna's authorship of the *Bodhisaṃbhāra Treatise* is generally well-acknowledged. We find it cited directly and indirectly in other works by Nāgārjuna. (The *Daśabhūmika Vibhāṣā* quotes from it extensively.) To our knowledge, neither the text nor the commentary are extant in either Sanskrit or Tibetan. Thus, as far as we know, the only surviving edition is the Chinese text preserved in the Taisho Tripiṭaka.

I should note here the basis for my choice of the Sanskrit reconstruction for the name of the Indian commentary author as "Bhikshu Vaśitva." This reconstruction was largely driven by the Chinese terminology choices made by Dharmagupta, the translator of the original Sanskrit edition. In the Indian commentary, there is a standard Mahāyāna list of ten types of "sovereign mastery" (*vaśitā*) translated by Dharmagupta as *zizai* (自在). The same two-character compound is used in translating the name of the commentary author, "Bhikshu Zizai" (比丘自在).

Additionally, the commentary author refers to himself by name in the body of the commentary itself (i.e., not just in a colophon). In this instance as well, we have Dharmagupta selecting the same Chinese characters to translate the commentary author's name as he used to translate the ten types of sovereign mastery (*vaśitā*). This more or less eliminates the possibility that the colophon's attribution to this Indian bhikshu might have simply been added later by individuals having no genuine basis for making that attribution.

Of course, it could go without saying that early translators often rendered multiple Sanskrit antecedents with a single Chinese term. I doubt, however, that the current circumstance involves multiple Sanskrit antecedents. In any case, the conjecture of "Īśvara" proposed by at least one academic, given its obvious Hindu connotation, seems to me to be extremely implausible as a name choice for a Buddhist monk. The provisional reconstruction as "Vaśitva" at least has the advantage of multiple evidentiary bases contained within the subject text itself.

On the Translation of This Text

There have been no previous attempts to produce a genuinely literal English translation of Nāgārjuna's *Bodhisaṃbhāra Treatise* of which I am aware.[1] As for previous translations of the commentary by Bhikshu Vaśitva, I don't believe this work has ever been rendered into any Western or Asian language. This should not be too surprising given that Dharmagupta's 609 CE Chinese text is extraordinarily and deceptively challenging in places. The difficulty of this text is due to extreme terseness in the *ślokas* and due to a good deal of surface inscrutability in the Classical Chinese style adopted by this South Indian translator monk.

As regards stylistic issues in this translation, specialists may notice my tendency to sometimes prefer translating the sense of both component glyphs in the Chinese binomes used by Dharmagupta to render what were probably single Sanskrit antecedent terms. This is deliberate, arising out of a desire to produce a text reflecting the meaning of the work as it would have presented to a Chinese Buddhist reader of the translated Sanskrit. I find this approach preferable to basing the translation largely on merely conjectural reconstructions of Sanskrit antecedent terms. Where the Sanskrit antecedents for the binomes in question are already obvious and well-established, then I tend more often to translate according to the known Sanskrit term. It is hoped that this has allowed my "binomial proliferation" of concepts to be reduced to a tolerable level.

On the Structure and Contents of the English Edition

As regards the contents of this English edition I have produced, there are a few points requiring explanation. First, because even Vaśitva's fine commentary seemed at points to be inadequate in laying out the intentions and implications of the work (this largely because it assumes a familiarity with the tradition not possessed by most Western readers), I felt compelled at some points to add a few additional explanatory paragraphs in endnotes which more usually would be reserved for notations recording emendations and other purely text-related issues.

To facilitate the reader's study of the text, I have inserted a table of contents, single-line synopses of each *śloka*, and also section headings flagging the main topics treated in the commentary. The reader should realize that the text as preserved in the Canon has no such outlining or subtitling. (Apparently such unadorned and

seamless "interweaving" of text and commentary was more-or-less
standard with palm-leaf manuscripts.)

I don't doubt that a closer and more reflective study of the text
may suggest numerous refinements in my rough outline's architec-
ture and in its implicit doctrinal judgments. Still, given the com-
plexity of Nāgārjuna's text and Vaśitva's commentary, I felt it was
better to at least provide the reader some sort of "signpost" outlining, even if imperfect, rather than to simply present two hundred
pages of unbroken and moderately abstruse translation.

Contents of Part One

Part One consists of a translation of all of Nāgārjuna's *ślokas*, for-
matted with their Chinese source-text verses in both traditional and
simplified scripts on the corresponding verso page. The inclusion
of both versions of Chinese script is intended to facilitate study of
Nāgārjuna's text by both Western Dharma students and bi-lingual
native readers of Chinese. In the case of the latter, the ready avail-
ability of both original text and English translation is often very
helpful in comprehending the unfamiliar technical terminology,
abstruse concepts, and refractory terseness typical of early sino-
Buddhist Classical Chinese texts.

As for the rationale in presenting a separate compilation of the
stanzas of the *Bodhisaṃbhāra Treatise* text itself, this is done because
no such edition is otherwise available in any language. To my mind,
a clean commentary-free presentation of this sort is both convenient
and necessary to facilitate easy access to the uninterrupted flow of
Nāgārjuna's work.

Contents of Part Two

Part Two consists of a repetition of each *śloka* followed by the
appropriate section of Bhikshu Vaśitva's commentary. Aside from
the *śloka* numbering and my one-line synopsis headings and topic
headings, this section reflects the translation of the Taisho text with
nothing added, nothing removed, and no alterations in sequence.
I emphasize this only because the closely interwoven format of
the text and its commentary in its Chinese edition is by no means
unequivocally straightforward in indicating which parts represent
Nāgārjuna's work and which parts represent Bhikshu Vaśitva's commentary. Indeed, it does require a reasonably attentive study of the
work to ascertain which is which. Even with a good deal of focus on

this problem, it is still possible that I may have mistakenly included a *śloka* or two merely quoted by Nāgārjuna from other texts (such as *The Ten Grounds Sutra*) as being integral to the *Bodhisaṃbhāra Treatise* text. The unbroken serial format of *Part Two* allows the reader to make his own judgment on this matter without being unduly influenced by the editorial choices inherent in the stanzas-only version contained in *Part One*.

In Summary

In Ārya Nāgārjuna's *Bodhisaṃbhāra Treatise*, we have a rare and beautiful Dharma jewel reflecting the essence of a bodhisattva's motivation, wisdom, skillful means, and practice. In Bhikshu Vaśitva's commentary, we have a fine setting for that jewel by which its facets are clearly displayed in their best light. I feel fortunate to have encountered these texts in personal circumstances conducive to comprehending at least their surface meanings and hope that this translation of the *Bodhisaṃbhāra Treatise* text and commentary will be useful to those studying the works of Nāgārjuna as guides to correct practice of the Bodhisattva Path.

It would be unrealistic for me to suppose that this translation might not benefit from further revisions. Suggestions for improvements from clergy, scholars, or Dharma students may be forwarded via website email and will certainly be very much appreciated.

Bhikshu Dharmamitra,
Spring, 2008

PART ONE:

THE TREATISE ON THE PROVISIONS FOR ENLIGHTENMENT

Ārya Nāgārjuna's
BODHISAṂBHĀRA TREATISE
(*Bodhisaṃbhāra Śāstra*)

菩提资粮论	菩提資糧論
圣者龙树本 比丘自在释	聖者龍樹本 比丘自在釋
大隋南印度三藏达磨笈多译	大隋南印度三藏達磨笈多譯

001
今于诸佛所合掌而顶敬
我当如教说佛菩提资粮

001
今於諸佛所合掌而頂敬
我當如教說佛菩提資糧

002
何能说无阙菩提诸资粮
唯独有诸佛别得无边觉

002
何能說無闕菩提諸資糧
唯獨有諸佛別得無邊覺

003
佛体无边德觉资粮为根
是故觉资粮亦无有边际

003
佛體無邊德覺資糧為根
是故覺資糧亦無有邊際

004
当说彼少分敬礼佛菩萨
是诸菩萨等次佛应供养

004
當說彼少分敬禮佛菩薩
是諸菩薩等次佛應供養

005
既为菩萨母亦为诸佛母
般若波罗蜜是觉初资粮

005
既為菩薩母亦為諸佛母
般若波羅蜜是覺初資糧

简體字　　　　　　　　繁体字

THE TREATISE ON
THE PROVISIONS FOR ENLIGHTENMENT

The Bodhisaṃbhāra Śāstra
By Ārya Nāgārjuna

**Translated into Chinese by the Great Sui Dynasty's
South Indian Tripiṭaka Master Dharmagupta (550?–619 CE)**

001

Now, in the presence of all the Buddhas,
With palms pressed together, I bow down my head in reverence.
I shall explain here in accordance with the teachings
The provisions essential for the bodhi of the Buddhas.

002

How would one be able to describe without omission
All of the provisions for the realization of bodhi?
This could only be accomplished by the Buddhas themselves,
For they, exclusively, have realized the boundless enlightenment.

003

The boundless qualities of a buddha's body
Are rooted in the provisions essential to enlightenment.
Therefore the provisions for enlightenment
Themselves have no bounds.

004

I shall then explain but a lesser portion of them.
I render reverence to the Buddhas and the Bodhisattvas.
It is all such bodhisattvas as these
To whom one should next make offerings, after the Buddhas.

005

Since it is the mother of the Bodhisattvas,
It is also the mother of the Buddhas:
The prajñāpāramitā
Is foremost among the provisions essential for enlightenment.

006

施戒忍进定及此五之馀
皆由智度故波罗蜜所摄

007

此六波罗蜜总菩提资粮
犹如虚空中尽摄于诸物

008

复有馀师意诸觉资粮者
实舍及寂智四处之所摄

009

大悲彻骨髓为诸众生依
如父于一子慈则遍一切

010

若念佛功德及闻佛神变
爱喜而受净此名为大喜

011

菩萨于众生不应得舍弃
当随力所堪一切时摄受

012

菩萨从初时应随堪能力
方便化众生令入于大乘

006

施戒忍進定及此五之餘
皆由智度故波羅蜜所攝

007

此六波羅蜜總菩提資糧
猶如虛空中盡攝於諸物

008

復有餘師意諸覺資糧者
實捨及寂智四處之所攝

009

大悲徹骨髓為諸眾生依
如父於一子慈則遍一切

010

若念佛功德及聞佛神變
愛喜而受淨此名為大喜

011

菩薩於眾生不應得捨棄
當隨力所堪一切時攝受

012

菩薩從初時應隨堪能力
方便化眾生令入於大乘

简體字　　　　　　　　繁体字

006

Because giving, moral virtue, patience, vigor, meditation,
And the others following from these five
All arise from the perfection of wisdom,
They are included within the pāramitās.

007

These six pāramitās
Encompass the provisions essential for bodhi,
They are comparable in this to empty space
Which entirely envelopes all things.

008

There is also the idea proposed by another master
That, as for the provisions for enlightenment,
Truth, relinquishment, cessation, and wisdom—
These four bases subsume them all.

009

The great compassion penetrates to the marrow of one's bones.
Thus one serves as a refuge for every being.
With a feeling as strong as a father's regard for his only son,
One's kindness extends universally to all beings.

010

If one brings to mind the qualities of a buddha
Or hears of a buddha's spiritual transformations,
One becomes purified through one's admiration and joyfulness.
This is what is meant by the great sympathetic joy.

011

In his relations with beings, the bodhisattva
Should not allow himself to forsake them.
As befits the abilities determined by his powers,
He should always strive to draw them in.

012

From the very beginning, the bodhisattva
Should accord with the power of his abilities
And use skillful means to instruct beings,
Causing them to enter the Great Vehicle.

013

化恒沙众生令得罗汉果
化一入大乘此福德为上

014

教以声闻乘及独觉乘者
以彼少力故不堪大乘化

015

声闻独觉乘及以大乘中
不堪受化者应置于福处

016

若人不堪受天及解脱化
便以现世利如力应当摄

017

菩萨于众生无缘能教化
当起大慈悲不应便弃舍

018

施摄及说法复听闻说法
亦行利他事此为摄方便

019

所作益众生不倦不放逸
起愿为菩提利世即自利

013

化恒沙眾生令得羅漢果
化一入大乘此福德為上

014

教以聲聞乘及獨覺乘者
以彼少力故不堪大乘化

015

聲聞獨覺乘及以大乘中
不堪受化者應置於福處

016

若人不堪受天及解脫化
便以現世利如力應當攝

017

菩薩於眾生無緣能教化
當起大慈悲不應便棄捨

018

施攝及說法復聽聞說法
亦行利他事此為攝方便

019

所作益眾生不倦不放逸
起願為菩提利世即自利

簡體字　　　　　　繁体字

013

Even if one taught beings as numerous as the Ganges' sands
So that they were caused to gain the fruit of arhatship,
Still, by instructing but a single person to enter the Great Vehicle,
One would generate merit superior to that.

014

Instructing through resort to the Śrāvaka Vehicle
Or through resort to the Pratyekabuddha Vehicle
Is undertaken where, on account of lesser abilities,
Beings are unable to accept instruction in the Great Vehicle.

015

Where even when relying on Śrāvaka or Pratyekabuddha Vehicles
In addition to the Great Vehicle teachings,
There are those who still cannot accept any such instruction,
One should strive to establish them in merit-creating situations.

016

If there be persons unable to accept
Instruction conducing either to the heavens or to liberation,
Favor them through bestowing present-life benefits.
Then, as befits one's powers, one should draw them in.

017

Where, with regard to particular beings, a bodhisattva
Has no conditions through which to instruct them,
He should draw forth the great kindness and compassion
And should refrain from abandoning them.

018

Drawing them in through giving, through explaining Dharma,
Through listening to them discuss the Dharma,
Or through endeavors beneficial to them—
These are skillful means through which to attract them.

019

In that which is done for the benefit of beings,
Do not succumb to either weariness or negligence.
Bring forth vows for the sake of realizing bodhi.
Benefiting the world is just benefiting self.

简體字	繁体字
020	020
入甚深法界灭离于分别	入甚深法界滅離於分別
悉无有功用诸处自然舍	悉無有功用諸處自然捨
021	021
利名赞乐等四处皆不着	利名讚樂等四處皆不著
反上亦无碍此等名为舍	反上亦無礙此等名為捨
022	022
菩萨为菩提乃至未不退	菩薩為菩提乃至未不退
譬如燃头衣应作是勤行	譬如燃頭衣應作是勤行
023	023
然彼诸菩萨为求菩提时	然彼諸菩薩為求菩提時
精进不应息以荷重担故	精進不應息以荷重擔故
024	024
未生大悲忍虽得不退转	未生大悲忍雖得不退轉
菩萨犹有死以起放逸故	菩薩猶有死以起放逸故
025	025
声闻独觉地若入便为死	聲聞獨覺地若入便為死
以断于菩萨诸所解知根	以斷於菩薩諸所解知根
026	026
假使堕泥犁菩萨不生怖	假使墮泥犁菩薩不生怖
声闻独觉地便为大恐怖	聲聞獨覺地便為大恐怖

简體字　　　　　　繁体字

020

Entering the extremely profound Dharma-realm,
One extinguishes mental discriminations.
As they are devoid of any useful function,
In all contexts, one naturally abides in equanimity.

021

Personal gain, reputation, praise, and happiness—
One refrains from attachment to any of these four points.
Nor do their opposites present any sort of obstacle.
This is the sort of conduct comprising equanimity.

022

So long as he has not yet gained irreversibility,
In the bodhisattva's striving for bodhi,
He should be as intensely diligent in practice
As someone whose turban has caught on fire.

023

Thus it is that those bodhisattvas,
When striving for the realization of bodhi,
Should not rest in their practice of vigor,
For they have shouldered such a heavy burden.

024

Until one develops the great compassion and the patiences,
Even though he may have gained irreversibility,
The bodhisattva is still subject to a form of "dying"
Occurring through the arising of negligence.

025

The grounds of the Śrāvakas or the Pratyekabuddhas,
If entered, constitute "death" for him
Because he would thereby sever the roots
Of the bodhisattva's understanding and awareness.

026

At the prospect of falling into the hell-realms,
The bodhisattva would not be struck with fright.
The grounds of the Śrāvakas and the Pratyekabuddhas
Do provoke great terror in him.

027
非堕泥犁中毕竟障菩提
声闻独觉地则为毕竟障

028
如说爱寿人怖畏于斩首
声闻独觉地应作如是怖

029
不生亦不灭非不生不灭
非俱不俱说空不空亦尔

030
随何所有法于中观不动
彼是无生忍断诸分别故

031
既获此忍已即时得授记
汝必当作佛便得不退转

032
已住不动诸菩萨得于法尔
不退智
彼智二乘不能转是故独得
不退名

033
菩萨乃至得诸佛现前住
牢固三摩提不应起放逸

简體字

027
非墮泥犁中畢竟障菩提
聲聞獨覺地則為畢竟障

028
如說愛壽人怖畏於斬首
聲聞獨覺地應作如是怖

029
不生亦不滅非不生不滅
非俱不俱說空不空亦爾

030
隨何所有法於中觀不動
彼是無生忍斷諸分別故

031
既獲此忍已即時得授記
汝必當作佛便得不退轉

032
已住不動諸菩薩得於法爾
不退智
彼智二乘不能轉是故獨得
不退名

033
菩薩乃至得諸佛現前住
牢固三摩提不應起放逸

繁体字

027

It is not the case that falling into the hell realms
Would create an ultimate obstacle to bodhi.
If one fell onto the grounds of the Śrāvakas or Pratyekabuddhas,
That would create an ultimate obstacle.

028

Just as is said of one who loves long life
That he is frightened at the prospect of being beheaded,
So too the grounds of the Śrāvakas and Pratyekabuddhas
Should provoke in one this very sort of fear.

029

As for "not produced and not destroyed,"
And "neither unproduced nor undestroyed,"
One denies assertions of "both" and "neither."
So too in cases involving "emptiness" and "non-emptiness."

030

No matter which "existent" dharma one encounters,
One persists therein in the contemplation, remaining unmoving.
That is the "unproduced-dharmas patience."
It is based on the severance of all mental discriminations.

031

Once one gains this patience,
One immediately receives the prediction:
"You will definitely become a buddha."
It is then that one achieves "irreversibility."

032

Those bodhisattvas already dwelling at the stage of immovability
Have gained irreversible wisdom cognizing all dharmas' reality.
As their wisdom cannot be turned back by two-vehicles adherents,
It is only at this point that they are designated as "irreversible."

033

Until the bodhisattva has gained
The solid samādhis
On the ground of all Buddhas' "direct presence,"
He should not allow any negligence to arise.

034
诸佛现前住牢固三摩提
此为菩萨父大悲忍为母

035
智度以为母方便为父者
以生及持故说菩萨父母

036
少少积聚福不能得菩提
百须弥量福聚胜乃能得

037
虽作小福德此亦有方便
于诸众生所应悉起攀缘

038
我有诸动作常为利众生
如是等心行谁能量其福

039
不爱自亲属及与身命财
不贪乐自在梵世及馀天

040
亦不贪涅盘为于众生故
此唯念众生其福谁能量

简體字

034
諸佛現前住牢固三摩提
此為菩薩父大悲忍為母

035
智度以為母方便為父者
以生及持故說菩薩父母

036
少少積聚福不能得菩提
百須彌量福聚勝乃能得

037
雖作小福德此亦有方便
於諸眾生所應悉起攀緣

038
我有諸動作常為利眾生
如是等心行誰能量其福

039
不愛自親屬及與身命財
不貪樂自在梵世及餘天

040
亦不貪涅槃為於眾生故
此唯念眾生其福誰能量

繁体字

034

The solid samādhis
On the ground of all Buddhas' "direct presence"
Serve for the bodhisattva as his father,
Whereas the great compassion and patiences serve as his mother.

035

As for the perfection of wisdom being his mother
And skillful means being his father,
It is because the one gives him birth and the other supports him
That they are said to be the bodhisattva's father and mother.

036

With but a lesser accumulation of merit
One remains unable to realize bodhi.
Only by collecting merit more massive than a hundred Sumerus
Can one succeed in achieving that realization.

037

Although one may perform but a minor meritorious deed,
Even in this, one possesses a skillful means:
Taking the sphere of "all beings" as the object,
One should generate a mental transformation of the conditions.

038

Where one reflects: "May whatever actions I undertake
Always be done for the welfare of beings,"
Who could measure the merit of he
Whose mental actions are of this sort?

039

Where one isn't constrained by fondness for relatives, retinue,
Body, life, or wealth,
Where one isn't held back by desiring pleasure in Iśvara's heavens,
Brahma-world heavens, or any other heavens,

040

Where one isn't constrained even by coveting nirvāṇa,
Where one's actions are done for the sake of other beings,
And where in all this, one thinks only of the welfare of beings,
Who then could measure the vastness of his merit?

041

无依护世间救护其苦恼
起如是心行其福谁能量

042

智度习相应如搆牛乳顷
一月复多月其福谁能量

043

佛所赞深经自诵亦教他
及为分别说是名福德聚

044

令无量众生发心为菩提
福藏更增胜当得不动地

045

随转佛所转最胜之法轮
寂灭诸恶刺是菩萨福藏

046

为利乐众生忍地狱大苦
何况馀小苦菩提在右手

047

起作不自为唯利乐众生
皆由大悲故菩提在右手

041

無依護世間救護其苦惱
起如是心行其福誰能量

042

智度習相應如搆牛乳頃
一月復多月其福誰能量

043

佛所讚深經自誦亦教他
及為分別說是名福德聚

044

令無量眾生發心為菩提
福藏更增勝當得不動地

045

隨轉佛所轉最勝之法輪
寂滅諸惡刺是菩薩福藏

046

為利樂眾生忍地獄大苦
何況餘小苦菩提在右手

047

起作不自為唯利樂眾生
皆由大悲故菩提在右手

簡體字   繁体字

041

When for those of the world without refuge or protection,
He rescues and protects them from their bitter afflictions—
When he raises forth such thoughts and actions as these,
Who could possibly measure his merit?

042

It would be so even in according with the perfection of wisdom
For only the moment of tugging forth a stream of cow's milk.
If one acted thus for a month or for many more months,
Who could possibly measure his merit?

043

Where one recites to himself or teaches to others
Those profound sutras praised by the Buddhas—
Also, where one interprets and explains them for others—
These are the bases of an accumulation of merit.

044

Through influencing countless beings
To generate the bodhi resolve,
One's treasury of merit increases yet more
And one becomes bound to gain "the ground of immovability."

045

Where one follows in turning what the Buddha turned,
The wheel of the supreme Dharma,
Thus clearing away all of the "noxious thorns,"
This creates the bodhisattva's treasury of merit.

046

Where, to benefit beings and make them happy,
One would endure even the sufferings of the great hells,
How much the more the other lesser sufferings,
It is as if bodhi lay in the palm of one's own right hand.

047

Where whatever one does, it is not for one's self,
But solely to benefit beings and make them happy—
Because this all arises from the great compassion,
It is as if bodhi lay in the palm of one's own right hand.

简體字	繁体字
048 智慧离戏论精进离懈怠 舍施离悭惜菩提在右手	**048** 智慧離戲論精進離懈怠 捨施離慳惜菩提在右手
049 无依无觉定圆满无杂戒 无所从生忍菩提在右手	**049** 無依無覺定圓滿無雜戒 無所從生忍菩提在右手
050 现在十方住所有诸正觉 我悉在彼前陈说我不善	**050** 現在十方住所有諸正覺 我悉在彼前陳說我不善
051 于彼十方界若佛得菩提 而不演说法我请转法轮	**051** 於彼十方界若佛得菩提 而不演說法我請轉法輪
052 现在十方界所有诸正觉 若欲舍命行顶礼劝请住	**052** 現在十方界所有諸正覺 若欲捨命行頂禮勸請住
053 若诸众生等从于身口意 所生施戒福及以思惟修	**053** 若諸眾生等從於身口意 所生施戒福及以思惟修
054 圣人及凡夫过现未来世 所有积聚福我皆生随喜	**054** 聖人及凡夫過現未來世 所有積聚福我皆生隨喜

048

Where wisdom is such that one abandons frivolous discourse,
Where vigor is such that one abandons indolence,
And where giving is such that one abandons miserliness,
It is as if bodhi lay in the palm of one's own right hand.

049

Where meditation is such that one is free of reliances or ideation,
Where morality is such that its practice is perfect and unmixed,
And where patience is such that one realizes non-production,
It is as if bodhi lay in the palm of one's own right hand.

050

In the abodes of all who have gained the right enlightenment,
Now abiding throughout the ten directions,
I appear there in the presence of them all,
And completely lay forth all my unwholesome deeds.

051

Where there are buddhas who have realized bodhi
In those realms throughout the ten directions,
But they have not yet proclaimed the Dharma,
I entreat them to turn the Dharma wheel.

052

Wherever there are those possessing the right enlightenment
Abiding in the present era in the ten directions' realms,
But now on the verge of relinquishing their lives and actions,
I bow down my head in reverence, beseeching them to remain.

053

Wherever there may be any beings
Who, by acts of body, mouth, or mind,
Have created any merit through giving, moral virtue,
And so forth, including through cultivation of meditation—

054

No matter whether they be āryas or common persons—
And no matter whether its creation is past, present, or future—
I am moved to rejoice
In all of that accumulated merit.

简體字	繁体字
055	055
若我所有福悉以为一抟	若我所有福悉以為一搏
迴与诸众生为令得正觉	迴與諸眾生為令得正覺
056	056
我如是悔过劝请随喜福	我如是悔過勸請隨喜福
及迴向菩提当知如诸佛	及迴向菩提當知如諸佛
057	057
说悔我罪恶请佛随喜福	說悔我罪惡請佛隨喜福
及迴向菩提如最胜所说	及迴向菩提如最勝所說
058	058
右膝轮着地一髀整上衣	右膝輪著地一髀整上衣
昼夜各三时合掌如是作	晝夜各三時合掌如是作
059	059
一时所作福若有形色者	一時所作福若有形色者
恒沙数大千亦不能容受	恒沙數大千亦不能容受
060	060
彼初发心已于诸小菩萨	彼初發心已於諸小菩薩
当起尊重爱犹如师父母	當起尊重愛猶如師父母
061	061
菩萨虽有过犹尚不应说	菩薩雖有過猶尚不應說
何况无实事唯应如实赞	何況無實事唯應如實讚

简體字   繁体字

055

If all of the merit I have created
Could be formed into a single ball,
I would bestow it on all beings through dedicating it
To causing them to gain the right enlightenment.

056

As for these actions I undertake in repenting transgressions,
In entreating and beseeching, in rejoicing in others' merit,
And so on, including in dedicating all merit to realizing bodhi—
One should realize they accord with all buddhas' own practices.

057

These acts of confession and repentance of my bad karmic deeds,
Of entreating the Buddhas, of rejoicing in others' merit,
And so on, including dedicating all merit to realizing bodhi—
These all accord with teachings set forth by the Victorious One.

058

Kneeling down with the right knee touching the ground
And the upper robe arranged to bare one shoulder,
Three times each day and three times each night,
Press the palms together and proceed in this manner.

059

The merit created in even a single instance of doing this,
If manifest in material form, would be so immense
That even a Ganges' sands of great chiliocosms
Would still be unable to contain it.

060

Having brought forth the initial resolve,
In relations with minor bodhisattvas,
One should bring forth for them veneration and cherishing
Comparable to that felt for the Guru and parents.

061

Although a bodhisattva may have committed transgressions,
One should still not speak about them,
How much the less so where there is no truth to the matter.
One should utter praises only where they are grounded in truth.

简體字	繁体字
062 若人愿作佛欲使不退转 示现及炽盛亦令生喜悦	062 若人願作佛欲使不退轉 示現及熾盛亦令生喜悅
063 未解甚深经勿言非佛说 若作如是言受最苦恶报	063 未解甚深經勿言非佛說 若作如是言受最苦惡報
064 无间等诸罪悉以为一抟 比前二种罪分数不能及	064 無間等諸罪悉以為一搏 比前二種罪分數不能及
065 于三解脱门应当善修习 初空次无相第三是无愿	065 於三解脫門應當善修習 初空次無相第三是無願
066 无自性故空已空何作相 诸相既寂灭智者何所愿	066 無自性故空已空何作相 諸相既寂滅智者何所願
067 于此修念时趣近涅盘道 勿念非佛体于彼莫放逸	067 於此修念時趣近涅槃道 勿念非佛體於彼莫放逸
068 我于涅盘中不应即作证 当发如是心应成熟智度	068 我於涅槃中不應即作證 當發如是心應成熟智度

062

Where someone has vowed to become a buddha
And one wishes to prevent his retreat from that resolve,
Reveal the way with such clarity he brims with intense vigor,
And cause him to be filled with delight.

063

Where one hasn't yet understood extremely profound scriptures,
One must not claim they were not spoken by a buddha.
If one makes statements of this sort,
One suffers the most bitter and horrible of karmic retributions.

064

If the karmic offenses generating "non-intermittent" retributions
Were all put together to form a single ball
And were compared to one formed from the above two offenses,
They would not amount to even the smallest fraction thereof.

065

One should skillfully cultivate
The three gates to liberation:
The first is emptiness, the next is signlessness,
And the third is wishlessness.

066

Because they have no self-existent nature, phenomena are empty.
If already empty, how could one establish any characteristic signs?
Since all characteristic signs are themselves in a state of cessation,
What could there be in them that the wise might wish for?

067

When cultivating the mindful awareness of these,
One draws close to those paths leading into nirvāṇa.
Do not bear in mind anything not resulting in a buddha's body
And, in that matter, one must not allow any negligence.

068

"In this matter of nirvāṇa,
I must not immediately invoke its realization."
One should initiate this sort of resolve,
For one must succeed in ripening the perfection of wisdom.

069

如射师放箭各各转相射
相持不令堕大菩萨亦尔

070

解脱门空中善放于心箭
巧便箭续持不令堕涅盘

071

我不舍众生为利众生故
先起如是意次后习相应

072

有着众生等久夜及现行
颠倒与诸相皆以痴迷故

073

着相颠倒者说法为断除
先发如是心次后习相应

074

菩萨利众生而不见众生
此亦最难事希有不可思

075

虽入正定位习应解脱门
未满本愿故不证于涅盘

069

如射師放箭各各轉相射
相持不令墮大菩薩亦爾

070

解脫門空中善放於心箭
巧便箭續持不令墮涅槃

071

我不捨眾生為利眾生故
先起如是意次後習相應

072

有著眾生等久夜及現行
顛倒與諸相皆以癡迷故

073

著相顛倒者說法為斷除
先發如是心次後習相應

074

菩薩利眾生而不見眾生
此亦最難事希有不可思

075

雖入正定位習應解脫門
未滿本願故不證於涅槃

简體字　　　　　　　　　繁体字

069

Just as an archer might shoot his arrows upwards,
Causing each in succession to strike the one before,
Each holding up the other so none are allowed to fall—
Just so it is with the great bodhisattva.

070

Into the emptiness of the gates to liberation,
He skillfully releases the arrows of the mind.
Through artful skillful means, arrows are continuously held aloft,
So none are allowed to fall back down into nirvāṇa.

071

"I shall not forsake beings,
But rather shall continue on for the sake of benefiting beings."
One first initiates this very sort of intention,
And thenceforth ensures that his practice corresponds thereto.

072

There are beings who have become inured to attachment
Throughout time's long night and in present actions as well.
Their coursing in inverted views regarding characteristic signs
Is in every case due to confusion wrought by delusion.

073

For those attached to marks and holding inverted views,
One explains the Dharma so such errors might be eliminated.
One first generates this very sort of resolve,
And thenceforth ensures that his practice corresponds thereto.

074

The bodhisattva benefits beings
And yet does not perceive the existence of any being.
This in itself is the most difficult of all endeavors
And is such a rarity as to be inconceivable.

075

Although one may have entered "the right and definite position,"
And one's practice may accord with the gates to liberation,
Because one has not yet fulfilled one's original vows,
One refrains from proceeding to the realization of nirvāṇa.

简體字	繁体字
076 若未到定位巧便力摄故 以未满本愿亦不证涅盘	076 若未到定位巧便力攝故 以未滿本願亦不證涅槃
077 极厌于流转而亦向流转 信乐于涅盘而亦背涅盘	077 極厭於流轉而亦向流轉 信樂於涅槃而亦背涅槃
078 应当畏烦恼不应尽烦恼 当为集众善以遮遮烦恼	078 應當畏煩惱不應盡煩惱 當為集眾善以遮遮煩惱
079 菩萨烦恼性不是涅盘性 非烧诸烦恼生菩提种子	079 菩薩煩惱性不是涅槃性 非燒諸煩惱生菩提種子
080 记彼诸众生此记有因缘 唯是佛善巧方便到彼岸	080 記彼諸眾生此記有因緣 唯是佛善巧方便到彼岸
081 如空及莲华峻崖与深坑 界不男迦柘亦如烧种子	081 如空及蓮華峻崖與深坑 界不男迦柘亦如燒種子
082 诸论及工巧明术种种业 利益世间故出生建立之	082 諸論及工巧明術種種業 利益世間故出生建立之

简體字   繁体字

076

Where one has not yet reached "the definite position,"
One holds himself back through the power of skillful means.
Because one has not yet fulfilled his original vows,
In this case too, he refrains from realization of nirvāṇa.

077

Though one abides in the ultimate renunciation for cyclic existence,
He nonetheless confronts cyclic existence directly.
Though one maintains faith and happiness in nirvāṇa,
He nonetheless turns his back on realization of nirvāṇa.

078

One should dread the afflictions,
But should not end the afflictions.
To gather the manifold forms of goodness, one should
Use blocking methods to fend off afflictions.

079

For the bodhisattva, afflictions accord with his nature.
He is not one who takes nirvāṇa as his very nature.
It is not the case that the burning up of the afflictions
Allows one to generate the seed of bodhi.

080

As for the predictions bestowed on those other beings,
These predictions involved specific causal circumstances.
They were solely a function of the Buddha's artfulness
In taking the perfection of skillful means "to the far shore."

081

Similes for their plight reference "empty space," "lotus flowers,"
"Precipitous cliffs," and "a deep abyss."
Their realms bar it. Analogies cite "non-virility" and "kācamaṇi,"
With an additional comparison made to "burnt seeds."

082

All of the treatises as well as the specialized skills,
The occult and mundane sciences, and the various trades—
Because they bring benefit to the world,
One brings them forth and establishes them.

简體字	繁体字
083 随可化众生界趣及生中 如念即往彼愿力故受生	083 隨可化眾生界趣及生中 如念即往彼願力故受生
084 于种种恶事及谄幻众生 应用牢铠钾勿厌亦勿惮	084 於種種惡事及諂幻眾生 應用牢鎧鉀勿厭亦勿憚
085 具足胜净意不谄亦不幻 发露诸罪恶覆藏众善事	085 具足勝淨意不諂亦不幻 發露諸罪惡覆藏眾善事
086 清净身口业亦清净意业 修诸戒学句勿令有缺减	086 清淨身口業亦清淨意業 修諸戒學句勿令有缺減
087 安住于正念摄缘独静思 用念为护己*心得无障心	087 安住於正念攝緣獨靜思 用念為護己*心得無障心
088 若起分别时当觉善不善 应舍诸不善多修诸善分	088 若起分別時當覺善不善 應捨諸不善多修諸善分
089 缘境心若散应当专念知 还于彼境中随动即令住	089 緣境心若散應當專念知 還於彼境中隨動即令住

083

Adapting to beings amenable to instruction,
To their worlds, rebirth destinies, and birth circumstances,
As befits one's reflections, one goes directly to them,
And, through power of vows, takes birth among them.

084

In the midst of all sorts of circumstances rife with evil,
And when among beings prone to guileful flattery and deceit,
One should don one's sturdy armor.
One must not yield to either loathing or fear.

085

One equips oneself with supremely pure intentions,
Does not resort to guileful flattery or deception,
Reveals the wrongs of his karmic offenses,
And conceals his many good deeds.

086

One purifies the karma of body and mouth
And also purifies the karma of the mind.
Cultivating observance of all passages in the moral-code training.
One must not allow any omissions or diminishment in this.

087

One establishes himself in right mindfulness,
Focuses on the object condition, and stills his thought in solitude.
Having put mindfulness to use as a guard,
The mind becomes free of any obstructive thoughts.

088

When discriminating thoughts arise,
One should realize which are good and which are unwholesome,
Should forsake any which are not good,
And extensively cultivate those which are good.

089

If the mind trained on the object becomes scattered,
One should focus one's mindful awareness,
Return it to that object,
And, whenever movement occurs, immediately cause it to halt.

简體字	繁体字
090 不应缓恶取而修于精进 以不能持定是故应常修	**090** 不應緩惡取而修於精進 以不能持定是故應常修
091 若登声闻乘及以独觉乘 唯为自利行不舍牢精进	**091** 若登聲聞乘及以獨覺乘 唯為自利行不捨牢精進
092 何况大丈夫自度亦度人 而当不发起俱致千倍进	**092** 何況大丈夫自度亦度人 而當不發起俱致千倍進
093 半时或别行一时行馀道 修定不应尔应缘一境界	**093** 半時或別行一時行餘道 修定不應爾應緣一境界
094 于身莫有贪于命亦勿惜 纵令护此身终是烂坏法	**094** 於身莫有貪於命亦勿惜 縱令護此身終是爛壞法
095 利养恭敬名一向勿贪着 当如然头衣勤行成所愿	**095** 利養恭敬名一向勿貪著 當如然頭衣勤行成所願
096 决即起胜利不可待明日 明日太赊远何缘保瞬命	**096** 決即起勝利不可待明日 明日太賒遠何緣保瞬命

090

One should refrain from laxity and from wrong attachment
Cultivated with intensity,
For they make it impossible to maintain concentration.
One should therefore remain constant in one's cultivation.

091

Even were one to take up the vehicle of the Śrāvakas
Or the vehicle of the Pratyekabuddhas,
And hence practice solely for one's own benefit,
One would still not relinquish the enduring practice of vigor.

092

How much the less could it be that a great man
Committed to liberate both himself and all others
Might somehow fail to generate
A measure of vigor a thousand *koṭis* times greater?

093

As for cultivating some other practice half the time
Or simultaneously practicing some other path,
One should not do this when cultivating meditative concentration.
One should rather focus exclusively on a single objective condition.

094

One must not indulge any covetousness regarding the body
And must not cherish even one's own life.
Even were one to allow any protectiveness toward this body,
It is but a dharma bound in the end to rot away.

095

One must never develop a covetous attachment
To offerings, reverence from others, or fame.
Rather one should strive diligently to fulfill one's vows,
Acting with the urgency of one whose turban has caught fire.

096

Acting resolutely and immediately, pull forth the supreme benefit.
In this, one cannot wait for tomorrow.
Tomorrow is too distant a time,
For how can one ensure survival even for the blink of an eye?

簡體字	繁体字
097 安住于正命如食爱子肉 于所食噉中勿爱亦勿嫌	**097** 安住於正命如食愛子肉 於所食噉中勿愛亦勿嫌
098 出家为何义我所作竟未 今思为作不如十法经说	**098** 出家為何義我所作竟未 今思為作不如十法經說
099 观有为无常若无我我所 所有诸魔业应觉而舍离	**099** 觀有為無常若無我我所 所有諸魔業應覺而捨離
100 根力与觉分神足正断道 及以四念处为修发精勤	**100** 根力與覺分神足正斷道 及以四念處為修發精勤
101 心与利乐善作传传生处 及诸恶浊根彼当善观察	**101** 心與利樂善作傳傳生處 及諸惡濁根彼當善觀察
102 我于善法中日日何增长 复有何损减彼应极观察	**102** 我於善法中日日何增長 復有何損減彼應極觀察
103 见他得增长利养恭敬名 微小悭嫉心皆所不应作	**103** 見他得增長利養恭敬名 微小慳嫉心皆所不應作

097

Having established oneself in right livelihood,
When eating, it is as if consuming the flesh of a cherished son.
One must not indulge in either affection for or disapproval of
Whatever food one has taken for the meal.

098

For what purpose has one left the home life?
Have I finished what is to be done or not?
Reflect now on whether or not one is doing the work,
Doing so as described in the Ten Dharmas Sutra.

099

Contemplate conditioned phenomena as impermanent,
As devoid of self, and as devoid of anything belonging to a self.
One must become aware of and withdraw from
All forms of demonic karmic activity.

100

Generate energetic diligence in order to cultivate
The roots, powers, limbs of enlightenment,
Bases of spiritual powers, right severances, the Path,
And the four stations of mindfulness.

101

The mind may serve as a source for the repeated generation
Of good deeds bestowing benefit and happiness
Or it may instead serve as the root of all sorts of evil and turbidity.
One should make it the focus of skillful analytic contemplation.

102

"From one day to the next, what increase has occurred
In my cultivation of good dharmas?"
"Also, what diminishment has occurred in this?"
Those should be the contemplations of utmost concern.

103

Whenever one observes someone else experiencing an increase
In offerings, reverences, or reputation,
Even the most subtle thoughts of stinginess and jealously
Should never be indulged.

104
不羡诸境界行痴盲瘖聋
时复师子吼怖诸外道鹿

105
奉迎及将送应敬所尊重
于诸法事中随顺而佐助

106
救脱被杀者自然增不减
善修明巧业自学亦教他

107
于诸胜善法牢固而受之
修行四摄事施衣及饮食

108
不违乞求者和合诸亲戚
眷属不乖离施宅及财物

109
父母及亲友随所应安置
所应安置处无上自在主

110
虽复是奴仆善说亦受取
应生最尊重施药愈诸病

104
不羨諸境界行癡盲瘖聾
時復師子吼怖諸外道鹿

105
奉迎及將送應敬所尊重
於諸法事中隨順而佐助

106
救脫被殺者自然增不減
善修明巧業自學亦教他

107
於諸勝善法牢固而受之
修行四攝事施衣及飲食

108
不違乞求者和合諸親慼
眷屬不乖離施宅及財物

109
父母及親友隨所應安置
所應安置處無上自在主

110
雖復是奴僕善說亦受取
應生最尊重施藥愈諸病

简體字　　　　　　繁体字

104

One should not cherish any aspect of the objective realms,
But rather should act as if dull-witted, blind, mute, and deaf.
Still, when timely, respond by roaring the lion's roar,
Frightening off the non-Buddhist deer.

105

In welcoming them on arrival and escorting them off as they go,
One should be reverential toward those worthy of veneration.
In all endeavors associated with the Dharma,
One should follow along, participate, and contribute assistance.

106

One rescues and liberates beings bound to be killed.
One's goodness increases and never decreases.
One well cultivates karmic works involving the sciences and skills,
Training in them oneself while also teaching them to others.

107

Adopt all of the supremely good dharmas,
Through persistent and solid practice.
Cultivate the four means of attraction,
Making gifts of robes and food and drink.

108

Do not turn away from those begging for alms.
Facilitate the uniting of close relatives.
Prevent estrangement between those of the same clan.
Make gifts of dwellings and of material possessions as well.

109

As for one's father, mother, relatives, and friends,
Provide them circumstances befitting their station.
Wherever one has given them such a suitable situation,
Treat them as supreme and independent sovereigns.

110

Although there may be yet others who are servants,
One speaks to them with goodness and, in effect, adopts them.
One should accord them the highest esteem
And provide them with medicines and treatment for all illnesses.

簡體字	繁体字
111 前行善业首细滑美妙言 善为正意语前后无不供	**111** 前行善業首細滑美妙言 善為正意語前後無不供
112 不坏他眷属慈眼观众生 亦不以嫌心皆如善亲友	**112** 不壞他眷屬慈眼觀眾生 亦不以嫌心皆如善親友
113 应当如所言即随如是作 如言若即作他人则生信	**113** 應當如所言即隨如是作 如言若即作他人則生信
114 应当拥护法觉察放逸者 及作金宝网罗覆于支提	**114** 應當擁護法覺察放逸者 及作金寶網羅覆於支提
115 有欲求婇女庄严以施之 亦与说佛德及施杂光璎	**115** 有欲求婇女莊嚴以施之 亦與說佛德及施雜光璎
116 造作佛形像端坐胜莲花 及于六法中修习同喜乐	**116** 造作佛形像端坐勝蓮花 及於六法中修習同喜樂
117 可供无不供为命亦不谤 佛之所说法及以说法人	**117** 可供無不供為命亦不謗 佛之所說法及以說法人

111

Be the first to act, taking the lead in good karmic deeds,
Speaking with smooth and sublime words,
Being skillful in discourse guided by right intention,
And having no one above or below to whom gifts are not given.

112

Avoid any harm to the retinue of others.
Instead regard beings with the eye of kindness.
Neither may one course in disapproving thoughts.
Instead treat everyone as a good relative or friend.

113

One should accord with the words he speaks,
Following them straightaway with concordant actions.
If one acts immediately in accordance with his words,
Others will be inclined then to develop faith.

114

One should support and protect the Dharma,
And should become aware of instances of neglect,
Even going so far as to build canopies graced by gold and jewels
Spreading over and covering the *caityas*.

115

For those wishing to obtain a maiden mate,
See to her adornment and assist in her presentation.
Speak to the parties about the qualities of the Buddha
And then give prayer beads gleaming in varying hues.

116

Create images of the Buddha
Sitting upright atop supremely fine lotus blossoms
And cultivate common delight and happiness
Through adherence to the six dharmas of community harmony.

117

Of those who may be given offerings, none are not given offerings.
Even for the sake of preserving one's life, one still does not slander
The Dharma spoken by the Buddha
Or the person who expounds the Dharma.

简體字	繁体字
118	**118**
金宝散教师及教师支提 若有忘所诵与念令不失	金寶散教師及教師支提 若有忘所誦與念令不失
119	**119**
未思所作已勿躁勿随他 外道天龙神于中皆莫信	未思所作已勿躁勿隨他 外道天龍神於中皆莫信
120	**120**
心应如金刚堪能通诸法 心亦应如山诸事所不动	心應如金剛堪能通諸法 心亦應如山諸事所不動
121	**121**
憙乐出世语莫乐依世言 自受诸功德亦应令他受	憙樂出世語莫樂依世言 自受諸功德亦應令他受
122	**122**
修五解脱入修十不净想 八大丈夫觉亦应分别修	修五解脫入修十不淨想 八大丈夫覺亦應分別修
123	**123**
天耳与天眼神足与他心 及与宿命住应修净五通	天耳與天眼神足與他心 及與宿命住應修淨五通
124	**124**
四神足为根欲进心思惟 四无量住持谓慈悲喜舍	四神足為根欲進心思惟 四無量住持謂慈悲喜捨

简體字   繁体字

118

Gold and jewels are distributed among teaching masters
And also among the *caityas* of teaching masters.
If there are those who forget what is to be recited,
One assists their remembrance, enabling them to stay free of error.

119

When one has not yet reflected on the right course of action,
One must not be impulsive and must not simply emulate others.
As for the non-Buddhists, gods, dragons, and spirits,
One must not invest one's faith in any of them.

120

One's mind should be like *vajra*,
Able to penetrate all dharmas.
One's mind should also be like a mountain,
Remaining unmoved in any circumstance.

121

Delight in world-transcending discourse
And do not take pleasure in worldly words.
Personally adopt all manner of meritorious qualities.
One should then influence others to adopt them as well.

122

Cultivate the five bases of liberation.
Cultivate the ten reflections on impurity.
The eight realizations of great men
Should also be the focus of analytic contemplation and cultivation.

123

The heavenly ear, the heavenly eye,
The bases of spiritual powers, the cognition of others' thoughts,
And the cognition of past lives and abodes—
One should cultivate purification of these five spiritual abilities.

124

The four bases of spiritual powers comprise their root.
They are zeal, vigor, mental focus, and contemplative reflection.
The four immeasurables govern them.
They are kindness, compassion, sympathetic joy, and equanimity.

125

四界如毒蛇六入如空村
五众如杀者应作如是观

126

重法及法师亦舍于法悭
教师勿卷秘听者勿散乱

127

无慢无希望唯以悲愍心
尊重恭敬意为众而说法

128

于闻无厌足闻已皆诵持
不诳尊福田亦令师欢喜

129

不应观他家心怀于敬养
勿以论难故习诵于世典

130

勿以瞋恚故毁呰诸菩萨
未受未闻法亦勿生诽谤

131

断除于憍慢当住四圣种
勿嫌于他人亦勿自高举

简體字

125

四界如毒蛇六入如空村
五眾如殺者應作如是觀

126

重法及法師亦捨於法慳
教師勿捲祕聽者勿散亂

127

無慢無希望唯以悲愍心
尊重恭敬意為眾而說法

128

於聞無厭足聞已皆誦持
不誑尊福田亦令師歡喜

129

不應觀他家心懷於敬養
勿以論難故習誦於世典

130

勿以瞋恚故毀呰諸菩薩
未受未聞法亦勿生誹謗

131

斷除於憍慢當住四聖種
勿嫌於他人亦勿自高舉

繁体字

125

The four elements are like poisonous serpents.
The six sense faculties are like an empty village.
The five aggregates are like assassins.
One should contemplate them in this way.

126

Esteem the Dharma and the masters of Dharma
And also relinquish any stinginess with the Dharma.
The instructing masters must not be tight-fisted or secretive
And those listening must not be mentally scattered or confused.

127

Free of arrogance and free of hopes,
Motivated solely by thoughts of compassion and pity,
With reverent and respectful mind,
Expound the Dharma for the community.

128

Be insatiable in learning
And always recite and retain what has been learned.
Do not deceive any among the venerable fields of merit.
Moreover, cause one's instructors to be delighted.

129

One should not pay visits to the houses of others
With a mind cherishing reverence or offerings.
One must not take up study and recitation of worldly texts
For the sake of debating challenging topics.

130

One must not be provoked by hatefulness or anger
Into defaming any bodhisattva.
As for dharmas not yet received or learned,
One must not initiate slanders in those cases either.

131

In order to cut off arrogance and pride,
One should abide in the four lineage bases of the ārya.
One must not course in disapproval of others
And must not allow oneself to become conceited.

132
若实不实犯不得发觉他
勿求他错失自错当觉知

133
佛及诸佛法不应分别疑
法虽最难信于中应信之

134
虽由实语死退失转轮王
及以诸天王唯应作实语

135
打骂恐杀缚终不怨责他
皆是我自罪业报故来现

136
应极尊重爱供养于父母
亦给侍和上恭敬阿阇梨

137
为信声闻乘及以独觉乘
说于最深法此是菩萨错

138
为信深大乘众生而演说
声闻独觉乘此亦是其错

简體字

132
若實不實犯不得發覺他
勿求他錯失自錯當覺知

133
佛及諸佛法不應分別疑
法雖最難信於中應信之

134
雖由實語死退失轉輪王
及以諸天王唯應作實語

135
打罵恐殺縛終不怨責他
皆是我自罪業報故來現

136
應極尊重愛供養於父母
亦給侍和上恭敬阿闍梨

137
為信聲聞乘及以獨覺乘
說於最深法此是菩薩錯

138
為信深大乘眾生而演說
聲聞獨覺乘此亦是其錯

繁体字

132

Whether or not someone has actually committed a transgression,
One must not reveal his situation to others.
Do not seek out the errors and faults of anyone else.
Rather one should become aware of one's own errors.

133

One should refrain from biased judgments and doubting
In fathoming the Buddha and the Dharma of the Buddhas.
Even though a dharma may be extremely difficult to believe,
One should nonetheless maintain faith in it.

134

Even though one might be put to death for speaking the truth,
Or might be forced to abdicate the throne of a universal monarch,
Or even that of a king among the gods,
One should still utter only truthful speech.

135

Even if beaten, cursed, or terrorized with death threats or captivity,
One must not hate or condemn others, but should instead reflect:
"This is all the product of my own karmic offenses.
This has happened as a result of karmic retribution."

136

One should, with the most ultimate respect and affection,
Provide offerings in support of one's father and mother.
Also supply the needs of and serve the *upādhyāyas*,
While extending reverence to the *ācāryas* as well.

137

When, for those who place their faith in the Śrāvaka Vehicle
Or those dedicated to the Pratyekabuddha Vehicle,
One discourses on the most profound of dharmas,
This, for a bodhisattva, is an error.

138

When, for believers in the profound Great-Vehicle teachings,
One discourses to those beings
On the Śrāvaka or Pratyekabuddha vehicles,
This too is an error for him.

简體字	繁体字
139 大人来求法慢缓不为说 而反摄受恶委任无信者	**139** 大人來求法慢緩不為說 而反攝受惡委任無信者
140 远舍所说错所说头多德 于彼当念知亦皆应习近	**140** 遠捨所說錯所說頭多德 於彼當念知亦皆應習近
141 等心平等说平等善安立 亦令正相应诸众生无别	**141** 等心平等說平等善安立 亦令正相應諸眾生無別
142 为法不为利为德不为名 欲脱众生苦不欲自身乐	**142** 為法不為利為德不為名 欲脫眾生苦不欲自身樂
143 密意求业果所作福事生 亦为成熟众舍离于自事	**143** 密意求業果所作福事生 亦為成熟眾捨離於自事
144 亲近善知识所谓法师佛 劝励出家者及以乞求辈	**144** 親近善知識所謂法師佛 勸勵出家者及以乞求輩
145 依止世论者专求世财者 信解独觉乘及以声闻乘	**145** 依止世論者專求世財者 信解獨覺乘及以聲聞乘

139

So too where some superior person comes seeking the Dharma,
But one delays and fails to provide him with teachings.
So too where, on the contrary, one takes in wrongdoers
Or delegates responsibilities to those who are untrustworthy.

140

One must abandon the errors mentioned above.
As for such herein-described meritorious practices as the *dhūtas*,
One ought to become knowledgeable about them
And then incorporate them into one's own practice.

141

Regard all equally in one's thoughts, speak equally for all,
Be uniformly equal in establishing all others in goodness,
And influence them all equally to accord with what is right.
Thus one refrains from making distinctions between any beings.

142

One works for the sake of Dharma and not for self-benefit.
One works to develop meritorious qualities, not for renown.
One wishes to liberate beings from suffering
And does not wish merely to ensure his own happiness.

143

With purposes kept secret, one seeks fruition in one's works.
When the results of one's merit-generating endeavors come forth,
Even then, one applies them to the ripening of the many
While abandoning preoccupation with one's own concerns.

144

Grow close to good spiritual friends,
Specifically, to the masters of Dharma, to the Buddhas,
To those who encourage one to leave the home life,
And to those who are seekers of alms.

145

Those who ground themselves in worldly treatises,
Those who exclusively seek worldly wealth,
Those with Pratyekabuddha Vehicle faith and understanding,
And those devoted to the Śrāvaka Vehicle—

146
此四恶知识菩萨应当知
复有应求者所谓四大藏

147
佛出闻诸度及于法师所
见之心无碍乐住空闲处

148
地水火风空悉与其相似
一切处平等利益诸众生

149
当善思惟义勤生陀罗尼
勿于听法者为作于障碍

150
恼中能调伏小事舍无馀
八种懈怠事皆亦应除断

151
莫作非分贪横贪不称意
离者皆令合无问亲非亲

152
于空而得空智者莫依行
若当得于空彼恶过身见

简體字

146
此四惡知識菩薩應當知
復有應求者所謂四大藏

147
佛出聞諸度及於法師所
見之心無礙樂住空閑處

148
地水火風空悉與其相似
一切處平等利益諸眾生

149
當善思惟義勤生陀羅尼
勿於聽法者為作於障礙

150
惱中能調伏小事捨無餘
八種懈怠事皆亦應除斷

151
莫作非分貪橫貪不稱意
離者皆令合無問親非親

152
於空而得空智者莫依行
若當得於空彼惡過身見

繁体字

146

As for these four types of unwholesome spiritual friends,
The bodhisattva should be aware of them as such.
There are, however, other circumstances one should seek out.
This refers specifically to the four great treasuries:

147

The emergence of buddhas; hearing the perfections explained;
Being able in the presence of a master of Dharma
To behold him with unobstructed mind;
And happily pursuing cultivation in a place of solitude.

148

Abide in a manner comparable to
Earth, water, fire, wind, and space,
Remaining thus uniformly equal under all circumstances
In providing benefit to all beings.

149

One should skillfully reflect upon the meanings
And diligently progress in the uses of the *dhāraṇīs*.
One must never create any sort of obstruction
To those seeking to hear the Dharma.

150

When embroiled in the afflictions, be able to overcome them.
Relinquish the lesser instances, retaining not a trace.
Regarding the eight cases involving indolence,
One should cut all of those off as well.

151

Do not covet what is not one's lot,
For unprincipled covetousness will not bring satisfaction.
Influence all who have become estranged to reconcile,
Whether or not they are one's own relations.

152

The wise must not base their practice
On getting at the "emptiness" in what is intrinsically empty.
In the case of one determined to get at that emptiness itself,
That wrong is even more extreme than viewing the body as a self.

简體字	繁体字
153 扫涂与庄严及多种鼓乐 香鬘等供具供养于支提	**153** 掃塗與莊嚴及多種鼓樂 香鬘等供具供養於支提
154 作种种灯轮供养支提舍 施盖及革屣骑乘车舆等	**154** 作種種燈輪供養支提舍 施蓋及革屣騎乘車輿等
155 专应喜乐(去)[法]乐知信佛得 喜乐给侍僧亦乐闻正法	**155** 專應喜樂(去)[法]樂知信佛得 喜樂給侍僧亦樂聞正法
156 前世中不生现在中不住 后际中不到如是观诸法	**156** 前世中不生現在中不住 後際中不到如是觀諸法
157 好事与众生不求彼好报 当为独忍苦不自偏受乐	**157** 好事與眾生不求彼好報 當為獨忍苦不自偏受樂
158 虽足大福报心不举不喜 虽贫如饿鬼亦不下不忧	**158** 雖足大福報心不舉不喜 雖貧如餓鬼亦不下不憂
159 若有已学者应极尊重之 未学令入学不应生轻蔑	**159** 若有已學者應極尊重之 未學令入學不應生輕蔑

简體字   繁体字

153

By sweeping and finishing floors, by providing adornments,
By furnishing many varieties of drums and music,
And by offering fragrances, flower garlands, and other gifts,
Contribute offerings to the *caityas*.

154

Create all sorts of lantern wheels
As offerings to the *caityas* and their buildings.
Provide canopies as well as sandals,
Horse-drawn carriages, sedan chairs, and the like.

155

One should especially find delight in the Dharma
And be happy knowing what is gained through faith in Buddha.
Delight in providing for and serving the monastic Sangha,
While also finding happiness through listening to right Dharma.

156

They do not arise in the past.
They do not abide in the present.
They do not go forward into the future.
Contemplate all dharmas in this manner.

157

Give to beings whatsoever is fine
And do not wish that they bestow anything fine in return.
One should prefer it be solely oneself who endures suffering
While not favoring oneself in the enjoyment of happiness.

158

Although replete with karmic rewards from immense merit,
The mind should not become lofty or overwhelmed with delight.
Although one may be as poverty-stricken as a hungry ghost,
One should still not become downcast or overcome with distress.

159

Accord the most ultimate degree of esteem
To those already accomplished in learning.
Inspire those as yet unlearned to devote themselves to study.
One should not behave in a manner belittling them.

160
戒具者恭敬破戒令入戒
智具者亲近愚者令住智

161
流转苦多种生老死恶趣
不怖此等畏当降魔恶智

162
所有诸佛土抟聚诸功德
为皆得彼故发愿及精进

163
恒于诸法中不取而行舍
此为诸众生受担欲荷负

164
正观于诸法无我无我所
亦勿舍大悲及以于大慈

165
胜过诸供养以供佛世尊
彼作何者是所谓法供养

166
若持菩萨藏及得陀罗尼
入深法源底是为法供养

160
戒具者恭敬破戒令入戒
智具者親近愚者令住智

161
流轉苦多種生老死惡趣
不怖此等畏當降魔惡智

162
所有諸佛土搏聚諸功德
為皆得彼故發願及精進

163
恒於諸法中不取而行捨
此為諸眾生受擔欲荷負

164
正觀於諸法無我無我所
亦勿捨大悲及以於大慈

165
勝過諸供養以供佛世尊
彼作何者是所謂法供養

166
若持菩薩藏及得陀羅尼
入深法源底是為法供養

简體字　　　　繁体字

160

Revere those perfect in observance of the moral precepts
And influence those who break precepts to take on the precepts.
Draw close to those perfect in wisdom
And influence those who act foolishly to abide in wisdom.

161

The sufferings of cyclic existence are of many kinds,
Involving birth, aging, death, and the wretched destinies.
One should not be frightened by the fearsomeness of these.
One must instead subdue demons and knowledge rooted in evil.

162

Amass every form of merit
In the lands of all the Buddhas.
Bring forth vows and proceed with vigor
So that everyone may succeed in reaching them.

163

Even in the midst of all dharmas, one is constant
In not seizing on them, thus coursing along in equanimity.
One takes on the burden, wishing to bear it on forth,
Proceeding in this manner for the sake of all beings.

164

Abide in the right contemplation of all dharmas
As devoid of self and as devoid of anything belonging to a self.
Even so, one must not relinquish the great compassion
Or one's reliance on the great kindness.

165

As for that which is superior even to using every sort of gift
In making offerings to the Buddha, the Bhagavān,
What sort of action might that be?
This refers specifically to making offerings of Dharma.

166

If one preserves the Bodhisattva Canon,
Even to the point of gaining realization of the *dhāraṇīs*—
If one enters into and reaches the bottom of Dharma's source—
This is what constitutes the offering of Dharma.

简體字	繁体字
167 应当依于义莫唯爱杂味 于深法道中善入莫放逸	**167** 應當依於義莫唯愛雜味 於深法道中善入莫放逸
168 如是此资粮恒沙等大劫 出家及在家当得满正觉	**168** 如是此資糧恒沙等大劫 出家及在家當得滿正覺

167

One should rely upon the meaning.
One must not cherish only the various flavors.
In the Path of the profound Dharma
One enters with skill and must not fall prey to negligence.

168

One cultivates these provisions in this manner
For kalpas as numerous as the Ganges' sands,
Doing so sometimes as a monastic, sometimes as a householder.
Thus one will succeed in perfecting the right enlightenment.

PART TWO:

THE BODHISAṂBHĀRA TREATISE COMMENTARY

The Early Indian Commentary On

Ārya Nāgārjuna's
Treatise on the Provisions for Enlightenment
(*Bodhisaṃbhāra Śāstra*)

Composed by Bhikshu Vaśitva
(*circa* 300–500 CE)

菩提資糧論卷第一

聖者龍樹本　比丘自在釋。

[6]大隋南印度三藏達[7]磨笈多譯。

今於諸佛所　　合掌而頂敬
我當如教說　　佛菩提資糧

[0517b16]　　佛者。於一切所應知中得覺。此為佛義。如所應知而知故。又於無智睡眠中覺故。覺者。[8]覺寤為義。以離無智睡故。又諸釋梵等不覺此覺。唯是名聲普遍三界者。所能覺故。一切諸佛乃覺此覺。以一切種遍智唯佛所知。非諸聲聞獨覺菩薩。以不共法具足故。

菩提资粮论卷第一

圣者龙树本　比丘自在释　。

[6]大隋南印度三藏达[7]磨笈多译。

今于诸佛所　　合掌而顶敬
我当如教说　　佛菩提资粮

[0517b16]　　佛者。于一切所应知中得觉。此为佛义。如所应知而知故。又于无智睡眠中觉故。觉者。[8]觉寤为义。以离无智睡故。又诸释梵等不觉此觉。唯是名声普遍三界者。所能觉故。一切诸佛乃觉此觉。以一切种遍智唯佛所知。非诸声闻独觉菩萨。以不共法具足故。

The Bodhisaṁbhāra Treatise Commentary

Bhikshu Vaśitva's Early Indian Commentary On

Ārya Nāgārjuna's
Treatise on the Provisions for Enlightenment
(Bodhisaṁbhāra Śāstra)

001 – The Homage to All Buddhas and the Declaration of Intent

Now, in the presence of all the Buddhas,
With palms pressed together, I bow down my head in reverence.
I shall explain here in accordance with the teachings
The provisions essential for the bodhi of the Buddhas.

Commentary:

On "Buddha," "Awakening," "Reverence," and "Bodhi"

"Buddhas," are those who have awakened to all which should be known. This is the meaning of "buddha." A "buddha" is so-called because his awareness accords with the manner in which things should be known and also because he has awakened from the sleep of ignorance.

"Awakening," has the meaning of coming into a state of awareness from the condition of sleep. Its application here is based on their abandonment of the slumber of ignorance. Moreover, it is in contrast to Śakra, Brahmā, and the others who have not succeeded in waking to this awakening. It is an awakening such as only those whose fame has spread universally throughout the three realms[2] have been able to awaken to.

It is only all of the Buddhas then who have qualified to awaken to this awakening. This is because the universal knowledge inhering in the knowledge of all modes is known only to the Buddhas. This is not the domain of the Śrāvaka-disciples, the Pratyekabuddhas, or the Bodhisattvas, this because it requires that one be equipped with the dharmas exclusive to a buddha.

繁體字

諸者。無闕故。謂過去未來現在等。頂者上分故。合掌者。攝手故敬者。向禮故。我說者。自分別故。如教者。彼彼經中種種已說。今亦如彼教說故。佛者。離無智故。菩提者。一切智智故。資糧者。能滿菩提法故。譬如世間瓶盈釜盈等。盈是滿義。如是以滿菩提法。為菩提資糧。又以持為義。譬如世間共行日攝於熱月攝於冷。攝是持義。如是以持菩提法。為菩提資糧。言資糧者即是持義。又以長養為義。譬如世間有能滿千或百或十。或唯自滿或難自滿。菩提資糧亦復如是。以長養菩提為義。

简体字

诸者。无阙故。谓过去未来现在等。顶者上分故。合掌者。摄手故敬者。向礼故。我说者。自分别故。如教者。彼彼经中种种已说。今亦如彼教说故。佛者。离无智故。菩提者。一切智智故。资粮者。能满菩提法故。譬如世间瓶盈釜盈等。盈是满义。如是以满菩提法。为菩提资粮。又以持为义。譬如世间共行日摄于热月摄于冷。摄是持义。如是以持菩提法。为菩提资粮。言资粮者即是持义。又以长养为义。譬如世间有能满千或百或十。或唯自满或难自满。菩提资粮亦复如是。以长养菩提为义。

"All" [buddhas] indicates that there are none left out. This refers then to those of the past, the future, and the present.

"Head" refers to the most elevated part. As for "with palms pressed together," it is through placing the palms together that one signifies respect. This is done during the formal expression of reverence.

"I shall explain" makes the clarifying distinction that it is oneself [who is the original author of these explanations].

"In accordance with the teachings" indicates that this has already been explained in all sorts of ways in one after another of the sutras and that now too, this shall be explained in accordance with those very teachings.

As for [last line's mention of] "the Buddhas," it indicates those who have abandoned ignorance.

"Bodhi" refers here to the wisdom of all-knowledge.

Definitions and Connotations of "Provisions"

"Provisions" refers to that by which one becomes able to bring the dharma of bodhi to fulfillment. By way of analogy, it is just as when things such as a jugs or measuring vessels are filled up. "Filled up" here simply means "filled to capacity." In this context, we are referring to fulfilling the dharmas required for realization of bodhi. It is on this basis that we speak of "provisions for bodhi."

"Provisions" also has the meaning of "to preserve" (lit. "to hold"). This is comparable to the case obtaining with those common worldly phenomena wherein the sun is held to be responsible for "maintaining" the heat and the moon is held to be responsible for "maintaining" the coolness. "Maintaining" here connotes "preservation." In this same way, it is based on their ability to preserve the dharmas of bodhi that these are "provisions" for bodhi. So when one speaks of "provisions," this is essentially a reference to "preservation."

Additionally, ["provisions"] also take "to raise and nurture" as the basis of their meaning. This is analogous to the situation in the world where there are those who are able to fulfill the needs of a thousand others, or perhaps a hundred, or perhaps ten, or perhaps only themselves, or perhaps the needs of themselves are even difficult to fulfill. The provisions essential to bodhi are themselves comparable in regard to this function. Thus their meaning derives from their ability to raise and nurture bodhi.

又以因為義。如舍城車等因中說言舍資糧城資糧車資糧。如是於生菩提因緣法中。說名菩提資糧。又以眾分具足為義。譬如祭祀分中杓火等具足名為祭祀。非不具足。亦如身分頭手足等具足得名為身。非不具足。施分亦如是。施者施物。受者迴向。此等具足名施資糧。非不具足。戒等資糧亦如是。是故眾分具足義。是資糧義。如是我說菩提資糧。是能滿者。持者。長養者。菩提因者。菩提分具足者。皆其義也。

何能說無闕　　菩提諸資糧
唯獨有諸佛　　別得無邊覺

又以因为义。如舍城车等因中说言舍资粮城资粮车资粮。如是于生菩提因缘法中。说名菩提资粮。又以众分具足为义。譬如祭祀分中杓火等具足名为祭祀。非不具足。亦如身分头手足等具足得名为身。非不具足。施分亦如是。施者施物。受者迴向。此等具足名施资粮。非不具足。戒等资粮亦如是。是故众分具足义。是资粮义。如是我说菩提资粮。是能满者。持者。长养者。菩提因者。菩提分具足者。皆其义也。

何能说无阙　　菩提诸资粮
唯独有诸佛　　别得无边觉

Then again, the meaning [of "provisions"] relies on "causation" as the basis of its meaning. This is just as with a building, a city wall, a cart, or other such things wherein, while [their construction is still only] in the causal phase, one speaks of the "provisions" (i.e. "supplies," or "materials") for [constructing] a building, the "provisions" for [constructing] a city wall, or the "provisions" for making a cart. In this same way, one speaks of the "provisions" for bodhi in reference to the dharmas serving as the causes and conditions for producing bodhi.

Furthermore, the meaning of "provisions" is based on the complete adequacy of the many essential parts. This is comparable to the essential parts required for performing ceremonial offerings wherein it is based on the complete adequacy of such things as a serving ladle, the cooking fire, and so forth that makes it possible to refer to performing a ceremonial offering. It is not the case that one can fail to have a complete adequacy of such things.

It is also just like when one relies on the complete presence of bodily parts such as the head, hands, feet, and so forth in referring to the existence of a body. It is not the case that one can fail to have complete adequacy in such things.

This is also the case in carrying out an act of giving wherein one has the benefactor, the gift, the recipient, and the transference [of merit]. When these sorts of things are perfectly adequate, one is then able to refer to the "provisions" for performing an act of giving. One cannot fail to have complete adequacy in such things. So too it is in the case of such things as the provisions essential to the moral precepts. And so it is that "complete adequacy of the many component parts" forms a basis for the meaning of "provisions."

Thus it is that in my explanation of the "provisions" for bodhi, this refers to: that which is able to bring about fulfillment; that which preserves; that which raises and nurtures; that which forms the causal basis for bodhi; and that which represents the complete adequacy of the component parts of bodhi. All of these concepts are inherent components of the meaning [of the term "provisions"].

---

002 – The Impossibility of Completely Describing the Provisions

How would one be able to describe without omission
All of the provisions for the realization of bodhi?
This could only be accomplished by the Buddhas themselves,
For they, exclusively, have realized the boundless enlightenment.

[0517c16] 何能者。何力也。若聲聞若菩薩少分覺知無力能故。若欲說諸菩提資糧無闕無餘。唯是諸佛別得無邊覺者。言無邊覺。謂非少分覺故。以佛世尊於無邊應知義中覺知無礙。是故佛名無邊覺者。又於欲樂及自疲苦斷常有無等邊見中。覺而不著。以所覺無邊。[9]是故佛名無邊覺者。問何故資糧唯佛能說。餘人不能答。

> 佛體無邊德　　覺資糧為根
> 是故覺資糧　　亦無有邊際

[0517c26] 佛體者。即佛身也。以彼佛體具足無邊功德故。說佛體無邊德。

[0517c16] 何能者。何力也。若声闻若菩萨少分觉知无力能故。若欲说诸菩提资粮无阙无馀。唯是诸佛别得无边觉者。言无边觉。谓非少分觉故。以佛世尊于无边应知义中觉知无碍。是故佛名无边觉者。又于欲乐及自疲苦断常有无等边见中。觉而不着。以所觉无边。[9]是故佛名无边觉者。问何故资粮唯佛能说。馀人不能答。

> 佛体无边德　　觉资粮为根
> 是故觉资粮　　亦无有边际

[0517c26] 佛体者。即佛身也。以彼佛体具足无边功德故。说佛体无边德。

COMMENTARY:

As for the phrase "How would one be able...?," this means to say: "How would one possess the power?" [This is brought up] because, in the case of the Śrāvaka-disciples and in the case of the Bodhisattvas, they possess only a lesser degree of awakening and knowing and so do not possess the requisite power or ability [to carry out this description]. If one wishes to describe the provisions for bodhi without allowing any omissions and with no factor remaining undescribed, it is only the Buddhas, exclusively, who could do this, for they are the ones who have realized the boundless enlightenment.

As for the reference to "boundless enlightenment," this is a statement indicating it is not the case that this involves a lesser degree of awakening. It is because the Buddhas, the Bhagavāns, have awakened to and know unimpededly the boundlessly many meanings which should be known that the Buddhas are therefore referred to here as those who have gained realization of the "boundless enlightenment."

Additionally, [the Buddhas] have awakened to and yet remain unattached to the views characterizing the [two] extreme bounds, views such as those which cling to the pleasures of desire or self-wearying asceticism, annihilationism or eternalism, existence or nonexistence, and so forth. Thus it is also because that to which they have awakened is free of extreme bounds that the Buddhas are referred to as having realized the boundless enlightenment.

Question: Why is it that it is only the Buddhas who are able to explain the provisions while other persons are not able to do so?

Response: (As below...)[3]

---

003 – Since a Buddha's Qualities are Boundless, So Too Are the Provisions

The boundless meritorious qualities of a buddha's body
Are rooted in the provisions essential to enlightenment.
Therefore the provisions for enlightenment
Themselves have no bounds.

COMMENTARY:

As for "a buddha's body," it refers here to a buddha's physical body.[4] It is because the body of a buddha is replete with a boundless number of meritorious qualities that it speaks here of "boundless meritorious qualities associated with a buddha's body."

繁體字

功德者。謂可稱讚義。若可稱讚則名功德。又是數
數作義。譬如數數誦習經書。彼則說名作功德者。
又是牢固義。譬如作繩。或合二為功。或合三為
功。又是增長義。譬如息利。或增二為功。或增三
為功。又是依止義。譬如諸物各以依止為功。如是
佛體為戒定等無邊差別功德依止故。說佛體有無邊
功德。覺資糧為根者。彼菩提資糧。與佛體無邊功
德為根本故。根者建立義。菩提者智也。根即資
糧。以彼資糧能建立一切智智。是故資糧為佛體根
本。良由佛體有無邊功德。須以無邊功德成彼佛
體。是故資糧亦無邊際。

简体字

功德者。谓可称赞义。若可称赞则名功德。又是数
数作义。譬如数数诵习经书。彼则说名作功德者。
又是牢固义。譬如作绳。或合二为功。或合三为
功。又是增长义。譬如息利。或增二为功。或增三
为功。又是依止义。譬如诸物各以依止为功。如是
佛体为戒定等无边差别功德依止故。说佛体有无边
功德。觉资粮为根者。彼菩提资粮。与佛体无边功
德为根本故。根者建立义。菩提者智也。根即资
粮。以彼资粮能建立一切智智。是故资粮为佛体根
本。良由佛体有无边功德。须以无边功德成彼佛
体。是故资粮亦无边际。

DEFINITION AND CONNOTATIONS OF "MERITORIOUS QUALITIES"

As for "meritorious qualities," it means "that which is praiseworthy." If something is praiseworthy, then it may be described as "a meritorious quality."

["Meritorious quality"] also connotes repetition of the associated [meritorious] action. This is comparable to when someone takes up the practice of repeated recitation of a sutra. Such a person is then appropriately described as one engaged in the creation of meritorious qualities.

["Meritorious quality"] also connotes "durability." This is comparable to when one makes a rope. In some cases one braids it by uniting two cords and deems it to be of appropriate "quality" and in some cases one braids it from three cords and deems it to be of appropriate "quality."

["Meritorious quality"] also connotes a relationship of "dependence" [upon noble bases]. This is comparable to things in general which are deemed to possess their meritorious quality based on that upon which they secondarily depend. In this same way, it is because the body of a buddha depends in turn upon the meritorious qualities inhering in the moral precepts, meditative concentration, and the other boundlessly many distinctly different meritorious qualities that one describes the body of a buddha as possessed of "boundless meritorious qualities."

ON "PROVISIONS" AS THE "ROOT" OF A BUDDHA'S "QUALITIES"

As for their being "rooted in the provisions essential to enlightenment," this is because the provisions involved in the acquisition of bodhi comprise the very root of the boundlessly many meritorious qualities associated with a buddha's body.

As for "root," it connotes "the ability to establish." As for "bodhi," that is a reference to wisdom. The root is just the provisions themselves, for the provisions have the ability to establish the wisdom founded on all-knowledge. Therefore the provisions serve as the very root of the body of a buddha.

It is especially on account of the fact that the body of a buddha is possessed of boundlessly many meritorious qualities that it is essential to employ boundlessly many meritorious qualities in perfecting that buddha body [for one's own future buddhahood]. Thus it is that the provisions themselves have no delimiting boundaries at all.

當說彼少分　　敬禮佛菩薩
是諸菩薩等　　次佛應供養

[0518a13]　　彼諸資糧無邊而智有邊。是以說彼資糧不
[1]能無闕。故言當說彼少分敬禮佛菩薩問應禮佛。
以一切眾生中最勝故。何義此中亦禮菩薩。答是諸
菩薩等次佛應供養故。諸菩薩等從初發心乃至覺場
皆應供養。菩薩有七種。一初發心。二正修行。三
得無生忍。四灌頂。五一生所繫。六最後生。七詣
覺場。此等菩薩於諸佛後次應供養。以身口意及外
物等而供養之。初發心者未得地。正修行者乃至七
地。

当说彼少分　　敬礼佛菩萨
是诸菩萨等　　次佛应供养

[0518a13]　　彼诸资粮无边而智有边。是以说彼资粮不
[1]能无阙。故言当说彼少分敬礼佛菩萨问应礼佛。
以一切众生中最胜故。何义此中亦礼菩萨。答是诸
菩萨等次佛应供养故。诸菩萨等从初发心乃至觉场
皆应供养。菩萨有七种。一初发心。二正修行。三
得无生忍。四灌顶。五一生所系。六最后生。七诣
觉场。此等菩萨于诸佛后次应供养。以身口意及外
物等而供养之。初发心者未得地。正修行者乃至七
地。

---

004 – Reverence to Buddhas and to Bodhisattvas, Those Also Worthy of Offerings

I shall then explain but a lesser portion of them.
I render reverence to the Buddhas and the Bodhisattvas.
It is all such bodhisattvas as these
To whom one should next make offerings, after the Buddhas.

COMMENTARY:

All of those provisions are boundless and yet one's own wisdom is bounded. Therefore, when embarking on the explanation of those provisions it is impossible to remain free of omissions. Therefore it states: "I shall then explain but a lesser portion of them. I render reverence to the Buddhas and the Bodhisattvas."

Question: One should pay reverence to the Buddhas, for it is they among all beings who are most superior. But what is the meaning here of claiming one should also revere bodhisattvas?

Response: This statement is made because all such bodhisattvas as these should be those to whom one makes offerings next after the Buddhas. All such bodhisattvas, from the time of their initial generation of the resolve [to gain bodhi] on forward until they arrive at the site of enlightenment—these are those to whom one should in every case make offerings.

THE SEVEN TYPES OF BODHISATTVAS

There are seven types of bodhisattvas:

1 – Those who have generated the initial resolve.
2 – Those who have taken up right cultivation.
3 – Those realizing the unproduced-dharmas patience.
4 – Those at the level of "anointing of the crown."
5 – Those abiding at the level of "one remaining life."
6 – Those at the level of their very last birth;
7 – Those who have approached the site of enlightenment.

The bodhisattvas of these sorts are those to whom one should make offerings next in sequence after having made offerings to the Buddhas. One uses body, mouth, mind together with outward things in making offerings to them.

"Those who have generated the initial resolve" have not yet reached any of the [bodhisattva] grounds. "Those who have taken up right cultivation" consists of those bodhisattvas who abide on all grounds up to and including the seventh ground. "Those who

繁體字

得無生忍者住第八地。灌頂者住第十地。一生所繫
者方入兜率陀。最後生者兜率陀處[2]住。詣覺場者
欲受用一切智智。於七種菩薩中。初發心菩薩一切
眾生皆應禮敬。何況餘者。何以故。深心寬大故。
如來教量故。初發心菩薩發菩提心時。於十方分無
減諸佛土無減諸眾生無減。以慈遍滿發菩提心。若
未度眾生我當度之。未解脫者我當解脫。未穌息者
我當蘇息。未寂滅者我當寂滅。應聲聞者我當令入
聲聞乘中。應獨覺者我當令入獨覺乘中。應大乘者
我當令入大乘之中。欲令眾生悉得寂滅。非為寂滅
少分眾生。以是深心寬大故。一切眾生皆應禮敬。

簡体字

得无生忍者住第八地。灌顶者住第十地。一生所系
者方入兜率陀。最后生者兜率陀处[2]住。诣觉场者
欲受用一切智智。于七种菩萨中。初发心菩萨一切
众生皆应礼敬。何况馀者。何以故。深心宽大故。
如来教量故。初发心菩萨发菩提心时。于十方分无
减诸佛土无减诸众生无减。以慈遍满发菩提心。若
未度众生我当度之。未解脱者我当解脱。未穌息者
我当苏息。未寂灭者我当寂灭。应声闻者我当令入
声闻乘中。应独觉者我当令入独觉乘中。应大乘者
我当令入大乘之中。欲令众生悉得寂灭。非为寂灭
少分众生。以是深心宽大故。一切众生皆应礼敬。

have realized the unproduced-dharmas patience" abide on the eighth ground [and above]. "Those at the level of 'anointment of the crown'" abide on the tenth ground. "Those at the level of 'one remaining life'" proceed then to enter the Tuṣita Heaven. "Those at the level of their very last birth" abide in the Tuṣita Heaven. "Those who have approached the site of enlightenment" are on the verge of putting to use the wisdom rooted in all-knowledge.

Among these seven types of bodhisattvas, even all those bodhisattvas who are at that level where they have generated the initial resolve are those to whom all beings should render reverence. How much the more so should this be true in the case of the remaining [six types of bodhisattvas]. Why is this the case? It is because they possess profound minds vast in the scope of their greatness. And it is because they possess the capacity to implement the teachings of the Tathāgatas.

When the bodhisattva at the level of initial generation of the resolve generates that resolve to realize bodhi, he becomes free of any deficiency in [his ability to course throughout] the ten directions, free of any deficiency in [his ability to visit] the buddhalands, and free of any deficiency in [his ability to interact with] all beings, this because, when he generates the bodhi-focused resolve, his kindness becomes universal in its extensiveness.

[Thus it is that he reflects], "In the case of those beings who have not yet gone across [to bodhi], I shall see that they are brought across. As for those beings who have not yet gained liberation, I shall see to their liberation. In those instances where beings have not yet been revived, I shall see to their being revived. In the case of those beings who have not yet realized cessation, I shall see that they realize cessation. Those who ought to become śrāvaka-disciples, I shall influence to enter the Śrāvaka-disciple Vehicle. Those who ought to become pratyekabuddhas, I shall influence to enter the Pratyekabuddha Vehicle. And as for those who ought to avail themselves of the Great Vehicle, I shall influence them to enter the Great Vehicle."

[These bodhisattvas] desire to influence all beings to realize cessation. It is not the case that they are motivated by the desire to bring but a lesser fraction of beings to the realization of cessation. Because this profound mind is so vast in the scope of its greatness, all beings should in every case be moved to offer them reverential respect.

何者為如來教量。如世尊說迦葉。譬如新月便應作
禮。非為滿月。如是迦葉。若信我者。應當禮敬諸
菩薩等。非為如來。何以故。從於菩薩出如來故。
又聲聞乘中亦說。

於彼知法者　　若老若年少　　應供養恭敬　　如梵志事火

[0518b12] 以是故。諸菩薩等。次於佛後皆應供養。如
偈。

紹持佛種者　　勝餘少分行　　是故諸菩薩　　次佛後供養
慈與虛空等　　普遍諸眾生　　是故最勝子　　次佛後供養
於諸眾生類　　大悲猶如子　　是故此佛子　　次佛後供養
悲心利眾生　　無二似虛空　　是故無畏者　　次佛後供養
一切時如父　　增長諸眾生　　是故諸菩薩　　次佛後供養

何者为如来教量。如世尊说迦叶。譬如新月便应作
礼。非为满月。如是迦叶。若信我者。应当礼敬诸
菩萨等。非为如来。何以故。从于菩萨出如来故。
又声闻乘中亦说。

于彼知法者　　若老若年少　　应供养恭敬　　如梵志事火

[0518b12] 以是故。诸菩萨等。次于佛后皆应供养。如
偈说。

绍持佛种者　　胜馀少分行　　是故诸菩萨　　次佛后供养
慈与虚空等　　普遍诸众生　　是故最胜子　　次佛后供养
于诸众生类　　大悲犹如子　　是故此佛子　　次佛后供养
悲心利众生　　无二似虚空　　是故无畏者　　次佛后供养
一切时如父　　增长诸众生　　是故诸菩萨　　次佛后供养

SUPPORTING CITATIONS FROM SCRIPTURE

What do we mean here by "[revering them because] they possess the capacity to implement the teachings of the Tathāgatas"? This is as expressed by the Bhagavān to Kāśyapa: "Just as one performs rites of ritual reverence on the new moon and not on the full moon, so too, Kāśyapa, should those having faith in me pay reverence to the bodhisattvas and not [exclusively] to the Tathāgatas themselves. And why? This is because it is from among the bodhisattvas that the Tathāgatas emerge."

This idea is also spoken of in [the teachings of] the Śrāvaka-disciple Vehicle:

As regards those knowledgeable about Dharma,
Whether they be old or young in years,
One should make offerings to them and pay reverence to them
In the manner of brahmacarins devoted to ritually serving fire.

It is for these sorts of reasons that one should make offerings to all bodhisattvas next in sequence after the Buddhas. This is as expressed in the following verses:

VERSES IN PRAISE OF BODHISATTVAS

Those who carry on the lineage of the Buddhas
Are superior to those cultivating lesser levels of conduct.
Thus it is that all of the Bodhisattvas,
Next after the Buddhas, are the recipients of offerings.

Their kindness is equal in scope to empty space
And extends universally to all of the beings.
Thus it is that those most supreme among their sons,
Next after the Buddhas, are the recipients of offerings.

In their relations with all types of beings,
Their great compassion is like that felt for one's son.
Thus it is that these sons of the Buddha,
Next after the Buddhas, are the recipients of offerings.

They benefit beings with the mind of compassion,
While, in [realization of] non-duality, they are like empty space.
Thus it is that these fearless ones,
Next after the Buddhas, are the recipients of offerings.

They are at all times like fathers
Striving to raise up all beings.
Thus it is that all bodhisattvas,
Next after the Buddhas, are the recipients of offerings.

繁體字

猶如地水火　　眾生常受用　　是故施樂者　　次佛後供養
唯為利眾生　　捨離自樂因　　是故彼一切　　次佛後供養
佛及佛之餘　　皆從初心出　　是故諸菩薩　　次佛後供養

[0518c01] 問尊者已正說資糧教緣起。今應說資糧體。

答

　既為菩薩母　　　亦為諸佛母
　般若波羅蜜　　　是覺初資糧

[0518c05] 　以般若波羅蜜是諸菩薩母故。為菩提初資糧。何以故。以最勝故。如諸身根中眼根最勝。諸身分中頭為最勝。諸波羅蜜中般若波羅蜜最勝亦如是。以般若波羅蜜最勝故。為初資糧。又前行故。如諸法中信為前行。諸波羅蜜中般若波羅蜜前行

簡体字

犹如地水火　　众生常受用　　是故施乐者　　次佛后供养
唯为利众生　　舍离自乐因　　是故彼一切　　次佛后供养
佛及佛之馀　　皆从初心出　　是故诸菩萨　　次佛后供养

[0518c01] 问尊者已正说资粮教缘起。今应说资粮体。

答

　既为菩萨母　　　亦为诸佛母
　般若波罗蜜　　　是觉初资粮

[0518c05] 　以般若波罗蜜是诸菩萨母故。为菩提初资粮。何以故。以最胜故。如诸身根中眼根最胜。诸身分中头为最胜。诸波罗蜜中般若波罗蜜最胜亦如是。以般若波罗蜜最胜故。为初资粮。又前行故。如诸法中信为前行。诸波罗蜜中般若波罗蜜前行

They are comparable to earth, to water, and to fire,
In that beings constantly put them to use.
Thus it is that those fond of giving,
Next after the Buddhas, present them with offerings.

Solely for the sake of benefiting beings,
They abandon the causes of personal happiness.
Thus it is that all of them,
Next after the Buddhas, are the recipients of offerings.

All Buddhas and all those following on the Buddhas,
Emerge from the generation of the initial resolve.
Thus it is that all of the Bodhisattvas,
Next after the Buddhas, are the recipients of offerings.

Question: The Venerable One has already rightly explained the causal bases for the arising of teachings on the provisions. Now he should explain what constitutes the substance of the provisions.

Response: (As below...)

MAIN DOCTRINAL SECTION: THE PROVISIONS
THE PERFECTION OF WISDOM AS SUBSUMING ALL PROVISIONS

005 – The Primary Provision: Prajñāpāramitā, Mother of Buddhas and Bodhisattvas

Since it is the mother of the Bodhisattvas,
It is also the mother of the Buddhas:
The prajñāpāramitā
Is the foremost among the provisions for enlightenment.

COMMENTARY:
ON THE SUPREMACY OF THE PERFECTION OF WISDOM

It is because the prajñāpāramitā is the mother of all bodhisattvas that it is foremost among the provisions for the acquisition of bodhi. How is this so? It is on account of its being the most supreme. In this sense, it is analogous to the eye, supreme among the body's sense faculties and is also analogous to the head, supreme among the parts of the body. Just so, the prajñāpāramitā abides in paramount supremacy among all of the pāramitās. Thus, it is on account of the prajñāpāramitā's supremacy that it is foremost among the provisions.

Additionally, [the prajñāpāramitā is supreme] because it is that which one must practice first. This is comparable to the case of faith which itself is that dharma among all dharmas which must be implemented first. Prajñāpāramitā's primacy in the practice of

繁體字

亦如是。以彼陀那若不迴向菩提。則非陀那波羅
蜜。如是尸羅等不迴向菩提亦非尸羅等波羅蜜。迴
向菩提即是般若。由般若前行故能迴向。以是前行
故。諸波羅蜜中般若波羅蜜。為菩提初資糧。又是
諸波羅蜜。三輪淨因體故。以般若波羅蜜為諸波羅
蜜三輪淨因體。是故般若波羅蜜。為菩提初資糧。
三輪淨者。菩薩於般若波羅蜜中行布施時。不念自
身。以離取自身故。不念受者差別。以斷一切處分
別故。不念施果。以諸法不來不出相故。如是菩薩
得三輪淨施。如淨施淨戒等亦如是。以此般若波羅
蜜是彼諸波羅蜜三輪淨因體故。般若波羅蜜為菩提
初資糧。

简体字

亦如是。以彼陀那若不迴向菩提。则非陀那波罗
蜜。如是尸罗等不迴向菩提亦非尸罗等波罗蜜。迴
向菩提即是般若。由般若前行故能迴向。以是前行
故。诸波罗蜜中般若波罗蜜。为菩提初资粮。又是
诸波罗蜜。三轮净因体故。以般若波罗蜜为诸波罗
蜜三轮净因体。是故般若波罗蜜。为菩提初资粮。
三轮净者。菩萨于般若波罗蜜中行布施时。不念自
身。以离取自身故。不念受者差别。以断一切处分
别故。不念施果。以诸法不来不出相故。如是菩萨
得三轮净施。如净施净戒等亦如是。以此般若波罗
蜜是彼诸波罗蜜三轮净因体故。般若波罗蜜为菩提
初资粮。

all of the pāramitās is just so. [Its stature as supreme therein] is due to the fact that, [when practicing *dāna*], if one does not transfer [the associated merit by dedicating it to the acquisition of bodhi], then it fails to qualify as *dāna* pāramitā (the perfection of giving). In this same manner, if one fails to transfer [the associated merit] from the practice of *śīla* and the other [pāramitas by dedicating it to the acquisition of bodhi], then that practice cannot qualify as *śīla* pāramitā (the perfection of moral virtue). So too it is with the other pāramitās as well.

The act of transferring [merit by dedicating it to the acquisition of bodhi] is itself just prajñā. It is because prajñā is the first among them which one practices that one thereby possesses the ability to carry out the transference [of merit through dedicating it to the acquisition of bodhi]. Thus it is on account of prajñāpāramitā's being the foremost practice among all of the pāramitās that it qualifies as foremost among the provisions for bodhi.

Also, it is because, in the practice of these pāramitās, [the prajñāpāramitā] is the very essence of the cause of purity in [one's understanding of] the three factors. It is because the prajñāpāramitā constitutes the very essence of the cause of purity in [one's understanding of] the three factors involved in all of the pāramitās that the prajñāpāramitā qualifies as the foremost among the provisions for bodhi.

Now, as for this "purity in [one's understanding of] the three factors," when the bodhisattva coursing in the prajñāpāramitā engages in the practice of giving, he does not hold in mind his own person, for he has abandoned any grasping at [even the concept of] his own person. Nor does he hold in mind any distinctions existing in the recipient [of that act of giving]. This is because he has severed all discriminations in all places. Nor does he hold in mind the karmic fruits of that act of giving, this because [he realizes that] all dharmas are characterized by neither coming nor going.

It is in this manner that the bodhisattva brings about the practice of giving wherein [his understanding of] the three factors has become purified. As it is with purity in giving, so too it is with purity in moral-virtue and with purity in the other [perfections]. It is because this prajñāpāramitā constitutes the very essence of the cause of purity in the three factors associated with all of the pāramitās that it therefore qualifies as the foremost among the provisions for bodhi.

又大果故。般若波羅蜜大果勝諸波羅蜜。 如經說

　菩提心福德　　及以攝受法　　於空若信解　　價勝十六分

[0518c27] 鞞羅摩經中大果因緣。此中應說。以是大果故。般若波羅蜜為菩提初資糧。問何故般若波羅蜜。得為菩薩母。答以能生故。方便所攝般若生諸菩薩。令求無上菩提。不求聲聞獨覺。以是生佛體因故。般若波羅蜜為菩薩母。又置於五波羅蜜中故。如言冥鉢囉膩波低也。冥為性。鉢囉膩波低為誦。即此性相是為摩多(摩多翻為母於字聲論中摩多字從冥鉢囉膩波低語中出冥是摩多體性鉢[1]囉膩波低是誦摩多義鉢囉膩波低正翻為置故以置為母義)譬如母生子。時或置床敷。或置地上。般若波羅蜜亦如是。生彼求菩提菩薩時。置於施等五波羅蜜中。以能置求菩提菩薩故。說般若波羅蜜為菩薩母。又以量故。如言茫摩泥也。茫為性摩泥為誦。即此性相是為摩多(於字聲論中摩多字又從茫摩泥語中出茫亦是體性摩泥是誦其義摩泥正翻為量故以量為母義)。譬如母生子已隨時籌量。如是我子以此食故身增。

又大果故。般若波罗蜜大果胜诸波罗蜜。 如经说

　菩提心福德　　及以摄受法　　于空若信解　　价胜十六分

[0518c27] 鞞罗摩经中大果因缘。此中应说。以是大果故。般若波罗蜜为菩提初资粮。问何故般若波罗蜜。得为菩萨母。答以能生故。方便所摄般若生诸菩萨。令求无上菩提。不求声闻独觉。以是生佛体因故。般若波罗蜜为菩萨母。又置于五波罗蜜中故。如言冥鉢罗腻波低也。冥为性。鉢罗腻波低为诵。即此性相是为摩多(摩多翻为母于字声论中摩多字从冥鉢罗腻波低语中出冥是摩多体性鉢[1]罗腻波低是诵摩多义鉢罗腻波低正翻为置故以置为母义)譬如母生子。时或置床敷。或置地上。般若波罗蜜亦如是。生彼求菩提菩萨时。置于施等五波罗蜜中。以能置求菩提菩萨故。说般若波罗蜜为菩萨母。又以量故。如言茫摩泥也。茫为性摩泥为诵。即此性相是为摩多(于字声论中摩多字又从茫摩泥语中出茫亦是体性摩泥是诵其义摩泥正翻为量故以量为母义)。譬如母生子已随时筹量。如是我子以此食故身增。

Additionally, it is on account of its great fruits. The great fruits brought about by the prajñāpāramitā are supreme over those deriving from any of the other pāramitās. This is as described in a sutra where it says:

The merit associated with the mind resolved on bodhi
And the dharmas employed for drawing in beings,
Compared with that from faith in or understanding of emptiness,
Is sixteen times greater in its value.

[Ideally], one should discuss at this point the causal factors associated with the great fruition as related in the *Vimalakīrti Sutra*. It is on account of its great fruits that the prajñāpāramitā is foremost among the provisions for the acquisition of bodhi.

THE PERFECTION OF WISDOM AS "MOTHER OF THE BODHISATTVAS"

Question: How is it that the prajñāpāramitā qualifies as "the mother of the Bodhisattvas"?

Response: It is on account of its ability to give birth to them. It is prajñā mediated by skillful means which brings about the birth of the bodhisattva. It causes him to seek the unsurpassed bodhi and to refrain from seeking the bodhi of the Śrāvaka-disciples and the Pratyekabuddhas. It is on account of its causing the birth of a buddha body that the prajñāpāramitā qualifies as "the mother of the Bodhisattvas."

Additionally, it is because of its "placement" within the [other] five pāramitās. [The etymology for the Sanskrit term for "mother" supports this "placement" interpretation.][5] This is analogous to when a mother gives birth to a child. At such time, she may do so in a way which places it on the cushions of a bed or else may do so in a way which places it on the ground. The prajñāpāramitā is comparable to this. When it gives birth to that bodhisattva who seeks bodhi, it does so in a way whereby [that bodhisattva] is placed in the midst of giving and the other five pāramitās. It is because it is able to effect such placement of the bodhisattva who seeks bodhi that the prajñāpāramitā qualifies as "the mother of the Bodhisattvas."

Additionally, it is on account of its serving as a means of "calculation." [The etymology for the Sanskrit term for "mother" also supports this "calculation" interpretation.][6]

By way of analogy, after a mother gives birth to a child, as befits the season, she calculates that, "If I proceed in this way, my child's body will grow through this approach to nutrition. If I proceed in

以此故損減。菩薩亦如是。以般若波羅蜜自量其身。我應如是布施。我應如是持戒等。以是自量因緣故。說般若波羅蜜為菩薩母。又以斟量故。譬如量物有鉢邏薩他。有阿宅迦。有突嚧[2]挐。有佉梨底等(如此間合升斗斛之類)斟量諸菩薩亦如是。此初發心。此修行。此得忍等。以斟量因緣故。說般若波羅蜜為菩薩母。又以修多羅中誦故。所謂於諸經中作母名誦。彼等經中有名稱遍諸佛國菩薩。名毘摩羅吉利帝。說伽他言(舊云維摩詰者不正)

　般若波羅蜜　菩薩仁者母　善方便為父　慈悲以為女

[0519a26] 　復有餘經。亦如是誦。以修多羅量故說。般若波羅蜜為菩薩母。問何故般若波羅蜜。亦為諸佛母。答以出生及顯示無障礙智故。過去未來現在諸佛。由般若波羅蜜阿含故。

以此故损减。菩萨亦如是。以般若波罗蜜自量其身。我应如是布施。我应如是持戒等。以是自量因缘故。说般若波罗蜜为菩萨母。又以斟量故。譬如量物有鉢逻萨他。有阿宅迦。有突嚧[2]挐。有佉梨底等(如此间合升斗斛之类)斟量诸菩萨亦如是。此初发心。此修行。此得忍等。以斟量因缘故。说般若波罗蜜为菩萨母。又以修多罗中诵故。所谓于诸经中作母名诵。彼等经中有名称遍诸佛国菩萨。名毘摩罗吉利帝。说伽他言(旧云维摩诘者不正)

　般若波罗蜜　菩萨仁者母　善方便为父　慈悲以为女

[0519a26] 　复有馀经。亦如是诵。以修多罗量故说。般若波罗蜜为菩萨母。问何故般若波罗蜜。亦为诸佛母。答以出生及显示无障碍智故。过去未来现在诸佛。由般若波罗蜜阿含故。

this other way, then it is likely to go into decline." So too it is with a bodhisattva. One uses the prajñāpāramitā to take the measure of one's own person, thinking, "I should go about the practice of giving in this way. I should go about the practice of upholding the moral precepts in this way." And so one continues along in this particular fashion. Thus it is on account of the causal circumstances involved in this sort of calculation that one speaks of the prajñāpāramitā as being "the mother of the Bodhisattvas."

Additionally, it is on account of its being the basis of "measuring out." This is comparable to having the various units of measure [such units as pints, quarts, gallons, and bushels][7] by which one makes measurements. So, too, it is with the Bodhisattvas [who "measure out" aspects of cultivation] in this same way, thinking, "This is the initial generation of the mind resolved on bodhi. This is the cultivation of the practices. This is the realization of the patiences." And so forth. Thus it is also on account of this causal basis associated with "measuring out" that one speaks of the prajñāpāramitā as being "the mother of the Bodhisattvas."

Additionally, it is because [the prajñāpāramitā] is inherent in one's recitation of the Sutras. This is a reference to the fact that, in the Sutras, "serving as a mother" [is etymologically implicit] in the term for "recitation." In those sutras, there is a famous bodhisattva named Vimalakīrti who travels to the lands of all buddhas. He uttered a gātha, saying:

The prajñāpāramitā
Is the mother of the Bodhisattvas, the humane ones.
Skillful means serves as their father,
And kindness and compassion are their daughters.

There are also other sutras in which this "recitation [as motherhood" relationship is implicit]. Hence it is also because the Sutras serve this function of "measuring out" [the prajñāpāramitā-infused concepts] that the prajñāpāramitā is said to serve as "the mother of the Bodhisattvas."

THE PERFECTION OF WISDOM AS "MOTHER OF THE BUDDHAS"

Question: How is it that the prajñāpāramitā is also "the mother of the Buddhas"?

Response: It is because it gives birth to and reveals unimpeded wisdom. All buddhas of the past, future and present come forth[8] on account of the prajñāpāramitā. It is on account of it that they have

繁體字

煩惱已盡當盡今盡以是出生故。般若波羅蜜為諸佛
母。顯示無障礙智者。以過去未來現在諸佛世尊顯
示無障礙智皆般若波羅蜜中顯。以是顯示無障礙智
故。諸佛[3]亦以般若波羅蜜為母此中有輸盧迦

由大悲相應	般若波羅蜜	於無為[4]險岸	佛子能超過
得到無等覺	利攝諸眾生	智度為母故	大人能如是
由得智度故	乃得成佛體	故為諸佛母	勝仙之所說

[0519b13]　何故此名般若波羅蜜。以不與聲聞獨覺共
故。名般若波羅蜜。於上更無所應知故。名般若波
羅蜜。此智到一切彼岸故。名般若波羅蜜。此般若
波羅蜜餘無能勝故。名般若波羅蜜。三世平等故。
名般若波羅蜜。虛空無邊平等故。名般若波羅蜜。
如是等勝因緣。如般若波羅蜜經中說。故名般若波
羅蜜。

簡体字

烦恼已尽当尽今尽以是出生故。般若波罗蜜为诸佛
母。显示无障碍智者。以过去未来现在诸佛世尊显
示无障碍智皆般若波罗蜜中显。以是显示无障碍智
故。诸佛[3]亦以般若波罗蜜为母此中有输卢迦

由大悲相应	般若波罗蜜	于无为[4]险岸	佛子能超过
得到无等觉	利摄诸众生	智度为母故	大人能如是
由得智度故	乃得成佛体	故为诸佛母	胜仙之所说

[0519b13]　何故此名般若波罗蜜。以不与声闻独觉共
故。名般若波罗蜜。于上更无所应知故。名般若波
罗蜜。此智到一切彼岸故。名般若波罗蜜。此般若
波罗蜜馀无能胜故。名般若波罗蜜。三世平等故。
名般若波罗蜜。虚空无边平等故。名般若波罗蜜。
如是等胜因缘。如般若波罗蜜经中说。故名般若波
罗蜜。

extinguished the afflictions in the past, will do so in the future, and now do so in the present. Because they are born forth from this, the prajñāpāramitā is therefore the mother of the Buddhas.

As for "revealing unimpeded wisdom," because the Buddhas, the Bhagavāns, of the past, future, and present manifest unimpeded wisdom, in every case, they are all born from within the prajñāpāramitā. It is on account of it that the Buddhas become able to manifest unimpeded wisdom. Hence the Buddhas too take the prajñāpāramitā as their mother. In this connection, we have ślokas as follows:

It is on account of that prajñāpāramitā
Which accords with the great compassion that,
Confronted with the perilous chasm of the unconditioned,
The sons of the Buddha are able to leap entirely beyond it.

They succeed in reaching the unequaled enlightenment
And in benefiting and drawing in all beings.
It is because the perfection of wisdom serves as their mother
That the great men are able to be thus.

It is through realization of the perfection of wisdom
That they are then able to perfect the body of a buddha.
Therefore it serves as the mother of the Buddhas.
So declared he who is supreme among all rishis.

Why is this referred to as the "prajñāpāramitā"?

It is because it is [a level of wisdom] not held in common with the Śrāvaka-disciples or the Pratyekabuddhas that it is referred to as the "prajñāpāramitā."

It is because there is nothing beyond it worth knowing that it is referred to as the "prajñāpāramitā."

It is because this wisdom reaches to the "other shore" of every matter that it is referred to as the "prajñāpāramitā."

It is because there is nothing anywhere else capable of vanquishing this prajñāpāramitā that it is referred to as the "prajñāpāramitā."

It is because it is uniformly equal in all of the three periods of time that it is referred to as the "prajñāpāramitā."

It is because it is uniformly equal throughout boundless space that it is referred to as the "prajñāpāramitā."

Such supreme causes and conditions as these are spoken of in the *Prajñāpāramitā Sutra*. It is on account of them that it is referred to as the "prajñāpāramitā."

[0519b20] 問已略說菩提初資糧。第二資糧今應說

施戒忍進定　　及此五之餘
皆由智度故　　波羅蜜所攝

[0519b23]　　此中陀那波羅蜜。為第二菩提資糧。以般若前行故。菩薩為菩提而行布施。是故施為第二資糧。於中生他身意樂。因名布施。非為作苦。彼有二種。謂財施法施。財施亦有二種。謂共識不共識。共識亦有二種。謂內及外。若施自身支節。若全身施。是為內施。若施男女妻妾及二足四足等。是為外施。不共識亦有二種。謂可食不可食。此有多種若施身內受用飲食等物。是為可食。若施身外受用香鬘所攝金銀珍寶衣服土田財物園池遊戲處等。是為不可食。

[0519b20] 问已略说菩提初资粮。第二资粮今应说

施戒忍进定　　及此五之馀
皆由智度故　　波罗蜜所摄

[0519b23]　　此中陀那波罗蜜。为第二菩提资粮。以般若前行故。菩萨为菩提而行布施。是故施为第二资粮。于中生他身意乐。因名布施。非为作苦。彼有二种。谓财施法施。财施亦有二种。谓共识不共识。共识亦有二种。谓内及外。若施自身支节。若全身施。是为内施。若施男女妻妾及二足四足等。是为外施。不共识亦有二种。谓可食不可食。此有多种若施身内受用饮食等物。是为可食。若施身外受用香鬘所摄金银珍宝衣服土田财物园池游戏处等。是为不可食。

Question: The foremost among the provisions for the acquisition of bodhi has now been explained in brief. Hence one should now proceed with explaining the second-tier provisions.

[**Response:** As below...]

SPECIFIC FORMULATIONS OF THE PROVISIONS

---

006 – Prajñā Includes the Remaining Five Perfections and Their Retinue

Because giving, moral virtue, patience, vigor, meditation,
And the others following from these five
All arise from the perfection of wisdom,
They are included within the pāramitās.

COMMENTARY:

THE SIX PERFECTIONS
THE PERFECTION OF GIVING

We are treating *dāna* pāramitā (the perfection of giving) herein as the second of the bodhi provisions because it is prajñā that takes primary priority in practice. The bodhisattva practices giving to realize bodhi. Hence giving is taken as the second of the provisions.

Through this practice, one facilitates both physical and mental happiness in other beings. That is why it is referred to as "giving." It is not that this is done to inflict suffering on others.

Giving is of two kinds: the giving of material wealth and the giving of Dharma. The giving of material wealth is itself of two types, namely that which is sentient and that which is insentient.

Sentient giving is also of two types, namely that which is "inward" (i.e. "personal") and that which is "outward" (i.e. "extra-personal"). If one gives the limbs of one's own body or if one gives one's entire body, this is what is meant by "inward" giving. If one were to give sons, daughters, wives, consorts, or any other of the two-legged or four-legged beings, this would be a case of "outward" giving.

"Insentient" is also of two types: consumable and inconsumable. In this there is much variety. Anything which when given may be used internally such as food and drink is "consumable."

When one gives things used outside the body such as anything in the category of fragrances and garlands, or such things as gold, silver, precious jewels, clothing, lands, wealth, gardens, ponds, places to stroll about and enjoy oneself, and so forth—these fall within the category of "inconsumable."

繁體字

然可受用法施。亦有二種。謂世間出世間。若因法施。於流轉中（舊云生死者非正翻名今改為流轉也已後諸云流轉者皆是此義）出生可愛身根境界。是為世間。若因法施果報。越度流轉。是為出世間。彼財施法施各有二種謂有著無著。若為自身。若為資生。若為勝果。悕望相續以財法施。是為有著。若為利益安樂一切眾生。若為無障礙智。是為無著。其餘更有無畏施等。亦隨順入財施中。彼二種施果及餘氣（謂津液也）具如大乘經說。此中當略說偈

飲食及被服	隨須皆布施	亦施花鬘燈	末香與音樂
或施諸美味	藥物及[5]猗枕	養病之所須	并醫人給侍
男女與妻妾	奴婢及倉庫	莊飾諸婇女	隨須皆布施
所有諸寶物	種種莊嚴具	象馬車乘等	妙物盡施之

简体字

然可受用法施。亦有二种。谓世间出世间。若因法施。于流转中（旧云生死者非正翻名今改为流转也已后诸云流转者皆是此义）出生可爱身根境界。是为世间。若因法施果报。越度流转。是为出世间。彼财施法施各有二种谓有着无着。若为自身。若为资生。若为胜果。悕望相续以财法施。是为有着。若为利益安乐一切众生。若为无障碍智。是为无着。其馀更有无畏施等。亦随顺入财施中。彼二种施果及馀气（谓津液也）具如大乘经说。此中当略说偈

饮食及被服	随须皆布施	亦施花鬘灯	末香与音乐
或施诸美味	药物及[5]猗枕	养病之所须	并医人给侍
男女与妻妾	奴婢及仓库	庄饰诸婇女	随须皆布施
所有诸宝物	种种庄严具	象马车乘等	妙物尽施之

Now, useful Dharma giving is itself of two kinds, mundane and supramundane. If it occurs that, on account of a given act of Dharma giving, a person comes to take rebirths in cyclic existence in a likeable body surrounded by enjoyable objective circumstances, this is an instance of "mundane" Dharma giving.

If the fruits of an act of Dharma giving conduce to transcendence of cyclic existence, that is an instance of "supramundane" Dharma giving.

The giving of material wealth and the giving of Dharma each involve two subtypes: "involving attachment" and "free of attachment." Where one gives either wealth or Dharma for one's own sake, for the sake of enhancing one's present situation, for the sake of some superior karmic result, or in order to ensure current karmic circumstances will continue on into the future, this is what is meant by giving "involving attachment."

Where giving is done for the sake of bringing benefit and happiness to all beings or is done for the sake of realizing unimpeded wisdom—these instances of giving are "free of attachment."

Additional sorts of giving include "the giving of fearlessness" and other types subsumed under "the giving of material wealth."[9] The karmic rewards and secondary effects of those two types of giving (material wealth and Dharma) are comprehensively explained in the Great Vehicle scriptures. We should describe them here briefly in verse:

Food and drink and clothing as well—
Adapting to circumstances, one gives these to all,
While also giving flowers, garlands, lamps,
Powdered fragrances and music.

One may give all manner of exquisite flavors,
Medicines, and fine pillows,
Whatever is needed by those recovering from illnesses,
Together with the services of physicians.

Sons and daughters, wives and consorts,
Servants and storehouses,
And well-adorned maidens—
As befits the circumstances, may all be given.[10]

All manner of precious things,
All sorts of articles of adornment,
Elephants and horses, carriages and such—
Such marvelous things may all be given.

繁體字

園林修道處　　池井集會堂　　土田并雜物　　客舍等皆施
若二足四足　　若復一洲渚　　村落與國都　　及王境悉施
施所玩好物　　利樂憪須者　　為諸眾生依　　怖者施無畏
施其所難捨　　手足眼耳鼻　　亦施心與頭　　舉身悉能捨
修行布施時　　常於受者所　　應生福田想　　亦如善眷屬
布施諸果報　　具足善聚集　　迴向為自他　　成佛及淨土
菩薩所行施　　正迴向佛體　　此菩薩陀那　　得名波羅蜜
若彼若此岸　　亦無能說者　　施果到於彼　　說為施彼岸

[0520a09] 今說施主差別

不貪於愛果　　悲故三輪淨　　正覺說彼施　　是為求菩提

簡体字

园林修道处　　池井集会堂　　土田并杂物　　客舍等皆施
若二足四足　　若复一洲渚　　村落与国都　　及王境悉施
施所玩好物　　利乐憪须者　　为诸众生依　　怖者施无畏
施其所难舍　　手足眼耳鼻　　亦施心与头　　举身悉能舍
修行布施时　　常于受者所　　应生福田想　　亦如善眷属
布施诸果报　　具足善聚集　　迴向为自他　　成佛及净土
菩萨所行施　　正迴向佛体　　此菩萨陀那　　得名波罗蜜
若彼若此岸　　亦无能说者　　施果到于彼　　说为施彼岸

[0520a09] 今说施主差别

不贪于爱果　　悲故三轮净　　正觉说彼施　　是为求菩提

Gardens, groves, places to cultivate the Path,
Ponds, wells, meeting halls,
Lands and fields with their various enhancements,
Guest houses and such—these may all be given.

Whether two-legged or four-legged beings,
Or perhaps even islands,
Villages, the capital of a country,
Or even the domain of a king—all may be given.

Giving things used in play,
Benefiting and pleasing those who wish for or need them,
One becomes one on whom beings can rely.
And for the frightened, one provides them fearlessness.

One may give what others find difficult to relinquish:
One's hands, feet, eyes, ear, or nose—
One may also give even one's heart or head—
One is able to give even one's entire body.

When one cultivates the practice of giving,
In reflecting on the recipients, one always
Should generate the thought of them as fields of merit
And also as belonging to one's own retinue of the good.

The karmic rewards resulting from giving,
Bring to completion the accumulation of goodness.
One dedicates it all for the sake of self and others,
That all may achieve buddhahood and reach the purelands.

That giving practiced by the bodhisattva
Is rightly dedicated to the gaining of a buddha's body.
This *dāna* of the bodhisattva
Is that worthy to be known as "pāramitā."

Whether it be that done "on the near shore" or "the far shore,"
Still, it is indescribable in the nature of its qualities.
Where the fruition of giving extends to perfection's "far shore,"
This is what qualifies as "the perfection of giving."[11]

THE VARIOUS TYPES OF BENEFACTORS

Now, we shall describe the distinctions among the various types
of benefactors:

One does not covet any pleasing karmic result.
It is done from compassion and with the three factors purified.[12]
The Rightly Enlightened One said: "Such giving
Is that which is done for the sake of seeking bodhi."

繁體字

我已作此事　正作當亦作　若作如是捨　傭賃非布施
貪增施果故　隨須即能捨　說為息利人　智念非施主
不貪增益果　唯以悲心施　此名真施主　餘皆是商販
如大雲遍雨　諸處等心施　此名大施主　餘皆是少分
施及施果報　哀愍與須者　施主於眾人　猶如其父母
不念所施物　受者及施者　而常樂布施　此名為施主
若不分別佛　菩提與菩薩　而為菩提施　彼當速成佛

[0520a26] 問已解釋陀那波羅蜜。今應說尸羅波羅蜜。答波羅蜜義如前解釋。尸羅義今當說。以尸羅故說為尸羅。言尸羅者謂習近也。此是體相。又本性義。

简体字

我已作此事　正作当亦作　若作如是舍　佣赁非布施
贪增施果故　随须即能舍　说为息利人　智念非施主
不贪增益果　唯以悲心施　此名真施主　馀皆是商贩
如大云遍雨　诸处等心施　此名大施主　馀皆是少分
施及施果报　哀愍与须者　施主于众人　犹如其父母
不念所施物　受者及施者　而常乐布施　此名为施主
若不分别佛　菩提与菩萨　而为菩提施　彼当速成佛

[0520a26] 问已解释陀那波罗蜜。今应说尸罗波罗蜜。答波罗蜜义如前解释。尸罗义今当说。以尸罗故说为尸罗。言尸罗者谓习近也。此是体相。又本性义。

Where one reflects, "I have performed such endeavors in the past,
Perform them now, and shall also perform them in the future"—
If one's relinquishing of possessions is done in this way,
It is as if done for hire and so does not qualify as "giving."

If, due to coveting some result beyond the act of giving,
A person becomes able to give because it suits his own needs,
He is said to be "one seeking to earn interest."
The wise are aware such persons do not qualify as benefactors.

When one doesn't covet some form of enhanced karmic result,
But rather gives with a mind imbued with compassion,
This person qualifies as a genuine benefactor.
The others are just businessmen engaged in buying and selling.

Where one is like those great clouds bringing rain to all places,
Giving with a mind of equal regard in all circumstances—
This is one who qualifies as a great benefactor.
The rest reach only a fraction of his stature.

In giving and the karmic result from giving,
One acts with heartfelt sympathy for those in need.
In relating to all the many people, the benefactor
Regards them all as if they were his own fathers and mothers.

One does not retain in his mind those things which are given,
The recipients of the gifts, or the one who does the giving,
But rather finds constant happiness in the act of giving.
It is those of this sort who are worthy to be known as benefactors.

Where someone makes no distinctions regarding buddhas,
Regarding bodhi, or regarding bodhisattvas,
And yet engages in giving for the sake of reaching bodhi—
That sort of person will swiftly gain realization of buddhahood.

The Perfection of Moral Virtue

Question: Having already explained the pāramitā of *dāna*, one should now explain *śīla* pāramitā (the perfection of moral virtue).
Response: The term "pāramitā" is as explained earlier.

Connotations and Associations of the Word Śīla

We shall now explain the meaning of *śīla*, referencing its various connotations as follows:

"Habituation." This refers to effects thereby produced at the level of both substance and characteristics, (i.e. "inwardly" and outwardly").

繁體字

如世間有樂戒苦戒等。又清涼義。為不悔因離心熱憂惱故。又安隱義。能為他世樂因故。又安靜義。能建立止觀故。又寂滅義。得涅槃樂因故。又端嚴義。以能莊飾故。又淨潔義。能洗惡戒垢故。又頭首義。能為入眾無怯弱因故。又讚歎義。能生名稱故。此戒是身口意善行所轉生。於中遠離殺生不與取欲邪行等。是三種身戒。遠離妄語破壞語麤惡語雜戲語等。是四種口戒。遠離貪瞋邪見等。是三種意戒。如是[1]等身口意善行所轉生十種戒。與貪瞋癡所生十種惡行為對治。彼十種惡行下中上常習近故。墮於地獄畜生閻摩世等。如前數十種善行戒。若不與覺分相應。

簡体字

如世间有乐戒苦戒等。又清凉义。为不悔因离心热忧恼故。又安隐义。能为他世乐因故。又安静义。能建立止观故。又寂灭义。得涅盘乐因故。又端严义。以能庄饰故。又净洁义。能洗恶戒垢故。又头首义。能为入众无怯弱因故。又赞叹义。能生名称故。此戒是身口意善行所转生。于中远离杀生不与取欲邪行等。是三种身戒。远离妄语破坏语麤恶语杂戏语等。是四种口戒。远离贪瞋邪见等。是三种意戒。如是[1]等身口意善行所转生十种戒。与贪瞋痴所生十种恶行为对治。彼十种恶行下中上常习近故。堕于地狱畜生阎摩世等。如前数十种善行戒。若不与觉分相应。

"Basic nature," as with people in the world described as "happy by nature," or "anguished by nature."

"Coolness" as in the case of one who leaves behind anguishing mind-inflaming afflictions [caused by immoral actions].

"Security," because it causes future-life happiness.

"Quiescence," because it is able to establish one in meditative calming and contemplation (śamatha-vipaśyanā).

"Cessation," because it is a cause for the bliss of nirvāṇa.

"Stateliness," because it is able to enhance outward appearance.

"Purity," because it is able to wash away the defilement of immoral actions.

"Primacy" because it enables abiding in the community free of any basis for timidity.

"Praiseworthiness," because it is able to bring about a fine reputation.

MORAL VIRTUE AS DEFINED BY THE TEN GOOD KARMIC DEEDS

These moral precepts derive from good actions on the part of the body, mouth, and mind. When acting in accordance with them, one abandons the killing of beings, the taking of what is not given, sexual misconduct, and so forth. These are the three moral precepts relating to the body.

One abandons lying, slanderous speech, harsh speech, and the various sorts of frivolous speech (gratuitous lewdness, useless banter, rumor-mongering, etc.). These are the four moral precepts associated with the mouth.

One abandons covetousness, hatefulness, and wrong views. These are the three moral precepts associated with the mind.

These ten types of moral precepts deriving from good conduct in body, mouth, and mind serve to counter the ten kinds of bad conduct generated through covetousness, hatefulness, and delusion. It is on account of constant and habitual proximity to actions reflective of the lower, middling, and higher degrees of those ten bad practices that one falls down into such places as the hell realms, the animal realms, and *yamaloka* (the hungry-ghost realms).

THE KARMIC EFFECTS OF MORAL VIRTUE

Now, as for the ten types of moral precepts reflective of good actions, so long as coursing in them is disconnected from factors generating enlightenment, constant and habitual proximity to the

繁體字

下中上常習近故。隨福上上差別。當得天人差別。
若與覺分相應十種善行。戒上上常習近多作。故當
得聲聞地及菩薩地中轉勝差別。又此菩薩戒聚。有
六十五種無盡。如無盡意經中說當知。又略說有二
種戒。謂平等種蒔戒。不平等種蒔戒。平等種蒔戒
者。以此善身口意積聚故。於生生中種蒔。若界若
富樂。若聲聞獨覺。若相報若淨土若成熟眾生。若
正遍覺等。彼皆說名平等種蒔戒。與此相違。名不
平等種蒔戒。

简体字

下中上常习近故。随福上上差别。当得天人差别。
若与觉分相应十种善行。戒上上常习近多作。故当
得声闻地及菩萨地中转胜差别。又此菩萨戒聚。有
六十五种无尽。如无尽意经中说当知。又略说有二
种戒。谓平等种莳戒。不平等种莳戒。平等种莳戒
者。以此善身口意积聚故。于生生中种莳。若界若
富乐。若声闻独觉。若相报若净土若成熟众生。若
正遍觉等。彼皆说名平等种莳戒。与此相违。名不
平等种莳戒。

lower, middling, and superior grades of such practice produces karmic effects reflecting the distinctions in the merit's relative superiority. As a consequence, one becomes bound to gain rebirth in the appropriately corresponding levels among gods and men.

Where linked to enlightenment-generating factors, constant, habitual, and often-repeated coursing in the ten good karmic actions done at the superior level of moral precept practice [produces the following karmic effects]: One becomes destined to gain the grounds of the Śrāvaka-disciples or the grounds of the Bodhisattvas at ever more superior levels of acquisition [as befits the quality and number of such karmic deeds].

Types of Moral Precepts
The Bodhisattva Precepts

Additionally, as for the collections of bodhisattva precepts, there are sixty-five different kinds of inexhaustibility associated with them as related in the *Akṣayamati Sutra*. One should become knowledgeable about this matter.[13]

Two Instances of Two-Fold Precept Classification
"Continuous" versus "Discontinuous" Moral Precepts

Also, there are in general two categories of moral-precepts, namely those which are "the same when transplanted" and those which are not "the same when transplanted." As for those which are "the same when transplanted," this refers for instance to where, on account of the accumulation of the good deeds of body, mouth, and mind, [that inclination toward moral behavior] is "transplanted" yet again in each succeeding life.

This concept may be applicable in relation to the realm [into which one is reborn], in relation to the karmic blessings [which one experiences in the subsequent rebirth], in relation to [one's tendency to take up] the Śrāvaka-disciple or the Pratyekabuddha [Paths], in relation to the process of mutual repayment [of karmic indebtedness], in relation to [one's association with particular] purelands, in relation to the ripening of [particular other] beings, in relation to the right and universal enlightenment, and so forth. All of these may be explained in terms of being associated with morality which is "the same when transplanted." Whatever stands in opposition to these [examples] corresponds to morality which is not "the same when transplanted."[14]

復有二種戒謂有作戒無作戒。若於有作中有所作者。名有作戒。與此相違名無作戒。復有九種戒。謂凡夫戒。外道五通戒。人戒。欲界天子戒。色界天子戒無色界天子戒。[2]諸學無學聲聞戒。獨覺戒。菩薩戒。凡夫戒者。入生處故盡。外道五通戒者。神通退故盡。人戒者。十善業道盡故盡。欲界天子戒者。福盡故盡。色界天子戒者。禪那盡故盡。無色界天子戒者。三摩鉢帝盡故盡。諸學無學聲聞戒者。究竟涅槃故盡。獨覺戒者。闕大悲故盡。菩薩戒者。則無有盡。

復有二种戒谓有作戒无作戒。若于有作中有所作者。名有作戒。与此相违名无作戒。复有九种戒。谓凡夫戒。外道五通戒。人戒。欲界天子戒。色界天子戒无色界天子戒。[2]诸学无学声闻戒。独觉戒。菩萨戒。凡夫戒者。入生处故尽。外道五通戒者。神通退故尽。人戒者。十善业道尽故尽。欲界天子戒者。福尽故尽。色界天子戒者。禅那尽故尽。无色界天子戒者。三摩鉢帝尽故尽。诸学无学声闻戒者。究竟涅盘故尽。独觉戒者。阙大悲故尽。菩萨戒者。则无有尽。

"Effortful" Versus "Effortless" Moral Precepts

There are yet another two primary categories of moral precept practice, namely "effortful" morality and "effortless" morality. If in one's actions, one must still rely on intentional effort to adhere to moral precepts, then this is what is referred to as "effortful" morality. The contrary case qualifies as "effortless" morality."[15]

A Nine-Fold Classification of Moral Precepts

There are yet another nine kinds of moral precepts, as follows:

1 – The moral precepts for the common person.
2 – The moral precepts of the non-Buddhists who have gained the five spiritual powers.
3 – The moral precepts of humans.
4 – The moral precepts of the desire-realm gods.
5 – The moral precepts of the form-realm gods.
6 – The moral precepts of the formless-realm gods.
7 – The moral precepts of Śrāvaka-disciples, both those still in training and those beyond training.
8 – The moral precepts of the Pratyekabuddhas.
9 – The moral precepts of the Bodhisattvas.

As for the moral precepts taken on by the common person, they cease completely to be in force upon entering the new rebirth location. In the case of the non-Buddhists who have gained the five spiritual powers, they cease completely at the time when they lose their spiritual powers. As for the precepts of humans, when the path of the ten good karmic deeds ceases to exist, then they too cease to exist. In the case of the precepts of the desire-realm gods, when their karmic blessings are exhausted, they too cease. In the case of the precepts of the form-realm gods, when their dhyāna concentration ceases, those precepts cease as well. In the case of the formless-realm gods, when their *samāpatti* (absorption) ceases, those precepts cease.

In the case of the precepts of Śrāvaka-disciples, both those still in training and those beyond training, when they reach their final nirvāṇa, those precepts then cease. In the case of the precepts of the Pratyekabuddhas, because those beings are deficient as regards the great compassion, their precepts come to an end [on reaching their final nirvāṇa]. As for the precepts observed by the Bodhisattvas, they never end.

以此戒能顯明諸戒故。種子相續無盡故。菩薩相續
無盡故。如來戒無盡故。以此因緣。菩薩戒者說名
無盡。諸菩薩戒。迴向菩提故。說名戒波羅蜜。此
中有輸盧[3]迦。

繁體字

猶如父愛功力子　　亦如自身愛壽命　　出離有愛戒亦爾
大心健者之所愛　　此戒牟尼習近已　　解脫於欲離有愛
似烏凡人所棄捨　　智者常當愛此戒　　此戒利益於自他
令身端嚴離憂乏　　此世他世勝莊嚴　　是戒智者當所愛
此戒不由於他力　　非不可得非乞求　　皆因自力而得之
是故上人愛此戒　　財物國境并土地　　自身肌肉及以頭
皆能捨之不捨戒　　為欲淨彼勝菩提　　假使從天墜於地
設令自地昇於天　　為滿離垢無染地　　應當決定不移動
若已滿足戒方便　　此時即得第二地　　既得離垢清淨地
是時成就心所欲

以此戒能显明诸戒故。种子相续无尽故。菩萨相续
无尽故。如来戒无尽故。以此因缘。菩萨戒者说名
无尽。诸菩萨戒。迴向菩提故。说名戒波罗蜜。此
中有输卢[3]迦

简体字

犹如父爱功力子　　亦如自身爱寿命　　出离有爱戒亦尔
大心健者之所爱　　此戒牟尼习近已　　解脱于欲离有爱
似乌凡人所弃舍　　智者常当爱此戒　　此戒利益于自他
令身端严离忧乏　　此世他世胜庄严　　是戒智者当所爱
此戒不由于他力　　非不可得非乞求　　皆因自力而得之
是故上人爱此戒　　财物国境并土地　　自身肌肉及以头
皆能舍之不舍戒　　为欲净彼胜菩提　　假使从天坠于地
设令自地升于天　　为满离垢无染地　　应当决定不移动
若已满足戒方便　　此时即得第二地　　既得离垢清净地
是时成就心所欲

Because these moral precepts are able to illuminate all other moral precepts, because the [karmic] seeds [planted through adopting them] continue on endlessly, because the Bodhisattvas themselves continue on endlessly, and because the precepts of the Tathāgatas are endless—it is for these reasons that the bodhisattva precepts are described as endless. It is because the moral-precepts of the Bodhisattvas are dedicated to the realization of [the utmost, right, and perfect] bodhi (anuttarasamyaksaṃbodhi) that they are said to define the "pāramitā" of moral virtue. In this connection, we have these ślokas:[16]

VERSES ON THE PERFECTION OF MORAL VIRTUE

Just as a father loves an accomplished and strong son,
And just as one cherishes one's very own life—
So too regard precepts by which love for existence is abandoned.
They are loved by the heroic stalwarts possessed of great minds.

After the Muni drew close to these precepts in practice,
He became liberated from desire and abandoned love for existence.
They are such as common men, like crows, are inclined to reject.
The wise, however, should constantly cherish these precepts.

These precepts bring benefit to both oneself and others,
Causing fine appearance and freedom from worry or privation.
In this life and ensuing lives, one is supreme in one's stateliness.
These precepts are such as the wise should cherish.

These precepts do not derive from the power of others.
They are not unobtainable and need not be begged from others.
In all cases, it is through one's own power that one gains them.
Therefore the superior person cherishes these precepts.

One's wealth, country, and lands,
One's own body, flesh, and even one's own head—
One could relinquish them all, but will not relinquish the precepts,
Acting thus for the sake of purifying that supreme bodhi.

Even were one faced with falling from the heavens to the ground,
Or even if one might raise one's own ground on up to the heavens,
To perfect the stainless ground free of all defilement,
One should remain resolute and refrain from being moved.

Once one has perfected the moral-precept methods,
One then immediately gains the second [bodhisattva] ground.[17]
Having gained the pure ground free of all defilement,
One may then accomplish whatever one wishes.

若復天人修羅世　　及畜生中可化者　　[4]善知教化方便已
隨念往彼利益之　　或以布施攝眾生　　或以愛語入其意
或復與其安隱利　　或與同事助其力　　或在人中為其主
或居天眾而自在　　彼彼方便引導之　　悉當安置於白法
具足實戒神通故　　便能乾竭於大海　　世間盡時火增盛
於剎那頃悉能滅　　觀於世間種種惱　　惱而生病由離親
智者有戒通方便　　為世親依示勝道

[0521a03] 問已解釋尸羅波羅蜜。今應說羼提波羅蜜。答此中羼提者。若身若心受諸苦樂。其志堪忍不高不下心無染濁。此名略說羼提。若自在說。則施設為三。謂身住持。心住持。法住持。於中身住持忍者。謂身所遭苦。若外有心無心不愛之觸。

若复天人修罗世　　及畜生中可化者　　[4]善知教化方便已
随念往彼利益之　　或以布施摄众生　　或以爱语入其意
或复与其安隐利　　或与同事助其力　　或在人中为其主
或居天众而自在　　彼彼方便引导之　　悉当安置于白法
具足实戒神通故　　便能乾竭于大海　　世间尽时火增盛
于刹那顷悉能灭　　观于世间种种恼　　恼而生病由离亲
智者有戒通方便　　为世亲依示胜道

[0521a03] 问已解释尸罗波罗蜜。今应说羼提波罗蜜。答此中羼提者。若身若心受诸苦乐。其志堪忍不高不下心无染浊。此名略说羼提。若自在说。则施设为三。谓身住持。心住持。法住持。于中身住持忍者。谓身所遭苦。若外有心无心不爱之触。

Whether it be within the worlds of gods, men, or *asuras,*
Or among those animals amenable to ripening,
Having become well aware of the means used in teaching,
As befits one's judgments, one goes there to benefit them.

Perhaps one resorts to giving in order to draw in beings.
Or uses pleasing words which penetrate their minds.
Or else provides them with the benefit of peaceful security,
Or engages in joint endeavors, thus enhancing their strengths.[18]

Perhaps one serves as a lord among men,
Or abides, sovereignly independent, among communities of gods.
In each of those places one uses skillful means to lead them along.
One should thus establish them all in adopting pristine dharmas.

By perfecting spiritual powers arising from genuine moral virtue,
One becomes able even to dry up the great sea.[19]
Thus when this world ends and the fires increase and spread,
In but a kṣaṇa's instant, one is able to extinguish them all.[20]

One contemplates the different afflictions of beings in the world.
Coursing in afflictions, they fall sick, and thus abandon relatives.
The wise, possessing moral virtue, powers, and skillful means,
Serve the world as a reliable relatives, teaching the supreme Path.

THE PERFECTION OF PATIENCE

Question: Having already explained the pāramitā of śīla, one should now explain kṣānti pāramitā (the perfection of patience).

Response: As intended herein, kṣānti refers to the ability of one's resolve to endure all manner of suffering and bliss, both physical and mental, without feeling either elevated or depressed, and without the mind being clouded by any defilement-induced turbidity.[21] This is a brief description of what is meant by kṣānti.

THE THREE TYPES OF PATIENCE

As interpreted by Vaśitva,[22] one may establish three categories [of patience] here: that sustained by the body, that sustained by the mind, and that sustained through Dharma.

PATIENCE SUSTAINED BY THE BODY

As for "patience sustained by the body," this refers to occasions when the body encounters painful sensations originating from without caused by disagreeable physical contacts inflicted by sentient or insentient agents. When in such instances, one remains able

所生身苦堪忍不計。此名身住持忍外所生者。謂以
食因緣故起怖瞋癡。及蚊虻蛇虎師子熊等二足四足
多足。諸有心物無量因緣逼惱於身。或復來乞手足
耳鼻頭目支節。而割截之。於此惡事心無悶亂亦無
動異。此名身住持忍。又暴風盛日寒熱雨雹擊觸因
緣。諸無心物來逼惱時。遍身苦切而能安受。此亦
名忍。又內身所起界動因緣故。風黃[1]痰癊及起所
生四百四病極為身苦。於逼惱時能忍不計。亦名身
住持忍。於中心住持忍者。若有罵詈瞋嫌呵責毀謗
挫辱欺誑等不愛語道。來逼惱時。其心不動亦無濁
亂。此名心住持忍。

所生身苦堪忍不計。此名身住持忍外所生者。谓以
食因缘故起怖瞋痴。及蚊虻蛇虎师子熊等二足四足
多足。诸有心物无量因缘逼恼于身。或复来乞手足
耳鼻头目支节。而割截之。于此恶事心无闷乱亦无
动异。此名身住持忍。又暴风盛日寒热雨雹击触因
缘。诸无心物来逼恼时。遍身苦切而能安受。此亦
名忍。又内身所起界动因缘故。风黄[1]痰癊及起所
生四百四病极为身苦。于逼恼时能忍不计。亦名身
住持忍。于中心住持忍者。若有骂詈瞋嫌呵责毁谤
挫辱欺诳等不爱语道。来逼恼时。其心不动亦无浊
乱。此名心住持忍。

to endure the physical pain without reckoning it [to be a problem], this qualifies as "patience sustained by the body."

As for [physical suffering] "originating from without," this may involve fear, hatred, or delusion arising in relation to obtaining sustenance, or else might involve mosquitoes, snakes, tigers, lions, bears, and other such two-legged, four-legged, or multi-legged sentient beings tormenting one's physical body in countless ways. It might also involve someone coming along, seeking to slice away one's hands, feet, ears, nose, head, eyes, or limbs.

When, with respect to these loathsome circumstances, one's mind is able to remain undiscouraged, unconfused, and unshaken, this qualifies as "patience sustained by the body."

Additionally, this may involve violent winds, blazing sun, cold, heat, rain, hail, or situations involving being physically struck. In instances where insentient phenomena torment and afflict the body so that even one's entire body may be subjected to intense pain and yet one remains able to endure it peacefully, this is [physical] patience [associated with "outwardly-originating" phenomena].

Also, in those instances when there arise in one's own body causal factors linked to changes in the sense realms—in instances when [internal] winds, bile, viscous disease-related fluids, or watery disease-related fluids generate the four hundred and four kinds of diseases—when in any of these circumstances the most extreme sorts of physical suffering arise and yet one remains able amidst such torment to endure it without reckoning it [to be a problem]— this too qualifies as "patience sustained by the body."

PATIENCE SUSTAINED BY THE MIND

Among these [three types of patience], "patience sustained by the mind" refers to circumstances wherein one's mind remains unmoving, free of turbidity, and free of confusion, this even when one is tormented and afflicted by those subjecting one to cursing, vilification, denunciation, slander, defamation, deception, or other sorts of disagreeable speech. This is what qualifies as "patience sustained by the mind."

Also, when one is touched by the eight worldly dharmas: gain, loss, esteem, disesteem, blame, praise, suffering, and happiness—if the mind is not elevated by them, is not cast down by them, and remains as unshaken as a mountain—this qualifies as "patience sustained by the mind."

繁體字

又八種世法所觸。謂得利失利好名惡名譏譽苦樂中。心無高下不動如山。是名心住持忍。又斷順眠瞋故。無殺害心。無結恨心。無鬪諍心。無訴訟心。自護護他。於眾生中慈心相應。與悲共行起歡喜意恒作捨心。此等亦名心住持忍。於中法住持忍者。於內於外如實觀察故。外者。謂罵詈殺害等。罵詈者。聲字和合同時不散。以剎那故。字空故。聲如響故。不可說次第相應義。此中無有罵詈。但諸餘凡夫虛妄分別而生瞋怒。若字與聲自性義中知不可得。心則隨順不相違背。平等忍受。此名法住持忍。又於殺害者所。當作是念。身非害者。身若無心。則如草木壁影等故。心亦非害者。以心非色。

简体字

又八种世法所触。谓得利失利好名恶名讥誉苦乐中。心无高下不动如山。是名心住持忍。又断顺眠瞋故。无杀害心。无结恨心。无鬪諍心。无诉讼心。自护护他。于众生中慈心相应。与悲共行起欢喜意恒作舍心。此等亦名心住持忍。于中法住持忍者。于内于外如实观察故。外者。谓骂詈杀害等。骂詈者。声字和合同时不散。以刹那故。字空故。声如响故。不可说次第相应义。此中无有骂詈。但诸馀凡夫虚妄分别而生瞋怒。若字与声自性义中知不可得。心则随顺不相违背。平等忍受。此名法住持忍。又于杀害者所。当作是念。身非害者。身若无心。则如草木壁影等故。心亦非害者。以心非色。

Then again, [mentally-sustained patience] is also operative when, having severed all latent traces of hatefulness, one remains free of murderous and injurious thoughts, enmity-ridden thoughts, contentious thoughts, and accusatory thoughts, when one takes care to protect both self and others, when one's relations with others involve a mind imbued with kindness, when one's actions are conjoined with compassion, when one's mind abides in delight, and when one courses constantly in equanimity. These instances too qualify as "patience sustained by the mind."

PATIENCE SUSTAINED THROUGH DHARMA

Among these [three types of patience], "patience sustained through Dharma" is operative through focusing reality-based analytic contemplation both inwardly and outwardly.

In cases where it is invoked outwardly, this refers to instances of being cursed, berated, slain, injured, and so forth. For example, when one [seizes on the idea that he] is being cursed or berated, the sound of a voice and a word come into simultaneous conjunction and fail to be analytically-dispersed [through reality-based perception]. However, because [continuity of these phenomena are falsely imputed on events enduring only for the micro-moment of a] kṣaṇa, because the words involved are devoid of any intrinsic reality, because the sound of the voice is comparable to a mere echo, and because one cannot speak of any sequence of real meaning inhering in any of this, there is in fact no [ultimately-apprehensible] scolding or berating going on at all.

But, [even though this is the reality perceived by the enlightened], everyone else, the common people, engage in false discriminations and, based on that, become filled with of rage. However, if one were to realize the inapprehensibility of any intrinsically real nature in the word, the sound, or the meaning, then the mind would simply go along with it, would not be inclined to oppose it, and would endure it patiently in a state of uniform even-mindedness. This is what is meant by "patience sustained through Dharma."

Also, regarding any individual inflicting death or injury, one should reflect thus: "It is not the case that the body itself is doing the harming since, being devoid of mind, the body is the same as grass, trees, a wall, a shadow, or other such things. Then again, it is not the case either that the mind is doing any harming, for the mind is something which, [by its very nature], is non-form and hence

繁體字

無所觸礙故。於第一義中無殺害者。作是觀時。不
見殺害。堪能忍之。此名法住持忍。內者。謂觀內
法時。作如是念。色如聚沫從緣而起。無動作故。
不自生故。空故。離我我所故。受如泡。想如陽
焰。行如芭蕉。識如幻。從緣而起。無動作故。不
自生故。剎那生滅故。空故。離我我所故。於中色
非我。色非我所。如是受想行識。識非我識非我
所。此等諸法從緣而生。若從緣生則自性無生。若
自性無生則無能害者。如是觀時。若內若外諸法自
性皆不可得。此名法住持忍。若於身心法中。作自
性觀時。

简体字

无所触碍故。于第一义中无杀害者。作是观时。不
见杀害。堪能忍之。此名法住持忍。内者。谓观内
法时。作如是念。色如聚沫从缘而起。无动作故。
不自生故。空故。离我我所故。受如泡。想如阳
焰。行如芭蕉。识如幻。从缘而起。无动作故。不
自生故。刹那生灭故。空故。离我我所故。于中色
非我。色非我所。如是受想行识。识非我识非我
所。此等诸法从缘而生。若从缘生则自性无生。若
自性无生则无能害者。如是观时。若内若外诸法自
性皆不可得。此名法住持忍。若于身心法中。作自
性观时。

is incapable of engaging in or resisting physical contact. Hence, in terms of ultimate reality, there is no entity engaging in any killing or harming."

When one performs this contemplation, one does not perceive the existence of any killing or harming and thus becomes able to patiently endure it. This is what is meant by "patience sustained through Dharma."

As for the meaning of "inwardly-focused" ["patience sustained through Dharma"], it refers to invoking this reflection in contemplating "inward" dharmas, as follows:[23]

"Physical form is comparable to a mass of sea foam. It arises from [the conjunction of] conditions. [It is devoid of any reality] because, [ultimately-speaking], there is no movement or action at all, because it is not self-generated, because it is empty [of any inherent existence], and because it is [a phenomenon existing entirely] apart from a self or anything belonging to a self.

"Feelings are comparable to a bubble. Perceptions are like mirages generated by the sun. Karmic formative factors are like the plantain [in their insubstantiality]. Consciousness is like a magically-conjured illusion and is something produced [solely from the conjunction] of conditions. [It is devoid of any reality] because, [ultimately-speaking], there is no movement or action at all, because it is not self-generated, because it is newly produced and destroyed in each succeeding $k\ṣana$ (micro-moment), because it is empty [of any inherent existence], and because it is [a phenomenon existing entirely] apart from a self or anything belonging to a self.

"Thus, in this situation, it is not the case that the physical form constitutes a self, nor is it the case that any physical form constitutes a thing belonging to a self. So, too, it is with [the aggregates of] feelings, perceptions, karmic formative factors, and consciousness. All of these dharmas are the product of conditions. If they are the product of conditions, then any [supposed] intrinsic nature in them is actually devoid of any [real] production at all. If there is no production of any intrinsic nature [in these phenomena], then there does not exist any ["being"] able to inflict harm."

When one contemplates in this manner, then one becomes unable to apprehend any intrinsic existence in any dharma, whether it be "inward-related" or "outward-related." This is what is meant by "patience sustained through Dharma." When one performs the contemplation searching for an inherently-existent nature anywhere

繁體字

即是順無生忍。此名略說羼提波羅蜜。如修多羅中
具說。此中有聖者頌

怨親及中人	悲念常平等	瞋因尚無有	何得瞋眾生
善修習常慈	眾生同己體	平等無有二	云何怒眾生
心常捨離瞋	多生於愛喜	健者既無礙	云何與世違
於諸眾生所	常求作利祐	云何[2]無瞋恚	得加眾生惡
世間八法觸	其心不動搖	譬如口吹山	應知彼得忍
深心離諸垢	礙事不能污	如泥泥虛空	應知彼得忍
於身無所愛	於命不亦貪	諸怨悉不能	動其相續志
於非可愛聲	安心猶如響	諸言亦如化	忍心便在手

简体字

即是顺无生忍。此名略说羼提波罗蜜。如修多罗中
具说。此中有圣者颂

怨亲及中人	悲念常平等	瞋因尚无有	何得瞋众生
善修习常慈	众生同己体	平等无有二	云何怒众生
心常舍离瞋	多生于爱喜	健者既无碍	云何与世违
于诸众生所	常求作利佑	云何[2]无瞋恚	得加众生恶
世间八法触	其心不动摇	譬如口吹山	应知彼得忍
深心离诸垢	碍事不能污	如泥泥虚空	应知彼得忍
于身无所爱	于命不亦贪	诸怨悉不能	动其相续志
于非可爱声	安心犹如响	诸言亦如化	忍心便在手

in the body, the mind, or dharmas, one immediately acquiesces in [the level of realization characteristic of] the unproduced-dharmas patience (anutpattika-dharma-kṣānti).

This amounts to a general explanation of kṣānti pāramitā. The complete explanation is such as one will find in the Sutras. We present herein verses by an ārya [Nāgārjuna?—Trans.]:

Verses on the Perfection of Patience

Toward adversaries, close relations, and persons in between,
One is compassionately mindful, always treating everyone equally.
As there is no existence even in the causes of hatefulness,
How could one be able to hold hatred for any being?

One skillfully cultivates constant kindness,
Regarding beings as identical in substance to oneself.
When uniformly even-minded and free of any dualities,
How could one become enraged at any being?

The mind constantly forsakes and abandons hatefulness
And, many times over, generates cherishing delight.
Since the heroic stalwarts remain free of any obstructiveness,
How could one act contrarily to those abiding in the world?

In all places where there are beings,
One constantly seeks to benefit and assist them.
How then could one free of hatefulness
Be able to visit evil on other beings?

Even when encountering the eight worldly dharmas,
His mind remains entirely unshaken.
Just as if one were to blow on a mountain [to move it],
So too should one comprehend how well he has realized patience.

With a profound mind, he has abandoned all defilement.
Hence obstructive circumstances remain unable to stain him.
Just as when one attempts to smear empty space with mud,
So too should one comprehend how well he has realized patience.

He does not cherish even his very own body.
Nor does he covet even his very own life.
All of his adversaries remain entirely unable
To shake the continuity of his resolve.

With regard to all those sounds which one might find unlikeable,
With his mind at peace, he regards them as but mere echoes.
All words too are like supernatural transformations.
Hence the mind realizing patience is controlled by his own hands.

繁體字

不於五眾中　　取我及命相　　身亦非我所　　應知彼得忍
若不見於我　　及我所自性　　便得無生忍　　佛子最安隱

[0521c16]　　問已解釋忍波羅蜜。今應說精進波羅蜜。
答勇健體相。勇健作業等。是為精進。於中諸菩薩
等。從初發心乃至究竟[3]覺場。建立一切菩提分
相應身口意善業。此名精進波羅蜜。又復若與諸凡
夫及學無學聲聞獨覺等。不共精進。此名精進波羅
蜜。精進有三種。謂身口意。彼身口精進。以心精
進而為前行。略說有三種福事。若身與福事相應。
是身精進。若口與相應。是口精進。若意與相應。
是意精進。

簡体字

不于五众中　　取我及命相　　身亦非我所　　应知彼得忍
若不见于我　　及我所自性　　便得无生忍　　佛子最安隐

[0521c16]　　问已解释忍波罗蜜。今应说精进波罗蜜。
答勇健体相。勇健作业等。是为精进。于中诸菩萨
等。从初发心乃至究竟[3]觉场。建立一切菩提分
相应身口意善业。此名精进波罗蜜。又复若与诸凡
夫及学无学声闻独觉等。不共精进。此名精进波罗
蜜。精进有三种。谓身口意。彼身口精进。以心精
进而为前行。略说有三种福事。若身与福事相应。
是身精进。若口与相应。是口精进。若意与相应。
是意精进。

He does not anywhere among the five aggregates
Seize on the existence of a "self" or on any sign of a "life."
Neither does he regard the body as belonging to some self.
Just so should one comprehend how well he has realized patience.

If one does not apprehend in any "self"
Or possessions of a self any sort of inherent existence,
One gains then realization of the unproduced-dharmas patience,
And becomes, among the Buddha's sons, the most serenely secure.

THE PERFECTION OF VIGOR

Question: Having already explained the pāramitā of patience, one should now explain the pāramitā of vigor (*vīrya*).

Response: This refers to heroically energetic strength in the substance and manifest aspects [of one's resolve] and to heroically energetic strength in the performance of karmic deeds and such. This is what is meant by "vigor."

In this connection, all bodhisattvas, from the time they generate the resolve on forward to when they arrive at the site of their ultimate enlightenment, establish every manner of good physical, verbal and mental karma, doing so in alignment with the factors conducing to enlightenment. It is this which qualifies as the pāramitā of vigor.

Also it is those instances of vigor not held in common with common folk, *śrāvaka*-disciples in or beyond training, or pratyekabuddhas which define what qualifies as the pāramitā of vigor.

THE THREE TYPES OF VIGOR

Vigor is of three types: physical, verbal, and mental. In the case of physical and verbal vigor, they rely on the prior initiation of mental vigor.

Briefly stated, there are three kinds of endeavors productive of karmic blessings. There is that in which the body is devoted to endeavors conducive to karmic blessings. There is that in which the mouth is devoted to such conducive endeavors. And there is that in which the mind is devoted to such conducive endeavors.

Also, where the body possesses energetic strength in its practice of whatever is beneficial to self and other, this qualifies as physical vigor. Where verbal actions demonstrate energetic strength in such endeavors, this is verbal vigor. Where the mind exhibits energetic strength in such endeavors, this is mental vigor.

又於若自利若利他善中身健行。是身精進。口健行
是口精進。意健行是心精進。復有三十二種菩薩精
進。謂不斷三寶種精進。成熟無量眾生精進。攝受
無量流轉精進無量供養給侍精進。聚集無量善根精
進。出生無量精進精進。善說令眾生歡喜精進。安
隱一切眾生精進。隨諸眾生所作精進。於諸眾生中
行捨精進。受諸戒學精進忍力調柔精進。出生諸禪
那三摩提三摩鉢帝精進。滿足無[1]著智慧精進。
成就四梵行精進。出生五神通精進。以一切佛土功
德成已佛土精進。降伏諸魔精進。如法降伏諸外論
師精進。滿足十力無畏等佛法精進。莊嚴身口意精
進。得度諸有所作精進。害諸煩惱精進。

又于若自利若利他善中身健行。是身精进。口健行
是口精进。意健行是心精进。复有三十二种菩萨精
进。谓不断三宝种精进。成熟无量众生精进。摄受
无量流转精进无量供养给侍精进。聚集无量善根精
进。出生无量精进精进。善说令众生欢喜精进。安
隐一切众生精进。随诸众生所作精进。于诸众生中
行舍精进。受诸戒学精进忍力调柔精进。出生诸禅
那三摩提三摩鉢帝精进。满足无[1]着智慧精进。
成就四梵行精进。出生五神通精进。以一切佛土功
德成已佛土精进。降伏诸魔精进。如法降伏诸外论
师精进。满足十力无畏等佛法精进。庄严身口意精
进。得度诸有所作精进。害诸烦恼精进。

THE BODHISATTVAS' THIRTY-TWO TYPES OF VIGOR

Then again, there are thirty-two kinds of bodhisattva vigor, as below:

1 – Vigor in preventing severance of the Three Jewels lineage.
2 – Vigor in ripening countless beings.
3 – Vigor in drawing in and adopting countless beings entrapped in cyclic existence.
4 – Vigor in making countless offerings to support and serve [the Three Jewels].
5 – Vigor in accumulating an immeasurable stock of roots of goodness.
6 – Vigor in generating an immeasurable reserve of vigor.
7 – Vigor in presenting skillful explanations [of Dharma] delightful to beings.
8 – Vigor in establishing all beings in serenely secure circumstances.
9 – Vigor in adapting to the various endeavors pursued by beings.
10 – Vigor in coursing in equanimity in the midst of beings.
11 – Vigor in taking on all aspects of the training in moral virtue.
12 – Vigor in developing one's power of patience to the point of abiding in mental pliancy.
13 – Vigor in acquisition of the dhyānas, samādhis, and samāpattis.
14 – Vigor in perfecting wisdom free of attachment.
15 – Vigor in perfecting "the four types of brahmacarya" [otherwise known as "the four immeasurable minds"].[24]
16 – Vigor in generating the five spiritual powers.
17 – Vigor in creating one's own buddhaland based on the qualities present in all other buddhalands.[25]
18 – Vigor in subduing all demons.
19 – Vigor in subduing in accordance with Dharma all non-Buddhist dialecticians.
20 – Vigor in perfecting the ten powers, the fearlessnesses, and the other dharmas exclusive to buddhas.
21 – Vigor in enhancing the quality of one's physical, verbal, and mental karma.
22 – Vigor in completing all endeavors one has begun.
23 – Vigor in wreaking destruction on all of one's afflictions.

未度者令度。未脫者令脫。未穌息者令穌息。未涅
槃者令涅槃精進。聚集百福相資糧精進。攝受一切
佛法精進。遊無邊佛土精進。見無量諸佛精進。此
諸精進從大悲出。離身口意故。住不取不捨故。得
不舉不下故。攝不生不起故。如是等三十二法具足
已。精進波羅蜜當得清淨滿足。此中亦有聖頌

彼諸施等波羅蜜	精進之力所成就	是故精進為根本
諸菩薩等得佛身	精進方便求菩提	我念精進勝方便
以其捨離精進已	方便不能作所作	若唯獨有一方便
則無策勤作事業	所作皆是精進作	是故精進勝方便

未度者令度。未脫者令脫。未穌息者令穌息。未涅
盘者令涅盘精进。聚集百福相资粮精进。摄受一切
佛法精进。游无边佛土精进。见无量诸佛精进。此
诸精进从大悲出。离身口意故。住不取不舍故。得
不举不下故。摄不生不起故。如是等三十二法具足
已。精进波罗蜜当得清净满足。此中亦有圣颂

彼诸施等波罗蜜	精进之力所成就	是故精进为根本
诸菩萨等得佛身	精进方便求菩提	我念精进胜方便
以其舍离精进已	方便不能作所作	若唯独有一方便
则无策勤作事业	所作皆是精进作	是故精进胜方便

24 – Vigor in escorting beyond [the sea of suffering] all who have not yet gone beyond it.

25 – Vigor in causing those not liberated to gain liberation.

26 – Vigor in reviving those not yet revived.[26]

27 – Vigor in bringing to nirvāṇa all who have not yet reached nirvāṇa.

28 – Vigor in accumulating the provisions generating the [buddha body's] hundred-fold signs of meritorious qualities (śata-puṇya-lakṣaṇa).

29 – Vigor in gathering in and integrating all buddha dharmas.

30 – Vigor in roaming to the boundlessly many buddhalands.

31 – Vigor in becoming able to see all of the immeasurably many buddhas.

32 – Vigor in making all such types of vigor issue forth from the great compassion.

[The ability to carry forward with such vigor] derives from transcendent body, mouth, and mind karma, from abiding in a state in which one grasps at nothing and forsakes no one, from becoming invulnerable to being either elated or downcast, and from developing the inward realization [that all dharmas] are not produced and do not arise at all.

Perfection of these thirty-two dharmas is the basis for total development of purity in the pāramitā of vigor.

We also present here verses composed by an ārya [Nāgārjuna?— TRANS.]:

VERSES ON THE PERFECTION OF VIGOR

All those pāramitās of giving and the rest
Are brought to their perfection by resorting to the power of vigor.
Therefore it is vigor that composes the very root
Of every bodhisattva's acquisition of a buddha's body.

Vigor is the means required in pursuing the quest for bodhi.
I remain mindful that vigor is supreme among skillful means,
For once a person abandons reliance on maintaining vigor,
Then skillful means are unable to accomplish anything at all.

Were one only able to have some other skillful means,
One would still have no goad spurring diligence in karmic deeds.
Everything one does is accomplished through reliance on vigor.
Therefore it is vigor that is supreme among skillful means.

繁體字

心有巧力為方便　此心從[2]於精進生　是故諸有所作事
皆以精進為根本　諸論及以工巧等　具精進故到彼岸
是故於諸所作中　精進最為成就者　所有自在及財物
精進之人則能得　是故諸有安樂事　皆以精進為得因
以有殊勝精進故　佛於聲聞為上首　是故此之精進力
最為勝因非餘行　勝上精進勇健者　於地地中雖同地
而彼恒得最勝上　是故常應起精進　佛在菩提樹下時
以精進故覺菩提　是故精進為根本　得佛身因前已說

[0522b06]　　問已略解釋精進波羅蜜。今應說禪那波羅
蜜。答禪那者。有四種禪那。謂有覺有觀離生喜
樂。遊於初禪。無覺無觀定生喜樂。遊第二禪。

簡体字

心有巧力为方便　此心从[2]于精进生　是故诸有所作事
皆以精进为根本　诸论及以工巧等　具精进故到彼岸
是故于诸所作中　精进最为成就者　所有自在及财物
精进之人则能得　是故诸有安乐事　皆以精进为得因
以有殊胜精进故　佛于声闻为上首　是故此之精进力
最为胜因非馀行　胜上精进勇健者　于地地中虽同地
而彼恒得最胜上　是故常应起精进　佛在菩提树下时
以精进故觉菩提　是故精进为根本　得佛身因前已说

[0522b06]　　问已略解释精进波罗蜜。今应说禅那波罗
蜜。答禅那者。有四种禅那。谓有觉有观离生喜
乐。游于初禅。无觉无观定生喜乐。游第二禅。

When the mind by ingenuity's power begets some skillful means
Such thoughts are in fact born forth from reliance upon vigor.
Therefore no matter what endeavor one performs,
In every case, it is vigor that forms its very basis.

All treatises as well as all works of artful skill,
Reach perfection's "other shore" by resort to the aid of vigor.
Therefore in all endeavors one seeks to carry through,
Vigor is most pivotal in bringing consummation.

In every form of freedom and in every sort of wealth,
It is the vigorous person who succeeds in gaining them.
Therefore every circumstance involving happiness
In every case takes vigor as the cause by which it is won.

It is through his especially supreme practice of vigor
That the Buddha became leader of all the Śrāvaka-disciples.
Therefore this power residing in the practice of vigor
Reigns as the supreme cause, unmatched by any other practice.

The valiantly strong, supreme in the practice of vigor,
On each and every ground, though at the same station as others,
Always succeed in becoming the most supreme among them all.
Therefore one should always raise forth the practice of vigor.

When the Buddha resided at the foot of the Bodhi Tree,
It was on account of vigor that he awakened then to bodhi.
Therefore it is vigor that forms the very basis.
The causes for winning a buddha's body are as described above.

THE PERFECTION OF DHYĀNA MEDITATION

Question: Having already presented a summary explanation of the pāramitā of vigor, one should now explain the pāramitā of dhyāna, [the perfection of meditative discipline].

Response: As for "dhyāna," there are four dhyānas, namely:

THE FOUR DHYĀNAS OF THE BODHISATTVAS

[1] Possessed of primary ideation (*vitarka*), possessed of mental discursion (*vicāra*), and possessed of that joy (*prīti*) and that bliss (*sukha*) that are generated through abandonment, one courses in the first dhyāna.[27]

[2] Having become free of primary ideation and free of mental discursion, and having become possessed of that joy (*prīti*) and that bliss (*sukha*) generated through concentration, one courses in the second dhyāna.[28]

離喜行捨念慧受樂。遊第三禪滅於苦樂捨念清淨不苦不樂。遊第四禪。於此四種禪那中。離證聲聞獨覺地。迴向佛地已。得名禪那波羅蜜。諸菩薩有十六種禪那波羅蜜。諸聲聞獨覺之所無有。何者十六種。謂不取實禪。不著味禪。大悲攀緣禪。三摩地迴轉禪。起作神通禪心堪能禪。諸三摩鉢帝禪。寂靜復寂靜禪。不可動禪。離惡對禪。入智慧禪。隨眾生心行禪。三寶種不斷禪。不退墮禪。一切法自在禪。破散禪。

離喜行舍念慧受乐。游第三禅灭于苦乐舍念清净不苦不乐。游第四禅。于此四种禅那中。离证声闻独觉地。迴向佛地已。得名禅那波罗蜜。诸菩萨有十六种禅那波罗蜜。诸声闻独觉之所无有。何者十六种。谓不取实禅。不着味禅。大悲攀缘禅。三摩地迴转禅。起作神通禅心堪能禅。诸三摩鉢帝禅。寂静复寂静禅。不可动禅。离恶对禅。入智慧禅。随众生心行禅。三宝种不断禅。不退堕禅。一切法自在禅。破散禅。

[3] Having abandoned joy, possessed of equanimity with respect to karmic formative factors (*saṃskāra-upekṣā*), possessed of mindfulness (*smṛti*), possessed of wise awareness (*samprajanya*), and experiencing blissful sensation (*sukha-vedanā*), one courses in the third dhyāna.[29]

[4] Having extinguished both suffering and bliss, abiding in equanimity, possessed of purified mindfulness, and experiencing sensations as neither suffering nor blissful, one courses in the fourth dhyāna.

When with respect to these four dhyānas, one has abandoned [the goal of using them as means to gain] realization of the grounds of the Śrāvaka-disciples and the Pratyekabuddhas and has instead dedicated one's efforts in them toward the ground of buddhahood, this qualifies as [practice directed toward] dhyāna pāramitā.

THE BODHISATTVAS' SIXTEEN TYPES OF DHYĀNA PĀRAMITĀ

The Bodhisattvas possess sixteen types of dhyāna pāramitā which are absent among the Śrāvaka-disciples and the Pratyekabuddhas. What are the sixteen? They are:

1 – The dhyāna of not seizing on anything as real.
2 – The dhyāna of refraining from any attachment to delectably blissful meditation states.
3 – The dhyāna wherein the great compassion initiates changes in objective circumstances.
4 – The dhyāna wherein samādhi turns back [its focus].
5 – The dhyāna of generating spiritual powers.
6 – The dhyāna of the mind's capacities.
7 – The dhyāna of all *samāpattis*.
8 – The dhyāna of quiescent stillness within quiescent stillness.
9 – The dhyāna of immovability.
10 – The dhyāna of employing antidotes to abandon evil.
11 – The dhyāna of entry into wisdom.
12 – The dhyāna of adaptation to beings' mental actions.
13 – The dhyāna preventing severance of the Three Jewels lineage.
14 – The dhyāna of invulnerability to retreating or falling.
15 – The dhyāna of sovereign mastery in all dharmas.
16 – The dhyāna of analytic deconstruction [of entities falsely imputed to possess intrinsic existence].

如是等十六種。是為禪那波羅蜜。不取實禪者。為
滿足如來禪故。不著味禪者。不貪自樂故。大悲攀
緣禪者。示現斷諸眾生煩惱方便故。三摩地迴轉禪
者。攀緣欲界為緣故。起作神通禪者。欲知一切眾
生心行故。心堪能禪者。成就心自在智故。諸三摩
鉢帝禪者。勝出諸色無色界故。寂靜復寂靜禪者。
勝出諸聲聞獨覺三摩鉢帝故。不可動禪者。究竟後
邊故。離惡對禪者。害諸熏習相續故。入智慧禪
者。出諸世間故。隨眾生心行禪者。度諸眾生故。
三寶種不斷禪者。如來禪無盡故。不退墮禪者。常
入定故。一切法自在禪者。諸業滿足故（第十六破散
禪本闕不解）。

如是等十六种。是为禅那波罗蜜。不取实禅者。为
满足如来禅故。不着味禅者。不贪自乐故。大悲攀
缘禅者。示现断诸众生烦恼方便故。三摩地迴转禅
者。攀缘欲界为缘故。起作神通禅者。欲知一切众
生心行故。心堪能禅者。成就心自在智故。诸三摩
鉢帝禅者。胜出诸色无色界故。寂静复寂静禅者。
胜出诸声闻独觉三摩鉢帝故。不可动禅者。究竟后
边故。离恶对禅者。害诸熏习相续故。入智慧禅
者。出诸世间故。随众生心行禅者。度诸众生故。
三宝种不断禅者。如来禅无尽故。不退墮禅者。常
入定故。一切法自在禅者。诸业满足故（第十六破散
禅本阙不解）。

Explanation of the Sixteen Types of Dhyāna Pāramitā

[Meditative discipline] of the sort exemplified by these sixteen varieties comprise what is meant by "the pāramitā of dhyāna."

"The dhyāna of not seizing on anything as real," is cultivated to perfect the dhyāna of the Tathāgatas.

"The dhyāna of refraining from any attachment to delectably blissful meditation states" is cultivated to avoid attachment to one's own bliss.

"The dhyāna wherein the great compassion initiates changes in objective circumstances" is cultivated to manifest skillful means capable of halting beings' afflictions.

"The dhyāna wherein samādhi turns back [the direction of its focus]" takes changing objective circumstances in the desire realm as its object.

"The dhyāna of generating spiritual powers," is cultivated to maintain awareness of the mental activity of all beings.

"The dhyāna of the mind's capacities," is cultivated to perfect the mind's sovereign mastery of wisdom.

"The dhyāna of all *samāpattis*," is cultivated to achieve supreme transcendence of the form and formless realms.

"The dhyāna of quiescent stillness within quiescent stillness," is cultivated to achieve supreme transcendence going beyond the *samāpattis* of *śrāvakas* and pratyekabuddhas.

"The dhyāna of immovability," is cultivated to reach the most ultimate limit.

"The dhyāna of employing antidotes to abandon evil," is cultivated to destroy the ability of habitual karmic propensities to continue on into the future.

"The dhyāna of entry into wisdom," is cultivated to transcend all mundane realms.

"The dhyāna of adaptation to beings' mental actions," is cultivated to facilitate the liberation of beings.

"The dhyāna preventing severance of the Three Jewels lineage," is cultivated to ensure the never-ending continuance of the dhyānas originating with the Tathāgatas.

"The dhyāna of invulnerability to retreating or falling," is cultivated through constant immersion in samādhi.

"The dhyāna of sovereign mastery in all dharmas," is cultivated for the sake of reaching perfect consummation of all of one's karmic works.[30]

又念淨。慧淨。趣淨。慚淨。持心希望淨。迴向菩
提淨。根淨。無依淨。不取實淨。起作神通淨。心
堪能淨。身遠離淨。內寂靜淨。外不行淨。有所得
見淨。無眾生無命無人淨。三界中不住淨。覺分門
淨。離翳光明淨。入智慧淨。因果不相違淨。業思
惟忍淨。開胞藏相智淨。攝方便前巧淨。菩提場障
礙淨。不著聲聞獨覺淨。

又念净。慧净。趣净。惭净。持心希望净。迴向菩
提净。根净。无依净。不取实净。起作神通净。心
堪能净。身远离净。内寂静净。外不行净。有所得
见净。无众生无命无人净。三界中不住净。觉分门
净。离翳光明净。入智慧净。因果不相违净。业思
惟忍净。开胞藏相智净。摄方便前巧净。菩提场障
碍净。不着声闻独觉净。

The Thirty-Two Types of Purity Forming the Bases of Dhyāna

In addition, we have:

1 – Purity in thought.
2 – Purity in wisdom.
3 – Purity in [the nature of] one's inclinations.
4 – Purity inhering in possessing a sense of shame.
5 – Purity in the aspirations sustaining the mind.
6 – Purity associated with dedication [of merit] to bodhi.
7 – Purity in one's faculties.
8 – Purity associated with freedom from dependencies.
9 – Purity associated with not seizing upon anything as real.
10 – Purity associated with the generation and implementation of spiritual powers.
11 – Purity in exercising the capacities of the mind.
12 – Purity associated with physical renunciation.
13 – Purity associated with inward stillness.
14 – Purity associated with refraining from external activity.
15 – Purity in one's views regarding perceptual apprehensibility.
16 – Purity through realization of the nonexistence of any being.
17 – Purity through realization of the nonexistence of any life.
18 – Purity through realization of the nonexistence of persons.
19 – Purity associated with having nowhere in the three realms in which one abides.
20 – Purity associated with the methods comprised by the factors conducive to enlightenment.
21 – Purity associated with the illumination through which one abandons the obscurations.
22 – Purity associated with entry into wisdom.
23 – Purity associated with having no inconsistencies regarding karmic cause-and-effect.
24 – Purity associated with bringing patience to one's contemplations on karma.
25 – Purity inherent in realizing the wisdom fathoming all aspects of the womb [from which buddhahood is born].[31]
26 – Purity associated with the preliminary expedient means used to attract [beings onto the Path].
27 – Purity associated with avoiding obstructiveness within any site dedicated to the realization of bodhi.
28 – Purity associated with refraining from attachment to [dharmas of] the Śrāvaka-disciples and the Pratyekabuddhas.

安住禪那出生光明淨。佛三摩地不散亂淨。觀自心
行淨。知諸眾生各各根如應說法淨（本闕二淨）。彼十
六種禪那波羅蜜由。此三十二淨故得清淨。得入如
來地。此中有輸盧迦

繁體字

若彼十六種	及三十二淨	與禪度相應	是為求菩提
到禪那彼岸	善知禪那業	智者五神通	出生不退墮
諸色無有盡	通達其實性	亦以勝天眼	普見諸色相
雖以淨天耳	遠聞諸音聲	智者通達知	聲非可言說
所有眾生心	觀其各各相	諸心猶如幻	了知其自性
眾生宿世住	如實能念知	諸法無過去	亦知其自性

安住禪那出生光明净。佛三摩地不散乱净。观自心
行净。知诸众生各各根如应说法净（本闕二净）。彼十
六种禪那波罗蜜由。此三十二净故得清净。得入如
来地。此中有输卢迦

简体字

若彼十六种	及三十二净	与禅度相应	是为求菩提
到禅那彼岸	善知禅那业	智者五神通	出生不退堕
诸色无有尽	通达其实性	亦以胜天眼	普见诸色相
虽以净天耳	远闻诸音声	智者通达知	声非可言说
所有众生心	观其各各相	诸心犹如幻	了知其自性
众生宿世住	如实能念知	诸法无过去	亦知其自性

29 – Purity associated with the radiance generated when peacefully abiding in dhyāna.

30 – Purity inhering in the freedom from mental scatteredness associated with the samādhis of the Buddha.

31 – Purity associated with contemplating the behavior of one's own mind.

32 – Purity associated with speaking Dharma well-suited to beings based on awareness of the karmic origins of each and every one of them.[32]

Those sixteen kinds of dhyāna involved in dhyāna pāramitā achieve their purification and ability to succeed in reaching the ground of the Tathāgatas based upon these thirty-two kinds of purity. In this connection we present *slokas* as follows:

VERSES ON DHYĀNA PĀRAMITĀ

Whenever those sixteen types [of dhyāna pāramitā]
Or those thirty-two sorts of purity
Correspond in practice to the perfection of dhyāna,
This is through being cultivated for the sake of bodhi.

When reaching the "other shore" of dhyāna's perfection,
And abiding in skillful awareness of the karmic works of dhyāna,
The wise employ the five spiritual powers
To bring about invulnerability to retreating or falling.

Though the manifestations of form are endless,
One commands a penetrating understanding of their actual nature
While also using the supremely realized heavenly eye
To universally perceive all of the characteristic features of forms.

Although one may resort to the purified heavenly ear
To hear all sounds even from a great distance,
The wise realize through their penetrating understanding
That [the true nature of] sounds is beyond the reach of words.

As for all the thoughts in the minds of beings,
One observes the features of each one of them.
[Realizing] all such thoughts are like magically-conjured illusions,
One completely comprehends the nature of their existence.

As for the previous-life abodes of beings,
One is able to remember them in accordance with reality,
[While realizing] all dharmas are devoid of any past existence
And remaining aware of the [actual] nature of their existence.

往詣俱知土　　見土具莊嚴　　土相如虛空　　了知其實性
眾生諸煩惱　　皆以亂心生　　是故勝智者　　[3]曠修諸禪定

[0523a01]　　問所解釋禪那波羅蜜者。略說已竟。今應次第說般若波羅蜜。答般若波羅蜜者。如前解釋。為初資糧中[1]說我今更釋其相。如先偈說。

　　施戒忍進定　　　此五種之餘
　　彼諸波羅蜜　　　智度之所攝

[0523a07]　　此餘有四波羅蜜謂[2]巧方便波羅蜜。願波羅蜜。力波羅蜜。智波羅蜜等。此四波羅蜜。皆是般若波羅蜜所攝。般若波羅蜜者。若佛世尊於菩提樹下。以一念相應智。覺了諸法。是般若波羅蜜。又是無礙相。以無身故。無邊相。等虛空故。無等等相。諸法無所得故。遠離相。畢竟空故。

繁體字

往詣俱知土　　见土具庄严　　土相如虚空　　了知其实性
众生诸烦恼　　皆以乱心生　　是故胜智者　　[3]旷修诸禅定

[0523a01]　　问所解释禅那波罗蜜者。略说已竟。今应次第说般若波罗蜜。答般若波罗蜜者。如前解释。为初资粮中[1]说我今更释其相。如先偈说。

　　施戒忍进定　　　此五种之馀
　　彼诸波罗蜜　　　智度之所摄

[0523a07]　　此馀有四波罗蜜谓[2]巧方便波罗蜜。愿波罗蜜。力波罗蜜。智波罗蜜等。此四波罗蜜。皆是般若波罗蜜所摄。般若波罗蜜者。若佛世尊于菩提树下。以一念相应智。觉了诸法。是般若波罗蜜。又是无碍相。以无身故。无边相。等虚空故。无等等相。诸法无所得故。远离相。毕竟空故。

简体字

One is able to go forth and visit *koṭīs* of [pure] lands,
Observing the complete adornment of those lands,
[Realizing] the features of the lands as like empty space,
And completely comprehending the nature of their existence.
All of the afflictions experienced by beings
In every case arise due to having chaotically scattered minds.
Therefore those possessed of supreme wisdom
Engage in extensive cultivation of all dhyāna absorptions.

The Perfection of Wisdom

Question: The summary explanation of dhyāna pāramitā has been completed. One should now, according to the sequence, explain the pāramitā of prajñā (the perfection of wisdom).

Response: As for the pāramitā of prajñā, it is as already explained earlier [in this commentary] wherein it was set forth as the foremost among the provisions [required for the acquisition of bodhi]. I now explain its marks once again. [In brief], they are just as described in that earlier verse which stated:

Giving, moral virtue, patience, vigor, and meditative discipline
As well as that which extends beyond these five—
All of those pāramitās
Are subsumed within the perfection of wisdom.[33]

"That which extends beyond these [five]" refers to four other pāramitās, namely: the pāramitā of skillful means, the pāramitā of vows, the pāramitā of the powers, and the pāramitā of the knowledges. These four pāramitās are all subsumed within the pāramitā of prajñā. As for the pāramitā of prajñā, it refers to that single thought-moment of comprehensive wisdom through which the Buddha, the Bhagavān, awakened to [the true nature of] all dharmas as he sat beneath the Bodhi Tree. This is what is meant by "prajñā pāramitā."

Additionally, [the perfection of wisdom] involves the following aspects:

It is unimpeded because it is independent of the body.

It is boundless because it is as vast as empty space.

It is equal to the unequaled because, in it, no dharma is perceptually apprehensible.

It is characterized by renunciation because of the ultimate emptiness [of all phenomena].

不可降伏相。無可得故。無句相。無名身故。無聚
合相。離來去故。無因相。離作者故。無生相。生
無有故。無去至相。離流轉故。無散壞相。離前後
際故。無染相。不可取故。無戲論相。離諸戲論
故。無動相。法界自體故。無起相。不分別故。無
量相。離量故。無依止相。依止無有故。無污相。
不出生故。不可測相。無邊際故。自然相。知諸法
自性故。又般若波羅蜜是聞慧相。及正[3]思入。彼
聞慧相。有八十種。謂樂欲等。正[*]思入。有三
十二種。謂安住奢摩他等。又般若波羅蜜。不與十
六種宿住等無明俱。如是等般若波羅蜜相。隨量已
說。若具說者乃有無量。

不可降伏相。无可得故。无句相。无名身故。无聚
合相。离来去故。无因相。离作者故。无生相。生
无有故。无去至相。离流转故。无散坏相。离前后
际故。无染相。不可取故。无戏论相。离诸戏论
故。无动相。法界自体故。无起相。不分别故。无
量相。离量故。无依止相。依止无有故。无污相。
不出生故。不可测相。无边际故。自然相。知诸法
自性故。又般若波罗蜜是闻慧相。及正[3]思入。彼
闻慧相。有八十种。谓乐欲等。正[*]思入。有三
十二种。谓安住奢摩他等。又般若波罗蜜。不与十
六种宿住等无明俱。如是等般若波罗蜜相。随量已
说。若具说者乃有无量。

It is unconquerable because nothing at all can be gotten at.

It is completely devoid of any sentence-based propositions because designations themselves are nonexistent entities.

It is devoid of any aggregation [of subsidiary components] because it transcends all coming hither and going thither.

It is free of any cause because it abandons [the concept of] any creative agent.

It is unproduced because production itself cannot be established as existing.

It involves no going anywhere because it has abandoned coursing in cyclic existence.

It is free of any disintegration because it transcends beginnings and endings.

It is stainless because it cannot even be grasped.

It is free of any frivolous discoursing because it has abandoned all frivolous discoursing.

It is unshakable because it is identical with the very substance of the entire Dharma realm.

It involves no arising because it does not engage in any discriminations.

It is immeasurable because it has transcended all means by which it might be measured.

It is free of any points of dependence because dependency itself does not exist.

It is free of defilement because it does not even come forth into existence.

It is unfathomable because it has no confining boundaries.

It is spontaneous because it is aware of the nature of all dharmas.

Additionally, prajñāpāramitā is marked by the wisdom derived from learning as well as by accessibility through right meditation. As for the aspects of wisdom derived from learning, there are eighty kinds, namely happiness, zeal, and so forth. As for [the aspects of] accessibility through right meditation, there are thirty-two kinds, namely stable abiding in *śamatha*, and so forth.

Also, prajñāpāramitā is not freighted by any of the sixteen kinds of delusion such as that originating in past lives, and so forth.

The aspects of prajñāpāramitā have been set forth here in accordance with limitations [of space]. Were one were to attempt to explain them completely, one would find they are limitless.

繁體字

此般若波羅蜜所攝方便善巧波羅蜜中。有八種善巧。所謂眾善巧。界善巧。入善巧。諦善巧。緣生善巧。三世善巧。諸乘善巧。諸法善巧。此中善巧波羅蜜無有邊際。又復隨於何等生趣。以何等行相。為菩提故。得自增長善根及調伏眾生。於彼彼生[4]趣彼彼行中。此一切處凡所應作種種方便。諸大人等所分別說。我今說彼經中微滴之分。若已作今作微少之善。能令[5]多多能令無量。此為方便。不自為己唯為眾生。此為方便。唯以陀那令諸波羅蜜滿足。此為方便。如是以尸羅攝諸生處。以羼提。莊嚴身口心

简体字

此般若波罗蜜所摄方便善巧波罗蜜中。有八种善巧。所谓众善巧。界善巧。入善巧。谛善巧。缘生善巧。三世善巧。诸乘善巧。诸法善巧。此中善巧波罗蜜无有边际。又复随于何等生趣。以何等行相。为菩提故。得自增长善根及调伏众生。于彼彼生[4]趣彼彼行中。此一切处凡所应作种种方便。诸大人等所分别说。我今说彼经中微滴之分。若已作今作微少之善。能令[5]多多能令无量。此为方便。不自为己唯为众生。此为方便。唯以陀那令诸波罗蜜满足。此为方便。如是以尸罗摄诸生处。以羼提。庄严身口心

THE ADDITIONAL FOUR PERFECTIONS COMPRISING THE TEN PERFECTIONS
THE PERFECTION OF SKILLFUL MEANS
THE EIGHT VARIETIES OF SKILLFUL MEANS

This pāramitā of skillful means is subsumed within the pāramitā of prajñā and involves eight primary categories, as follows:

1 – Skillful means related to the aggregates.
2 – Skillful means related to the sense realms.
3 – Skillful means related to the sense bases.
4 – Skillful means related to the truths.
5 – Skillful means related to conditioned arising.
6 – Skillful means related to the three periods of time.
7 – Skillful means related to the vehicles [for liberation].
8 – Skillful means related to dharmas.

THE SCOPE OF WHAT SHOULD BE EXPLAINED

Within these particular spheres, the skillful means pāramitā is boundless in its applications. Additionally, as befits the circumstances associated with whichever rebirth destinies and whichever aspects of cultivation are at hand, for the sake of bodhi, one augments one's own roots of goodness while working to train beings. What precisely should be done in each and every one of those rebirth destinies, what precisely one should take up in terms of practice, and how precisely one should proceed in each of these given circumstances—the great eminences have already explained these matters in detail. I shall now set forth only a tiny drop of what is set forth on these matters in the Sutras.

SKILLFUL MEANS AS WHATEVER INCREASES GOOD AND STEMS FROM ALTRUISM

If there has been in the past or is now in the very present even the slightest bit of goodness in a person's actions and one is able to cause it to become ever greater and then is able to cause it to become immeasurable, this is a function of skillful means. If it is not something undertaken for one's own sake but rather is something undertaken for the sake of beings, this is skillful means.

THE SIX PERFECTIONS AS SKILLFUL MEANS

If one is able only by resort to *dāna* to bring about perfection in the pāramitās, then this a skillful means. In this same manner, one may resort to *śīla* as a basis through which one draws in beings. One may employ *kṣānti* to grace one's physical, verbal, and mental

為於菩提。以毘梨耶安住精進。以禪那不退於禪。以般若捨離無為。以慈為作依護。以悲不棄流轉。以喜能忍不喜樂事。以捨發起諸善。以天眼攝取佛眼。以天耳滿足佛耳。以他心智知各各根。以宿住念知三世無礙。以自在通得如來自在通。以入眾生心欲知諸行相。已度還入。無染而染捨擔更擔。無量示量最勝現[6]劣。以方便故涅槃相應而墮[7]在流轉。雖[8]行涅槃。不畢竟寂滅。

为于菩提。以毘梨耶安住精进。以禅那不退于禅。以般若舍离无为。以慈为作依护。以悲不弃流转。以喜能忍不喜乐事。以舍发起诸善。以天眼摄取佛眼。以天耳满足佛耳。以他心智知各各根。以宿住念知三世无碍。以自在通得如来自在通。以入众生心欲知诸行相。已度还入。无染而染舍担更担。无量示量最胜现[6]劣。以方便故涅盘相应而堕[7]在流转。虽[8]行涅盘。不毕竟寂灭。

karma and facilitate acquisition of bodhi. One may focus on *vīrya* to establish oneself in vigor. One may devote oneself to the cultivation of dhyāna so as to avoid falling away from the dhyānas. Or one may resort to prajñā as the means by which to relinquish [any attachment to] the unconditioned.

THE FOUR IMMEASURABLE MINDS AS SKILLFUL MEANS

One may cultivate kindness so as to become one upon whom beings can rely and to become one who will afford them protection. One may devote oneself to compassion so as to avoid forsaking those entrapped in cyclic existence. One may cultivate sympathetic joy so as to endure circumstances in which one does not delight. One may train in equanimity as the means through which to develop every manner of goodness.

THE SPIRITUAL POWERS AS SKILLFUL MEANS

One uses the heavenly eye to assemble the bases for acquisition of the buddha eye. One uses the heavenly ear to perfect the buddha ear. One uses knowledge of others' thoughts to become aware of the faculties of each being. One uses recall of past lives to gain unimpeded knowledge of the three periods of time. One uses sovereign mastery of spiritual powers to gain the sovereign mastery of spiritual powers unique to the Tathāgatas. Through accessing the mental aspirations of beings, one becomes aware of all aspects of their actions.

THE PARADOXICAL SKILLFUL MEANS OF BODHISATTVAS IN CYCLIC EXISTENCE

Having already achieved liberation, one may turn around and enter [cyclic existence] yet again. Even though free of defilement, one nonetheless becomes exposed to defilement. Having already successfully thrown down all burdens, one may [voluntarily] take them up yet again. Having ascended to the limitless, one may then nonetheless manifest signs of limitation. Having ascended to the highest level of supremacy, one may nonetheless manifest as possessing inferior capacities.

As a function of skillful means, even though one's realization corresponds to realization of nirvāṇa, one may nonetheless drop back down into the midst of cyclic existence. Even though one courses in realization of nirvāṇa, one nonetheless refrains from opting for the ultimate and final cessation.

繁體字

現行四[9]魔。而超過諸魔。達四諦智及觀無生。而不入正位。雖行憒閙。而不行順眠煩惱。雖行遠離。而不依身心盡。雖行三界。而於界中不行世諦。雖行於空。而一切時恒求佛法。雖行無為。而不於無為作證。雖行[10]六通。而不盡漏。雖現聲聞獨覺威儀。而不捨樂欲佛法。如是等巧方便波羅蜜中。所有教化眾生方便。彼等方便是菩薩教化巧方便住處應知。此中有輸盧迦

畜生道中諸苦惱	地獄餓鬼生亦然	於流轉中相應受
眾生種種諸過惡	此等苦聚不能障	於眾生處起哀[11]愍
諸佛便說彼菩薩	一切世間無礙悲	

简体字

现行四[9]魔。而超过诸魔。达四谛智及观无生。而不入正位。虽行愦闹。而不行顺眠烦恼。虽行远离。而不依身心尽。虽行三界。而于界中不行世谛。虽行于空。而一切时恒求佛法。虽行无为。而不于无为作证。虽行[10]六通。而不尽漏。虽现声闻独觉威仪。而不舍乐欲佛法。如是等巧方便波罗蜜中。所有教化众生方便。彼等方便是菩萨教化巧方便住处应知。此中有输卢迦

畜生道中诸苦恼	地狱饿鬼生亦然	于流转中相应受
众生种种诸过恶	此等苦聚不能障	于众生处起哀[11]愍
诸佛便说彼菩萨	一切世间无碍悲	

Although one may manifest practice involving the four types of demon-related influences [involving afflictions, the aggregates, death, and sixth desire heaven deities], one nonetheless transcends every form of demonic influence. Even though one has already gained a penetrating understanding of the wisdom fathoming the four truths, and even though one courses in contemplation of the unproduced, one nonetheless refrains from entering the "right and fixed position" [which would make final Śrāvaka-vehicle nirvāṇa unavoidably certain].

Even though one may take up practice in the midst of the vexing boisterousness [of cyclic existence], one still refrains from actions rooted in latent afflictions. Even though one courses in renunciation, one refrains from reliance on practices which would bring about complete cessation of body and mind. Although one does course along in the midst of the three realms, one nonetheless refrains from practice dominated by worldly truth.

Even though one's practice is rooted in emptiness, nonetheless, one constantly focuses on the quest for the dharmas of a buddha. Even though one courses in the unconditioned, one nonetheless avoids opting for realization of the unconditioned. Even though one implements the six spiritual powers, one nonetheless refrains from ending all outflow impurities. Even though one manifests the refined comportment of the Śrāvaka-disciples and Pratyekabuddhas, one nonetheless refrains from relinquishing one's delight in and zeal for the dharmas of a buddha.

Such practices within the skillful-means pāramitā are those used as skillful means in instructing beings. All of these skillful means are artful methods dwelt in by bodhisattvas as they carry on their teaching endeavors. This being the case, one should become aware of them. In this connection, we present ślokas as follows:

VERSES ON THE PERFECTION OF SKILLFUL MEANS

They course in the bitter afflictions of animal rebirth,
Doing so in hell realms and hungry ghost births as well,
Undergoing in corresponding cyclic-existence circumstances
All manner of transgressions and evil wrought by beings.

Such accumulations of sufferings still do not obstruct
Their drawing forth deeply-felt pity as they abide among beings.
Thus the Buddhas proclaimed that all those bodhisattvas
Implement unimpeded compassion in the midst of all worlds.

繁體字

論中若有善該綜
皆以愛語授與之
攝已復令常相續
令其調伏而受教
若不厭於染境樂
極逼惱處亦不捨
是人未離世間法
而有無邊諸苦事
若於聲聞出家者
或置十種妙力乘
若應觀察現見果
丈夫難事皆能為
此乘諸佛所讚歎
以說勝妙善道故

眾多別人所作業
戒財聞修寂調等
勝仙說為住善道
或現男身化女人
愍其無道令入道
或有信解於無我
但作如此觀察轉
當於受彼苦果時
便置安隱寂靜處
令其當得正覺乘
如其所作正安置
依彼種種巧方便
百千功德而莊嚴

工巧等明及餘事
以此功德攝化他
或現女身化男子
令其調伏而受教
隨眾生門種種化
及知諸法離自性
於業及果生信順
不喜諸苦所逼切
或復置於緣覺道
或得寂靜及天趣
如是從初至究竟
捨離一切愛不愛
能生世間極淨信

简体字

论中若有善该综
皆以爱语授与之
摄已复令常相续
令其调伏而受教
若不厌于染境乐
极逼恼处亦不舍
是人未离世间法
而有无边诸苦事
若于声闻出家者
或置十种妙力乘
若应观察现见果
丈夫难事皆能为
此乘诸佛所赞叹
以说胜妙善道故

众多别人所作业
戒财闻修寂调等
胜仙说为住善道
或现男身化女人
愍其无道令入道
或有信解于无我
但作如此观察转
当于受彼苦果时
便置安隐寂静处
令其当得正觉乘
如其所作正安置
依彼种种巧方便
百千功德而庄严

工巧等明及馀事
以此功德摄化他
或现女身化男子
令其调伏而受教
随众生门种种化
及知诸法离自性
于业及果生信顺
不喜诸苦所逼切
或复置于缘觉道
或得寂静及天趣
如是从初至究竟
舍离一切爱不爱
能生世间极净信

Wherever any manner of goodness is contained in treatises
Describing the many karmic works undertaken by others—
Just such skills, arts, clarities and other sorts of matters—
They pass on all those teachings, employing pleasing words.

Morality, wealth, learning, meditation, trainings, and the rest—
They use these meritorious qualities to attract and teach others.
Having drawn them in, they then cause them to continue,
Teaching words of the Supreme Rishi so they abide in good paths.

They may manifest in the body of a woman in instructing men,
Causing them to be subdued and thus accept the teachings.
Or they may manifest in the body of a man in instructing women,
Causing them to be subdued and thus accept the teachings.

Where they're not yet disgusted with defiled sorts of pleasures,
They pity their having no path and cause them to enter the Path.
Adapting to beings' ways, they use all manner of fitting teachings,
And even in the most tormenting places still don't forsake them.

Where some might believe and understand nonexistence of self
And could realize dharmas have no inherently-existent nature—
For this sort of person who hasn't yet abandoned worldly dharmas,
They simply provide these contemplations to turn them around.

Where some could believe and accord with karma and its effects,
And yet are oppressed by countless circumstances of suffering,
They should [be instructed] as they endure those bitter effects,
So they will no longer find joy in being driven along by sufferings.

When encountering *śrāvaka*-disciple monastics,
One may provide them safe places to cultivate stillness,
Or may establish them in the path of pratyekabuddhas,
Or may establish them in the vehicle of the ten sublime powers.

One may cause them to gain the right-enlightenment vehicle,
To realize quiescent stillness, or even course in celestial destinies.
As appropriate, one contemplates presently observed effects,
And, as befits their capabilities, correctly establishes them in that.

In this fashion, from the beginning on through to the end,
One is able to do whatever a great man would find difficult.
Relying on all of those different sorts of skillful means,
One forsakes every manner of like and dislike.

This vehicle is such as all the Buddhas do praise.
It is graced with a hundred thousand meritorious qualities.
It is able to generate in worldlings the ultimate form of pure faith,
This because it explains the path of supremely sublime goodness.

於緣覺乘聲聞乘　　及以天世諸乘中
皆以十善而成熟　　亦於人乘成熟人

[0523c23]　　　　已解釋[*]巧方便波羅蜜。我今當說願波
羅蜜。諸菩薩最初有十大願。所謂供養給侍諸佛無
餘。是第一大願。於彼佛所持大正法。攝受正覺普
護正教。是第二大願。諸世界中諸佛出興。始從住
兜率宮乃至[12]退墮。入胎住胎初生出家。證正覺
請轉法輪入大涅槃。皆往其所受行供養初不捨離。
是第三大願。諸菩薩行曠大無量。不[1]雜諸波羅蜜
所攝善淨諸地。出生總分別分同相異相共轉不共轉
等諸菩薩行。如實如[2]地道說。修治波羅蜜教誡教
授。授已住持。發起出生如是等心。是第四大願。

于缘觉乘声闻乘　　及以天世诸乘中
皆以十善而成熟　　亦于人乘成熟人

[0523c23]　　　　已解释[*]巧方便波罗蜜。我今当说愿波
罗蜜。诸菩萨最初有十大愿。所谓供养给侍诸佛无
余。是第一大愿。于彼佛所持大正法。摄受正觉普
护正教。是第二大愿。诸世界中诸佛出兴。始从住
兜率宫乃至[12]退堕。入胎住胎初生出家。证正觉
请转法轮入大涅盘。皆往其所受行供养初不舍离。
是第三大愿。诸菩萨行旷大无量。不[1]杂诸波罗蜜
所摄善净诸地。出生总分别分同相异相共转不共转
等诸菩萨行。如实如[2]地道说。修治波罗蜜教诫教
授。授已住持。发起出生如是等心。是第四大愿。

In the vehicles of śrāvaka-disciples and pratyekabuddhas
As well as in all vehicles in both the heavens and the world—
In all cases, one uses the ten good deeds to bring about ripening,
Employing them too to ripen people in the vehicle of humanity.

THE PERFECTION OF VOWS
THE TEN BODHISATTVA VOWS

Having completed the explanation of the pāramitā of skillful means, I shall now explain the pāramitā of vows. All bodhisattvas establish themselves from the very outset in ten great vows, namely:

1 – The vow to make offerings to and serve the needs of all buddhas without exception. This is the first of the great vows.

2 – The vow, in the place of those buddhas, to uphold the great right Dharma, to embrace the right enlightenment, and to comprehensively protect the orthodox teaching. This is the second of the great vows.

3 – One vows that, whenever buddhas come forth into any world, starting with their dwelling in the Tuṣita Heaven palace, proceeding on through to their descent into the womb, to their dwelling in the womb, to their first taking birth, to their subsequent leaving of the home life, to their realization of the right enlightenment, to their being requested to turn the Dharma wheel, and to their finally entering the great nirvāṇa—in all those circumstances, one resolves to go wherever they are, to adopt their practices, and to make offerings to them, never departing from them during that entire time. This is the third of the great vows.

4 – The practices of the bodhisattva are vast, are beyond measure, are free of admixture [with inferior teachings], are subsumed within the pāramitās, and are such as one skillfully purifies on the stages [of the Bodhisattva Path]. As for the general and specific distinctions, the identical and differentiating aspects, and the shared and unshared practices associated with the bodhisattva practices—one vows to teach them in accordance with reality and in accordance with the path coursing through the stages, teaching [all beings] the methods for cultivating the pāramitās, remonstrating with them, and passing on the teachings to them in such a way that, having received them, they will abide in and uphold them. The generation of the resolve to act accordingly is the fourth of the great vows.

無餘眾生界。有色無色有想無想。卵生胎生濕生化
生。三界同入六趣共居。諸生順去名色所攝。無餘
眾生界皆悉成熟。令入佛法。斷除諸趣。安立於一
切智智。是第五大願。無餘諸世界曠大無量。若細
若麁若橫若倒若平住等。同入共居順去。十方分分
猶如帝網。入於分分以智順行。是第六大願。一切
土即一土。一土即一切土。平等清淨無量國土。普
皆莊嚴離諸煩惱。淨道具足無量智相。眾生充滿入
佛上妙境界。隨眾生心示現令其歡喜。是第七大
願。為與諸菩薩同一心故。為不共善根聚集故。為
與諸菩薩同一攀緣常不離菩薩平等故。為發起自心
入如來威神故。為得不退行神通故。為遊行諸世界
故。為影到諸大眾[3]論故。為自身順入諸生處故。
為具足

无餘众生界。有色无色有想无想。卵生胎生湿生化
生。三界同入六趣共居。诸生顺去名色所摄。无餘
众生界皆悉成熟。令入佛法。断除诸趣。安立于一
切智智。是第五大愿。无餘诸世界旷大无量。若细
若麁若横若倒若平住等。同入共居顺去。十方分分
犹如帝网。入于分分以智顺行。是第六大愿。一切
土即一土。一土即一切土。平等清净无量国土。普
皆庄严离诸烦恼。净道具足无量智相。众生充满入
佛上妙境界。随众生心示现令其欢喜。是第七大
愿。为与诸菩萨同一心故。为不共善根聚集故。为
与诸菩萨同一攀缘常不离菩萨平等故。为发起自心
入如来威神故。为得不退行神通故。为游行诸世界
故。为影到诸大众[3]论故。为自身顺入诸生处故。
为具足

繁體字

简体字

5 – One vows to enter all realms of beings without exception, including those possessed of form, those devoid of form, those possessed of thought, those devoid of thought, those which are egg-born, womb-born, moisture-born, and transformationally born—one vows to enter equally into all three realms, abiding together with beings in the six destinies of rebirth, going wherever beings have taken birth. One vows to ripen without exception all types of beings included in the sphere of name-and-form, causing them to enter the Dharma of the Buddha, doing so in order to cut off all of the [worldly] paths. Thus one works to establish them in the wisdom of all-knowledge. This is the fifth of the great vows.[34]

6 – The realm inclusive of all worlds without exception is incalculably vast. Whether refined, coarse, laterally-structured, suspended, or arranged with beings living on flat terrains—one vows to enter them all identically and abide therein. All of different sectors of existence throughout the ten directions are interconnected in the manner of the net-like canopy of Indra. One vows to enter into each and every one of those sectors, employing wisdom to which one adapts in one's practice. This is the sixth of the great vows.[35]

7 – In order to realize all lands as being identically subsumed within any single land and any single land as being identically manifest in all other lands, one vows to equally purify all of the incalculably many worlds, universally adorning them all while abandoning all afflictions. One refines the purity of one's practice of the Path and perfects the limitlessly numerous aspects of wisdom. Beings all entirely enter the supremely sublime mind state of the Buddhas. One adapts to the minds of beings and, in doing so, manifests for them in whatever ways will bring them delight. [The resolve to proceed in this way] is the seventh of the great vows.[36]

8 – One vows to become of identical mind with that of the Bodhisattvas, doing so in order to assemble those roots of goodness not yet held in common with them, doing so in order to transform circumstances in ways identical to the Bodhisattvas while never abandoning the uniform equality realized by bodhisattvas, doing so in order to develop one's mind in a way that it may access the awesome spirituality of the Tathāgatas, doing so in order to gain undiminishing spiritual powers, doing so in order to become able to roam to all worlds, doing so in order to influence the discourse in the great [Dharma] assemblies, doing so in order to adaptively enter all stations of rebirth, doing so in order to perfect one's practice of

不思議大乘故。為行菩薩行故。是第八大願。為昇
不退轉行菩薩行故。為身口意業不空故。即於見時
令決定佛法故。為[4]即出一音聲時[5]令入智慧故。
為即於信時令轉煩惱故。為得如大藥王身故。為行
諸菩薩行故。是第九大願。為於諸世界中正覺阿耨
多羅三藐三菩提故。為於一毛道中及餘一切毛道
中。皆現出生坐道場轉法輪大般涅槃故。為以智慧
入佛大境界威神故。為於一切眾生界如其深心佛應
出時開悟令得寂靜而示現故。為正覺一法一切法[6]
悉涅槃相故。為出一音聲令諸眾生心歡喜故。為現
大涅槃而不斷行力故。為現大智慧地安立諸法故。
為以佛境界法智神通普遍諸世界故。是第十大願。

不思议大乘故。为行菩萨行故。是第八大愿。为升
不退转行菩萨行故。为身口意业不空故。即于见时
令决定佛法故。为[4]即出一音声时[5]令入智慧故。
为即于信时令转烦恼故。为得如大药王身故。为行
诸菩萨行故。是第九大愿。为于诸世界中正觉阿耨
多罗三藐三菩提故。为于一毛道中及馀一切毛道
中。皆现出生坐道场转法轮大般涅盘故。为以智慧
入佛大境界威神故。为于一切众生界如其深心佛应
出时开悟令得寂静而示现故。为正觉一法一切法[6]
悉涅盘相故。为出一音声令诸众生心欢喜故。为现
大涅盘而不断行力故。为现大智慧地安立诸法故。
为以佛境界法智神通普遍诸世界故。是第十大愿。

the inconceivable and ineffable Great Vehicle, and doing so in order to implement the practices of the Bodhisattvas. This is the eighth of the great vows.[37]

9 – One vows to ascend to non-retreating implementation of the bodhisattva practices, doing so in order to cause one's karmic deeds of body, mouth, and mind to not be done in vain, doing so in order that, immediately upon being seen by them, beings will be caused to become resolved on the Dharma of buddhahood, doing so in order that, immediately upon hearing a single sound from one's voice, beings will be caused to develop wisdom, doing so in order that, immediately on generating faith, beings will be caused to have their afflictions transformed, doing so in order that he will gain a body serving beings in the manner of the great king of medicine trees, and doing so in order to implement the practices of the Bodhisattvas. This is the ninth of the great vows.

10 – One vows to achieve the right enlightenment and manifest the realization of *anuttarasamyaksaṃbodhi* in all worlds, doing so in order to manifest in every one of one's own hair pores the appearance of a buddha coming forth into the world, sitting at the site of enlightenment, turning the wheel of Dharma, and entering the great *parinirvāṇa*.

One does so in order to become able to utilize wisdom to access the great mind-state of the Buddhas replete with awesome spiritual powers, doing so in order to become able, in the realms of all beings, to manifest in whichever manner best adapts to their most profound aspirations, in whichever manner best adapts to whichever timing is appropriate for the appearance of a buddha to them, and in whichever manner allows them to become awakened and then achieve quiescent stillness.

One does so in order to gain that right enlightenment wherein a single dharma is realized as identical with all dharmas, and all dharmas are realized as nirvāṇa-like in character. One does so in order to become able with the creation of but a single sound to cause the minds of all beings to become delighted. One does so in order to manifest the great nirvāṇa even while still not cutting off implementation of the powers, does so in order to manifest the ground of great wisdom and to become established in all dharmas, and does so in order to become able to manifest universally in all worlds the mind-state, the Dharma, the wisdom, and the spiritual powers of a buddha. This is the tenth of the great vows.

如是等大欲大出生十大願為首。滿此十大願已。建立菩薩阿僧祇百千餘願。得住菩薩歡喜地。此名願波羅蜜。已解釋願波羅蜜。我今當說力波羅蜜。此中略說諸菩薩有七種力。謂福報生力。神通力。信力。精進力。念力。三摩提力。般若力

[0524b11] 福報生力者。如十小象力當一龍象力。十龍象力當一香象力。十香象力當一大香象力。十大香象力當一大力士力。十大力士力當一半那羅延力。十半那羅延力當一那羅延力。十那羅延力當一大那羅延力。十大那羅延力當一過百劫菩薩力。十過百劫菩薩力當一過百千劫菩薩力。十過百千劫菩薩力

如是等大欲大出生十大愿为首。满此十大愿已。建立菩萨阿僧只百千馀愿。得住菩萨欢喜地。此名愿波罗蜜。已解释愿波罗蜜。我今当说力波罗蜜。此中略说诸菩萨有七种力。谓福报生力。神通力。信力。精进力。念力。三摩提力。般若力

[0524b11] 福报生力者。如十小象力当一龙象力。十龙象力当一香象力。十香象力当一大香象力。十大香象力当一大力士力。十大力士力当一半那罗延力。十半那罗延力当一那罗延力。十那罗延力当一大那罗延力。十大那罗延力当一过百劫菩萨力。十过百劫菩萨力当一过百千劫菩萨力。十过百千劫菩萨力

Great vows such as these ten characterized by great zeal and great manifestations in the world comprise the foremost class of vows.[38] After one has fulfilled these ten great vows, one establishes *asaṃkhyeyas* of hundreds of thousands of other bodhisattva vows. Thus one comes to abide on the bodhisattva's "ground of joyfulness" (*pramudita-bhūmi*). This is what is meant by the pāramitā of vows.

THE PERFECTION OF POWERS

Having completed the explanation of the pāramitā of vows, we now explain the pāramitā of the powers. Generally speaking, the Bodhisattvas possess seven kinds of powers, as follows:

1 – The power produced through karmic reward.
2 – The power of the supernatural powers.
3 – The power of faith.
4 – The power of vigor.
5 – The power of mindfulness.
6 – The power of the samādhis.
7 – The power of prajñā.

As for "the power produced through karmic reward," [one may describe it in this way]: It requires the power of ten small elephants to equal the power of a single *mahānāga* (lit. "dragon elephant"), requires the power of ten *mahānāgas* to equal the power of a single *gandha-hastin* (lit. "fragrance elephant"), requires the power of ten such *gandha-hastins* to equal the power of a single "great *gandha-hastins*", and requires the power of ten great *gandha-hastins* to equal the power of a single "greatly powerful eminence" (*mahābalavān*).

It requires the power of ten greatly powerful eminences to equal the power of a demi-*nārāyaṇa*, requires the power of ten demi-*nārāyaṇas* to equal the power of a single *nārāyaṇa*, requires the power of ten *nārāyaṇas* to equal the power of a single great *nārāyaṇa*, requires the power of ten great *nārāyaṇas* to equal the power of a single bodhisattva who has already coursed through one hundred kalpas [on the Bodhisattva Path].

It requires the power of ten bodhisattvas who have already coursed through one hundred kalpas to equal the power of a single bodhisattva who has already coursed through one hundred thousand kalpas, requires the power of ten bodhisattvas who have already coursed through one hundred thousand kalpas to equal

當一得忍菩薩力。十得忍菩薩力當一最後生菩薩
力。住此力已。菩薩即於生時能行七步。十最後生
菩薩生時力。乃當菩薩少年時力。菩薩住此力已。
趣菩提場成等正覺。得正覺已。以過百千功德力
故。成就如來正遍知一種處非處力。如是等十力成
就。此名諸佛菩薩及餘少分眾生福報生力

[0524b25] 　　神通力者。謂四神足善修多作已。以此希
有神通力故。得調伏諸眾生等。彼以希有神力。顯
現若色若力若住持等。若諸眾生。應以此色像得調
伏者。即以此色像。於彼彼眾生所。示現或佛色像
或獨覺色像或聲聞色像。如是或釋梵護世轉輪王等
色像。若復諸餘色像。乃至畜生色像。為調伏眾生
故。示現如是色像。

当一得忍菩萨力。十得忍菩萨力当一最后生菩萨
力。住此力已。菩萨即于生时能行七步。十最后生
菩萨生时力。乃当菩萨少年时力。菩萨住此力已。
趣菩提场成等正觉。得正觉已。以过百千功德力
故。成就如来正遍知一种处非处力。如是等十力成
就。此名诸佛菩萨及馀少分众生福报生力

[0524b25] 　　神通力者。谓四神足善修多作已。以此希
有神通力故。得调伏诸众生等。彼以希有神力。显
现若色若力若住持等。若诸众生。应以此色像得调
伏者。即以此色像。于彼彼众生所。示现或佛色像
或独觉色像或声闻色像。如是或释梵护世转轮王等
色像。若复诸馀色像。乃至畜生色像。为调伏众生
故。示现如是色像。

the power of a bodhisattva who has already realized the patiences, and requires the power of ten bodhisattvas who have already realized the patiences to equal the power of a single bodhisattva in his last birth.

When [a bodhisattva] abides in a state endowed with this degree of power, he is able to walk the seven steps immediately on taking birth. It takes the power of ten of these bodhisattvas in their last birth to equal the power of that same bodhisattva when he has reached his youthful years. When a bodhisattva possesses this degree of power, he proceeds to the site of bodhi and gains the realization of the right enlightenment. After he has gained the right enlightenment, he utilizes power exceeding even that inhering in the hundred thousand meritorious qualities to bring about the perfection of the right and universal knowledge of the Tathāgata and but one of the powers, "the power to know what can be as what can be and what cannot be as what cannot be." When he has proceeded in this manner on through to the realization of all ten of the ten powers, it is this degree of power which constitutes that of the Buddhas, that of [some] of the Bodhisattvas, and that of but a small fraction of other beings who have gained this "power produced through karmic reward."

As for "the power of the supernatural powers," this refers to the four bases of spiritual power (ṛddhi-pāda). After those [bodhisattvas] have skillfully cultivated and implemented them time and time again, they are able to employ these supernatural powers in the training of beings. They employ the power of supernatural powers to manifest whichever forms, whichever powers, whichever sustaining capacity, and so forth as may be required to suit the occasion.

In an instance where particular beings should succeed in being trained and subdued by encountering a particular physical appearance, then they immediately employ just this particular physical appearance in manifesting where those particular beings reside, manifesting then perhaps in the form of a buddha, perhaps in the form of a pratyekabuddha, or perhaps in the form of a śrāvaka-disciple. Thus, in this very manner, they may manifest in the form of Śakra, Brahmā, a world-protector, a wheel-turning king, or in some other such physical form. If it be appropriate that they appear in yet another type of physical form, even to the point of manifesting in the physical form of an animal, this for the sake of training beings, then they manifest in just such a physical form.

繁體字

若有多力憍慢瞋怒兇惡自高眾生。應以此力得調伏者。即現此力。或大力士力。或四分那羅延力。或半那羅延力。或[7]一那羅延力。以此力故。須彌山王高十六萬八千踰闍那。寬八萬四千踰闍那。以三指舉取。如舉菴摩勒果擲置他方世界。而四天王天及三十三天等無所嬈惱。於菩薩力亦不減損。又此三千大千世界雖復寬曠。從於水界乃至有頂。置之手掌經劫而住。於諸神通道。具足示現如是等力。若有憍慢增上慢瞋怒兇惡自高眾生。說法調伏令離憍慢增上慢瞋怒兇惡等。彼得如是神足住持智已。以此住持智。有所住持。隨意皆得若以大海為牛迹。即成牛迹。若以牛迹為大海。即成大海。

简体字

若有多力憍慢瞋怒凶恶自高众生。应以此力得调伏者。即现此力。或大力士力。或四分那罗延力。或半那罗延力。或[7]一那罗延力。以此力故。须弥山王高十六万八千逾闍那。宽八万四千逾闍那。以三指举取。如举菴摩勒果掷置他方世界。而四天王天及三十三天等无所娆恼。于菩萨力亦不减损。又此三千大千世界虽复宽旷。从于水界乃至有顶。置之手掌经劫而住。于诸神通道。具足示现如是等力。若有憍慢增上慢瞋怒凶恶自高众生。说法调伏令离憍慢增上慢瞋怒凶恶等。彼得如是神足住持智已。以此住持智。有所住持。随意皆得若以大海为牛迹。即成牛迹。若以牛迹为大海。即成大海。

Thus, if there be a very strong, arrogant, hateful, cruelly evil and self-important being who rightly should be trained and sub-dued by power of this sort, then [those bodhisattvas] immediately manifest just such power [to accomplish just this purpose], perhaps manifesting with the power possessed by a great powerful emi-nence (*mahābalavān*), perhaps manifesting with four increments of the power of a *nārāyaṇa*, perhaps manifesting with the power of a demi-*nārāyaṇa*, or perhaps manifesting with the power of one who is a full *nārāyaṇa*.

Employing this sort of power, they are able to pick up with just three fingers Sumeru, that king of mountains which is a hundred and sixty-eight thousand yojanas high and eighty-four thousand yojanas in breadth, doing so with the same ease that they might pick up a mango fruit. They can then toss it off into the worlds of some other region while still not disturbing any of the gods in the Heaven of the Four Heavenly Kings or any of the gods in the Heaven of the Thirty-three. In doing this, the powers of such bodhisattvas are not diminished in the slightest.

Additionally, even though this great trichiliocosm is vast in its breadth, [these bodhisattvas] are able to place in the palm of the hand everything from the water realms on up to the peak of exis-tence, holding it there for an entire kalpa. Pursuing the path of the spiritual powers, they perfect the ability to manifest powers of just these sorts.

Thus, if there be an arrogant being of overweening pride, one who is prone to hateful rages and who is cruel, evil, and self-impor-tant, [then those bodhisattvas are able to employ their spiritual powers as the circumstance requires, thus being able to success-fully] speak Dharma for them, thus training and subduing them, causing them thereby to abandon their arrogance, overweening pride, hateful rages, cruelty, evil, and such.

After they have gained the knowledge of how to invoke the bases of the spiritual powers, they freely employ this knowledge of how to invoke them. Thus, in an instance where there is that which should be invoked, they succeed in bringing about whatso-ever they wish to bring about. If they wish to transform a great ocean into [the puddle formed by] the hoof print of a cow, then it immediately becomes just such a hoof-print [puddle]. If they wish to make a hoof-print [puddle] into a great sea, then they are able to immediately transform it into a great sea.

若以劫燒為水聚者。即成水聚。若以水聚為火聚
者。即成火聚。若以火聚為風聚者。即成風聚。若
以風聚為火聚者。即成火聚。如是若以此住持。隨
所住持下中上法。既住持已。無有人能震動隱沒。
所謂若釋若梵若魔及餘世間同法者。除佛世尊。於
眾生類中。無有眾生於菩薩所住持法震動隱沒。以
住持力故。為彼種種勝上喜踊尊敬眾生說法。彼神
足力高出自在。過魔煩惱入佛境界。覺諸眾生。聚
集宿世善根資糧。魔及魔身天等不能障礙。此名菩
薩神通力

[0524c28]　　信力者。於佛法僧及菩薩行中。信解一向
不可沮壞。若惡魔作佛身來。隨於何法欲壞其信。

若以劫烧为水聚者。即成水聚。若以水聚为火聚
者。即成火聚。若以火聚为风聚者。即成风聚。若
以风聚为火聚者。即成火聚。如是若以此住持。随
所住持下中上法。既住持已。无有人能震动隐没。
所谓若释若梵若魔及馀世间同法者。除佛世尊。于
众生类中。无有众生于菩萨所住持法震动隐没。以
住持力故。为彼种种胜上喜踊尊敬众生说法。彼神
足力高出自在。过魔烦恼入佛境界。觉诸众生。聚
集宿世善根资粮。魔及魔身天等不能障碍。此名菩
萨神通力

[0524c28]　　信力者。于佛法僧及菩萨行中。信解一向
不可沮坏。若恶魔作佛身来。随于何法欲坏其信。

If they wish to transform the burning [up of the world which occurs at the end] of the kalpa into bodies of water, then it immediately turns into bodies of water. If they wish to transform bodies of water into a fiery conflagration, then they immediately become a fiery conflagration. If they wish to transform a fiery conflagration into a whirlwind, then it immediately becomes a whirlwind. If they wish to transform a whirlwind into a fiery conflagration, then it immediately becomes a fiery conflagration.

In this manner, if they have some [manifestation of spiritual power] which they have invoked, then no matter what they have invoked, whether it be a lesser, middling, or superior sort of dharma, having already succeeded in invoking it, it becomes such as no person is able to disturb or cause to disappear. This is to say then that even if it were Śakra, Brahmā, a demon, or someone from another world system possessed of identical dharmas, aside from a buddha, one of the Bhagavāns, there is no being whatsoever anywhere among all of the classes of other beings that would possess the ability to disturb [that manifestation of spiritual powers] or cause it to disappear.

On account of the power to invoke [such manifestations of spiritual power, these bodhisattvas] are able to speak Dharma for all of those beings brought into an attitude of reverence by observing all of those different sorts of supremely ascendant [manifestations of spiritual power which cause them] to jump up in delight [on observing them].

In their exercise of the power of spiritual powers, they invoke them with sovereign mastery at the highest level. They go beyond the afflictions produced through the influence of demons and enter into that very state of mind possessed by the Buddhas themselves. They [employ such powers] in the awakening of beings and in the accumulation of the provisions [for the acquisition of bodhi], bringing to bear the roots of goodness accumulated across the course of previous lives. [These powers are such as] the demons and the demonically-influenced celestial beings are unable to impede. This is what constitutes "the power of the supernatural powers" possessed by the Bodhisattvas.

As for "the power of faith," they possess such faith and understanding in the Buddha, the Dharma, the Sangha, and the bodhisattva conduct as can never be obstructed or damaged. Even if an evil demon were to appear in the body of a buddha, it does not matter

菩薩以信解力故。彼不能動菩薩信力。此名信力

[0525a03] 精進力者。菩薩若發起精進。與彼彼善法相應時。於彼彼處得牢固力。隨所受行若天若人不能動壞令其中止。此名精進力

[0525a06] 念力者。住彼彼法處其心安止。諸餘煩惱不能散亂。以念力持故破諸煩惱。彼諸煩惱不能破壞菩薩所念。此名念力

[0525a09] 三摩提力者。於憒鬧中行遠離行。諸有音聲及語道所出。不為聲刺障礙初禪。行善覺觀不礙二禪。生於愛喜不礙三禪。成熟眾生攝受諸法未曾捨廢不礙四禪。如是遊四種禪。諸禪惡對不能破壞。雖遊諸禪。而不隨禪生。此名菩薩三摩提力

[0525a15] 般若力者。謂世出世法中不可壞智。於生生中不由師教。

菩萨以信解力故。彼不能动菩萨信力。此名信力

[0525a03] 精进力者。菩萨若发起精进。与彼彼善法相应时。于彼彼处得牢固力。随所受行若天若人不能动坏令其中止。此名精进力

[0525a06] 念力者。住彼彼法处其心安止。诸馀烦恼不能散乱。以念力持故破诸烦恼。彼诸烦恼不能坏菩萨所念。此名念力

[0525a09] 三摩提力者。于愦闹中行远离行。诸有音声及语道所出。不为声刺障碍初禅。行善觉观不碍二禅。生于爱喜不碍三禅。成熟众生摄受诸法未曾舍废不碍四禅。如是游四种禅。诸禅恶对不能破坏。虽游诸禅。而不随禅生。此名菩萨三摩提力

[0525a15] 般若力者。谓世出世法中不可坏智。于生生中不由师教。

which dharma in which he attempted to damage such faith, for the bodhisattva is possessed of such power of faith and understanding that [such a demon] remains utterly unable to shake the power of faith possessed by that bodhisattva. This is what is meant by "the power of faith."

As for "the power of vigor," in an instance where the bodhisattva invokes his practice of vigor, in whichever of those good dharmas to which it is applied, he succeeds in gaining in just such circumstances the power of enduring solidity of practice. No matter which practice he has undertaken, no god or person is able to shake him in that practice, damage that practice, or cause him to cease that practice. This is what is meant by "the power of vigor."

As for "the power of mindfulness," in whichever of those various dharmas his mind has become established, no extraneous afflictive circumstance is able to cause him to become scattered. Through the sustaining power of mindfulness, he is able to break all afflictions. Thus none of those afflictions are able to break or cause the deterioration of the bodhisattva's mindfulness. This is what is meant by "the power of mindfulness."

As for "the power of samādhi," even in the midst of vexing boisterousness, he continues to course in renunciation [of worldly matters]. In any instance where there may be extraneous noise or conversations, his coursing in the first dhyāna remains unimpeded by the piercings of such noises. Involvement in wholesome ideation and mental discursion does not impede his coursing in the second dhyāna. The arising of enjoyable blissful states does not impede his coursing in the third dhyāna. His ripening of beings and accumulation of all manner of dharmas are never forsaken and do not impede his coursing in the fourth dhyāna. In this manner, he roams in the four dhyānas. In doing so, the evil opposing states encountered in the practice of the dhyānas remain unable to damage or undermine his practice. Although he does roam about within the dhyānas, still, he refrains from taking rebirth in those realms corresponding to the dhyānas. This is what is meant by the bodhisattva's "power of samādhi."

As for "the power of prajñā," this refers to wisdom which remains undamaged even in the midst of all manner of worldly and world-transcending dharmas. In life after life, he is [so able to remain wisely guided by prajñā] that he need not resort to the teachings of a guru.

諸所作業工巧明處。乃至世間最勝難作難忍。菩薩
皆得現前。若出世法救度於世。菩薩智慧隨順入
已。彼天人阿修羅眾不能破壞。此名般若力。如是
等菩薩七力已略解說。若欲具演無有邊際。此名菩
薩力波羅蜜。已解釋力波羅蜜。我今當說智波羅
蜜。此中若世間所行書論印算數等。及[1]界論（謂
風黃痰[2]癊等性）方論（謂醫方論）治諸乾痟[3]顛狂
鬼持等病。破諸蠱毒。又作戲笑所攝文章談謔等。
令生歡喜。出生村城園苑陂湖池井華果藥物及林叢
等。示現金銀摩尼琉璃貝[4]（石白如貝）[5]玉珊瑚等
寶性。入於日月薄蝕星宿地動夢怪等事。建立相諸
身分支節等。

諸所作业工巧明处。乃至世间最胜难作难忍。菩萨
皆得现前。若出世法救度于世。菩萨智慧随顺入
已。彼天人阿修罗众不能破坏。此名般若力。如是
等菩萨七力已略解说。若欲具演无有边际。此名菩
萨力波罗蜜。已解释力波罗蜜。我今当说智波罗
蜜。此中若世间所行书论印算数等。及[1]界论（谓
风黄痰[2]癊等性）方论（谓医方论）治诸乾痟[3]颠狂
鬼持等病。破诸蛊毒。又作戏笑所摄文章谈谑等。
令生欢喜。出生村城园苑陂湖池井华果药物及林丛
等。示现金银摩尼琉璃贝[4]（石白如贝）[5]玉珊瑚等
宝性。入于日月薄蚀星宿地动梦怪等事。建立相诸
身分支节等。

All sorts of livelihoods, all of the arts and skills, all of the abilities in the higher clarities, and even the world's most supreme, most difficult to perform, and most difficult to endure abilities—the bodhisattva has them all manifest for him as abilities he is free to exercise. In the case of those world-transcending dharmas with which one rescues and liberates beings in the world, once the bodhisattva's wisdom has entered into them, they become such as no group of gods, men, or *asuras* can overturn or interfere with.

This is what is meant by "the power of prajñā." These seven bodhisattva powers have only been briefly explained. If one wished to expound on them completely, that would involve a boundlessly-long discussion. This is what is meant by the bodhisattva's pāramitā of the powers.

THE PERFECTION OF KNOWLEDGES

Having finished the discussion of the pāramitā of the powers, I shall now explain the pāramitā of the knowledges, as follows:

[The bodhisattva] understands the various traditions operative in the world, including those set forth in the classics and philosophical treatises, including printing, mathematics, and so forth, including the treatises devoted to the physical elements,[39] including the treatises devoted to medical prescriptions,[40] including the means for treating wasting diabetes, the means for treating insanity, the means for performing exorcisms in cases of possession by ghosts, and the means for treating other such pathologies, including the means for breaking the effects of poisonings associated with black magic.

Additionally, he knows how to write humorous works and how to converse in a satirical manner, these for the sake of causing people to be delighted.[41]

He knows how to establish villages, cities, parks and gardens, dikes, lakes, ponds, wells, floral gardens, orchards, medicinal plant gardens, forests, groves, and other such projects.

He possesses a manifest knowledge of the nature of gems as it relates to gold, silver, *maṇi* jewels, *vaiḍūrya*, alabaster,[42] jade, coral, and other such precious things.

His knowledge includes such phenomena as solar and lunar eclipses, the stars and their constellations, seismology, and the oddities experienced in dreams, these as well as the physiognomic signs present in the body and its limbs and appendages.

知於禁戒行處禪那神通無量無色處。及餘正覺相應
利樂眾生等彼岸。又復知諸世界成壞。隨世界成隨
世界壞皆悉了知。又知業集故世界成。業盡故世界
壞。知世界若干時成住。知世界若干時壞住。知諸
地界水界風界火界若大若小若無量等差別。知極細
微塵。亦知所有微塵聚集微塵分散。知世界中所有
地微塵數。如是亦知水火風等微塵數。知所有眾生
身微塵數國土身微塵數。知諸眾生麁身細身差別。
乃至亦知微塵合成地獄畜生餓鬼阿修羅天人等身。
知欲色無色界成壞。及知彼小大無量等差別。知眾
生身中業身報身色身。

知于禁戒行处禅那神通无量无色处。及馀正觉相应
利乐众生等彼岸。又复知诸世界成坏。随世界成随
世界坏皆悉了知。又知业集故世界成。业尽故世界
坏。知世界若干时成住。知世界若干时坏住。知诸
地界水界风界火界若大若小若无量等差别。知极细
微尘。亦知所有微尘聚集微尘分散。知世界中所有
地微尘数。如是亦知水火风等微尘数。知所有众生
身微尘数国土身微尘数。知诸众生麁身细身差别。
乃至亦知微尘合成地狱畜生饿鬼阿修罗天人等身。
知欲色无色界成坏。及知彼小大无量等差别。知众
生身中业身报身色身。

His knowledge includes the points of practice related to the moral precepts, includes the dhyānas, the spiritual powers, the [four] immeasurables, and the formless realm stations. It includes as well perfected understanding of the other aspects of right enlightenment useful in bringing benefit and happiness to beings.

He understands as well the manner in which all worlds are created and destroyed while also completely understanding the developments arising as a consequence of their creation and destruction.

He also understands that it is on account of the accumulation of karma that worlds are created and that it is on account of the exhaustion of such karma that worlds are destroyed. Thus he understands how it is that, at a particular time, a particular world comes into existence and understands as well how it is that, at a particular time, that particular world meets its destruction.

He also understands the innumerable variations in the greater and lesser manifestation of the elemental phases of earth, water, wind, and fire.[43]

He has knowledge of the most extremely minute particles, understanding as well how all of these minute particles come together and how all of these minute particles come apart and disperse.

He knows even the number of all minute particles residing in the "earth" elemental phase comprising the physical world, and knows as well in this same manner the number of minute particles abiding in the "water," "fire," and "wind" elemental phases.

He knows the number of such minute particles present in the bodies of all beings, the number of such minute particles present in the bodies contained in a single country, and knows the distinctions involved in both the coarse bodies and subtle bodies of beings, this even to the point of also having knowledge of the extremely minute particles which come together to form the bodies of those residing in the hells, among the animals, among the hungry ghosts, among the asuras, among the gods, and among men.

He understands how it is that the desire realm, form realm, and formless realm are produced and destroyed, even to the point of knowing the immeasurable number of great and small distinctions involved therein.

His knowledge extends to knowledge of the bodies of beings, including their karmic-action creating bodies, their karmic-reward experiencing bodies, and their form bodies.

知國土身中小大染淨。及撗住倒住平住等方網差別
[0525b14]　　知業報身中差別名字身。知聲聞獨覺菩薩
身中差別名字身。知如來身中正覺身願身化身住持
身。形色相好莊嚴身威光身意念身福身法身。知智
身中若善分別若如理思惟。若果相應攝若世出世。
若安立三乘若共法不共法。若[6]出道非[*]出道若學
無學。知法身中平等不動。安立世諦處所名字。安
立眾生非眾生法。安立佛法聖眾。知虛空身中無量
身入。一切處非身真實無邊無色身差別。

知国土身中小大染净。及撗住倒住平住等方网差别
[0525b14]　　知业报身中差别名字身。知声闻独觉菩萨
身中差别名字身。知如来身中正觉身愿身化身住持
身。形色相好庄严身威光身意念身福身法身。知智
身中若善分别若如理思惟。若果相应摄若世出世。
若安立三乘若共法不共法。若[6]出道非[*]出道若学
无学。知法身中平等不动。安立世谛处所名字。安
立众生非众生法。安立佛法圣众。知虚空身中无量
身入。一切处非身真实无边无色身差别。

He also understands the middling, lesser, and greater degrees of defilement in the physical "bodies" of particular countries and lands, this extending even to such [worlds] as have evolved in a lateral direction, those suspended in an inverted fashion, and those which abide on level terrains. He knows as well the distinctions involved in the net-like spatial inter-relationship [of those worlds].

He knows the distinctions and designations involved in the karma-creating bodies and karmic-reward-experiencing bodies. He also knows the distinctions and designations in the bodies of the Śrāvaka-disciples, the Pratyekabuddhas, and the Buddhas.

He knows among the bodies of the Tathāgatas, the right-enlightenment body, the vow body, the transformation body, and the primary sustaining body, understanding as well the physical forms, major marks, and minor characteristics which adorn their bodies. He also understands the awesome-light body, the mind-body, the karmic-blessings body, and the Dharma body.

He also knows with respect to the wisdom body the specifics involved in the making of skillful distinctions and in the carrying on of contemplative endeavors, knowing those matters associated with fruition of karma, including the associated mundane aspects and world-transcending aspects, including the matter of the establishment of the Three Vehicles, the matter of dharmas held in common and dharmas which are not held in common, including matters associated with the world-transcending path and the paths which do not bring about transcendence of the world, including matters associated with those still in training as well as those who have gone beyond training.

He knows with respect to the Dharma body the matter of its uniformly even equality [in all places] and the matter of its remaining entirely unmoving. He knows the matters associated with the establishment of the worldly truth and its associated designations, and knows the matters associated with the establishment of dharmas associated with beings and with non-beings.

He knows the matters associated with the establishment of the Buddhas, the Dharma, and the Ārya Sangha. He knows with respect to the empty-space body that immeasurable body's [acquisition of the ten] universal bases, knows that which is not real with respect to these [various types of bodies], and knows the distinctions involved in the bodies associated with the boundless-space and other formless [absorptions].

繁體字

得出生如是等身智。又得命自在心自在眾具自在業自在願自在信解自在神通自在智自在生自在法自在。得如是等十自在已。為不思議智者無量智者不退智者。如是等智有八萬四千行相。是菩薩所知智波羅蜜。如是隨分解釋智波羅蜜。若欲具演。唯佛世尊。乃能解說

　　此六波羅蜜　　　總菩提資糧

　　猶如虛空中　　　盡攝於諸物

[0525c03] 如所解釋六波羅蜜中。總攝一切菩提資糧。譬如虛空行住諸物。有識無識悉攝在中。如是其餘聞資糧[7]等諸資糧攝在六波羅蜜中。同相無異。應知

简体字

得出生如是等身智。又得命自在心自在众具自在业自在愿自在信解自在神通自在智自在生自在法自在。得如是等十自在已。为不思议智者无量智者不退智者。如是等智有八万四千行相。是菩萨所知智波罗蜜。如是随分解释智波罗蜜。若欲具演。唯佛世尊。乃能解说

　　此六波罗蜜　　　总菩提资粮

　　犹如虚空中　　　尽摄于诸物

[0525c03] 如所解释六波罗蜜中。总摄一切菩提资粮。譬如虚空行住诸物。有识无识悉摄在中。如是其馀闻资粮[7]等诸资粮摄在六波罗蜜中。同相无异。应知

He has succeeded in developing such knowledges as these with respect to the various sorts of bodies [described in the passages above.

Additionally, he has succeeded in gaining sovereign mastery of the lifespan (*āyur-vaśitā*), sovereign mastery of the mind (*citta-vaśitā*), sovereign mastery of equipage (*pariṣkāra-vaśitā*), sovereign mastery of karmic actions (*karma-vaśitā*), sovereign mastery of vows (*praṇidhāna-vaśitā*), sovereign mastery of faith and understanding (*adhimukti-vaśitā*), sovereign mastery of spiritual powers (*ṛddhi-vaśitā*), sovereign mastery of the knowledges (*jñāna-vaśitā*), sovereign mastery of rebirths (*upapatti-vaśitā*), and sovereign mastery of Dharma (*dharma-vaśitā*).

Having gained ten such types of sovereign mastery, he then becomes one possessed of inconceivable and ineffable knowledges, becomes one possessed of immeasurably many knowledges, and becomes one possessed of the knowledges whereby he remains invulnerable to retreating [from the path to buddhahood]. Knowledges of these sorts involve eighty-four thousand practice-related aspects. It is this which constitutes the pāramitā of the knowledges known by the bodhisattva.

We have presented in this fashion a categorized explanation of the pāramitā of the knowledges. If one wished to expound on the matter completely, it would be only the Buddha, the Bhagavān, who would be qualified to present that explanation.

---

007 – The Six Perfections, Like Space, Comprehensively Subsume Bodhi's Provisions

These six pāramitās
Encompass the provisions essential for bodhi,
They are comparable in this to empty space
Which entirely envelopes all things.

COMMENTARY:

The six pāramitās as explained above comprehensively subsume the provisions for bodhi. This is analogous to the way in which, in empty space, all things possessed of or devoid of consciousness which travel about and abide in it are all contained within it. Thus all of the other sorts of provisions such as the "learning" provision are contained within the six pāramitās. One should realize that they all share this same common feature [of being subsumed therein]. [In this respect], they are no different.

復有餘師意　　諸覺資糧者
實捨及寂智　　四處之所攝

[0525c15]　又一論師作[8]是念。一切菩提資糧皆實處捨處寂處智處所攝。實者不虛誑相。實即是戒。是故實為尸羅波羅蜜。捨即布施。是故捨處為[9]陀那波羅蜜。寂者即心不濁。若心不[10]濁。愛不愛事所不能動是故寂處為羼提波羅蜜及禪那波羅蜜。智處還為般若波羅蜜毘梨耶波羅蜜。遍入諸處以無精進。則於諸處無所成就。是故毘梨耶波羅蜜成就諸事。是故一切資糧皆入四[11]處。問如經說。以慈資糧得無礙心。以捨資糧得斷憎愛。於中慈悲有何差別。答

復有餘師意　　諸觉资粮者
实舍及寂智　　四处之所摄

[0525c15]　又一论师作[8]是念。一切菩提资粮皆实处舍处寂处智处所摄。实者不虚诳相。实即是戒。是故实为尸罗波罗蜜。舍即布施。是故舍处为[9]陀那波罗蜜。寂者即心不浊。若心不[10]浊。爱不爱事所不能动是故寂处为羼提波罗蜜及禅那波罗蜜。智处还为般若波罗蜜毘梨耶波罗蜜。遍入诸处以无精进。则于诸处无所成就。是故毘梨耶波罗蜜成就诸事。是故一切资粮皆入四[11]处。问如经说。以慈资粮得无碍心。以舍资粮得断憎爱。于中慈悲有何差别。答

AN ALTERNATIVE SCHEMA: THE FOUR MERIT BASES INCLUDE ALL PROVISIONS

008 – Another Exegete's Opinion: The Four Merit Bases Subsume All Provisions

There is also the idea proposed by another master
That, as for the provisions for enlightenment,
Truth, relinquishment, cessation, and wisdom—
These four bases subsume them all.

COMMENTARY:

Additionally, there is a treatise master who sets forth the idea that all provisions requisite for bodhi are included within "the truth basis" (*satya*), "the relinquishment basis" (*tyāga*), "the cessation basis" (*upaśama*), and "the wisdom basis" (*prajñā*).

As for "truth," it is characterized by refraining from falseness and deception. Truth then is just moral virtue. Hence "the truth [basis]" is [identifiable with] the pāramitā of *śīla*.

As for "relinquishment," it is just "giving." Hence "the relinquishment basis" is [identifiable with] the pāramitā of *dāna*.

As for "cessation," it is just an absence of turbidity in the mind. If the mind is not turbid, then it is such as matters connected with affections and antipathies are unable to move. Hence "the cessation basis" is integral to both the pāramitā of *kṣānti* (the perfection of patience) and the pāramitā of dhyāna (the perfection of meditative discipline).

"The wisdom basis" is [identifiable with] the pāramitā of prajñā (the perfection of wisdom).

The pāramitā of *vīrya* (the perfection of vigor) pervasively permeates all of these "bases," for if there were to be an absence of vigor, then there would be no accomplishment of anything at all. Hence the pāramitā of *vīrya* is that which brings all endeavors to completion.

It is for these sorts of reasons that all of the provisions [may be described as being] entirely subsumed within "the four bases" (*adhiṣṭhāna*).[44]

Question: According to the statements in the Sutras, it is on account of the kindness (*maitrī*) provision that one gains a mind free of any obstructiveness and it is on account of the relinquishment (*tyāga*) provision that one succeeds in cutting off detestation and affection. What in all of this differentiates "kindness" from "compassion"?

Response: (As below...)

大悲徹骨髓　　為諸眾生依
如父於一子　　慈則遍一切

[0525c28]　　若入生死嶮道。墮地獄畜生餓鬼諸趣。在惡邪見網。覆愚癡稠林。行邪徑非道。猶如盲闇。非出離中見為出離。為老病死憂悲苦惱諸賊執持。入[1]魔意稠林。去佛意遠者。菩薩大悲。穿於自身皮肉及筋。徹至骨髓。為諸眾生而作依處。令此眾生得度如是生死曠野險難惡路。置於一切智城無畏之宮。譬如長者唯一福子而遭病苦。愛徹皮肉入於骨髓。但念何時得其病愈。悲亦如是。唯於苦眾生中起。慈者遍於一切眾生中起。又復慈故於諸眾生得無礙心。悲故於生死中無有疲厭。

大悲彻骨髓　　为诸众生依
如父于一子　　慈则遍一切

[0525c28]　　若入生死嶮道。墮地狱畜生饿鬼诸趣。在恶邪见网。覆愚痴稠林。行邪径非道。犹如盲暗。非出离中见为出离。为老病死忧悲苦恼诸贼执持。入[1]魔意稠林。去佛意远者。菩萨大悲。穿于自身皮肉及筋。彻至骨髓。为诸众生而作依处。令此众生得度如是生死旷野险难恶路。置于一切智城无畏之宫。譬如长者唯一福子而遭病苦。爱彻皮肉入于骨髓。但念何时得其病愈。悲亦如是。唯于苦众生中起。慈者遍于一切众生中起。又复慈故于诸众生得无碍心。悲故于生死中无有疲厌。

繁體字

简体字

THE FOUR IMMEASURABLES AS ESSENTIAL ATTRIBUTES OF THE BODHISATTVA

009 – The Great Compassion and the Great Kindness

The great compassion penetrates to the marrow of one's bones.
Thus one serves as a refuge for every being.
With a feeling as strong as a father's regard for his only son,
One's kindness extends universally to all beings.

COMMENTARY:

When one enters the perilous path of cyclic births and deaths, one falls into the destinies of the hell-dwellers, animals, and hungry ghosts and abides in the net of wrong and perverse views. Covered over by the canopy of a thickly-grown forest of delusions, one courses along on an erroneous track which is not the Path and abides in a darkness [so deep it is] like that of the blind. One sees a means of escape in what is not in fact a means of escape. One instead is seized and held by the insurgents of aging, sickness, death, worry, lamentation, and bitter affliction. One then enters the thickly-grown forest of demonic intentions.

As for these who have departed so far from the intentions of the Buddhas, the bodhisattva feels for them such great compassion that it pierces his body, goes on through his skin, through his flesh, into his sinews, and penetrates even into the very marrow of his bones. Thus he is able to become for all beings one in whom they can take refuge. He causes those beings to be able to pass on through just such a dangerous, difficult, and terrible road as this which traverses the vast wilderness of cyclic births and deaths. He then establishes them in the city of all-knowledge where they abide within the palace of fearlessness.

This is comparable to the circumstance of an elder whose single blessed son has become afflicted with the suffering of some sickness. The love felt for his son penetrates his skin and flesh and enters the very marrow of his bones. He is only able to think, "Oh when will it be that he will be able to recover from his illness?!" Compassion (*karuṇa*), too, is just like this. It is such as one feels only for those beings who are caught in suffering. As for kindness (*maitrī*), it is a feeling which, when it arises, extends universally to all beings.

Moreover, it is on account of kindness that one develops a mind free of any obstruction in relating to beings. It is on account of compassion that one experiences no weariness or disgust as one works within the sphere of cyclic births and deaths.

繁體字

又慈於善人中生。悲於不善人中生。又菩薩慈增長
故不著己樂。則生大慈。悲增長故捨諸支節及命。
則生大悲

　　若念佛功德　　　及聞佛神變
　　愛喜而受淨　　　此名為大喜

[0526a15]　　若念佛功德者。於中何者是佛功德。謂諸
佛世尊無量百千俱致劫中。聚集善根故。不護身口
意業故。五種應知中斷疑故。四種答難中無失故。
三十七助菩提法教授故。十二分緣生中因緣覺故。
教九教故。四種住持具足故。得四無量故。滿足六
波羅蜜故。

簡体字

又慈于善人中生。悲于不善人中生。又菩萨慈增长
故不着己乐。则生大慈。悲增长故舍诸支节及命。
则生大悲

　　若念佛功德　　　及闻佛神变
　　爱喜而受净　　　此名为大喜

[0526a15]　　若念佛功德者。于中何者是佛功德。谓诸
佛世尊无量百千俱致劫中。聚集善根故。不护身口
意业故。五种应知中断疑故。四种答难中无失故。
三十七助菩提法教授故。十二分缘生中因缘觉故。
教九教故。四种住持具足故。得四无量故。满足六
波罗蜜故。

Then again, kindness is generated with respect to those persons who are good whereas compassion is generated even for people not inclined toward goodness.

Furthermore, because the kindness of the bodhisattva grows ever greater, he does not cherish any attachment to his own happiness. This then culminates in the generation of "the great kindness" (mahā-maitrī). Because one's compassion grows ever greater, one may then give up even his own limbs and even his own life. This then culminates in the generation of "the great compassion" (mahā-karuṇa).[45]

---

010 – The Great Sympathetic Joy

If one brings to mind the qualities of a buddha
Or hears of a buddha's spiritual transformations,
One becomes purified through one's admiration and joyfulness.
This is what is meant by the great sympathetic joy.

COMMENTARY:

As for "If one brings to mind the qualities of a buddha," what are those "qualities of a buddha"? [One experiences sympathetic joy on account of the following qualities]:

1 – Because all buddhas, the Bhagavāns, have worked to accumulate roots of goodness across the course of countless hundreds of thousands of koṭīs of kalpas.
2 – Because of their being unprotective of the risks to their own physical, verbal, and mental karma.
3 – Because of their severing doubts regarding the five categories of things which should be known.
4 – Because of their remaining free of any error in the four kinds of responses to challenging questions.
5 – Because of their teaching of the thirty-seven dharmas assisting realization of bodhi.
6 – Because of their awakening to the causes and conditions comprising the twelve-fold chain of conditioned arising.
7 – Because of their presenting instruction through the nine categories of teaching text.
8 – Because of their perfection in the four modes of abiding and sustaining [the Dharma].
9 – Because of their having realized the four immeasurables.
10 – Because of their having perfected the six pāramitās.

說菩薩十地故。出世五眾成滿故。四無畏十力十八不共佛法具足故。無邊境界故。自心自在轉故。無厭足法故。得如金剛三摩地故。不虛說法故。無能壞法故。世間導師故。無能見頂故。無與等故。無能勝故。不可[2]思法故。得大慈大悲大喜大捨故。百福相故。無量善根故。無邊功德故。無量功德故。無數功德故。不可分別功德故。希有功德故。不共功德故。

说菩萨十地故。出世五众成满故。四无畏十力十八不共佛法具足故。无边境界故。自心自在转故。无厌足法故。得如金刚三摩地故。不虚说法故。无能坏法故。世间导师故。无能见顶故。无与等故。无能胜故。不可[2]思法故。得大慈大悲大喜大舍故。百福相故。无量善根故。无边功德故。无量功德故。无数功德故。不可分别功德故。希有功德故。不共功德故。

11 – Because of their having explained the ten bodhisattva grounds.

12 – Because of their having completely established the five-fold world-transcending Sangha (monks, nuns, novice monks, novice nuns, probationary novice nuns).

13 – Because of their perfection of the dharmas possessed by buddhas, including the four fearlessnesses, the ten powers, and the eighteen dharmas exclusive to buddhas.

14 – Because of their possession of the boundless state of mind.

15 – Because of their sovereign mastery in the transformation of their own minds.

16 – Because of their methods for remaining free of weariness [in teaching beings].

17 – Because of their having realized the *vajra*-like samādhi.

18 – Because of their being free of falseness in explaining the Dharma.

19 – Because of their Dharma's invulnerability to refutation.

20 – Because of their serving as guides for beings in the world.

21 – Because of their possessing the "summit" mark atop the head, the peak of which none can view.

22 – Because of their being such as none can equal.

23 – Because of their being such as none can overcome.

24 – Because of their possessing the inconceivable Dharma.

25 – Because of their having developed the great kindness, great compassion, great sympathetic joy, and great equanimity.

26 – Because of their possession of the hundred-fold marks of merit.

27 – Because of their possession of countless roots of goodness.

28 – Because of their possession of boundlessly-expansive meritorious qualities.

29 – Because of their possession of incalculably vast merit.

30 – Because of their possession of countless meritorious qualities.

31 – Because of their possession of meritorious qualities [so subtle and numerous that they] surpass one's ability to distinguish them.

32 – Because of their possession of rarely-encountered meritorious qualities.

33 – Because of their possession of meritorious qualities not held in common [with any other class of beings].

如是等名。念佛諸[3]功德

[0526b01] 　　　化諸眾生故。起神通變現。隨所應度眾生。隨眾生身。隨其形量長短寬狹。隨其色類種種差殊。隨其音聲清淨分別。諸佛世尊以種種希有神通。如其所行如其信欲。以彼彼方便差別神變。而教化之。聞此事已愛喜受淨。名為大喜。於中[4]心勇名愛。愛心遍身名喜。喜心覺樂名受。於受樂時念正覺者大神通德。其心不濁名淨。彼心淨時喜意充滿名為大喜。彼登少分乘者。雖亦有喜。以不[5]共故得大喜名。問菩薩應捨眾生。為不應捨。答

如是等名。念佛诸[3]功德

[0526b01] 　　　化诸众生故。起神通变现。随所应度众生。随众生身。随其形量长短宽狭。随其色类种种差殊。随其音声清净分别。诸佛世尊以种种希有神通。如其所行如其信欲。以彼彼方便差别神变。而教化之。闻此事已爱喜受净。名为大喜。于中[4]心勇名爱。爱心遍身名喜。喜心觉乐名受。于受乐时念正觉者大神通德。其心不浊名净。彼心净时喜意充满名为大喜。彼登少分乘者。虽亦有喜。以不[5]共故得大喜名。问菩萨应舍众生。为不应舍。答

繁體字

简体字

Qualities such as these are what is intended [when the text says]: "If one brings to mind the qualities of a buddha."

For the sake of teaching beings, the Buddhas manifest various sorts of spiritual transformations. Adapting to whichever beings are amenable to being brought across to liberation, they accord with the type of body possessed by such beings, appropriately adjusting their size, height, and build, according with distinctions in the forms possessed by those beings, and adapting as well to their language and to the various levels of karmic purity possessed by those beings.

The Buddhas, the Bhagavāns, employ all sorts of rare spiritual superknowledges to accord with the activities of beings and to accord with the types of beliefs and desires they possess. Thus they employ many different types of spiritual transformations, manifesting distinctly different sorts of skillful means in efforts to teach those beings.

In a case where, on hearing of these matters, one is moved to feel such admiration and joy that one experiences karmic purification as this occurs, this becomes what may be described as "the great sympathetic joy." In this, it is the welling up of mental feelings which is referred to as "admiration." When that sensation of admiration pervades the entire body, it becomes what is referred to as "joy." When through the mind of joyfulness, one experiences happiness, this is what is referred to as the process of "becoming" [purified].

When one experiences such happiness on calling to mind the great superknowledges possessed by those who have achieved the right enlightenment, one's mind then becomes free of turbidity. It is this which is referred to as "purification." When one's mind becomes "purified," it is pervaded by the mental sensation of joyfulness. This is what is meant when one refers to "the great sympathetic joy."

Although those dedicated to the lesser-scope vehicles of liberation also possess this concept of sympathetic joy within their doctrines, [what we are speaking of here] is not held in common with them. It is this concept discussed here which alone which is worthy to be known as "the great sympathetic joy."

Question: Should the bodhisattva exercise equanimity with respect to beings, or not?

Response: (As below...)

菩薩於眾生　　不應得捨棄
當隨力所堪　　一切時攝受

[0526b13]　　菩薩摩訶薩常念利樂諸眾生等。若為貪瞋癡所惱。[6]登於慳悋破戒恚恨懈怠亂心惡智之道。入於異路。此等眾生所不應捨。於一切時說施戒修。隨力所能應當攝受。不應捨棄

菩薩從初時　　應隨堪能力
方便化眾生　　令入於大乘

[0526b19]　　此登大乘菩薩於眾生中。隨所堪能從初應作。如前方便波羅蜜中所說方便。應當精勤以諸方便教化眾生置此大乘。問何故菩薩但以大乘教化眾生。不以聲聞獨覺乘也。答

菩萨于众生　　不应得舍弃
当随力所堪　　一切时摄受

[0526b13]　　菩萨摩诃萨常念利乐诸众生等。若为贪瞋痴所恼。[6]登于悭悋破戒恚恨懈怠乱心恶智之道。入于异路。此等众生所不应舍。于一切时说施戒修。随力所能应当摄受。不应舍弃

菩萨从初时　　应随堪能力
方便化众生　　令入于大乘

[0526b19]　　此登大乘菩萨于众生中。随所堪能从初应作。如前方便波罗蜜中所说方便。应当精勤以诸方便教化众生置此大乘。问何故菩萨但以大乘教化众生。不以声闻独觉乘也。答

011 – The Great Equanimity

In his relations with beings, the bodhisattva
Should not allow himself to forsake them.
As befits the abilities determined by his powers,
He should always strive to draw them in.

COMMENTARY:

The bodhisattva, *mahāsattva*, is constantly motivated by the intention to bring benefit and happiness to beings. In cases where, afflicted by covetousness, hatefulness, and delusion, they go forth on the road of miserliness, precept-breaking, hostility, indolence, mental scatteredness, and intelligence devoted to the pursuit of evil—in cases where they go down the road of such aberrant behaviors as these—one should still refrain from forsaking such beings. One should always persist in speaking to them about the cultivation of giving and the cultivation of moral virtue. In accordance with one's abilities, one should strive to draw them in. Thus one should not forsake them.

SUBSIDIARY ASPECTS OF THE PROVISIONS
SKILLFUL MEANS AS ESSENTIAL STRATAGEMS FOR THE TEACHING OF BEINGS

012 – The Role of Skillful Means

From the very beginning, the bodhisattva
Should accord with the power of his abilities
And use skillful means to instruct beings,
Causing them to enter the Great Vehicle.

COMMENTARY:

Even from the very beginning, this bodhisattva who has entered the Great Vehicle should accomplish whatever he is able to do as he interacts with beings, resorting to whichever expedients are consistent with the earlier commentary on the skillful means pāramitā. He should be energetically diligent in employing all manner of skillful-means techniques to instruct beings and establish them in this Great Vehicle.

Question: Why is it that the bodhisattva [first] resorts only to the Great Vehicle in instructing beings and does not instead choose to offer instruction in the doctrines of the Śrāvaka-disciple and Pratyekabuddha vehicles?

Response: (As below...)

化恒沙眾生　　令得羅漢果
化一入大乘　　此福德為上

[0526b26]　　若教化恒河沙等眾生。得阿羅漢果。此大乘福。勝過彼聲聞等乘教化福。以種子無盡故。此所有種子。能為餘眾生等。作菩提心方便。亦以出生聲聞獨覺故。此福勝彼。此福勝者。大乘於聲聞獨覺乘為上故。又菩提心。有無量無數福德故。又由大乘。三寶種不斷故。是故欲求大福。應以大乘教化眾生。不以餘乘。問諸摩訶薩豈唯以大乘教化眾生。不以聲聞獨覺乘耶。[7]答

教以聲聞乘　　及獨覺乘者
以彼少力故　　不堪大乘化

化恒沙众生　　令得罗汉果
化一入大乘　　此福德为上

[0526b26]　　若教化恒河沙等众生。得阿罗汉果。此大乘福。胜过彼声闻等乘教化福。以种子无尽故。此所有种子。能为馀众生等。作菩提心方便。亦以出生声闻独觉故。此福胜彼。此福胜者。大乘于声闻独觉乘为上故。又菩提心。有无量无数福德故。又由大乘。三宝种不断故。是故欲求大福。应以大乘教化众生。不以馀乘。问诸摩诃萨岂唯以大乘教化众生。不以声闻独觉乘耶。[7]答

教以声闻乘　　及独觉乘者
以彼少力故　　不堪大乘化

繁體字

简体字

A Bodhisattva's Varying Teachings Addressing Varying Capacities

013 – The Superior Merit Arising from Teaching the Great Vehicle

Even if one taught beings as numerous as the Ganges' sands
So that they were caused to gain the fruit of arhatship,
Still, by instructing but a single person to enter the Great Vehicle,
One would generate merit superior to that.

COMMENTARY:

Even were one to instruct a Ganges' sands number of beings so that they gained the fruit of arhatship, still, this merit derived from teaching the Great Vehicle is supreme over that generated in teachings associated with the vehicles of the Śrāvaka-disciples and the others. This is because the karmic seeds thereby set down are inexhaustible. All of these karmic seeds are able in turn to redound to the benefit of yet other beings, thus constituting expedients by which they too generate the mind resolved on realizing bodhi.

Also, it is because the former involves the production of śrāvaka-disciples and pratyekabuddhas that this latter sort of merit is superior to that. As for this merit being supreme, this is because the Great Vehicle is in fact superior to the vehicles of the Śrāvaka-disciples and the Pratyekabuddhas. It is also because the mind resolved on bodhi possesses immeasurably fine and innumerably many meritorious qualities. It is also because it is solely on account of the Great Vehicle that one is able to prevent the lineage of the Three Jewels from being cut off entirely [during the Dharma-ending age].

It is for these reasons that, if one desires to gain a great measure of merit, one should resort to the Great Vehicle in instructing beings and should refrain from resorting to the teachings of the other vehicles.

Question: How could it be that all of the Mahāsattvas would resort only to the Great Vehicle in instructing beings and would somehow never employ the vehicles of the Śrāvaka-disciples and the Pratyekabuddhas in doing so?

Response: (As below...)

014 – The Two Vehicles Are Taught Only to Those of Lesser Abilities

Instructing through resort to the Śrāvaka Vehicle
Or through resort to the Pratyekabuddha Vehicle
Is undertaken where, on account of lesser abilities,
Beings are unable to accept instruction in the Great Vehicle.

繁體字

[0526c08]　　若中下意眾生。捨利他事闕於大悲。不堪
以大乘化者。乃以聲聞獨覺乘。而化度之。問若有
眾生。不可以三乘化者。於彼應捨為不捨也。答

　　聲聞獨覺乘　　　及以大乘中
　　不堪受化者　　　應置於福處

[0526c14]　　若有眾生。喜樂生死憎惡解脫。不堪以聲
聞獨覺及大乘化者。應當教化置於梵乘四梵行中。
若復不堪梵乘化者。應當教化置於天乘十善業道。
及施等福事中。不應捨棄。問若有眾生喜樂世樂。
於三福事無力能行。於彼人所當何所作。答

簡体字

[0526c08]　　若中下意众生。舍利他事阙于大悲。不堪
以大乘化者。乃以声闻独觉乘。而化度之。问若有
众生。不可以三乘化者。于彼应舍为不舍也。答

　　声闻独觉乘　　　及以大乘中
　　不堪受化者　　　应置于福处

[0526c14]　　若有众生。喜乐生死憎恶解脱。不堪以声
闻独觉及大乘化者。应当教化置于梵乘四梵行中。
若复不堪梵乘化者。应当教化置于天乘十善业道。
及施等福事中。不应舍弃。问若有众生喜乐世乐。
于三福事无力能行。于彼人所当何所作。答

COMMENTARY:

In the case of beings possessing only middling or inferior levels of resolve, they have relinquished any endeavors devoted to the benefit of others and are deficient in the great compassion. Thus they are such as are not amenable to the use of Great Vehicle doctrines in teaching them. Then and only then does one resort to the vehicles of the Śrāvaka-disciples and the Pratyekabuddhas, employing those teachings then to instruct such beings and bring them across to liberation.

Question: In the event that one encounters beings who cannot be taught through resort to any of the Three Vehicles, should one then utterly forsake them or not?

Response: (As below...)

---

015 – Teach Meritorious Deeds to Those Incapable of the Three Vehicles

Where even when relying on Śrāvaka or Pratyekabuddha Vehicles
In addition to the Great Vehicle teachings,
There are those who still cannot accept any such instruction,
One should strive to establish them in merit-creating situations.

COMMENTARY:

In an instance where one encounters beings who delight in the sphere of cyclic births and deaths, who detest and abhor [a life devoted to] liberation, and who therefore are not amenable to accepting the teachings of the Śrāvaka, Pratyekabuddha, or Great Vehicles, one should employ teaching techniques by which they will be established in the four practices of Brahmā associated with the vehicle of Brahmā.

If these beings are such as cannot be taught even by resort to the vehicle associated with Brahmā, one should employ teachings which may establish them in the path of the ten types of good karma associated with the celestial [rebirth] vehicle or, [if even that is untenable], in merit-generating endeavors such as giving and so forth. [In any case], one should refrain from just forsaking them entirely.

Question: If there be beings who delight in worldly pleasures and who have no strength by which they are able to act in accordance with the three merit-generating circumstances, what should one do on encountering such people?[46]

Response: (As below...)

若人不堪受　　天及解脫化
便以現世利　　如力應當攝

[0526c22]　　若有眾生。專求欲樂不觀他世。趣向地獄
餓鬼畜生。不可教化令生天解脫者。亦當愍彼智如
小兒。如其所應現世攝受。隨己力能以施等攝之。
愍而不捨。問若菩薩於此似小兒相諸眾生所。無有
方便可得攝化。當於彼人應何所作。答

菩薩於眾生　　無緣能教化
當起大慈悲　　不應便棄捨

[0527a01]　　若菩薩於喜樂罪惡可愍眾生中。無有方便
能行攝化。菩薩於彼當起子想興大慈悲。無有道理
而得捨棄。問已說於眾生中應須攝受。未知攝受方
便云何。答

若人不堪受　　天及解脫化
便以現世利　　如力应当摄

[0526c22]　　若有众生。专求欲乐不观他世。趣向地狱
饿鬼畜生。不可教化令生天解脱者。亦当愍彼智如
小儿。如其所应现世摄受。随己力能以施等摄之。
愍而不舍。问若菩萨于此似小儿相诸众生所。无有
方便可得摄化。当于彼人应何所作。答

菩萨于众生　　无缘能教化
当起大慈悲　　不应便弃舍

[0527a01]　　若菩萨于喜乐罪恶可愍众生中。无有方便
能行摄化。菩萨于彼当起子想兴大慈悲。无有道理
而得舍弃。问已说于众生中应须摄受。未知摄受方
便云何。答

繁體字

簡体字

016 – Benefit and Slowly Draw in Those Unfit for Liberation or Celestial Rebirth

If there be persons unable to accept
Instruction conducing either to the heavens or to liberation,
Favor them through bestowing present-life benefits.
Then, as befits one's powers, one should draw them in.

COMMENTARY:

Where there are beings who exclusively dedicate themselves to seeking desire-based pleasures, who do not contemplate the import of ensuing lifetimes, who are bound for the realms of the hell-dwellers, hungry ghosts, or animals, and whom one cannot subject to instruction bringing rebirth in the heavens or spiritual liberation, still, one should feel pity for their child-like level of wisdom. One should then adapt to whatever is appropriate for them and employ present-life priorities to draw them in. In accordance with one's own powers and abilities, one uses giving and so forth to draw them in. One should have pity on them and not forsake them.

Question: If a bodhisattva encounters these child-like beings for whom no skillful means may succeed in drawing them in and instructing them, what should he do with such people?

Response: (As below...)

017 – One Generates Kindness and Compassion for Those One Cannot Assist

Where, with regard to particular beings, a bodhisattva
Has no conditions through which to instruct them,
He should draw forth the great kindness and compassion
And should refrain from abandoning them.

COMMENTARY:

If a bodhisattva finds he has no skillful means whatsoever by which he is able to draw in and instruct those pitiable beings who delight in the evils of karmic transgressions, that bodhisattva should initiate a reflection through which he regards them as if they were his own sons. He should implement the great kindness and compassion. There is no Path-concordant principle by which one may rationalize abandoning them.

Question: It has already been explained that one should find it essential to attract beings [to the Path]. It is not yet clear, however, by which skillful means one might succeed in drawing them in.

Response: (As below...)

施攝及說法　　復聽聞說法
亦行利他事　　此為攝方便

[0527a07]　　　諸菩薩為攝受眾生故。或以布施為攝方便。或受他所施。或為他說法。或聽他說法。或行利他。或以愛語。或以同事。或說諸明處。或教以工巧。或示現作業。或令病者得愈。或救拔險難。如是等名為攝受眾生方便。當以此諸方便攝受眾生。不應棄捨。問以如是等攝受方便。攝眾生已成就何利。答

所作益眾生　　不倦不放逸
起願為菩提　　利世即自利

[0527a16]　　　此中菩薩作願利益世間者。發如是意。凡利世間事

施摄及说法　　复听闻说法
亦行利他事　　此为摄方便

[0527a07]　　　诸菩萨为摄受众生故。或以布施为摄方便。或受他所施。或为他说法。或听他说法。或行利他。或以爱语。或以同事。或说诸明处。或教以工巧。或示现作业。或令病者得愈。或救拔险难。如是等名为摄受众生方便。当以此诸方便摄受众生。不应弃舍。问以如是等摄受方便。摄众生已成就何利。答

所作益众生　　不倦不放逸
起愿为菩提　　利世即自利

[0527a16]　　　此中菩萨作愿利益世间者。发如是意。凡利世间事

THE FOUR MEANS OF ATTRACTION AS ESSENTIAL BODHISATTVA METHODS

018 – The Means of Attraction

Drawing them in through giving, through explaining Dharma,
Through listening to them discuss the Dharma,
Or through endeavors beneficial to them—
These are skillful means through which to attract them.[47]

COMMENTARY:

For the sake of drawing in beings, bodhisattvas:

May employ giving as a skillful means to attract them,
May accept gifts bestowed by them,
May explain Dharma for them,
May listen to them speak about the Dharma,
May carry out actions which benefit them,
May speak to them in a way which they find pleasing,
May undertake joint endeavors together with them,
May explain specialized fields of learning for them,
May teach them special skills,
May appear among them pursuing a particular livelihood,
May cure them when they are sick, or
May rescue them from perilous difficulties.

It is endeavors of these sorts which qualify as skillful means for the attraction of beings. One should resort to these various sorts of skillful means to draw beings [into the Path]. One should not abandon them.

Question: What are the benefits accomplished through having successfully used such means of attraction to draw beings [into the Path]?

Response: (As below...)

019 – The Need for Tirelessness, Vows, Realization that Other-Benefit is Self-Benefit

In that which is done for the benefit of beings,
Do not succumb to either weariness or negligence.
Bring forth vows for the sake of realizing bodhi.
Benefiting the world is just benefiting self.

COMMENTARY:

In this matter of the bodhisattva's vowing to benefit the world, he reflects in this manner: "Whatever endeavors might redound

繁體字

我皆應作。立此誓已。於諸眾生所作事中。不應疲
倦不應放逸。又當作[1]念。若利世間即是自利。是
故菩薩於利樂眾生因緣。不應棄捨。問已[2]說菩薩
常應利樂眾生。不應行捨。於諸法中為捨不捨。答

　　入甚深法界　　　滅離於分別

　　悉無有功用　　　諸處自然捨

[0527a24]　　法界者。即是緣生。是故先說。如來若出
不出。此法界法[3]性常住。所謂緣生。又如先說。
阿難陀。緣生甚深證亦甚深。是故入此甚深法界菩
薩。滅一切有無等二邊。攝取方便智已。即斷諸動
念戲論分別。離諸取相。

简体字

我皆应作。立此誓已。于诸众生所作事中。不应疲
倦不应放逸。又当作[1]念。若利世间即是自利。是
故菩萨于利乐众生因缘。不应弃舍。问已[2]说菩萨
常应利乐众生。不应行舍。于诸法中为舍不舍。答

　　入甚深法界　　　灭离于分别

　　悉无有功用　　　诸处自然舍

[0527a24]　　法界者。即是缘生。是故先说。如来若出
不出。此法界法[3]性常住。所谓缘生。又如先说。
阿难陀。缘生甚深证亦甚深。是故入此甚深法界菩
萨。灭一切有无等二边。摄取方便智已。即断诸动
念戏论分别。离诸取相。

to the benefit of the world—in every case, those are endeavors I should carry out." Having made this vow, in those endeavors done for beings, one should not allow oneself to yield to weariness. Nor should one allow oneself to fall into negligence.

One should also reflect thus: "When one benefits the world one is thereby just benefiting oneself as well." Hence, when the bodhisattva is involved in endeavors aimed at benefiting beings and making them happy, he should refrain from abandoning them.

Question: It has already been explained that the bodhisattva should constantly strive for the benefit and happiness of beings and that in doing so, he should refrain from coursing in equanimity [where "equanimity" is synonymous with "indifference" or "renunciation" or "abandonment"]. However, as regards dharmas [as aspects of existence], should one practice equanimity with respect to them, or not?

Response: (As below...)

MORE ON EQUANIMITY AS PRACTICED BY THE BODHISATTVA

020 – Entering the Dharma Realm, Discriminations Cease, Equanimity Ensues

Entering the extremely profound Dharma realm,
One extinguishes mental discriminations.
As they are devoid of any useful function,
In all contexts, one naturally abides in equanimity.

COMMENTARY:

As for "the Dharma realm," it is identical with the sphere of conditioned arising. Hence, as has been stated before: "Whether or not the Tathāgata came forth [into the world], the very nature of this Dharma realm (*dharmatā*) would nonetheless constantly abide. It is [the very essence of] the so-called 'conditioned arising'."

Again, as has also been stated before, [the Buddha stated]: "Ānanda, conditioned arising is extremely profound. Moreover, its apprehension is a matter of extreme profundity as well."

Thus the bodhisattva who enters [the mind-state cognizing] this extremely profound Dharma realm thereby brings about the cessation of all such duality-based extremes as "existence," "non-existence," and so forth. Once one develops the associated facilitating wisdom, one immediately cuts off all mind-moving frivolous discourse and mental discrimination. Thus one abandons all seizing on any aspects [of objective phenomena].

諸心意識行處皆不復行。乃至行佛行菩提行菩薩
行涅槃處皆亦不行。則於諸法無復功用。於諸法
中。[4]得寂靜[5]復寂靜[6]心無分別心。是名第一義
捨。此即菩薩無分別也。已說出世間捨。我今當說
世間捨

　利名讚樂等　　四處皆不著
　反上亦無礙　　此等名為捨
[0527b07]　　　於利養名聞讚歎安樂等中無[7]所繫著。與
此相反無利無名[8]毀苦等中亦不退礙。捨離愛憎處
中而住無復分別。此名第二[9]說世間捨。問若菩薩
於諸法中。作第一義捨者。為菩提故如然頭衣。如
是勤行云何可得。答

　菩薩為菩提　　乃至未不退
　譬如燃頭衣　　應作是勤行

繁體字

諸心意识行处皆不复行。乃至行佛行菩提行菩萨
行涅盘处皆亦不行。则于诸法无复功用。于诸法
中。[4]得寂静[5]复寂静[6]心无分别心。是名第一义
舍。此即菩萨无分别也。已说出世间舍。我今当说
世间舍

　利名赞乐等　　四处皆不着
　反上亦无碍　　此等名为舍
[0527b07]　　　于利养名闻赞叹安乐等中无[7]所系着。与
此相反无利无名[8]毁苦等中亦不退碍。舍离爱憎处
中而住无复分别。此名第二[9]说世间舍。问若菩萨
于诸法中。作第一义舍者。为菩提故如然头衣。如
是勤行云何可得。答

　菩萨为菩提　　乃至未不退
　譬如燃头衣　　应作是勤行

简体字

In all those circumstances where the intellectual mind consciousness would ordinarily be active, it ceases to be active, even to the point that it is no longer active in the midst of practices focused on buddhahood, in the midst of bodhi practices, in the midst of bodhisattva practices, or in the realization of nirvāṇa.[48]

When this occurs, [mental discriminations] no longer serve any function. In the midst of dharmas, one realizes a mind state marked by stillness within stillness, a mind state devoid of mental discriminations. This is the equanimity conforming to ultimate truth (*paramārtha*).

Having already discussed the transcendent form of equanimity, I shall now explain equanimity in the sphere of the mundane.

---

021 – Equanimity as Remaining Unimpeded by the Eight Worldly Dharmas

Personal gain, reputation, praise, and happiness—
One refrains from attachment to any of these four points.
Nor do their opposites present any sort of obstacle.
This is the sort of conduct comprising equanimity.

COMMENTARY:

One retains no attachment to concerns over the receipt of beneficial gains, fame, praise, or happiness. Nor is one inclined to retreat or find any obstacle in the opposite conditions involving loss, ill repute, disparagement, or suffering.[49] One relinquishes both fondness and loathing. One abides in the midst of such conditions and yet remains free of any further mental discriminations. This is what is meant by the second type, equanimity amidst the mundane.

Question: If a bodhisattva were [to allow himself] to abide in ultimate-truth equanimity in the midst of dharmas, given the need to be as urgently energetic in pursuing bodhi as someone whose turban has caught fire, how could such diligent practice even be possible?

Response: (As below...)

INDISPENSABILITY OF DILIGENCE AND VIGOR FOR A BODHISATTVA

---

022 – The Need for Diligence So Long as Irreversibility Hasn't Been Gained

So long as he has not yet gained irreversibility,
In the bodhisattva's striving for bodhi,
He should be as intensely diligent in practice
As someone whose turban has caught on fire.

繁體字

[0527b14]　　雖於諸法應如是捨。而菩薩決定修行如然頭衣。乃至未得不退轉菩提菩薩。為菩提故應當勤行。於中菩薩有五種不退菩提因緣應知。何者為五。如華聚等經中說。若聞具足大願諸菩薩及佛世尊名號[10]故。若願生彼佛世尊國土故。是為[11]二種因緣。受持及說般若波羅蜜等深經故。是為第三因緣。修習現前住等三摩提及隨喜得者故。是為第四因緣。此四因緣說未得忍菩薩不退轉。若此菩薩住菩薩不動地已得無生忍。說為究竟決定不退[12]轉。問若此四種因緣中。隨以一因緣。菩薩得不退轉者。先說如然頭衣應當勤行。彼云何成。答

简体字

[0527b14]　　虽于诸法应如是舍。而菩萨决定修行如然头衣。乃至未得不退转菩提菩萨。为菩提故应当勤行。于中菩萨有五种不退菩提因缘应知。何者为五。如华聚等经中说。若闻具足大愿诸菩萨及佛世尊名号[10]故。若愿生彼佛世尊国土故。是为[11]二种因缘。受持及说般若波罗蜜等深经故。是为第三因缘。修习现前住等三摩提及随喜得者故。是为第四因缘。此四因缘说未得忍菩萨不退转。若此菩萨住菩萨不动地已得无生忍。说为究竟决定不退[12]转。问若此四种因缘中。随以一因缘。菩萨得不退转者。先说如然头衣应当勤行。彼云何成。答

COMMENTARY:

Although one should abide in this sort of equanimity in the midst of dharmas, the bodhisattva still continues to engage in resolute cultivation as intensely energetic as someone whose turban has caught fire. So long as the bodhisattva has not yet achieved irreversibility in his quest for bodhi, he should be diligent in the practices through which realization of bodhi is gained.

One should be aware of five circumstances related to bodhisattva "irreversibility" in pursuit of bodhi. What are the five? They are as described in such sutras as the *Accumulation of Blossoms Sutra*:

1 – [Irreversibility] based on hearing the names of those bodhisattvas or buddhas, the Bhagavāns, who are equipped with the great vows. This is the first of the causal circumstances.[50]

2 – [Irreversibility] based on vowing to be reborn in the buddhalands of those buddhas, the Bhagavāns. This is the second of the causal circumstances.[51]

3 – [Irreversibility] based on accepting, bearing in mind, or discoursing on such profound sutras as the Prajñāpāramitā Sutras. This is the third of the causal circumstances.

4 – [Irreversibility] based on cultivating such samādhis as are associated with [the sixth bodhisattva ground], "the ground of direct presence" (*abhimukha-bhūmi*), or on cultivating sympathetic joy in someone else's realization of such samādhis. This is the fourth of the causal circumstances.

These four circumstances are described as constituting the irreversibility of bodhisattvas who have not yet realized the patiences.

5 – When these bodhisattvas come to abide on [the eighth bodhisattva ground], "the ground of immovability" (*acala-bhūmi*), they succeeded in realizing the "unproduced-dharmas patience" (*anutpattika-dharma-kṣānti*). This is what is described as constituting "ultimate and definite irreversibility." This is the fifth of the causal circumstances.[52]

Question: The bodhisattva can gain irreversibility through any of those [first] four causal circumstances, and yet you claim that one should pursue diligent practice with the energetic intensity of someone whose turban has caught fire. This being the case, how could one be able to succeed [in maintaining that level of energetic diligence given that irreversibility has already been so easily achieved]?

Response: (As below...)

然彼諸菩薩　　為求菩提時
精進不應息　　以荷重擔故

[0527b29]　雖復四因緣中隨一因緣菩薩皆得不退。而
精進不應休息。由先作是言。我當令諸眾生皆得涅
槃。以荷如是重擔故。於其中間精進不息。問何故
於其中間精進不得休息。答

未生大悲忍　　雖得不退轉
菩薩猶有死　　以起放逸故

[0527c06]　於四因緣中隨何因緣。得不退轉菩薩。[13]
彼未生大悲乃至未得無生忍。[14]中間受業力死生
者。由入放逸故。是以菩薩應當勤行如然頭衣。為
得無生忍故。於其中間精進不息

[0527c10]　問菩薩復有何死。答

然彼诸菩萨　　为求菩提时
精进不应息　　以荷重担故

[0527b29]　虽复四因缘中随一因缘菩萨皆得不退。而
精进不应休息。由先作是言。我当令诸众生皆得涅
盘。以荷如是重担故。于其中间精进不息。问何故
于其中间精进不得休息。答

未生大悲忍　　虽得不退转
菩萨犹有死　　以起放逸故

[0527c06]　于四因缘中随何因缘。得不退转菩萨。[13]
彼未生大悲乃至未得无生忍。[14]中间受业力死生
者。由入放逸故。是以菩萨应当勤行如然头衣。为
得无生忍故。于其中间精进不息

[0527c10]　问菩萨复有何死。答

023 – Bodhisattvas' Ceaseless Vigor in Seeking Bodhi Is Due to Heavy Responsibility

Thus it is that those bodhisattvas,
When striving for the realization of bodhi,
Should not rest in their practice of vigor,
For they have shouldered such a heavy burden.

COMMENTARY:

Although the bodhisattva may succeed in reaching irreversibility through any of the [first] four causal circumstances [described above], he should still continue on with vigor, refraining from resting, this because he previously uttered these words: "I shall cause all beings to gain realization of nirvāṇa." Because he has taken on such a heavy burden, he continues on with unremitting vigor during the interim.

Question: Why is it that, during the interim, one continues on with vigor, not allowing himself to rest?
Response: (As below...)

THE DANGERS TO A BODHISATTVA OF NEGLIGENCE: SPIRITUAL DEATH

024 – Prior to Compassion and Patience, the Bodhisattva Life Remains Imperiled

Until one develops the great compassion and the patiences,
Even though he may have gained irreversibility,
The bodhisattva is still subject to a form of "dying"
Occurring through the arising of negligence.

COMMENTARY:

No matter which of the [first] four causal circumstances the bodhisattva avails himself of, he will succeed in gaining irreversibility. However, so long as he has not yet generated the great compassion and so long as he has not yet realized the unproduced-dharmas patience, during the interim period, he remains subject to the power of his karma. As for the arising of this "death," it would arise on account of entering into a state of negligence. It is for this reason that the bodhisattva should become so diligent in his practice aimed at realization of the unproduced-dharmas patience that he acts with the urgency of one whose turban has caught fire. Thus it is that he exerts himself with unresting vigor during the interim.[53]

Question: What additional sort of "death" is this to which the bodhisattva remains subject?
Response: (As below...)

聲聞獨覺地　　　若入便為死
以斷於菩薩　　　諸所解知根

[0527c13]　　如前所說四種因緣。隨何因緣得不退轉。此菩薩未有大悲未得忍。未過聲聞獨覺地。或以惡友力怖生死苦故。或受生中間故。或劫壞時間瞋嫌菩薩毀謗正法故。失菩提心。起聲聞獨覺地心已。或於聲聞解脫。若獨覺解脫作證。彼斷菩薩根。所謂大悲。是以諸菩薩及佛世尊。名為[15]說解知死。問此應思量菩薩。為畏住泥犁。為畏墮聲聞獨覺地。答

假使墮泥犁　　　菩薩不生怖
聲聞獨覺地　　　便為大恐怖

[0527c23]　菩薩設住泥犁。與無數百千苦俱。

声闻独觉地　　　若入便为死
以断于菩萨　　　诸所解知根

[0527c13]　　如前所说四种因缘。随何因缘得不退转。此菩萨未有大悲未得忍。未过声闻独觉地。或以恶友力怖生死苦故。或受生中间故。或劫坏时间瞋嫌菩萨毁谤正法故。失菩提心。起声闻独觉地心已。或于声闻解脱。若独觉解脱作证。彼断菩萨根。所谓大悲。是以诸菩萨及佛世尊。名为[15]说解知死。问此应思量菩萨。为畏住泥犁。为畏堕声闻独觉地。答

假使堕泥犁　　　菩萨不生怖
声闻独觉地　　　便为大恐怖

[0527c23]　菩萨设住泥犁。与无数百千苦俱。

---

025 – Falling onto the Śrāvaka or Pratyekabuddha Grounds is Fatal for a Bodhisattva

The grounds of the Śrāvakas or the Pratyekabuddhas,
If entered, constitute "death" for him
Because he would thereby sever the roots
Of the bodhisattva's understanding and awareness.

COMMENTARY:

No matter which of the above four circumstances is relied upon, one may succeed through that means in gaining "irreversibility." However, so long as this bodhisattva does not yet possess the great compassion and realization of the patiences, he has not yet succeeded in moving beyond *śrāvaka* and pratyekabuddha stations.

Thus it could occur that he might lose the resolve to realize bodhi through the powerful influence of bad friends, through terror of the sufferings inherent in cyclic births and deaths, through taking births in an intervening period [when Dharma is not present in the world], or through hatred of bodhisattvas or slander of right Dharma during the deterioration of the kalpa.

Having subsequently generated resolve focused on *śrāvaka-*disciple or pratyekabuddha stations, he could gain the liberation of either the Śrāvaka-disciples or the Pratyekabuddhas. That would amount to the severance of the roots of bodhisattvahood, namely, the great compassion. It is for this reason that the Bodhisattvas and the Buddhas, the Bhagavāns, have identified such an occurrence as constituting the death of all understanding and awareness.[54]

Question: It is appropriate here to contemplate this question: Would the bodhisattva be more frightened by the prospect of dwelling in the hell-realms or instead by the prospect of falling down onto the grounds of the Śrāvaka-disciples and Pratyekabuddhas?

Response: (As below...)

---

026 – The Bodhisattva Fears the Two-Vehicles' Grounds More Than the Hells

At the prospect of falling into the hell-realms,
The bodhisattva would not be struck with fright.
The grounds of the Śrāvakas and the Pratyekabuddhas
Do provoke great terror in him.

COMMENTARY:

If the bodhisattva were confronted with the prospect of abiding in the hell-realms amidst their countless hundreds of thousands of

不比墮聲聞獨覺地怖畏。問何故如此。答

　　非墮泥犁中　　　畢竟障菩提
　　聲聞獨覺地　　　則為畢竟障

[0527c27]　　設入泥犁。於正覺道。不能作畢竟障礙。住泥犁時。乃至惡業盡邊。於菩提道暫為障礙。菩薩若墮聲聞獨覺地。則畢竟不生故。聲聞獨覺地。於正覺道乃為障礙。由是義故。菩薩入於泥犁。不比墮聲聞獨覺地怖畏。問其怖如何。答

　　如說愛壽人　　　怖畏於斬首
　　聲聞獨覺地　　　應作如是怖

[0528a06] 經中佛世尊作如是說。如愛壽人怖畏斬首。菩薩欲求無上菩提。

不比墮声闻独觉地怖畏。问何故如此。答

　　非墮泥犁中　　　毕竟障菩提
　　声闻独觉地　　　则为毕竟障

[0527c27]　　设入泥犁。于正觉道。不能作毕竟障碍。住泥犁时。乃至恶业尽边。于菩提道暂为障碍。菩萨若墮声闻独觉地。则毕竟不生故。声闻独觉地。于正觉道乃为障碍。由是义故。菩萨入于泥犁。不比墮声闻独觉地怖畏。问其怖如何。答

　　如说爱寿人　　　怖畏于斩首
　　声闻独觉地　　　应作如是怖

[0528a06] 经中佛世尊作如是说。如爱寿人怖畏斩首。菩萨欲求无上菩提。

sufferings, he would not find this more frightening than the prospect of falling down onto the grounds of the Śrāvaka-disciples and
Pratyekabuddhas.

Question: Why is this the case?

Response: (As below...)

---

027 – Whereas Hells Don't Block Buddhahood, Two Vehicles' Grounds Do

It is not the case that falling into the hell realms
Would create an ultimate obstacle to bodhi.
If one fell onto the grounds of the Śrāvakas or Pratyekabuddhas,
That would create an ultimate obstacle.

COMMENTARY:

In the event that one were to fall into the hell realms (lit. *"niraya"*),
this would still not present an ultimate obstacle to the right-enlightenment Path. During that time when one abides in the hell realms,
it *does* present a *temporary* obstacle to the acquisition of bodhi which
endures only until one's evil karma has been exhausted.

However, in the event that the bodhisattva falls down onto the
grounds of the Śrāvaka-disciples and Pratyekabuddhas, that then
does result in [the bodhi of a buddha] *never* being able to manifest.
Thus the Śrāvaka-disciple and Pratyekabuddha grounds do constitute an obstacle to realizing the right enlightenment.

It is on account of the implications of this that, when faced with
the prospect of falling into the hell realms, the bodhisattva does not
become as frightened as he would at the prospect of falling down
onto the grounds of the Śrāvaka-disciples and Pratyekabuddhas.

Question: What is the nature of his fearfulness?

Response: (As below...)

---

028 – The Bodhisattva Should Fear Two-Vehicles Grounds Like the Gallows

Just as is said of one who loves long life
That he is frightened at the prospect of being beheaded,
So too the grounds of the Śrāvakas and Pratyekabuddhas
Should provoke in one this very sort of fear.

COMMENTARY:

The Buddha, the Bhagavān, spoke in this way in the sutras. Just
as a person fond of living becomes frightened at the prospect of
beheading, given that the bodhisattva aspires to the unsurpassed

怖畏聲聞獨覺地。亦應如此。是故菩薩雖入泥犁。不比墮聲聞獨覺地怖畏。問已說未得無生忍諸菩薩障礙法。此菩薩云何得無生忍。答

> 不生亦不滅　　非不生不滅
>
> 非俱不俱說　　空不空亦爾

[0528a13]　　此中菩薩觀緣生時作是念。有緣[1]生法但施設。如無生中有生。是故生者自體不成。自體不成故生則非有。如生自體非有。彼滅為二。二俱無體如生滅。彼不生不滅為二。亦二俱無體。彼生滅二種中。生不生滅不滅亦不有互相違故。

怖畏声闻独觉地。亦应如此。是故菩萨虽入泥犁。不比堕声闻独觉地怖畏。问已说未得无生忍诸菩萨障碍法。此菩萨云何得无生忍。答

> 不生亦不灭　　非不生不灭
>
> 非俱不俱说　　空不空亦尔

[0528a13]　　此中菩萨观缘生时作是念。有缘[1]生法但施设。如无生中有生。是故生者自体不成。自体不成故生则非有。如生自体非有。彼灭为二。二俱无体如生灭。彼不生不灭为二。亦二俱无体。彼生灭二种中。生不生灭不灭亦不有互相违故。

form of bodhi, he too should experience just such fearfulness at the prospect of entering the grounds of the Śrāvaka-disciples or Pratyekabuddhas. It is for this reason that, although he might be faced with entering the hell realms, the bodhisattva would not become as frightened at that prospect as he would become fearful at the prospect of falling down onto the grounds of the Śrāvaka-disciples or Pratyekabuddhas.

Question: The dharmas obstructing the bodhisattva who has not yet realized the unproduced-dharmas patience have now already been described. How then does this bodhisattva succeed in realizing the unproduced-dharmas patience?

Response: (As below...)

The Bodhisattva's Unproduced-Dharmas Patience and Irreversibility

029 – The Tetralemma-Transcending Contemplation of Dharmas

As for "not produced and not destroyed,"
And "neither unproduced nor undestroyed,"
One denies assertions of "both" and "neither."
So too in cases involving "emptiness" and "non-emptiness."

COMMENTARY:

When the bodhisattva contemplates the sphere of conditioned arising, he reflects, "Wherever dharmas arising from [the coming together] of conditions are held to 'exist,' that 'existence' is based solely on conceptual consensus. Therefore, whatever is 'produced' cannot be validly established as having any inherent existence. Because its inherent existence cannot be validly established, then the process of 'production' is itself devoid of inherent existence.

"If there is no intrinsic reality to the process of production, then 'destruction' is itself but a matter of [interdependent] dual concepts.

"As with 'production' and 'destruction,' simultaneous affirmation and negation is also devoid of any substantial existence. So too with the concepts of nonproduction and nondestruction which themselves are based on dual concepts devoid of any substantial existence.

"In those cases which involve the dual concepts of production and destruction as with 'both production and nonproduction,'" and 'both destruction and nondestruction,'—those too are devoid of any real existence, this because they involve a simultaneity of opposing concepts.

空亦如是。如有者無自體故。彼不空及空不空亦
爾。問若作是念。以緣生故諸法無自體者。何故復
作是念。亦無有緣生法。答

　　隨何所有法　　　於中觀不動

　　彼是無生忍　　　斷諸分別故

[0528a24]　　　　如是菩薩如實觀緣生時。得離諸法自體
見。離自體見故。即斷取法自體。得[2]斷法自體時
作是念。非無內外法。而無法自體。雖有緣生法。
但如葦束幻夢。若法從緣生。彼自體不生。作是觀
已。若沙門若波羅門。所不能動而不取證。彼以樂
觀無生法。斷諸分別故。說名無生忍。

空亦如是。如有者无自体故。彼不空及空不空亦
尔。问若作是念。以缘生故诸法无自体者。何故复
作是念。亦无有缘生法。答

　　随何所有法　　　于中观不动

　　彼是无生忍　　　断诸分别故

[0528a24]　　　　如是菩萨如实观缘生时。得离诸法自体
见。离自体见故。即断取法自体。得[2]断法自体时
作是念。非无内外法。而无法自体。虽有缘生法。
但如苇束幻梦。若法从缘生。彼自体不生。作是观
已。若沙门若波罗门。所不能动而不取证。彼以乐
观无生法。断诸分别故。说名无生忍。

"So too it is in the case of the concept of being 'empty [of inherent existence],' for wherever [one might posit that] there is some supposed 'existence,' that is a case devoid of any intrinsic substantiality. Those concepts of 'non-emptiness' as well as 'both emptiness and non-emptiness' are just the same in this respect."

Question: If one reflected in this manner, concluding that, "because they are merely products of conditions, all dharmas are devoid of any inherent existence," how could one persist in this reflection? [Persisting in the contemplation would necessitate the conclusion that], "Not even the dharma of conditioned co-production exists."

Response: (As below...)

---

030 – Unshakable Contemplation in the Unproduced-Dharmas Patience

No matter which "existent" dharma one encounters,
One persists therein in the contemplation, remaining unmoving.
That is the "unproduced-dharmas patience."
It is based on the severance of all mental discriminations.

COMMENTARY:

When this bodhisattva contemplates conditioned co-production in accordance with reality, he succeeds in abandoning the view that any dharma possesses any intrinsic substance of its own. Through abandoning the view imputing intrinsically-existent substantiality, one straightaway cuts off any seizing on an intrinsically-existent substantiality in any dharma.

Once one succeeds in cutting off [the view] imputing intrinsic substantiality to dharmas,[55] one then reflects, "It is not the case that there are no inward-related or outward-related dharmas. However, there is no intrinsically existent substantiality associated with those dharmas. Although the dharmas produced through conditioned-coproduction do exist, that "existence" abides only in the manner of a bundled sheaf of reeds, a magical conjuration, or a mere dream. Wherever dharmas are produced from conditions, no intrinsic substantiality is actually 'produced.'"

Once one has carried out this contemplation, one becomes such as no śramaṇa or brahman is able to move and yet one refrains from seizing on [this level of] realization. Because one takes pleasure in contemplating the dharma of non-production and because one severs all mental discriminations, this is described as the

此菩薩即住菩薩不動地。偈言

　既獲此忍已　　　即時得授記

　汝必當作佛　　　便得不退轉

[0528b04]　　得此無生忍故。即於得時非前非後。諸佛現前授記作佛。汝於來世。於爾所時某世界某劫中。當為某如來應正遍知。此名菩薩不退轉。問從住初地乃至七地諸菩薩。皆決定向三菩提。何故不說為不退轉。唯說住不動地菩薩。為不退轉。答

　已住不動諸菩薩　　　得於法爾不退智

　彼智二乘不能轉　　　是故獨得不退名

[0528b12]　　此謂所有信等出世間善根。諸聲聞獨覺乃至住第七地菩薩。不能障礙令其退轉。

此菩萨即住菩萨不动地。偈言

　既获此忍已　　　即时得授记

　汝必当作佛　　　便得不退转

[0528b04]　　得此无生忍故。即于得时非前非后。诸佛现前授记作佛。汝于来世。于尔所时某世界某劫中。当为某如来应正遍知。此名菩萨不退转。问从住初地乃至七地诸菩萨。皆决定向三菩提。何故不说为不退转。唯说住不动地菩萨。为不退转。答

　已住不动诸菩萨　　　得于法尔不退智

　彼智二乘不能转　　　是故独得不退名

[0528b12]　　此谓所有信等出世间善根。诸声闻独觉乃至住第七地菩萨。不能障碍令其退转。

"unproduced-dharmas patience." Having gained this realization, this bodhisattva immediately comes to abide on the "unmoving" bodhisattva ground (acala bhūmi).

The verses state:

---

031 – The Prediction and Irreversibility Come with Unproduced-Dharmas Patience

Once one gains this patience,
One immediately receives the prediction:
"You will definitely become a buddha."
It is then that one achieves "irreversibility."

COMMENTARY:

On account of having gained this unproduced-dharmas patience, immediately at the time of realization, neither before nor after, the Buddhas manifest directly before one and make the prediction that one will become a buddha, stating: "In a future life, at this particular time, in this particular world, and in this particular kalpa, you will become the Tathāgata known as such-and-such, endowed with right and universal knowledge." For the bodhisattva, this qualifies as the achievement of irreversibility.

Question: All of those bodhisattvas on the first through the seventh grounds are definitely progressing toward saṃbodhi. Why then are they not declared to be "irreversible"? Why does one instead only describe the [eighth-stage] bodhisattva dwelling on the "unmoving ground" (acala bhūmi) as "irreversible"?

Response: (As below...)

---

032 – Only This "Stage of Immovability" Guarantees Definite "Irreversibility"

Those bodhisattvas already dwelling at "the stage of immovability"
Have gained irreversible wisdom cognizing all dharmas' reality.
As their wisdom cannot be turned back by Two-vehicles adherents,
It is only at this point that they are designated as "irreversible."[56]

COMMENTARY:

This alludes to all of the roots of world-transcending goodness [possessed by those bodhisattvas], including faith and the rest.[57] (The five root-faculties are: faith, vigor, mindfulness, concentration, and wisdom.) The Śrāvaka-disciples, pratyekabuddhas, and bodhisattvas on up through the seventh ground are unable to obstruct [these bodhisattvas] and cause them to turn back in retreat.[58]

繁體字

故名不退轉。非餘十種菩薩為三菩提於諸法中不退
轉也。已說不退轉因緣。此中又得殊勝授[3]記。大
乘中說四種授記。謂未發菩提心授記共發菩提心授
記。隱覆授記。現前授記。是為四種授記。於中未
發菩提心授記者。其人利根具增上信。諸佛世尊以
無礙佛眼觀已。而為授記。共發菩提心授記者。成
熟善根種菩提種先已修習。其根猛利得增上行。但
欲解脫諸眾生故。即發心時入不退轉。無墮落法離
八不閑(謂八難也)。此人或聞自授記。於六波羅蜜
不發精進。如其不聞更發精進為令不聞。欲使他人
聞其授記。斷疑心故。佛以威神隱覆授記。

簡体字

故名不退转。非馀十种菩萨为三菩提于诸法中不退
转也。已说不退转因缘。此中又得殊胜授[3]记。大
乘中说四种授记。谓未发菩提心授记共发菩提心授
记。隐覆授记。现前授记。是为四种授记。于中未
发菩提心授记者。其人利根具增上信。诸佛世尊以
无碍佛眼观已。而为授记。共发菩提心授记者。成
熟善根种菩提种先已修习。其根猛利得增上行。但
欲解脱诸众生故。即发心时入不退转。无墮落法离
八不闲(谓八难也)。此人或闻自授记。于六波罗蜜
不发精进。如其不闻更发精进为令不闻。欲使他人
闻其授记。断疑心故。佛以威神隐覆授记。

It is for this reason that, [from this point on, these bodhisattvas] are designated as "irreversible." It is not the case that those [previous] other seven[59] levels of bodhisattvas are "irreversible" in their quest for *saṃbodhi* as they course along in the midst of dharmas.

We have already discussed the causal circumstances involved in irreversibility. There is herein the additional factor of gaining the especially supreme form of prediction [of buddhahood]. In the Great Vehicle, one speaks of four types of predictions, namely:

1 – Predictions bestowed prior to generating the resolve to realize bodhi;
2 – Predictions bestowed simultaneously with the generation of the resolve to realize bodhi;
3 – Predictions the bestowal of which remain concealed; and
4 – Predictions the bestowal of which involve "direct presence."

These are the four kinds of predictions. Among these, as for "predictions bestowed prior to generating the resolve to realize bodhi," this refers to cases involving individuals with sharp faculties and especially superior faith. When the Buddhas, the Bhagavāns, observe them with the unimpeded buddha eye, they may then bestow on them a prediction [of future buddhahood].

As for "predictions bestowed simultaneously with the generation of the resolve to realize bodhi," this occurs in instances where someone has completely ripened their roots of goodness, has planted the seeds of bodhi, and has already carried out cultivation to such a degree that their faculties are fiercely sharp and they have developed especially superior forms of practice. Because they wish only to liberate all beings, immediately upon generating the resolve, they then enter the state of irreversibility wherein they become free of any dharmas conducive to falling away and leave behind the eight difficulties.[60] It may be that this person then hears the bestowal of his own prediction [of buddhahood].

There are cases where someone has not yet become vigorous in cultivating the six perfections and, so long as he fails to hear [a prediction of his future buddhahood], he will continue to develop a greater level of vigor in such practice. In order to prevent such a person from hearing [a prediction] while still wishing to cause others to hear that person's prediction so that their doubts might be cut off, the Buddha may employ his awesome spiritual powers to bestow a "concealed prediction" [of buddhahood].

若菩薩成熟出世五根。得無生忍。住菩薩不動地。
彼即現前授記。是為四種授記。彼得無生忍菩薩已
決定故。諸佛世尊現前授記。又別有密意授記。以
為第五。如法華經說

我等皆隨喜　大仙密意語　如授記聖者　無畏舍利弗
我等亦當得　成佛世無上　復以密意語　說無上正覺

[0528c06]　　　以何義故。說此別語授記。有論師說。為
令未入決定聲聞乘者發菩提心故。又已發菩提心初
業菩薩等。畏流轉苦。欲於聲聞涅槃取滅度者。為
令牢固菩提心故。又有異佛土菩薩。於此聚集。授
記時到。以相似名。為彼授記故。諸師如是分別別
語授記。於中實義唯佛世尊。乃能知之

若菩萨成熟出世五根。得无生忍。住菩萨不动地。
彼即现前授记。是为四种授记。彼得无生忍菩萨已
决定故。诸佛世尊现前授记。又别有密意授记。以
为第五。如法华经说

我等皆随喜　大仙密意语　如授记圣者　无畏舍利弗
我等亦当得　成佛世无上　复以密意语　说无上正觉

[0528c06]　　　以何义故。说此别语授记。有论师说。为
令未入决定声闻乘者发菩提心故。又已发菩提心初
业菩萨等。畏流转苦。欲于声闻涅盘取灭度者。为
令牢固菩提心故。又有异佛土菩萨。于此聚集。授
记时到。以相似名。为彼授记故。诸师如是分别别
语授记。于中实义唯佛世尊。乃能知之

In an instance where a bodhisattva has ripened the world-transcendent five root-faculties, has realized the unproduced-dharmas patience, and has come to abide on the bodhisattva ground of immovability (acala bhūmi), he may immediately receive the "direct presence" type of prediction.

These are the four kinds of predictions. Because those bodhisattvas who have realized the unproduced-dharmas patience have already become definite [in their irreversibility], the Buddhas, the Bhagavāns, manifest directly before them and bestow on them this [latter type of] prediction of buddhahood.

There is yet another [prediction type], the prediction arising based on "secret intention." It may be regarded as a fifth type of prediction. It is such as is found in the Lotus Sutra, wherein it states:

> We all experience sympathetic joy
> On hearing the Great Rishi's secretly-intentioned words.
> As exemplified in the prediction given to that ārya,
> The fearless Śāriputra.
>
> We, too, should be able
> To become buddhas, unsurpassed in the world,
> And should also have resort to the secretly-intentioned words
> Devoted to the unsurpassed right enlightenment.

What is the meaning implicit in the utterance of these "specially-spoken" predictions? There are treatise masters stating that they are set forth to cause those in the Śrāvaka Vehicle not yet established in the "definite [position]" to generate the mind resolved on bodhi.

There are others supposing that this is done for the sake of solidifying the determination of newly-resolved beginning bodhisattvas who, frightened at the prospect of cyclic existence's sufferings, may be tempted to opt for the cessation of the Śrāvaka-disciple's nirvāṇa.

Then again, [some suppose that] similarly-named bodhisattvas from other buddhalands were in attendance at the [Dharma] assembly when the time came for bestowing predictions and the Buddha then bestowed these predictions on them, [but not actually on any of the Buddha's arhat disciples].

Various commentators make these sorts of discriminating judgments regarding such "specially-spoken" predictions. The real meaning behind these circumstances is such as only the Buddhas, the Bhagavāns, are able to know.

菩薩乃至得　　諸佛現前住
牢固三摩提　　不應起放逸

[0528c15]　　諸佛現前三摩提得已而住者。謂現在諸佛現其前住三摩提也。三摩提者。平等住故。菩薩乃至未得此三摩提。其間不應放逸。以未得三摩提。菩薩猶墮惡趣。未離不閑故。是故為得此三摩提。不應放逸。若得三摩提。彼諸怖畏皆得解脫。此三摩提有三種。謂色攀緣。法攀緣。無攀緣。於中若攀緣如來形色相好莊嚴身。而念佛者。是色攀緣三摩提。若復攀緣十名號身十力無畏不共佛法等無量色類佛之功德。

菩萨乃至得　　诸佛现前住
牢固三摩提　　不应起放逸

[0528c15]　　诸佛现前三摩提得已而住者。谓现在诸佛现其前住三摩提也。三摩提者。平等住故。菩萨乃至未得此三摩提。其间不应放逸。以未得三摩提。菩萨犹堕恶趣。未离不闲故。是故为得此三摩提。不应放逸。若得三摩提。彼诸怖畏皆得解脱。此三摩提有三种。谓色攀缘。法攀缘。无攀缘。于中若攀缘如来形色相好庄严身。而念佛者。是色攀缘三摩提。若复攀缘十名号身十力无畏不共佛法等无量色类佛之功德。

---

033 – No Negligence Can Be Indulged Prior to the "Direct Presence" Ground

Until the bodhisattva has gained
The solid samādhis
On the ground of all Buddhas' "direct presence,"
He should not allow any negligence to arise.

COMMENTARY:

As for the samādhi involving "the direct presence of all Buddhas," this is referring to that samādhi in which all Buddhas of the present era manifest directly in one's presence as one abides [on the ground of "direct presence"] (*abhimukha-bhūmi*).[61] "Samādhi," is a designation referring to abiding in a uniformly even [and profoundly deep] mind state.

During that period when the bodhisattva has not yet gained these samādhis, he should not allow himself to become negligent. This is because, so long as he has not gained these samādhis, the bodhisattva is still vulnerable to falling into the wretched destinies and has still not transcended vulnerability to the [eight] difficult [rebirth] circumstances. Therefore, in order to be able to gain these samādhis, one must not indulge any negligence. Once one gains these samādhis, he is liberated from all such fearsome circumstances.

These samādhis are of three kinds, namely:

1 – Those involving mental transformation of form-based objective conditions.
2 – Those involving mental transformation of Dharma-related objective conditions.
3 – Those involving no mental transformation of any objective conditions whatsoever.

Where, through mindfulness of the Buddha, one [employs visualizations to] mentally manipulate objective conditions involving the shape, appearance, major marks, or minor characteristics adorning the Tathāgata's body, this is a samādhi involving "mental transformation of form-based objective conditions."

Beyond this, where, through mindfulness of the Buddha, one [employs visualization to] mentally manipulate objective conditions associated with the ten names [of a buddha], the ten powers possessed by [a buddha's] body, the fearlessnesses, the dharmas exclusive to a buddha, or any of the other immeasurably many qualities

繁體字

而念佛者。是法攀緣三摩提。若復不攀緣色。不攀
緣法。亦不作意念佛。亦無所得。遠離諸相空三摩
提。此[4]名無攀緣三摩提。於中初發心菩薩。得
色攀緣三摩提。已入行者法攀緣。得無生忍者無攀
緣。此等名得決定。自在故

　　諸佛現前住　　　牢固三摩提
　　此為菩薩父　　　大悲忍為母

[0529a03]　　此所說三種現。在佛現前住三摩提。攝諸
菩薩功德及諸佛功德故。說名諸菩薩父。大悲者。
於生死流轉中。不生疲倦故。又於聲聞獨覺地險
岸。護令不墮故。說名為母。忍者。得忍菩薩。於
諸流轉苦及諸惡眾生中。不厭流轉。不捨眾生及菩
提。以不生厭。是故此忍

簡体字

而念佛者。是法攀缘三摩提。若复不攀缘色。不攀
缘法。亦不作意念佛。亦无所得。远离诸相空三摩
提。此[4]名无攀缘三摩提。于中初发心菩萨。得
色攀缘三摩提。已入行者法攀缘。得无生忍者无攀
缘。此等名得决定。自在故

　　诸佛现前住　　　牢固三摩提
　　此为菩萨父　　　大悲忍为母

[0529a03]　　此所说三种现。在佛现前住三摩提。摄诸
菩萨功德及诸佛功德故。说名诸菩萨父。大悲者。
于生死流转中。不生疲倦故。又于声闻独觉地险
岸。护令不堕故。说名为母。忍者。得忍菩萨。于
诸流转苦及诸恶众生中。不厌流转。不舍众生及菩
提。以不生厌。是故此忍

of a form-body buddha, this is a samādhi involving "mental trans-formation of Dharma-related objective conditions."

Beyond this, where one does not mentally manipulate form-based conditions, does not mentally manipulate Dharma-related conditions, does not engage in any intellect-directed mindfulness-of-the-Buddha, does not apprehend any [conditioned dharmas] at all, and abandons even the samādhis focused on the emptiness of signs, this is what is meant by a samādhi "involving no mental transformation of any objective conditions whatsoever."

Among these, the newly-resolved bodhisattva gains samādhis involving the mental transformation of form-based objective conditions. One who has already entered the [bodhisattva] practices gains samādhis involving the mental transformation of Dharma-related objective conditions. Those who have gained the unproduced-dharmas patience have gone beyond all mental transformation of objective conditions. It is these last who have reached the "definite" state [of bodhisattva irreversibility], this by virtue of their sover-eign mastery [of the bodhisattva practices].[62]

---

034 – Samādhis Are a Bodhisattva's Father, Compassion and Patience Are Mother

The solid samādhis
On the ground of all Buddhas' "direct presence"
Serve for the bodhisattva as his father,
Whereas the great compassion and patiences serve as his mother.

COMMENTARY:

Because these previously-described three types of samādhis manifesting on the ground of the Buddhas' "direct presence" focus on the qualities of the Bodhisattvas as well as the qualities of the Buddhas, they are said to serve as the bodhisattva's father.

As for the great compassion, because it prevents one from becom-ing weary while coursing in cyclic births and deaths, and also because it protects one from falling down the treacherous precipice onto the grounds of the Śrāvaka-disciples and the Pratyekabuddhas, it is said to serve as the bodhisattva's mother.

As for the patiences, even in the midst of the sufferings of cyclic existence and the evil beings therein, the bodhisattva who has gained the patiences does not become disgusted with cyclic exis-tence and does not forsake either beings or bodhi. Because, avail-ing himself of them, he does not become disgusted, these patiences

又為諸菩薩母。更有別偈說

　智度以為母　　方便為父者
　以生及持故　　說菩薩父母

[0529a12]　　以般若波羅蜜生諸菩薩法故。佛說般若波羅蜜為菩薩母。諸菩薩法從般若波羅蜜生已。為巧方便所持。不令趣向聲聞獨覺地險岸。以是持菩提故。說巧方便為菩薩父。問菩薩以幾許福能得菩提。答

　少少積聚福　　不能得菩提
　百須彌量福　　聚勝乃能得

[0529a19]菩提者。謂一切智智。彼智與[1]無應知等。應知與虛空等。虛空無邊故應知亦無邊。以有邊福不能得無邊智。是故少少積聚福。不能得菩提。

又为诸菩萨母。更有别偈说

　智度以为母　　方便为父者
　以生及持故　　说菩萨父母

[0529a12]　　以般若波罗蜜生诸菩萨法故。佛说般若波罗蜜为菩萨母。诸菩萨法从般若波罗蜜生已。为巧方便所持。不令趣向声闻独觉地险岸。以是持菩提故。说巧方便为菩萨父。问菩萨以几许福能得菩提。答

　少少积聚福　　不能得菩提
　百须弥量福　　聚胜乃能得

[0529a19]菩提者。谓一切智智。彼智与[1]无应知等。应知与虚空等。虚空无边故应知亦无边。以有边福不能得无边智。是故少少积聚福。不能得菩提。

繁體字

简体字

also serve as the bodhisattva's mother. There is yet another verse explaining the matter thus:

---

035 – Wisdom as Mother and Means as Father is Due to Giving Birth and Support

As for the perfection of wisdom being his mother
And skillful means being his father,
It is because the one gives him birth and the other supports him
That they are said to be the bodhisattva's father and mother.

COMMENTARY:

It is because the prajñāpāramitā gives birth to all of the dharmas of a bodhisattva that the Buddha declared the prajñāpāramitā to be the mother of the bodhisattva. After the bodhisattva dharmas have been born from the prajñāpāramitā, they are sustained by skillful means. Thus [the bodhisattva] is prevented from wandering over the treacherous embankment plunging on down to the grounds of the Śrāvaka-disciples and the Pratyekabuddhas. It is because these [skillful means] sustain [him in his progress toward] bodhi that one asserts that skillful means serve as the father of the bodhisattva.

Question: How much merit is required to enable the bodhisattva's acquisition of bodhi?

Response: (As below...)

MERIT AS INDISPENSABLE TO A BODHISATTVA'S FUTURE BUDDHAHOOD

---

036 – Only Merit Greater Than a Hundred Sumerus Would Be Adequate for Bodhi

With but a lesser accumulation of merit
One remains unable to realize bodhi.
Only by collecting merit more massive than a hundred Sumerus
Can one succeed in achieving that realization.

COMMENTARY:

As for "bodhi," this refers to the realization of wisdom corresponding [in its breadth and depth] to all-knowledge. That knowledge is commensurate with all that should be known.[63] "What should be known" is in turn commensurate with empty space. Because empty space is infinite, what should be known is also infinite. Were one to resort to only a finite amount of merit, that would be inadequate for the realization of infinite knowledge. It is for this reason that a lesser accumulation of merit cannot enable the realization of bodhi.

云何得[2]百須彌量福。聚集乃能得

[0529b07]　　問若如是者。百須彌量福聚無有故。亦無一人能得菩提。答

　雖作小福德　　此亦有方便　　於諸眾生所　　應悉起攀緣

[0529b11]　　若此菩薩雖作小福。以有方便成大福聚。或以飲食捨[3]與眾生。或以華香鬘等奉如來像。彼諸福德。於一切世界所攝諸眾生所。悉作攀緣。我以此福。令諸眾生皆得無上正覺。復以此福。與諸眾生共之。如是等福。共諸眾生迴向菩提。是名菩薩方便。如是迴向。其福得成無量無數無邊。以是故彼一切智智雖是無邊。還以此相無邊福故能得

[0529b19]　　復有別義

我有諸動作　　[4]常為利眾生　　如是等心行　　誰能量其福

云何得[2]百须弥量福。聚集乃能得

[0529b07]　　问若如是者。百须弥量福聚无有故。亦无一人能得菩提。答

虽作小福德　　此亦有方便　　于诸众生所　　应悉起攀缘

[0529b11]　　若此菩萨虽作小福。以有方便成大福聚。或以饮食舍[3]与众生。或以华香鬘等奉如来像。彼诸福德。于一切世界所摄诸众生所。悉作攀缘。我以此福。令诸众生皆得无上正觉。复以此福。与诸众生共之。如是等福。共诸众生迴向菩提。是名菩萨方便。如是迴向。其福得成无量无数无边。以是故彼一切智智虽是无边。还以此相无边福故能得

[0529b19]　　复有别义

我有诸动作　　[4]常为利众生　　如是等心行　　谁能量其福

繁體字

简体字

Why must one gain merit equal to a hundred Sumerus? Because only then does one become able to gain the realization of bodhi.

Question: Were this the case, because an accumulation of merit the measure of a hundred Sumerus could not exist, there would not be even one single person capable of realizing bodhi.

Response: (As below...)

MEANS FOR ACCUMULATING AN IMMENSE STOCK OF MERIT

037 – Through Skillful Means, a Minor Deed Generates Great Merit

Although one may perform but a minor meritorious deed,
Even in this, one possesses a skillful means:
Taking the sphere of "all beings" as the object,
One should generate a mental transformation of the conditions.

COMMENTARY:

Although this bodhisattva may perform but a minor meritorious deed, by resorting to a skillful means, he becomes able thereby to produce a great collection of merit. For instance, he may give drink or food to beings or may offer up flowers, incense, garlands, and so forth to images of the Tathāgata. In doing so, he takes all of that merit he has thereby created and, taking all being in all worlds as the object of this reflection, he mentally transforms the objective conditions, reflecting thus: "I dedicate this merit to all beings to cause them to realize the unsurpassed, right enlightenment."

He then, [through mental reflection], bestows this merit on all beings. It is the bestowing of such merit on all beings and dedicating it to bodhi as he does so which constitutes the bodhisattva's skillful means herein. By performing this type of dedication of merit, his own merit becomes immeasurable, incalculable, and infinite in scope. Thus, even though [his goal of] omniscience-based wisdom is so infinite in scope, he is still able to gain it by availing himself of this merit which, generated in this manner, becomes correspondingly infinite in scope.

There are other concepts to be considered here: [As below...]

038 – How Could One Measure the Merit of Such Universally-Dedicated Deeds?

Where one reflects: "May whatever actions I undertake
Always be done for the welfare of beings,"
Who could measure the merit of he
Whose mental actions are of this sort?

繁體字

[0529b22] 菩薩於晝及夜。常起如是心行。若我所有動作[5]善身口意。皆為度諸眾生故。脫諸眾生故。[6]穌息諸眾生故。寂滅諸眾生故起。及為令眾生滿足一切智智。得至一切智智故。彼如是具足大悲。安住善巧方便。所有福聚唯除諸佛。何人能量。是故具此福者能得菩提

[0529b28] 問何故此福復是無量。答

不愛自親屬　　及與身命財　　不貪樂自在　　梵世及餘天
亦不貪涅槃　　為於眾生故　　此唯念眾生　　其福誰能量

[0529c04] 此中菩薩行六度行時。於己男女及與親屬。若金銀等財。若自壽命。若支節分。若具足身。若身心樂。若天人自在。若梵身天。若無色天。乃至涅槃。為眾生故皆亦不愛。唯於眾生愍念不捨。

简体字

[0529b22] 菩萨于昼及夜。常起如是心行。若我所有动作[5]善身口意。皆为度诸众生故。脱诸众生故。[6]穌息诸众生故。寂灭诸众生故起。及为令众生满足一切智智。得至一切智智故。彼如是具足大悲。安住善巧方便。所有福聚唯除诸佛。何人能量。是故具此福者能得菩提

[0529b28] 问何故此福复是无量。答

不爱自亲属　　及与身命财　　不贪乐自在　　梵世及馀天
亦不贪涅盘　　为于众生故　　此唯念众生　　其福谁能量

[0529c04] 此中菩萨行六度行时。于己男女及与亲属。若金银等财。若自寿命。若支节分。若具足身。若身心乐。若天人自在。若梵身天。若无色天。乃至涅盘。为众生故皆亦不爱。唯于众生愍念不舍。

COMMENTARY:

Both day and night, the bodhisattva constantly initiates mental actions of this sort, reflecting: "May all my good deeds arising through body, mouth, and mind be generated for the sake of taking all beings on across [the sea of suffering], for the sake of liberating all beings, for the sake of reviving all beings, and for the sake of establishing all beings in cessation. May they also be for the sake of instigating beings to fulfill [the requisites for] omniscience-based wisdom so that they may realize that omniscience-based wisdom."

When he has thus perfected the great compassion and abides well-established in excellent implementation of skillful means, who aside from the Buddhas could gauge the amount of merit he accumulates? Therefore, one who equips himself with merit in this manner thereby becomes able to achieve realization of bodhi.

Question: How might this merit become even more incalculably vast?

Response: (As below...)

---

039 – When Free of Attachments, When Not Coveting Even the Heavens—

Where one isn't constrained by fondness for relatives, retinue,
Body, life, or wealth,
Where one isn't held back by desiring pleasure in Iśvara's heavens,
Brahma-world heavens, or any other heavens,

---

040 – Not Coveting Nirvāṇa, Yet Caring for Others, Who Could Gauge Such Merit?

Where one isn't constrained even by coveting nirvāṇa,
Where one's actions are done for the sake of other beings,
And where in all this, one thinks only of the welfare of beings,
Who then could measure the vastness of his merit?

COMMENTARY:

When this bodhisattva engages in the six-perfections practices, because he does so for the sake of beings, he indulges no cherishing even of his own sons, daughters, retinue, indulges no cherishing of his gold, silver, or other wealth, indulges no cherishing of his life, limbs, entire body, physical and mental pleasures, pleasures of the Iśvara heavens, Brahma-kāyika Heavens, or formless-realm heavens, and indulges no cherishing even of nirvāṇa. It is only with respect to the welfare of other beings that he is sympathetically mindful and unforsaking.

我當何為令此眾生小兒凡夫無智翳膜所覆盲者。脫
三界獄安置常樂涅槃無畏城中。如是菩薩行利樂
事。於諸眾生無因而愛。所有福德何人能量又偈言
　無依護世間　救護其苦惱　起如是心行　其福誰能量
[0529c14]　　此菩薩常以大悲。作如是念。今此世間無
救無護。遍行六趣入三苦火。無有歸依此彼馳走。
身心諸病常有苦惱。無依護者我當與作依處。救其
身心所受諸苦。起此心行。所有福德何人能量
　智度習相應　如搆牛乳頃　一月復多月　其福誰能量
[0529c21]　　此般若波羅蜜。能生諸佛菩薩。及成就諸
佛菩薩法。

我当何为令此众生小儿凡夫无智翳膜所覆盲者。脱
三界狱安置常乐涅盘无畏城中。如是菩萨行利乐
事。于诸众生无因而爱。所有福德何人能量又偈言
　无依护世间　救护其苦恼　起如是心行　其福谁能量
[0529c14]　　此菩萨常以大悲。作如是念。今此世间无
救无护。遍行六趣入三苦火。无有归依此彼驰走。
身心诸病常有苦恼。无依护者我当与作依处。救其
身心所受诸苦。起此心行。所有福德何人能量
　智度习相应　如搆牛乳顷　一月复多月　其福谁能量
[0529c21]　　此般若波罗蜜。能生诸佛菩萨。及成就诸
佛菩萨法。

He thinks, "How shall I be able to influence these beings, these child-like common people blinded by the cataracts of ignorance? How shall I be able to cause them to gain liberation from the prison of the three realms so that they become established in the constant bliss of nirvāṇa's city of fearlessness?"

When this bodhisattva thus carries out such endeavors bestowing benefit and happiness on others, and when, even without any particular instigating cause, he nonetheless still acts toward beings with such cherishing kindness—who could possibly measure the extent of his merit?

There are yet more such verses as follows:

---

041 – Rescuing and Protecting the Vulnerable, Who Could Measure Such Merit?

When for those of the world without refuge or protection,
He rescues and protects them from their bitter afflictions—
When he raises forth such thoughts and actions as these,
Who could possibly measure his merit?

COMMENTARY:

This bodhisattva, constantly resorting to the great compassion, contemplates thus: "Those now abiding in the world have no one to rescue or protect them. They wander everywhere throughout the six rebirth destinies, plunging into the fires of the three types of suffering.[64] Having no place of refuge, they chase about hither and thither. In all of their physical and mental sicknesses, they are constantly beset by bitter afflictions. For those without refuge or protection I shall be a place of refuge, rescuing them from their physical and mental sufferings."

When he raises forth these thoughts and actions, who could possibly measure the extent of his merit?

---

042 – So It Is in a Moment Aligned with Wisdom. If Longer, Who Could Gauge It?

It would be so even in according with the perfection of wisdom
For only the moment of tugging forth a stream of cow's milk.
If one acted thus for a month or for many more months,
Who could possibly measure his merit?

COMMENTARY:

This prajñāpāramitā is able to give birth to all buddhas and bodhisattvas and perfect all dharmas of buddhas and bodhisattvas.

繁體字

菩薩若於搆牛乳頃。思惟修習彼之福聚。尚無有量。何況若一日夜二日夜三日夜。乃至七日夜半月一月。若復多月修習相應。所有福聚何人能量

　　佛所讚深經　　　自誦亦教他
　　及為分別說　　　是名福德聚

[0529c28]　　甚深者。謂甚深經。與空相應出於世間。彼是甚深。又復分別緣生故。緣生者即是法。法者即是如來身。彼與如來身相應者。是甚深經。諸佛世尊之所讚歎。若自誦[1]若教他誦。若為他解說無希望心。但欲不隱沒如來身故。如來身者即是法身。欲令久住故。彼所有福誰能得量

　　令無量眾生　　　發心為菩提
　　福藏更增勝　　　當得不動地

简体字

菩萨若于搆牛乳顷。思惟修习彼之福聚。尚无有量。何况若一日夜二日夜三日夜。乃至七日夜半月一月。若复多月修习相应。所有福聚何人能量

　　佛所赞深经　　　自诵亦教他
　　及为分别说　　　是名福德聚

[0529c28]　　甚深者。谓甚深经。与空相应出于世间。彼是甚深。又复分别缘生故。缘生者即是法。法者即是如来身。彼与如来身相应者。是甚深经。诸佛世尊之所赞叹。若自诵[1]若教他诵。若为他解说无希望心。但欲不隐没如来身故。如来身者即是法身。欲令久住故。彼所有福谁能得量

　　令无量众生　　　发心为菩提
　　福藏更增胜　　　当得不动地

If a bodhisattva were to reflect upon it or put it into practice even only for that brief moment in which one might tug forth a stream of milk from a cow, just the accumulation of merit produced by that mental reflection or action would be beyond measure. How much the more would this be so where he continued on for one, two, or three days and nights, or perhaps for seven days and nights, a half month, or a month?

If he continued on for even more months in cultivating the corresponding practices, who could possibly measure his accumulation of merit?

---

043 – Recitation and Teaching of Profound Sutras Creates Massive Merit

Where one recites to himself or teaches to others
Those profound sutras praised by the Buddhas—
Also, where one interprets and explains them for others—
These are the bases of an accumulation of merit.

COMMENTARY:

As for what is extremely "profound," this is a reference to extremely profound sutras devoted to emptiness and transcendence of the world. Those qualify as extremely profound.

Then again, it refers to those providing analytic explanations of conditioned arising. Conditioned arising itself is synonymous with Dharma. As for the Dharma, that itself is identical with the very body of the Tathāgata. Whatsoever may be identified with the very body of the Tathāgata—it is these which are the extremely profound sutras, and it is these which are praised by all of the Buddhas, the Bhagavāns.

Where one recites them to himself, teaches others to recite them, explains them for others with a mind seeking nothing in return, where one does so wishing solely to prevent the Tathāgata's body from disappearing, this because the body of the Tathāgata is just the Dharma body itself, and if one does this hoping to cause it to long abide, who could possibly measure his merit?

---

044 – Through Inspiring Bodhi Resolve, Superior Merit and Eighth Stage Are Assured

Through influencing countless beings
To generate the bodhi resolve,
One's treasury of merit increases yet more
And one becomes bound to gain "the ground of immovability."

[0530a08]　　　此有善巧方便菩薩。先以四攝事攝諸眾生。知彼眾生受我言已。然後教令發菩提心。如是具足善巧方便菩薩。令諸眾生發菩提心。彼所有福無人能量。以無量故。又令諸眾生發菩提心故。福藏更為增勝。言福藏者。福無盡故。以能至無盡故不可盡。不動地者。以不可動故名不動地。此中菩薩令他發菩提心故。於生生中。菩提心不動不失。以令他發菩提心故。此心即為不動地因

　　隨轉佛所轉　　最勝之法輪　　寂滅諸惡刺　　是菩薩福藏

[0530a19]　　　如佛世尊。於婆[2]囉奈城仙人住處鹿林中。轉法輪已。於彼最勝法輪隨順而轉。亦為福藏。此隨順轉有三種因緣。謂於如來所說深經。與空相應出於世間。若持若說

[0530a08]　　　此有善巧方便菩萨。先以四摄事摄诸众生。知彼众生受我言已。然后教令发菩提心。如是具足善巧方便菩萨。令诸众生发菩提心。彼所有福无人能量。以无量故。又令诸众生发菩提心故。福藏更为增胜。言福藏者。福无尽故。以能至无尽故不可尽。不动地者。以不可动故名不动地。此中菩萨令他发菩提心故。于生生中。菩提心不动不失。以令他发菩提心故。此心即为不动地因

　　随转佛所转　　最胜之法轮　　寂灭诸恶刺　　是菩萨福藏

[0530a19]　　　如佛世尊。于婆[2]罗奈城仙人住处鹿林中。转法轮已。于彼最胜法轮随顺而转。亦为福藏。此随顺转有三种因缘。谓于如来所说深经。与空相应出于世间。若持若说

COMMENTARY:

Here we have a bodhisattva possessed of excellent skillful means who first draws in beings through resorting to the four means of attraction. Then, once he knows, "Those beings will now accept my words," he afterwards teaches them in a manner causing them to generate the resolve to gain bodhi.

As for this sort of bodhisattva who, entirely equipped with excellent skillful means, instigates beings to generate the mind resolved on bodhi—his merit becomes so extensive that no one could possibly measure it. Because it has become immeasurable and because he then instigates yet more beings to generate the mind resolved on bodhi, his treasury of merit becomes yet more surpassingly extensive.

When one refers here to a "treasury of merit," it is because one's [reserves of] merit have become inexhaustible. It is because [it is in the nature of such actions that] they are able to cause [one's merit] to become so endless that it does indeed become "inexhaustible."

As for "the ground of immovability," it is termed "ground of immovability" because, once one reaches it, [his mind and its resolve] can no longer be moved. Because the bodhisattva herein has caused others to generate the mind resolved on bodhi, in life after life, his own resolve to gain bodhi remains unshakable and is never lost. It is on account of instigating others to generate the mind resolved on bodhi that [these actions of] his own mind become the cause for reaching "the ground of immovability," [the eighth of the ten bodhisattva grounds].

---

045 – Turning the Dharma Wheel and Stilling Heterodoxies Makes a Merit Treasury

Where one follows in turning what the Buddha turned,
The wheel of the supreme Dharma,
Thus clearing away all of the "noxious thorns,"
This creates the bodhisattva's treasury of merit.

COMMENTARY:

When one follows along in turning the wheel of the supreme Dharma, following the example of the Buddha, the Bhagavān, in the Deer Park at Varanasi where the rishis dwelt—this too creates a treasury of merit.

This "following along in turning [the wheel of Dharma]" corresponds to three circumstances involving preservation, explanation,

繁體字

及順法行法。若於如是等經。持令不失。是為第一
隨順轉法輪。為有根器眾生。分別演說。是為第二
隨順轉法輪。如彼經中所說。依法修行。是為第三
隨順轉法輪。寂滅諸惡刺者。佛教惡刺所謂外道邪
見。及以惡魔欲界自在。憎惡解脫。若四眾中或有
異人。非法說法。非律說律。非師教說師教。是為
佛教內惡刺。應當如法折伏彼等。摧慢破見令法熾
然。此名寂滅諸惡刺。以寂滅惡刺。故名為菩薩福
藏

為利樂眾生　　忍地獄大苦
何況餘小苦　　菩提在右手

[0530b05] 若菩薩著牢固鎧。常為利樂

简体字

及顺法行法。若于如是等经。持令不失。是为第一
随顺转法轮。为有根器众生。分别演说。是为第二
随顺转法轮。如彼经中所说。依法修行。是为第三
随顺转法轮。寂灭诸恶刺者。佛教恶刺所谓外道邪
见。及以恶魔欲界自在。憎恶解脱。若四众中或有
异人。非法说法。非律说律。非师教说师教。是为
佛教内恶刺。应当如法折伏彼等。摧慢破见令法炽
然。此名寂灭诸恶刺。以寂灭恶刺。故名为菩萨福
藏

为利乐众生　　忍地狱大苦
何况馀小苦　　菩提在右手

[0530b05] 若菩萨着牢固铠。常为利乐

and cultivation in accordance with the Dharma in the profound sutras brought into the world by the Tathāgata to set forth the emptiness teachings:

1) Where one preserves such sutras so as to prevent their disappearance, this is the first type of "following along in turning the wheel of Dharma."

2) Where, for the sake of beings capable of retaining them, one provides analytic explanations as one expounds [the Dharma taught in these sutras], this is the second type of "following along in turning the wheel of Dharma."

3) Where one cultivates [the Path] in accordance with the Dharma as set forth in those sutras, this is the third type of "following along in turning the wheel of Dharma."

As for "clearing away all those 'noxious thorns,'" the Buddha taught that "noxious thorns" refers specifically to the erroneous views of non-Buddhists and also to the actions of evil demons and denizens of the desire realm's sovereign independence heavens who abhor the prospect of beings gaining liberation.

It could be as well that, in the midst of the four-fold assembly, there are unorthodox persons proclaiming non-Dharma to be Dharma, proclaiming what doesn't conform to the moral codes to be in conformity with the moral codes, and proclaiming that not taught by the Guru to have been taught by the Guru. These are what make up the "noxious thorns" within the Buddhist domain.

In a manner consistent with Dharma, one should vanquish individuals of this sort [in doctrinal debate], shattering their arrogance and demolishing their views, thus causing [the torch of] Dharma to blaze brightly on. This is what is meant by "clearing away the noxious thorns." Through doing away with such "noxious thorns," one establishes the bodhisattva's treasury of merit.

---

046 – Where One Is Willing to Suffer the Hells for Beings, Bodhi Is at Hand

Where, to benefit beings and make them happy,
One would endure even the sufferings of the great hells,
How much the more the other lesser sufferings,
It is as if bodhi lay in the palm of one's own right hand.

COMMENTARY:

This refers to instances where the bodhisattva dons the durable armor [of patience], works constantly to promote the benefit and

眾生。發精勤意。於一眾生為令解脫故。雖住阿毘
至大地獄中。經劫辛苦堪忍不動。況餘小苦。菩薩
能忍如是等苦。當知菩提如住右掌

　　起作不自為　　　唯利樂眾生
　　皆由大悲故　　　菩提在右手

[0530b11]菩薩諸所起作。若布施等。由大悲故。唯為
利樂眾生。亦為令眾生得涅槃故。終不為身微少樂
事。彼亦是大悲者。如是大人。當知菩提到其右手

　　智慧離戲論　　　精進離懈怠
　　捨施離慳惜　　　菩提在右手

[0530b17] 　　問前已解釋陀那等諸波羅蜜。今復解釋有
何所[3]為。[0530b19] 　　答前多為修行者解釋。今為無
所得忍智光者解釋。

众生。发精勤意。于一众生为令解脱故。虽住阿毘
至大地狱中。经劫辛苦堪忍不动。况馀小苦。菩萨
能忍如是等苦。当知菩提如住右掌

　　起作不自为　　　唯利乐众生
　　皆由大悲故　　　菩提在右手

[0530b11]菩萨诸所起作。若布施等。由大悲故。唯为
利乐众生。亦为令众生得涅盘故。终不为身微少乐
事。彼亦是大悲者。如是大人。当知菩提到其右手

　　智慧离戏论　　　精进离懈怠
　　舍施离悭惜　　　菩提在右手

[0530b17] 　　问前已解释陀那等诸波罗蜜。今复解释有
何所[3]为。[0530b19] 　　答前多为修行者解释。今为无
所得忍智光者解释。

happiness of beings, generates intensely diligent resolve, and, in order to bring about the liberation of all beings, is able to endure unflinchingly even the ordeal of passing through kalpas of bitter suffering in the great *avīci* hells, how much the more the other lesser sufferings.

When a bodhisattva is able to endure even such sufferings as these, one should realize that is as if bodhi already lay in the palm of his own right hand.

---

047 – Where Actions Are Selfless, Altruistic, and Compassionate, Bodhi Is at Hand

Where whatever one does, it is not for one's self,
But solely to benefit beings and make them happy—
Because this all arises from the great compassion,
It is as if bodhi lay in the palm of one's own right hand.

COMMENTARY:

When the bodhisattva initiates any endeavor such as giving, because it arises from the great compassion, it is solely for the sake of benefiting and bringing happiness to beings while also being aimed at instigating those beings to gain nirvāṇa. It is never for the sake of creating even the slightest sort of pleasure for himself.

Thus such people are also possessed of the great compassion. One should realize then that, for a person of such greatness, it is as if bodhi has already arrived in the palm of his own right hand.

THE BODHI-GENERATING POWER OF THE FULLY-DEVELOPED SIX PERFECTIONS

---

048 – Where Wisdom, Vigor, and Giving Are Transcendent, Bodhi Is at Hand

Where wisdom is such that one abandons frivolous discourse,
Where vigor is such that one abandons indolence,
And where giving is such that one abandons miserliness,
It is as if bodhi lay in the palm of one's own right hand.

COMMENTARY:

Question: *Dāna* (giving) and the other pāramitās were already explained earlier. Why are they now explained yet again?

Response: The earlier explanation was primarily for the benefit of those taking up the cultivation of these practices. Now, however, they are described in reference to those possessing the light of wisdom associated with that patience in which no phenomenon's [intrinsic existence] is deemed apprehensible.[65]

以覺知一道相故。彼智遠離戲論。以不捨軛故。彼
精進遠離懈怠。以除貪故。彼施遠離慳惜。如是菩
薩。當知菩提到其右手

　　無依無覺定　　　圓滿無雜戒
　　無所從生忍　　　菩提在右手

繁體字

[0530b25]　　若菩薩善成就禪那波羅蜜已。此定不依三
界。其相寂靜無有思覺。又圓滿尸羅無雜無濁。迴
向菩提無有磨滅。又善成就般若波羅蜜已。緣生法
中住無生忍。根本勝故無有退轉。當知菩提住其右
掌

[0530c01]　　問已說修行及得忍菩薩積聚諸福[4]田。此
福聚能得菩提。云何初發心菩薩。積聚諸福[5]田。
此福聚能得菩提。答

以觉知一道相故。彼智远离戏论。以不舍轭故。彼
精进远离懈怠。以除贪故。彼施远离悭惜。如是菩
萨。当知菩提到其右手

　　无依无觉定　　　圆满无杂戒
　　无所从生忍　　　菩提在右手

简体字

[0530b25]　　若菩萨善成就禅那波罗蜜已。此定不依三
界。其相寂静无有思觉。又圆满尸罗无杂无浊。迴
向菩提无有磨灭。又善成就般若波罗蜜已。缘生法
中住无生忍。根本胜故无有退转。当知菩提住其右
掌

[0530c01]　　问已说修行及得忍菩萨积聚诸福[4]田。此
福聚能得菩提。云何初发心菩萨。积聚诸福[5]田。
此福聚能得菩提。答

It is because they have realized the singular character of the Path that their wisdom demonstrates abandonment of all frivolous disputation. It is because they do not set aside the yoke [of the bodhisattva practices] that their vigor demonstrates abandonment of all indolence. It is because they have gotten rid of covetousness that their giving demonstrates abandonment of all miserliness.

One should realize that, for a bodhisattva of this sort, it is as if bodhi has come to rest in the palm of his own right hand.

---

049 – Where Meditation, Moral Virtue, and Patience Are Perfected, Bodhi Is at Hand

Where meditation is such that one is free of reliances or ideation,
Where morality is such that its practice is perfect and unmixed,
And where patience is such that one realizes non-production,
It is as if bodhi lay in the palm of one's own right hand.

COMMENTARY:

In a case where a bodhisattva has perfected dhyāna pāramitā, this meditative absorption does not rely upon anything in the three realms. It is quiescently still in character and is devoid of any contemplative ideation.

Also, one's observance of śīla is perfect, so much so that one's practice involves no adulteration [by the defilements] and no turbidity. [The merit of such practice] is dedicated to bodhi and [the precept practice itself] becomes invulnerable to any diminishment in quality.

Moreover, once one has well perfected prajñāpāramitā, one abides in the unproduced-dharmas patience even in the midst of dharmas produced through conditioned arising.

Due to the supremacy of the foundations, [such bodhisattvas] become unretreating [in their practice]. One should realize that, [for a practitioner of this sort], it is as if bodhi has come to rest in the palm of his own right hand.

Question: It has already been explained how those bodhisattvas established in cultivation or possessed of the unproduced-dharmas patience have collected their merit fields, that accumulation of merit through which they become able to realize bodhi. How then is it that the bodhisattvas who have only just brought forth the initial resolve are able to accumulate the merit field, this aggregation of merit by which they become able to realize bodhi?

Response: (As below...)

現在十方住　　　所有諸正覺
我悉在彼前　　　陳說我不善

[0530c06] 若有現在諸佛世尊。於十方世間無所障礙。以本願力為利眾生故住。今於彼等實證者前。發露諸罪。若我無始流轉已來。於其前世及現在時。或自作惡業。或教他或隨喜。以貪瞋癡起身口意。我皆陳說不敢覆藏。悉當永斷終不更作

於彼十方界　　　若佛得菩提
而不演說法　　　我請轉法輪

[0530c14] 　若佛世尊滿足大願。於菩提樹下。證無上正覺已。少欲靜住。不為世間轉[6]於法輪。我當勸請彼佛

現在十方住　　　所有诸正觉
我悉在彼前　　　陈说我不善

[0530c06] 若有现在诸佛世尊。于十方世间无所障碍。以本愿力为利众生故住。今于彼等实证者前。发露诸罪。若我无始流转已来。于其前世及现在时。或自作恶业。或教他或随喜。以贪瞋痴起身口意。我皆陈说不敢覆藏。悉当永断终不更作

于彼十方界　　　若佛得菩提
而不演说法　　　我请转法轮

[0530c14] 　若佛世尊满足大愿。于菩提树下。证无上正觉已。少欲静住。不为世间转[6]于法轮。我当劝请彼佛

How a Bodhisattva Creates the Merit Essential to Buddhahood Through Purification of Bad Karma

050 – One Confesses All Bad Deeds in the Presence of All Buddhas

In the abodes of all who have gained the right enlightenment,
Now abiding throughout the ten directions,
I appear there in the presence of them all,
And completely lay forth all my unwholesome deeds.

COMMENTARY:

One reflects: "I go before all of the Buddhas of the present era throughout the interconnected worlds of the ten directions, going to where, through the power of their original vows, they now abide for the benefit of beings.

"In the presence of all those exemplars of genuine realization, I lay forth all of my karmic offenses: including throughout beginningless cyclic existence on up to the present all transgressions committed in previous lives and the present life; including all transgressions committed myself as well those undertaken by others at my behest; including all transgressions committed by others, but nonetheless joyfully approved of by me; including all transgressions arising through desire, hatefulness, or delusion; and including all transgressions committed through body, mouth, or mind.

"I completely confess and describe all those transgressions I have committed, not daring to conceal any of them. I now vow to cease all such bad deeds forever, and vow to refrain from ever committing them again."

Through Entreating the Buddhas to Turn the Dharma Wheel

051 – One Entreats the Buddhas to Turn the Dharma Wheel

Where there are buddhas who have realized bodhi
In those realms throughout the ten directions,
But they have not yet proclaimed the Dharma,
I entreat them to turn the Dharma wheel.

COMMENTARY:

One reflects: "Wherever there may be a buddha, a *bhagavān*, who has fulfilled the great vow, who dwells beneath a bodhi tree, who has realized the unsurpassed enlightenment, who abides in stillness with few needs, and who has not yet turned the Dharma wheel for the sake of the world, I shall go there to entreat that buddha, that

世尊轉佛法輪。利益多人安樂多人。憐愍世間為於
大眾。利樂天人

現在十方界　　所有諸正覺
若欲捨命行　　頂禮勸請住

[0530c20]　　若佛世尊世間無礙。在於十方證菩提轉法
輪安住正法。所應化度眾生化度已訖。欲捨命行。
我當頂禮彼佛世尊請住久時。利益多人安樂多人。
憐愍世間為於大眾。利樂天人

若諸眾生等　　從於身口意
所生施戒福　　及以思惟修
聖人及凡夫　　過現未來世
所有積聚福　　我皆生隨喜

世尊转佛法轮。利益多人安乐多人。怜愍世间为于
大众。利乐天人

现在十方界　　所有诸正觉
若欲舍命行　　顶礼劝请住

[0530c20]　　若佛世尊世间无碍。在于十方证菩提转法
轮安住正法。所应化度众生化度已讫。欲舍命行。
我当顶礼彼佛世尊请住久时。利益多人安乐多人。
怜愍世间为于大众。利乐天人

若诸众生等　　从于身口意
所生施戒福　　及以思惟修
圣人及凡夫　　过现未来世
所有积聚福　　我皆生随喜

bhagavān, to set turning the Buddha's Dharma wheel to benefit and bring happiness to the multitude."

This is done out of pity for beings in the world, is done for the members of the Great Assembly, and is done with the wish that benefit and happiness will be bestowed on both gods and men.

THROUGH BESEECHING THE BUDDHAS TO REMAIN IN THE WORLD

052 – One Beseeches the Buddhas to Remain in the World

Wherever there are those possessing the right enlightenment
Abiding in the present era in the ten directions' realms,
But now on the verge of relinquishing their lives and actions,
I bow down my head in reverence, beseeching them to remain.

COMMENTARY:

One reflects: "Wherever there are buddhas, *bhagavāns,* dwelling in the interconnected worlds throughout the ten directions—where they have already gained realization of bodhi, have already turned the Dharma wheel, have already established right Dharma, and have already finished instructing and liberating all of those beings whom they should instruct and bring across to liberation—when they are on the verge of relinquishing their lives and their activities, I shall go there and bow down my head in reverence before those buddhas, those *bhagavāns,* beseeching them to remain for a long time, benefiting and bringing happiness to the multitudes."

This too is done out of pity for beings in the world, is done for the members of the Great Assembly, and is done with the wish that benefit and happiness will be bestowed on both gods and men.

THROUGH ACCORDANT REJOICING IN MERIT CREATED BY OTHERS

053 – All Merit Created by Beings Through Giving on Through to Meditation—

Wherever there may be any beings
Who, by acts of body, mouth, or mind,
Have created any merit through giving, moral virtue,
And so forth, including through cultivation of meditation—[66]

054 – Whether Created by Āryas or Common People, I Rejoice in It All

No matter whether they be āryas or common persons—
And no matter whether its creation is past, present, or future—
I am moved to rejoice[67]
In all of that accumulated merit.

繁體字

[0530c28]　若諸眾生施戒修等所作福事。從身口意之所出生。已聚現聚及以當聚。聲聞獨覺諸佛菩薩諸聖人等。及以凡夫所有諸福。我皆隨喜。如是隨喜。是先首者。勝住者。殊[1]異者。[2]最上者。勝攝者。美妙者。無上者。無等者。無等等者。如是隨喜乃名隨喜

　　若我所有福　　悉以為一搏
　　迴與諸眾生　　為令得正覺

[0531a07]　若我無始流轉已來。於佛法僧及別人邊。所有福聚。乃至施與畜生一搏之食。若歸依善根。若悔過善根。若勸請善根。若隨喜善根。彼皆稱量共為一搏。我為諸眾生故。迴向菩提皆悉捨與。以此善根。令諸眾生

簡体字

[0530c28]　若诸众生施戒修等所作福事。从身口意之所出生。已聚现聚及以当聚。声闻独觉诸佛菩萨诸圣人等。及以凡夫所有诸福。我皆随喜。如是随喜。是先首者。胜住者。殊[1]异者。[2]最上者。胜摄者。美妙者。无上者。无等者。无等等者。如是随喜乃名随喜

　　若我所有福　　悉以为一抟
　　迴与诸众生　　为令得正觉

[0531a07]　若我无始流转已来。于佛法僧及别人边。所有福聚。乃至施与畜生一抟之食。若归依善根。若悔过善根。若劝请善根。若随喜善根。彼皆称量共为一抟。我为诸众生故。迴向菩提皆悉舍与。以此善根。令诸众生

COMMENTARY:

One reflects: "In whatever circumstance beings engage in merit-generating endeavors through giving, moral virtue, or other forms of cultivation, whether such merit arises from body, mouth, or mind, whether it be accumulated in the past, accumulated in the present, or accumulated in the future, whether it be created by the likes of the Śrāvaka disciples, the Pratyekabuddhas, the Buddhas, the Bodhisattvas, the Āryas, or the common people—I accord with and rejoice in all of that merit."

Accordant rejoicing of this sort [especially rejoices as well in that merit which is foremost, that which is paramount, that which is especially distinctive, that which is most superior, that which is supreme in what it subsumes, that which is lovely in its sublimity, that which has no other which stands above it, that which has no equal, and that which is equal even to the unequalled. It is just such accordant rejoicing as this which, then and only then, qualifies as [genuine] accordant rejoicing.

THROUGH TRANSFERENCE OF MERIT

055 – I Dedicate All Merit to All Beings That They Might Realize Bodhi

If all of the merit I have created
Could be formed into a single ball,
I would bestow it on all beings through dedicating it
To causing them to gain the right enlightenment.

COMMENTARY:

One reflects: "I dedicate all of that merit I have ever accumulated in my interactions with the Buddha, the Dharma, the Sangha, and other persons across the course of my cyclic existence from the beginningless past on forward to the present, including even any merit created through giving a morsel of food to an animal. I dedicate all of that merit, including all of that created through roots of goodness associated with taking the Refuges, roots of goodness based on repentance of transgressions, roots of goodness based on entreating [buddhas to turn the Dharma wheel and remain in the world], and roots of goodness based on accordant rejoicing [in the merit of others]. Were it possible to take all of that merit, measure it out and form it into a ball, I would take [the merit arising from] these roots of goodness and, dedicating it to bodhi, would give all of it to all beings, this with the intention of causing all beings to

繁體字

證無上正覺。得一切智智

　我如是悔過　勸請隨喜福　及迴向菩提　當知如諸佛

[0531a15]　　　　若我為諸眾生迴向菩提善根。若悔過善根。若勸轉法輪善根。若請長壽善根。若隨喜善根。彼皆稱量為一摶已。如過去未來現在諸佛世尊為菩薩時。已作迴向當作迴向。我亦如是以諸善根迴向菩提。以此迴向善根。令我及諸眾生當[3]證無上正覺。我今更略說

　說悔我罪惡　請佛隨喜福　及迴向菩提　如最勝所說

[0531a23]　　　自有罪惡盡皆說悔。及請佛轉法輪。住壽長時隨喜諸福。迴向福等。如前迴向為菩提故。如最勝人所說。

簡体字

证无上正觉。得一切智智

　我如是悔过　劝请随喜福　及迴向菩提　当知如诸佛

[0531a15]　　　　若我为诸众生迴向菩提善根。若悔过善根。若劝转法轮善根。若请长寿善根。若随喜善根。彼皆称量为一抟已。如过去未来现在诸佛世尊为菩萨时。已作迴向当作迴向。我亦如是以诸善根迴向菩提。以此迴向善根。令我及诸众生当[3]证无上正觉。我今更略说

　说悔我罪恶　请佛随喜福　及迴向菩提　如最胜所说

[0531a23]　　　自有罪恶尽皆说悔。及请佛转法轮。住寿长时随喜诸福。迴向福等。如前迴向为菩提故。如最胜人所说。

realize the unsurpassed right enlightenment and gain the wisdom associated with all-knowledge."

BUDDHA'S OWN ACTS: REPENT, ENTREAT, BESEECH, REJOICE, DEDICATE

056 – To Repent, Entreat, Beseech, Rejoice, and Dedicate Accords with Buddhas' Acts

As for these actions I undertake in repenting transgressions,
In entreating and beseeching, in rejoicing in others' merit,
And so on, including in dedicating all merit to realizing bodhi—
One should realize they accord with all buddhas' own practices.

COMMENTARY:

Whether it be roots of goodness based on my dedication of merit to bodhi on behalf of beings, roots of goodness based on repentance of transgressions, roots of goodness based on exhortation to turn the wheel of Dharma, roots of goodness based on requesting the Buddhas to extend their lifespans, or roots of goodness based on rejoicing in others' merit—after measuring it all out and forming it into a single ball—then, just as all past, future, and present buddhas, those bhagavāns, have dedicated merit in the past while on the Bodhisattva Path and will dedicate merit in the future, so too do I now, in the very same way, take all those roots of goodness and dedicate them to bodhi, intending that the roots of goodness thus dedicated might cause myself and all beings to gain realization of the unsurpassed right enlightenment. (Adopting the voice of Nāgārjuna) "I shall now briefly summarize this":

057 – To Repent, Entreat, Beseech, Rejoice, and Dedicate Accords with Their Teachings

These acts of confession and repentance of my bad karmic deeds,
Of entreating the Buddhas, of rejoicing in others' merit,
And so on, including dedicating all merit to realizing bodhi—
These all accord with teachings set forth by the Victorious One.

COMMENTARY:

As for these acts such as confession and repentance of one's bad karmic deeds, such as requesting buddhas to turn the Dharma wheel, such as requesting them to remain with extended lives for a long time, such as rejoicing in others' merit, and such as the dedication of merit—because they are in accord with the past deeds [performed by the Buddhas] in their own dedication of merit to bodhi [and so forth], they conform to the teachings as they were presented

如是迴向問又彼迴向。應云何作。答

　　右膝輪著地　　　一[4]髖整上衣
　　晝夜各三時　　　合掌如是作

[0531a29]　　當自清淨著淨潔服。澡洗手足裙衣圓整。於一髖上整理上著衣已。用右膝輪安置於地。合掌一心離分別意。若如來塔所若像所。若於虛空攀緣諸佛如在前住。作是意已。如前所說。若晝若夜[5]各三時作

　　一時所作福　　　若有形色者
　　恒沙數大千　　　亦不能容受

[0531b07]　　於彼所說六時迴向中。若分別一時所作於中福德。

如是迴向问又彼迴向。应云何作。答

　　右膝轮着地　　　一[4]髖整上衣
　　昼夜各三时　　　合掌如是作

[0531a29]　　当自清净着净洁服。澡洗手足裙衣圆整。于一髖上整理上着衣已。用右膝轮安置于地。合掌一心离分别意。若如来塔所若像所。若于虚空攀缘诸佛如在前住。作是意已。如前所说。若昼若夜[5]各三时作

　　一时所作福　　　若有形色者
　　恒沙数大千　　　亦不能容受

[0531b07]　　于彼所说六时迴向中。若分别一时所作于中福德。

by the Victorious One (*jina*). Hence one carries out [just such actions and] just such dedication of merit oneself.

Question: How should one go about [carrying out such acts], including such dedication of merit?

Response: (*As below...*)

THE CORRECT CEREMONIAL PROCEDURE FOR PERFORMING THESE DEEDS

058 – Thrice Daily, Thrice Nightly, Kneeling with Shoulder Bared, Palms Together

Kneeling down with the right knee touching the ground
And the upper robe arranged to bare one shoulder,
Three times each day and three times each night,
Press the palms together and proceed in this manner.

COMMENTARY:

Having bathed, one should don clean robes, wash one's hands and feet, and arrange the robe so that it hangs even all around. Then, having arranged the upper robe so that the [right] shoulder is bared, bring down the right knee so that it touches the floor, place the palms together, abandon all discriminating thought, and focus the mind so that one abides in a single-minded mental state.

This may be done before a stupa dedicated to the Tathāgata or may be done before his image. Alternatively, it may be done by visualizing in a manner whereby one lays hold of and arranges the objective conditions [in the visual field of the mind's eye] so that the Buddha appears as if abiding in empty space directly before one. Then, having engaged in this mental act, proceed as described above, performing these acts [of repentance and so forth until we come to dedication of merit] three times each day and three times each night.

059 – Merit From But a Single Instance of This Would Be Incalculably Immense

The merit created in even a single instance of doing this,
If manifest in material form, would be so immense
That even a Ganges' sands of great chiliocosms
Would still be unable to contain it.

COMMENTARY:

Regarding the above-described six-times-daily dedication of merit [along with its associated practices of repentance and so forth], were one to analyze the merit created through but a single instance

諸佛世尊如實見者所說。彼若有色如穀等聚者。其
福積集無有限量。雖如[6]恒伽沙等大三千界盡其邊
際。亦不能容受。以彼迴向福與虛空界等迴向故。
乃至一時迴向。猶有如是福聚。況多迴向。雖是初
發心菩薩由迴向力故亦成大福。還以如是相福聚
故。漸次能得菩提

[0531b15] 問已說諸菩薩得成大福方便。今欲護福用。
何方便。答

　　彼初發心已　　　於諸小菩薩
　　當起尊重愛　　　猶如師父母

[0531b19] 　　彼初發心菩薩。若欲護自善根及自身者。
於諸初發心菩薩。當起至極尊重愛敬之心。猶如世
尊一切智師及

诸佛世尊如实见者所说。彼若有色如谷等聚者。其
福积集无有限量。虽如[6]恒伽沙等大三千界尽其边
际。亦不能容受。以彼迴向福与虚空界等迴向故。
乃至一时迴向。犹有如是福聚。况多迴向。虽是初
发心菩萨由迴向力故亦成大福。还以如是相福聚
故。渐次能得菩提

[0531b15] 问已说诸菩萨得成大福方便。今欲护福用。
何方便。答

　　彼初发心已　　　于诸小菩萨
　　当起尊重爱　　　犹如师父母

[0531b19] 　　彼初发心菩萨。若欲护自善根及自身者。
于诸初发心菩萨。当起至极尊重爱敬之心。犹如世
尊一切智师及

of performing this act, the Buddhas, the Bhagavāns, have described it as they themselves have observed its reality, explaining that, were one to give that merit a physical form whereby it became like a heap of grain kernels, that accumulation of merit would be boundlessly large in its volume. Thus, although one might attempt to place it within a number of great trichiliocosms equaling the sand grains of the Ganges River, it would so completely exhaust those bounds that they would be unable to contain it.

Because one performs this dedication of merit employing an amount of merit equal in scope to the entire realm of empty space, even in a single instance of such an act of dedication, there would still be a leftover accumulation of merit equal to what was just described. How much the more so would this be the case in multiple instances of performing such an act of merit dedication.

Thus, although one might be a bodhisattva who has only recently generated the initial resolve to gain bodhi, due to the power inherent in such an act of merit dedication, one still creates a huge measure of merit. Consequently, because one draws upon such an accumulation of merit, one gradually becomes able to achieve the realization of bodhi.

Question: Now that the skillful means used by bodhisattvas in the creation of a massive amount of merit have already been explained, if one wishes to guard this merit, what skillful means should one employ?

Response: (As below...)

RIGHT BODHISATTVA PRACTICES AND PERILOUS KARMIC ERRORS TO BE AVOIDED

060 – Revere and Cherish Minor Bodhisattvas As One Respects Guru and Parents

Having brought forth the initial resolve,
In relations with minor bodhisattvas,
One should bring forth for them veneration and cherishing
Comparable to that felt for the Guru and parents.

COMMENTARY:

If initial-resolve bodhisattvas wish to preserve both their own roots of goodness and their own persons, they should raise forth thoughts of the most ultimate veneration and cherishing respectfulness in all relations with other initial-resolve bodhisattvas, bringing forth toward them an attitude comparable to that maintained toward the Bhagavān, the Master of All-knowledge, and toward

繁體字

自所生父母。如是以初發心菩薩為首。於諸菩薩亦
應如是極作愛重。若異於此則自身及善根皆悉滅
盡。如世尊經中曾說我不見餘一法障礙菩薩及滅盡
善根。如於菩薩起瞋心者。若菩薩雖於百劫積集善
根。由此瞋菩薩心故。皆悉滅盡。是故於諸菩薩應
起尊重。猶如教師

　　菩薩雖有過　　　猶尚不應說
　　何況無實事　　　唯應如實讚

[0531c01]　　若菩薩毀訾行大乘人罪過。令得惡名。所
有生生善法皆悉滅盡。不得增長白法。是故諸菩薩
等雖有過惡。為護自善根命故。不應顯說。何況無
實。譬如王罪。

簡体字

自所生父母。如是以初发心菩萨为首。于诸菩萨亦
应如是极作爱重。若异于此则自身及善根皆悉灭
尽。如世尊经中曾说我不见馀一法障碍菩萨及灭尽
善根。如于菩萨起瞋心者。若菩萨虽于百劫积集善
根。由此瞋菩萨心故。皆悉灭尽。是故于诸菩萨应
起尊重。犹如教师

　　菩萨虽有过　　　犹尚不应说
　　何况无实事　　　唯应如实赞

[0531c01]　　若菩萨毁訾行大乘人罪过。令得恶名。所
有生生善法皆悉灭尽。不得增长白法。是故诸菩萨
等虽有过恶。为护自善根命故。不应显说。何况无
实。譬如王罪。

their own birth parents. Having thus taken those other initial-resolve bodhisattvas as the first object of concern, they should then also raise forth just such thoughts of ultimate veneration and cherishing respectfulness toward all other bodhisattvas as well.[68]

Were one to act in a manner varying from this, one's very own person could become destined for destruction along with all of one's previously-established roots of goodness. This is just as stated in the scriptures by the Bhagavān himself when he stated, "I see no other single dharma so effective in obstructing a bodhisattva and completely destroying all of his roots of goodness as the act of generating hateful thoughts toward other bodhisattvas." Thus, even though a bodhisattva might have already accumulated a hundred kalpas' worth of roots of goodness, because of this thought of hatefulness toward other bodhisattvas, all of that merit becomes utterly destroyed.

It is for this reason that one should bring forth thoughts of profound veneration for bodhisattvas, thoughts which are comparable to those reserved for the Guru.

061 – Don't Discuss a Bodhisattva's Faults; Utter Only Truth-Based Praise

Although a bodhisattva may have committed transgressions,
One should still not speak about them,
How much the less so where there is no truth to the matter.
One should utter praises only where they are grounded in truth.

COMMENTARY:

If a bodhisattva speaks disparagingly of persons who practice the Great Vehicle by describing their karmic transgressions, thus causing them to gain a bad reputation, all of his own good dharmas accumulated across the course of lifetimes become entirely destroyed. One then finds it impossible to bring about the growth of pristine dharmas.

Therefore, although there may be bodhisattvas or the likes of them who have committed various forms of karmic transgressions, one should not discuss those matters in a way that reveals them to others, this in order to protect the life of one's own roots of goodness. How much the less might one do so in instances where there is no actual truth to such matters. The care one adopts in these circumstances is comparable to that observed regarding the crimes of a king.

繁體字

如經中說。有菩薩清淨活命無可毀呰。而彼達[7]摩比丘[8]妄說其惡故。於七十劫中受泥犁報又於六萬生中為貧窮人。常受盲瘂[9]癩病惡瘡。是故於菩薩所。若有惡若無惡。皆不得說。彼有實德唯應稱揚。為自善根增長故。亦為餘人生信故

若人願作佛　　　欲使不退轉

示現及熾盛　　　亦令生喜悅

[0531c13]　　若有眾生已發願求菩提。唯欲令其不退。而有人愚癡瞋恚及貪。自朋黨故作如是言。何用長行菩薩難行之行。其涅槃樂平等相似。行聲聞行疾得涅槃。此等後當說其果報。若以種種譬喻顯佛功德令入其心。是為示現。令其具足精進諸菩薩行。是為熾盛。欲令精進更增疾利。為說正覺功德

简体字

如经中说。有菩萨清净活命无可毁呰。而彼达[7]摩比丘[8]妄说其恶故。于七十劫中受泥犁报又于六万生中为贫穷人。常受盲瘂[9]癩病恶疮。是故于菩萨所。若有恶若无恶。皆不得说。彼有实德唯应称扬。为自善根增长故。亦为馀人生信故

若人愿作佛　　　欲使不退转

示现及炽盛　　　亦令生喜悦

[0531c13]　　若有众生已发愿求菩提。唯欲令其不退。而有人愚痴瞋恚及贪。自朋党故作如是言。何用长行菩萨难行之行。其涅盘乐平等相似。行声闻行疾得涅盘。此等后当说其果报。若以种种譬喻显佛功德令入其心。是为示现。令其具足精进诸菩萨行。是为炽盛。欲令精进更增疾利。为说正觉功德

An example of this principle is described in a sutra: There once was a bodhisattva named "Pure Livelihood," one whose conduct was beyond criticism. Even so, a bhikshu named "Dharma" claimed falsely[69] that he had committed evil deeds. As karmic retribution, the bhikshu suffered seventy kalpas of punishments in the hells and then underwent sixty thousand additional lifetimes of continually being reborn in poverty, blind, mute, and covered with loathsome leprosy sores.[70]

Therefore, in one's interactions with bodhisattvas, no matter whether or not they have fallen into karmic offenses, one must always refrain from spreading rumors about them. And only when such persons actually do possess meritorious qualities should one proclaim such matters to others. This behavior is observed for the sake of the growth of one's own roots of goodness and also for the sake of allowing other people to develop faith.

---

062 – To Prevent Retreat from Bodhi, Show the Way, Promote Vigor, Inspire Delight

Where someone has vowed to become a buddha
And one wishes to prevent his retreat from that resolve,
Reveal the way with such clarity he brims with intense vigor,
And cause him to be filled with delight.

COMMENTARY:

Suppose there is a being who has already generated the vow to seek bodhi and one wishes only to prevent him from retreating from his resolve, yet some other person affected by delusion, hatefulness, covetousness or partisanship has approached him, saying: "What is the use in cultivating for such a long time the difficult practices of the bodhisattva conduct? The bliss of their nirvāṇa is so similar as to be uniformly equal to what we promote. Practice the Śrāvaka-disciple practices to gain swift realization of nirvāṇa."

After those promoting such positions have spoken, one should describe the karmic fruits of practice. If one uses all sorts of analogies to make manifest the meritorious qualities of one who gains buddhahood, causing these matters to penetrate his consciousnesses, it is this which serves to "reveal the way with clarity."

If one causes him to become full of vigor in the bodhisattva practices, it is this which amounts to causing him to "brim with intense vigor." Wishing to cause that vigor to enhance the swiftness of his progress, one describes to him the meritorious qualities of the right

大神通事。是為喜悅。如是令彼不捨[10]菩提之心

　　未解甚深經　　　勿言非佛說
　　若作如是言　　　受最苦惡報

[0531c23]　　甚深經者。謂佛所說與空無相無願相應。除無量斷常等邊見。滅我人眾生壽者等自性。顯如來大神通希有功德。於此經律若未證知。勿以癡。故言非佛說。何以故佛世尊說。若謗如來所說之經。惡果最苦

　　無間等諸罪　　　悉以為一摶
　　比前二種罪　　　分數不能及

[0532a01]　　世尊於不退輪經中說。五無間業所有諸罪。若斷三千大千世界中諸眾生命所有罪報。若[*]恒伽河沙等佛世尊滅度已所有支提。或壞或燒若障礙過去未來現在諸佛法眼所有罪報。

大神通事。是为喜悦。如是令彼不舍[10]菩提之心

　　未解甚深经　　　勿言非佛说
　　若作如是言　　　受最苦恶报

[0531c23]　　甚深经者。谓佛所说与空无相无愿相应。除无量断常等边见。灭我人众生寿者等自性。显如来大神通希有功德。于此经律若未证知。勿以痴。故言非佛说。何以故佛世尊说。若谤如来所说之经。恶果最苦

　　无间等诸罪　　　悉以为一抟
　　比前二种罪　　　分数不能及

[0532a01]　　世尊于不退轮经中说。五无间业所有诸罪。若断三千大千世界中诸众生命所有罪报。若[*]恒伽河沙等佛世尊灭度已所有支提。或坏或烧若障碍过去未来现在诸佛法眼所有罪报。

enlightenment, including the matter of great spiritual powers. It is this which "causes him to be filled with delight."

It is via these means that one may influence someone to refrain from abandoning his resolve to gain bodhi.

---

063 – Don't Claim Buddhas Didn't Utter the Profound Sutras; Retribution is Severe

Where one hasn't yet understood extremely profound scriptures,
One must not claim they were not spoken by a buddha.
If one makes statements of this sort,
One suffers the most bitter and horrible of karmic retributions.

COMMENTARY:

"Extremely profound scriptures," refers to teachings spoken by the Buddha on emptiness, signlessness, and wishlessness, teachings dispensing with countless extreme views such as annihilationism and eternalism, teachings demolishing the concept of any inherent nature in a self, others, beings, or a life, and those teachings revealing the Tathāgata's great spiritual powers and rare qualities.

Where one has not yet developed a realization-based knowledge of such scriptures and moral codes, one must not, relying on one's own delusions, claim, "These were not spoken by a buddha. Why would a buddha, a *bhagavān*, speak in this way?" If one does so and thus slanders scriptures spoken by the Tathāgatas, one reaps the most horribly bitter of karmic fruits.

---

064 – Not Even the "Non-intermittent Offenses" Can Compare to These Two Offenses

If the karmic offenses generating "non-intermittent" retributions
Were all put together to form a single ball
And were compared to one formed from the above two offenses,[71]
They would not amount to even the smallest fraction thereof.

COMMENTARY:

In the *Irreversible Wheel Sutra*, the Bhagavān described the offenses associated with the five types of non-intermittent karmic retributions,[72] taking as examples: the karmic offense of cutting short the lives of all beings in a great trichiliocosm; the offense of demolishing or burning down all *caityas* erected after the passing into cessation of a Ganges sands number of buddhas, *bhagavāns*; and the offense of creating an obstruction to [the manifestation of] the Dharma eye of all buddhas of the past, future, and present.[73]

如是等過皆悉搏聚。若於未解深經而起執著言非佛說。及菩薩發菩提願已而令退菩提心。此二種罪。彼前五無間等罪聚比之。百分不及千分不及。乃至數分柯羅分算分譬喻分優波尼沙陀分亦不及。以是罪相故。為護自身及自善根。勿作此二種罪

[0532a11]問已說菩薩護自善根。何者是修道勝義。答

　　於三解脫門　　　應當善修習

　　初空次無相　　　第三是無願

[0532a14] 於中菩薩行般若波羅蜜時。應修三解脫門。最初應修空解脫門。為破散諸見故。第二無相解脫門。為不取諸分別攀緣意故。第三無願解脫門。為超過欲界色界無色界故

[0532a18] 問何故此等名解脫門。

如是等过皆悉搏聚。若于未解深经而起执着言非佛说。及菩萨发菩提愿已而令退菩提心。此二种罪。彼前五无间等罪聚比之。百分不及千分不及。乃至数分柯罗分算分譬喻分优波尼沙陀分亦不及。以是罪相故。为护自身及自善根。勿作此二种罪

[0532a11]问已说菩萨护自善根。何者是修道胜义。答

　　于三解脱门　　　应当善修习

　　初空次无相　　　第三是无愿

[0532a14] 于中菩萨行般若波罗蜜时。应修三解脱门。最初应修空解脱门。为破散诸见故。第二无相解脱门。为不取诸分别攀缘意故。第三无愿解脱门。为超过欲界色界无色界故

[0532a18] 问何故此等名解脱门。

繁體字

簡体字

Suppose that one were to take all such karmic transgressions and collect them together [as a single entity]. Then suppose that one generated a fixed view regarding profound sutras one hadn't understood and claimed they weren't spoken by a buddha, while also [incurring the karmic offense of] causing one equipped with the bodhi vow to retreat from their resolve to realize bodhi.

If one were to take the karmic offenses associated with these latter two acts and make a comparison, the former mass of offenses which generate the five types of non-intermittent retribution would not amount to even a hundredth part, not to a thousandth part, and so forth, even to the point that it would not amount to a numerable fraction, a *kalā*-based fraction, a calculable fraction, a fraction describable only by analogy, or an *upaniṣad*-based fraction [of the karmic offenses associated with these latter acts].

Due to the character of these karmic offenses and the need to guard one's own person and one's own roots of karmic goodness, one must not commit either of these two types of karmic offenses.

Question: Now that the means by which a bodhisattva preserves his roots of goodness have already been explained, what is the ultimate truth to which cultivation of the Path is devoted?

Response: (As below...)

THE THREE GATES TO LIBERATION

065 – One Should Cultivate the Three Gates to Liberation

One should skillfully cultivate
The three gates to liberation:
The first is emptiness, the next is signlessness,
And the third is wishlessness.

COMMENTARY:

As the bodhisattva herein practices the prajñāpāramitā, he should cultivate the three gates to liberation. At the very beginning, he should cultivate the "emptiness" (*śūnyatā*) gate to liberation, this for the sake of refuting all views. The second is the "signlessness" (*ānimitta*) gate to liberation which is undertaken to eliminate seizing upon discriminations or thoughts intent on manipulating objective conditions. The third is the "wishlessness" (*apraṇihita*) gate to liberation taken up to facilitate stepping completely beyond the desire realm, form realm, and formless realm.[74]

Question: Why are these referred to as "gates to liberation"?

答

無自性故空　　已空何作相
諸相既寂滅　　智者何所願

[0532a21]　　以緣生故法無自性。此名為空。以其空故心無攀緣。則是無相。離諸相故則無所願。又若法從緣生。彼自性無生。以自性無生故。彼法是空。若法是空彼中無相。相無有故彼是無相。若無有相彼中心無所依。以無依故於三界中。心無所願

於此修念時　　趣近涅槃道

勿念非[1]佛體　　於彼莫放逸

[0532a29]　修此三解脫門時。若非方便所攝。

答

无自性故空　　已空何作相
诸相既寂灭　　智者何所愿

[0532a21]　　以缘生故法无自性。此名为空。以其空故心无攀缘。则是无相。离诸相故则无所愿。又若法从缘生。彼自性无生。以自性无生故。彼法是空。若法是空彼中无相。相无有故彼是无相。若无有相彼中心无所依。以无依故于三界中。心无所愿

于此修念时　　趣近涅盘道

勿念非[1]佛体　　于彼莫放逸

[0532a29]　修此三解脱门时。若非方便所摄。

Response: (As below...)

THE BASES FOR THE DESIGNATIONS: EMPTINESS, SIGNLESSNESS, WISHLESSNESS

066 – Dharmas Are "Empty" of Inherent Existence, Hence Signless, Hence Wishless

Because they have no self-existent nature, phenomena are empty.
If already empty, how could one establish any characteristic signs?
Since all characteristic signs are themselves in a state of cessation,
What could there be in them that the wise might wish for?

COMMENTARY:

Because dharmas are produced from [a mere conjunction of] conditions, they are devoid of any inherent nature of their own. This is what we refer to as "emptiness" [of inherent existence].

Because [dharmas] are empty [of inherent existence], the mind refrains from [imputation-based] seizing upon objective conditions. Hence [dharmas] are "signless."

It is on account of having abandoned all [mental imputation of] characteristic signs that one finds there is nothing to provoke any wishes. [Hence dharmas are said to be "wishless."]

Then again, given that dharmas are only "produced" from [subsidiary] conditions, then its [supposed] "inherently existing nature" is not produced [in the first place]. Because its "inherent nature" is not produced at all, that dharma is "empty" of inherent existence.

If a dharma is "empty," there are no signs abiding in it. Because such signs are devoid of any existence, [that dharma] is "signless."

If that dharma is devoid of any signs, then the mind finds nothing in it upon which it might rely. Because it has nothing upon which it might rely, the mind finds nothing anywhere in the three realms for which it might wish. [Hence we speak of "wishlessness."]

BODHISATTVA USE OF EXPEDIENTS TO RESTRAIN NIRVĀṆA WHILE ON THE PATH

067 – As These Tend Toward Nirvāṇa, Focus on the Causes Leading to Buddhahood

When cultivating the mindful awareness of these,
One draws close to those paths leading into nirvāṇa.
Do not bear in mind anything not resulting in a buddha's body
And, in that matter, one must not allow any negligence.[75]

COMMENTARY:

When one cultivates these three gates to liberation, if one fails to exert restraining control through the use of skillful means, one

則趣近涅槃。雖應修習。莫墮餘菩提處。當求無所
得忍。應住善巧方便

我於涅槃中　　不應即作證
當發如是心　　應成熟智度

[0532b05] 發如是心。我當利益諸眾生。度脫諸眾生。
雖修三解脫門。不應於涅槃作證。然我為學般若波
羅蜜故。於三解脫門中。專應成熟。我應修空。不
應證空。我應修無相。不應證無相。我應修無願。
不應證無願

如射師放箭　　各各轉相射
相持不令墮　　大菩薩亦爾

[0532b12] 　　譬如射師善學射已。放箭空中。續放後箭
各各相射。彼箭遂多。空中相持。不令墮地

則趣近涅盘。虽应修习。莫墮馀菩提处。当求无所
得忍。应住善巧方便

我于涅盘中　　不应即作证
当发如是心　　应成熟智度

[0532b05] 发如是心。我当利益诸众生。度脱诸众生。
虽修三解脱门。不应于涅盘作证。然我为学般若波
罗蜜故。于三解脱门中。专应成熟。我应修空。不
应证空。我应修无相。不应证无相。我应修无愿。
不应证无愿

如射师放箭　　各各转相射
相持不令墮　　大菩萨亦尔

[0532b12] 　　譬如射师善学射已。放箭空中。续放后箭
各各相射。彼箭遂多。空中相持。不令墮地

draws close to entering nirvāṇa. Although one should cultivate [these gates to liberation], one must not fall into a circumstance conducing to entering those other [paths to] nirvāṇa. One should strive to realize that patience wherein nothing whatsoever is apprehensible even as one continues to abide in the artful exercise of skillful means.

---

068 – Resolve to Abstain from Nirvāṇa; Rather Ripen the Perfection of Wisdom

"In this matter of nirvāṇa,
I must not immediately invoke its realization."
One should initiate this sort of resolve,
For one must succeed in ripening the perfection of wisdom.

COMMENTARY:

One generates just this sort of thought: "I shall bring about the benefit and liberation of all beings. Although I shall cultivate the three gates to liberation, I still must refrain from opting for the ultimate realization of nirvāṇa.

"Thus, as I strive to train in the prajñāpāramitā, my cultivation of these three gates to liberation should be done with the exclusive aim of ripening [my development of the prajñāpāramitā]. Consequently, although I should cultivate emptiness, I must still avoid opting for the ultimate realization of emptiness. I should cultivate signlessness, but still should avoid opting for the ultimate realization of signlessness. I should cultivate wishlessness, but still should avoid opting for the ultimate realization of wishlessness."

---

069 – The Great Bodhisattva Is Like the Skillful Archer Keeping His Arrows Aloft

Just as an archer might shoot his arrows upwards,
Causing each in succession to strike the one before,
Each holding up the other so none are allowed to fall—
Just so it is with the great bodhisattva.

COMMENTARY:

This is analogous to a hypothetical instance wherein a well-trained archer might release his arrows into the sky in succession, continuously releasing them so that each succeeding arrow supports the one before. As those arrows grow more numerous, they hold themselves up in the sky so that none are allowed to fall back down to the ground.

解脫門空中　　善放於心箭
巧便箭續持　　不令墮涅槃

[0532b16]　　　　如是此菩薩大射者。以學修空無相無願弓。於三解脫門空中。放心箭已。又以悲愍眾生巧方便箭。展轉相續。於三界虛空中。持彼心箭。不令墮涅槃。城

[0532b20]　問云何復令彼心不墮涅槃。答

我不捨眾生　　為利眾生故
先起如是意　　次後習相應

[0532b23]若我於三解脫門。善成熟已。欲取涅槃如在手掌。然我以小兒凡夫猶如飲乳。不能自向涅槃城者。未涅槃故。我於涅槃不應獨入。我當如是發起精進。隨我所作。唯為利益諸眾生故。亦為諸眾生得涅槃故。先應如是起作。次即心與三解脫門隨順

解脱门空中　　善放于心箭
巧便箭续持　　不令堕涅盘

[0532b16]　　　　如是此菩萨大射者。以学修空无相无愿弓。于三解脱门空中。放心箭已。又以悲愍众生巧方便箭。展转相续。于三界虚空中。持彼心箭。不令堕涅盘。城

[0532b20]　问云何复令彼心不堕涅盘。答

我不舍众生　　为利众生故
先起如是意　　次后习相应

[0532b23]若我于三解脱门。善成熟已。欲取涅盘如在手掌。然我以小儿凡夫犹如饮乳。不能自向涅盘城者。未涅盘故。我于涅盘不应独入。我当如是发起精进。随我所作。唯为利益诸众生故。亦为诸众生得涅盘故。先应如是起作。次即心与三解脱门随顺

070 – Even in Realizing Emptiness, the Mind's Arrows Never Fall to Nirvāṇa's Ground

Into the emptiness of the gates to liberation,
He skillfully releases the arrows of the mind.
Through artful skillful means, arrows are continuously held aloft,
So none are allowed to fall back down into nirvāṇa.

COMMENTARY:

In this fashion, this bodhisattva, this great archer, through his training and cultivation in the use of the bow of emptiness, signlessness, and wishlessness—having released arrows of the mind into the emptiness of the three gates to liberation and having also used the artful skillful means arrows of compassionate pity for beings—continues on releasing them into the emptiness of the three realms. He thus causes his mind's arrows to be suspended [in that sky] and so does not allow them to fall back down into the city of nirvāṇa.

Question: Why does he continue to prevent his mind from falling down into nirvāṇa?

Response: (As below...)

071 – One Makes the Altruistic Vow and Thenceforth Accords Therewith

"I shall not forsake beings,
But rather shall continue on for the sake of benefiting beings."
One first initiates this very sort of intention,
And thenceforth ensures that his practice corresponds thereto.

COMMENTARY:

[The bodhisattva reflects]: "In an instance where I have already skillfully ripened my cultivation of the three gates to liberation, I might wish to just go ahead and seize nirvāṇa just as if it already lay here in the palm of my hand. However, because these child-like common people are [just as helpless] as if they were still being nursed, they are unable to make their way to the city of nirvāṇa on their own. Because they have not yet gained nirvāṇa, it is not right that I alone be able to enter nirvāṇa.

"Accordingly, I should draw upon the practice of vigor and thenceforth, in all that I do, my actions should be motivated solely by the intention to benefit all beings while also working to facilitate their eventual nirvāṇa."

First, one should initiate actions in this way. Next, even as the mind abides in the three gates to liberation, one acts accordingly,

相應。隨順者順後義也。若不如是。彼之心箭。無
巧方便攝故。行三解脫門時。即墮聲聞解脫。若獨
覺解脫中。今更有巧方便

　　有著眾生等　　久夜及現行
　　顛倒與諸相　　皆以癡迷故

[0532c05]　　小兒凡夫諸眾生等。以癡迷故。於無始際
流轉久夜。著四顛倒。無常謂常苦謂樂。不淨謂淨
無我謂我。及於內外眾界入中。計我我所。謂有所
得。久夜行已及現在行

　　著相顛倒者　　說法為斷除
　　先發如是心　　次後習相應

[0532c11]　　如是諸眾生等。以癡迷故。起我我所二種
計著。

相应。随顺者顺后义也。若不如是。彼之心箭。无
巧方便摄故。行三解脱门时。即堕声闻解脱。若独
觉解脱中。今更有巧方便

　　有着众生等　　久夜及现行
　　颠倒与诸相　　皆以痴迷故

[0532c05]　　小儿凡夫诸众生等。以痴迷故。于无始际
流转久夜。着四颠倒。无常谓常苦谓乐。不净谓净
无我谓我。及于内外众界入中。计我我所。谓有所
得。久夜行已及现在行

　　着相颠倒者　　说法为断除
　　先发如是心　　次后习相应

[0532c11]　　如是诸众生等。以痴迷故。起我我所二种
计着。

acting in a manner directly corresponding [to that stated resolve]. "Proceeds accordingly" here simply refers to "thenceforth acting accordingly."

If one fails to proceed in this fashion [wherein one resolves to act solely for the welfare of all beings], when one practices the three gates to liberation, the arrows of one's mind will immediately fall back down into the liberation sought by the Śrāvaka-disciples or the Pratyekabuddhas, this because one's mind is not controlled by such skillful means.

Now there are yet more skillful means approaches [to follow in Nāgārjuna's ensuing text].

---

072 – Beings Abide in Attachment, Cherishing Inverted Views Caused by Delusion

There are beings who have become inured to attachment
Throughout time's long night and in present actions as well.
Their coursing in inverted views regarding characteristic signs
Is in every case due to confusion wrought by delusion.

COMMENTARY:

Throughout the long night of beginningless cyclic existence the child-like common people and all beings have remained attached to the four inverted views, this on account of confusion wrought by delusion. Thus they take the impermanent to be permanent, the suffering to be pleasurable, the impure to be pure, and non-self to be self, even to the point that, in the sphere of the inward and outward aggregates, sense realms, and sense bases, they reckon the existence of a self, appurtenances of a self and hold the opinion that there exists something which might be gained. Having carried on in this way throughout time's long night, they still carry on this way even on into the present.

---

073 – Speak Dharma to Eliminate Attachments to Marks and Inverted Views

For those attached to marks and holding inverted views,
One explains the Dharma so such errors might be eliminated.
One first generates this very sort of resolve,
And thenceforth ensures that his practice corresponds thereto.

COMMENTARY:

On account of the confusion wrought by delusion, all beings such as these generate the two types of reckoning attaching to the

繁體字

又於色等無所有中。妄起分別取相。生四種邪顛倒。我為說法令其斷除。先發如是心已。然後於三解脫門中。修習相應。若異此而修三解脫門者。則趣近涅槃道

> 菩薩利眾生　　而不見眾生
> 此亦最難事　　希有不可思

[0532c18]　　菩薩起眾生想。此亦最難不可思。未曾有如畫虛空。於最勝義中本無眾生。此菩薩不知不得。而為利樂眾生故。勤行精進。唯除大悲。何處更有如此難事

> 雖入正定[2]位　　習應解脫門
> 未滿本願故　　不證於涅槃

[0532c24]　　此應思量。若到正定位菩薩。以三十二法故入正定位。

簡体字

又于色等无所有中。妄起分别取相。生四种邪颠倒。我为说法令其断除。先发如是心已。然后于三解脱门中。修习相应。若异此而修三解脱门者。则趣近涅盘道

> 菩萨利众生　　而不见众生
> 此亦最难事　　希有不可思

[0532c18]　　菩萨起众生想。此亦最难不可思。未曾有如画虚空。于最胜义中本无众生。此菩萨不知不得。而为利乐众生故。勤行精进。唯除大悲。何处更有如此难事

> 虽入正定[2]位　　习应解脱门
> 未满本愿故　　不证于涅盘

[0532c24]　　此应思量。若到正定位菩萨。以三十二法故入正定位。

existence of a self and appurtenances of a self. Additionally, in the midst of forms and other such phenomena wherein nothing whatsoever exists, they erroneously generate discriminations, seize upon their aspects, and develop the four types of inverted views.

[One resolves:] "I shall proclaim Dharma for their sakes, thus influencing them to eliminate [these errors]." Having first initiated this sort of resolve, one proceeds thereafter in cultivating the directly corresponding practices even as one courses in the three gates to liberation. If one strays from this approach in one's cultivation of the three gates to liberation, then one draws close to that path leading directly into nirvāṇa.

---

074 – Bodhisattvas Help Beings, yet Perceive No Beings, and in This Are Inconceivable

The bodhisattva benefits beings
And yet does not perceive the existence of any being.
This in itself is the most difficult of all endeavors
And is such a rarity as to be inconceivable.

COMMENTARY:

The bodhisattva's raising forth of the idea of a "being" is in itself the most difficult and inconceivable of phenomena. It is as unprecedented as being able to paint a mural in empty space. At the level of the ultimate truth (paramārtha), there are basically no "beings" at all. This bodhisattva does not course in any awareness of them and does not even apprehend them as existent entities. Nonetheless, for the sake of bringing benefit and happiness to beings, he proceeds with the diligent practice of vigor. With the sole exception of the great compassion, where could there be any other endeavor so difficult as this?

---

075 – Though Realizing Definite Stage and Gates to Liberation, One Avoids Nirvāṇa

Although one may have entered "the right and definite position,"
And one's practice may accord with the gates to liberation,
Because one has not yet fulfilled one's original vows,
One refrains from proceeding to the realization of nirvāṇa.

COMMENTARY:

We should reflect upon the situation of a bodhisattva who has reached "the right and definite position."[76] This right and definite position is reached through reliance on thirty-two dharmas.[77] One

繁
體
字

與解脫門相應時。中間未滿本願。為證涅槃為不
證。以世尊經中說云。四大可令改異。無有入正定
位。菩薩中間未滿本願證於涅槃。是故到正定位菩
薩。未滿本願不證涅槃

　若未到定位　　巧便力攝故
　以未滿本願　　亦不證涅槃

[0533a03]　　若初發心菩薩。未到正定位。彼以巧方便
所攝故。修三解脫門時。中間未滿本願。亦不證涅
槃

　極厭於流轉　　而亦向流轉
　信樂於涅槃　　而亦背涅槃

[0533a08]　　此菩薩於流轉中。以三種熾火故。應極厭
離。不應起心迯避流轉。當於眾生為子想故。

简
体
字

与解脱门相应时。中间未满本愿。为证涅盘为不
证。以世尊经中说云。四大可令改异。无有入正定
位。菩萨中间未满本愿证于涅盘。是故到正定位菩
萨。未满本愿不证涅盘

　若未到定位　　巧便力摄故
　以未满本愿　　亦不证涅盘

[0533a03]　　若初发心菩萨。未到正定位。彼以巧方便
所摄故。修三解脱门时。中间未满本愿。亦不证涅
盘

　极厌于流转　　而亦向流转
　信乐于涅盘　　而亦背涅盘

[0533a08]　　此菩萨于流转中。以三种炽火故。应极厌
离。不应起心迯避流转。当于众生为子想故。

might ask: "During that time when he has already reached the right and definite position, when his level of practice is entirely in accord with the gates to liberation, could it be that, before having fulfilled his original vows, he might go ahead and opt for the ultimate realization of nirvāṇa or not?"

The Bhagavān stated in the sutras, "Even supposing that the four great elements themselves might be changed into something completely different, there is still not the slightest possibility that a bodhisattva who has entered the right and definite position might take up the ultimate realization of nirvāṇa during that interim period prior to fulfillment of his original vows." Therefore, so long as a bodhisattva who has reached the right and definite position has not yet fulfilled his original vows, he will not take up the ultimate realization of nirvāṇa.[78]

---

076 – Prior to Definite Stage, As One Fulfills Vows, Skillful Means Restrain Nirvāṇa

Where one has not yet reached "the definite position,"
One holds himself back through the power of skillful means.
Because one has not yet fulfilled his original vows,
In this case too, he refrains from realization of nirvāṇa.

COMMENTARY:

As for the initial-resolve bodhisattva who hasn't yet reached the right and definite position, because he holds himself back through artful use of skillful means as he cultivates the three gates to liberation and during the time he's not yet fulfilled his original vows, he too refrains from realization of nirvāṇa.

---

077 – One Rejects Yet Faces Cyclic Existence, Has Faith in but Abstains From Nirvāṇa

Though one abides in the ultimate renunciation for cyclic existence,
He nonetheless confronts cyclic existence directly.
Though one maintains faith and happiness in nirvāṇa,
He nonetheless turns his back on realization of nirvāṇa.

COMMENTARY:

Through the three types of blazing vigor, the bodhisattva should develop the most ultimate degree of renunciation for cyclic existence.[79] Still, one should not develop a state of mind inclined to run away from and avoid cyclic existence. Rather, one should instead develop a contemplation viewing beings as if they were one's very

而向流轉。及應信樂涅槃。如覆護舍宅故。然復應
背涅槃。為滿一切智智故。於流轉中若有厭離。則
於涅槃亦有信樂。若不向流轉不背涅槃未滿本願。
修習解脫門時。則於涅槃作證

　　應當畏煩惱　　　不應盡煩惱
　　當為集眾善　　　以遮遮煩惱

[0533a17]　　以是流轉因故。應畏煩惱。不應畢竟盡於
煩惱。若斷煩惱。則不得集菩提資糧。是故菩薩以
遮制法遮諸煩惱。由遮煩惱令其無力故。得集菩提
資糧善根。以集善根故滿足本願。能到菩提

[0533a22]　問何故不以斷滅故滅諸煩惱。答

　　菩薩煩惱性　　　不[1]是涅槃性
　　非燒諸煩惱　　　生菩提種子

而向流转。及应信乐涅盘。如覆护舍宅故。然复应
背涅盘。为满一切智智故。于流转中若有厌离。则
于涅盘亦有信乐。若不向流转不背涅盘未满本愿。
修习解脱门时。则于涅盘作证

　　应当畏烦恼　　　不应尽烦恼
　　当为集众善　　　以遮遮烦恼

[0533a17]　　以是流转因故。应畏烦恼。不应毕竟尽于
烦恼。若断烦恼。则不得集菩提资粮。是故菩萨以
遮制法遮诸烦恼。由遮烦恼令其无力故。得集菩提
资粮善根。以集善根故满足本愿。能到菩提

[0533a22]　问何故不以断灭故灭诸烦恼。答

　　菩萨烦恼性　　　不[1]是涅盘性
　　非烧诸烦恼　　　生菩提种子

own children, thus enabling the capacity to face cyclic existence directly.

One should also develop that faith and happiness in nirvāṇa which looks on it like a home offering shelter and protection. Even so, one should turn one's back on the ultimate realization of nirvāṇa, this for the sake of perfecting the wisdom of all-knowledge.

If one has developed renunciation for cyclic existence, then one will also maintain faith and happiness in relation to nirvāṇa. If one fails to confront cyclic existence directly and fails also to turn one's back on the ultimate realization of nirvāṇa, then even before having fulfilled one's original vows, while cultivating the gates to liberation, one will proceed with realization of nirvāṇa.

---

078 – Dread But Don't End Afflictions; Block Them to Gather Good Karma

One should dread the afflictions,
But should not end the afflictions.
To gather the manifold forms of goodness, one should
Use blocking methods to fend off afflictions.

COMMENTARY:

Because they are the cause of cyclic existence, one should indeed dread the [negative influence of] afflictions. However, one should not bring a complete and final end to afflictions. If one cuts off afflictions completely, one cannot succeed in accumulating the provisions essential to bodhi. Hence the bodhisattva uses blocking and controlling methods to fend off the afflictions.

It is through fending off the afflictions and thus rendering them powerless that one succeeds in accumulating the roots of goodness comprising the provisions essential for bodhi. It is through collecting such roots of goodness that one fulfills one's original vows and thence becomes able to reach realization of bodhi.

Question: Why does one not deliberately destroy the afflictions by cutting them off entirely?

Response: (As below...)

---

079 – A Bodhisattva Is Better Served by Afflictions than by Nirvāṇa

For the bodhisattva, afflictions accord with his nature.
He is not one who takes nirvāṇa as his very nature.
It is not the case that the burning up of the afflictions
Allows one to generate the seed of bodhi.

[0533a25]　　　如諸聲聞聖人等。涅槃為性。以攀緣涅槃。得沙門果故。諸佛不以涅槃為性。諸佛煩惱為性。以菩提心由此生故。聲聞獨覺燒諸煩惱。不生菩提心種子。以二乘心種子無流故。是故煩惱為如來性。以有煩惱眾生發菩提心。出生佛體故不離煩惱

[0533b02]　　問若燒煩惱。不生菩提心種子者。何故法華經中。與燒煩惱諸聲聞等授記。答

　　記彼諸眾生　　　此記有因緣
　　唯是佛善巧　　　方便到彼岸

[0533b06]　　　不知[2]成就何等眾生。彼中因緣唯佛所知。以到調伏彼岸。不共餘眾生相似故。

[0533a25]　　　如諸声闻圣人等。涅盘为性。以攀缘涅盘。得沙门果故。诸佛不以涅盘为性。诸佛烦恼为性。以菩提心由此生故。声闻独觉烧诸烦恼。不生菩提心种子。以二乘心种子无流故。是故烦恼为如来性。以有烦恼众生发菩提心。出生佛体故不离烦恼

[0533b02]　　问若烧烦恼。不生菩提心种子者。何故法华经中。与烧烦恼诸声闻等授记。答

　　记彼诸众生　　　此记有因缘
　　唯是佛善巧　　　方便到彼岸

[0533b06]　　　不知[2]成就何等众生。彼中因缘唯佛所知。以到调伏彼岸。不共馀众生相似故。

COMMENTARY:

For those such as the Śrāvaka-Vehicle Āryas, nirvāṇa serves as their very nature, for it is through pursuing nirvāṇa that they succeed in gaining "the fruits of the śramaṇa" (i.e. arhatship).

The Buddhas, on the other hand, do not take nirvāṇa as the very nature [of their path]. For the Buddhas, it is instead the afflictions which correspond to the nature [of their path]. This is because the mind resolved on bodhi arises from these [afflictions].

The Śrāvaka-disciples and the Pratyekabuddhas burn up the afflictions and so do not create that seed comprising the bodhi mind, for the seed generated by the resolve of the Two-Vehicles practitioner is free of any capacity to course on in cyclic existence.

It is for these reasons that the afflictions [can be said to] correspond to the very nature of the Tathāgatas' [path]. It is by virtue of their possessing afflictions that beings generate the resolve to gain bodhi. It is in order to succeed in developing the body of a buddha that [the Mahāyāna practitioner] refrains from entirely abandoning the afflictions.

Question: If by burning up the afflictions, one cannot subsequently generate the resolve to gain the bodhi [of a buddha], why were predictions bestowed on Śrāvaka-Vehicle disciples in the *Lotus Sutra*?

Response: (As below...)

THE UNTENABILITY OF THE BUDDHA PATH AFTER TWO-VEHICLES IRREVERSIBILITY

080 – Predictions Such as in the Lotus Sutra Were Situation-Specific Expedients

As for the predictions bestowed on those other beings,
These predictions involved specific causal circumstances.
They were solely a function of the Buddha's artfulness
In taking the perfection of skillful means "to the far shore."[80]

COMMENTARY:

One does not know which particular beings were being assisted in their development by those predictions.[81] The causes and conditions associated with those events are known only by the Buddha because:

1) They represent the "farthest shore" (i.e. "the most extreme expression") of his training methods.

2) They represent circumstances dissimilar to those of any other beings.

而彼不生菩提心種子者。以入無為正定位故。如經
說

　　如空及蓮華　　　峻崖與深坑
　　界不男迦柘　　　亦如燒種子

[0533b11]　　　如虛空中不生種子。如是於無為中。不曾
生佛法。亦不當生。如高原曠野不生蓮華。如是聲
聞獨覺入無為正定位中。不生佛法。峻崖者。於一
切智智城道中。有二峻崖。所謂聲聞地峻崖。獨覺
地峻崖。聲聞獨覺若有一切智者。則非菩薩二峻崖
也。深坑者。如丈夫善學跳擲。雖墮深坑安隱而
住。若不善學。而墮深坑便死坑內。如是菩薩修習
無為善相應故。雖修無為而不墮無為中。

而彼不生菩提心种子者。以入无为正定位故。如经
说

　　如空及莲华　　　峻崖与深坑
　　界不男迦柘　　　亦如烧种子

[0533b11]　　　如虚空中不生种子。如是于无为中。不曾
生佛法。亦不当生。如高原旷野不生莲华。如是声
闻独觉入无为正定位中。不生佛法。峻崖者。于一
切智智城道中。有二峻崖。所谓声闻地峻崖。独觉
地峻崖。声闻独觉若有一切智者。则非菩萨二峻崖
也。深坑者。如丈夫善学跳掷。虽堕深坑安隐而
住。若不善学。而堕深坑便死坑内。如是菩萨修习
无为善相应故。虽修无为而不堕无为中。

繁體字

简体字

3) They involve beings who do not generate the resolve to achieve buddhahood, this due to having already entered [the irreversible] "right and definite position" [utterly wedded to] the unconditioned.

This circumstance is the same as that described in the Sutras [as summed up in the following śloka].

---

081 – Analogies for Incompatibility of Two-Vehicles Irreversibility and Buddhahood

Similes for their plight reference "empty space," "lotus flowers," "Precipitous cliffs," and "a deep abyss."
Their realms bar it. Analogies cite "non-virility" and "kācamaṇi,"
With an additional comparison made to "burnt seeds."[82]

COMMENTARY:

Just as one cannot grow seeds in empty space, so too one has never been able to generate growth in the dharmas of buddhahood in the sphere of the unconditioned, nor would one ever be able to succeed in producing their growth therein. In just the same way as one cannot grow lotus blossoms in the vast wilderness of the high plains, so too the Śrāvaka-disciples and the Pratyekabuddhas who have entered the unconditioned's "right and definite position" (samyaktva niyāma) cannot produce the dharmas of buddhahood.

As for the comparison to "precipitous cliffs," there are two precipitous cliffs along the path to the city of the wisdom of all-knowledge. Specifically, they are the precipitous cliff overhanging the ground of the Śrāvaka-disciples and the precipitous cliff overhanging the ground of the Pratyekabuddhas. If śrāvaka-disciples and pratyekabuddhas possessed all-knowledge, [their grounds] would not constitute two precipitous cliffs for the bodhisattva.

Now, as for the comparison to "a deep abyss," a well-trained mountain climber (lit. "a man trained in jumping and leaping"), even when descending into a deep abyss could still abide safely therein. However, when one not well trained in this stumbles down into a deep abyss, he dies down inside that abyss.

In this same way, because the bodhisattva has cultivated the practice of abiding in the unconditioned in a skillful manner, even though he cultivates the unconditioned, he does not plummet on down into the unconditioned. However, the Śrāvaka-disciples and others do not train with comparable skillfulness as they practice immersion in the unconditioned. This being the case, they consequently plummet on down into the unconditioned.

聲聞等修習無為不善相應。則墮無為中。界者。聲
聞繫在無為界故。不復能於有為中行。是故彼中不
生菩提之心。不男者。如根敗丈夫於五欲利不復有
利。如是聲聞具無為法。於諸佛法利亦無有利。迦
柘者。如迦柘珠。諸天世間雖善修理彼迦柘珠。終
不能為鞞琉璃寶。如是聲聞雖復具諸戒學頭多功德
三摩提等。終不能坐覺場證無上正覺。亦如燒種子
者。如被燒種子。雖置地中水澆日[3]暖。終不能
生。如是聲聞燒煩惱種子已。於三界中亦無生義。
以如是等經故。當知聲聞得無為法已。不生菩提之
心。[0533c10]問得力菩薩於眾生中。云何應修行。答

　　諸論及工巧　　　明術種種業
　　利益世間故　　　出生建立之

声闻等修习无为不善相应。则堕无为中。界者。声
闻系在无为界故。不复能于有为中行。是故彼中不
生菩提之心。不男者。如根败丈夫于五欲利不复有
利。如是声闻具无为法。于诸佛法利亦无有利。迦
柘者。如迦柘珠。诸天世间虽善修理彼迦柘珠。终
不能为鞞琉璃宝。如是声闻虽复具诸戒学头多功德
三摩提等。终不能坐觉场证无上正觉。亦如烧种子
者。如被烧种子。虽置地中水浇日[3]暖。终不能
生。如是声闻烧烦恼种子已。于三界中亦无生义。
以如是等经故。当知声闻得无为法已。不生菩提之
心。[0533c10]问得力菩萨于众生中。云何应修行。答

　　诸论及工巧　　　明术种种业
　　利益世间故　　　出生建立之

As for the statement: "Their realms [bar it]," the Śrāvaka-disciples are so tied up within the realm of the unconditioned that they have no facility to course about within the sphere of the conditioned. Therefore those in their midst do not generate the mind resolved on bodhi.

As for the comparison to "non-virility," just as an impotent man no longer finds any satisfaction in the advantages available in the sphere of the five desires, so too, those śrāvaka-disciples who have equipped themselves with the dharma of the unconditioned find no further satisfaction in the advantages associated with the dharmas of buddhahood.

As for the comparison to "kācamaṇi" (common quartz crystals), in the same way that no one in the heavens or in the world, though skilled in the gem-finishing arts, is ever able to transform kācamaṇi crystals into vaiḍūrya gems, so too, even though these śrāvaka-disciples continue to be equipped with all such meritorious qualities as inhere in the moral-precept training and the dhūta [ascetic] practices, including also the samādhis and such, they will still never succeed in being able to sit at the site of the enlightenment and bring about realization of the unsurpassed right enlightenment.

As for the statement: "An additional comparison is made to burnt seeds,'" just as a burnt seed never becomes able to sprout even though planted in the soil, watered, and warmed by the sun, so too it is with the Śrāvaka-disciples. After they have burned up the seeds of the afflictions, there is no longer any conceptual possibility that they might ever be able to be born again into the three realms.

Based on such citations from sutras, one should realize that, once a śrāvaka-disciple gains the dharmas of the unconditioned, he will no longer have any ability to generate the mind resolved on bodhi.

Question: How should the bodhisattva who has gained the powers go about carrying out his cultivation in the midst of beings?

Response: (As below...)

How the Bodhisattva with Powers Should Cultivate Among Beings

082 – To Benefit the World, Bring Forth and Treatises, Skills, Sciences, Trades

All of the treatises as well as the specialized skills,
The occult and mundane sciences, and the various trades—
Because they bring benefit to the world,
One brings them forth and establishes them.

繁體字

[0533c13]　　於中書印算數。鑛論醫論。能滅鬼持被毒論等。出生村城園苑河泉陂池花果藥林論等。顯示金銀真珠鞞琉璃貝石（石白如貝）珊瑚寶性論等。記說日月星曜地動夢相論等。相諸身分支節論等。如是等無量諸論。能與世間為利樂者。劫轉壞時悉皆滅沒。劫轉生時還於人間出生建立。如木鐵瓦銅作等。工巧非一。能滅鬼持顛狂被毒。霍亂不消食諸逼惱等。種種明術雕畫繡織作等。種種事業。能與世間為利樂者。皆亦出生及令建立

　　隨可化眾生　　界趣[4]及生中
　　如念即往彼　　願力故受生

[0533c25]　諸摩訶薩隨何世界。

简体字

[0533c13]　　于中书印算数。鑛论医论。能灭鬼持被毒论等。出生村城园苑河泉陂池花果药林论等。显示金银真珠鞞琉璃贝石（石白如贝）珊瑚宝性论等。记说日月星曜地动梦相论等。相诸身分支节论等。如是等无量诸论。能与世间为利乐者。劫转坏时悉皆灭没。劫转生时还于人间出生建立。如木铁瓦铜作等。工巧非一。能灭鬼持颠狂被毒。霍乱不消食诸逼恼等。种种明术雕画绣织作等。种种事业。能与世间为利乐者。皆亦出生及令建立

　　随可化众生　　界趣[4]及生中
　　如念即往彼　　愿力故受生

[0533c25]　诸摩诃萨随何世界。

COMMENTARY:

This refers to treatises on book printing, mathematics, metallurgy, medical treatises, to treatises on exorcism for ghost-possession and rescuing victims of poisoning, and to treatises on the establishment of towns and cities, gardens, rivers and springs, lakes and ponds, flowers and fruit, medicinal herbs, forests, and so forth.

This also refers to gemological treatises revealing the nature of such things as gold, silver, pearls, *vaiḍūrya* (beryl), alabaster, and coral, to treatises which record and describe such things as the movements of the sun, moon, stars, sunlight, and the earth, and also to those treatises devoted to signs occurring in dreams.

It is also referencing treatises on the physiognomy of all parts of the body and the limbs. All of the countless sorts of treatises such as these comprise what is intended here.

All of those things which are able to be of benefit to the world are entirely destroyed during the deterioration of the kalpa. As the kalpa develops again, these things are brought forth and established again among people. The specialized skills of importance include creating things from wood, iron, clay, and copper and are not of a single sort.

This includes all of the different sorts of occult and mundane sciences including the ability to perform exorcisms in cases of ghost-possession, the ability to do away with insane behavior, the ability to cure cases of poisoning, cases of acute digestive afflictions and indigestion, and cases involving all of the other different sorts of pressing afflictions.

Also, making things which involve carving, painting, embroidery, weaving, and such, including all of the different sorts of livelihoods. Whatsoever is able to bring benefit and happiness to the world—one brings forth and establishes all of these things.

---

083 – Adapting to Various Beings, Per One's Vows, One Takes Birth Among Them

Adapting to beings amenable to instruction,
To their worlds, rebirth destinies, and birth circumstances,
As befits one's reflections, one goes directly to them,
And, through power of vows, takes birth among them.

COMMENTARY:

Wherever there are beings amenable to instruction, *mahāsattvas* adapt to whichever world those beings inhabit, adapt to whichever

若天人等趣。若婆羅門剎帝利鞞舍等生。於彼彼
處。若有可化眾生。為起無量思念。欲化彼等眾生
故。隨彼色類長短寬狹音聲果報。得令眾生受化之
事。即應作願。起彼色類長短寬狹音聲果報。令彼
眾生速受化故

　　於種種惡事　　　及諂幻眾生

　　應用牢鎧[1]鉀　　　勿厭亦勿憚

[0534a04]　　若以罵[2]詈恐動嫌恨鞭打繫閉訶責如是等
惡事加我。及諸眾生無量諂幻知不可化。以彼等故
不應自緩鎧鉀。亦勿厭流轉。勿憚求菩提。又應發
如是心。我不為無諂無幻眾生而著鎧鉀。我正為彼
等眾生著此鎧鉀。我當作如是事發起精進。為令彼
等眾生速得建立無諂無幻故。應當如是自牢鎧鉀
問已說得力菩薩修行。云何未得力菩薩修行。答

若天人等趣。若婆罗门刹帝利鞞舍等生。于彼彼
处。若有可化众生。为起无量思念。欲化彼等众生
故。随彼色类长短宽狭音声果报。得令众生受化之
事。即应作愿。起彼色类长短宽狭音声果报。令彼
众生速受化故

　　于种种恶事　　　及谄幻众生

　　应用牢铠[1]钾　　　勿厌亦勿惮

[0534a04]　　若以骂[2]詈恐动嫌恨鞭打系闭诃责如是等
恶事加我。及诸众生无量谄幻知不可化。以彼等故
不应自缓铠钾。亦勿厌流转。勿惮求菩提。又应发
如是心。我不为无谄无幻众生而着铠钾。我正为彼
等众生着此铠钾。我当作如是事发起精进。为令彼
等众生速得建立无谄无幻故。应当如是自牢铠钾
问已说得力菩萨修行。云何未得力菩萨修行。答

rebirth destiny they abide in, be it as a god, a man, or a being in another destiny, and adapt to whichever birth circumstance they are born into, whether as a brahman, as a *kṣatriya*, as a *vaiśya*, or as in another birth circumstance. Then, focusing on those places in which such beings dwell, they contemplate them in accordance with the immeasurable minds, this out of a wish to teach such beings.

When [those mahāsattvas] observe that circumstances conducive to instruction have developed, they adapt to the physical forms of those beings, including their height, build, voice, and karmic retribution circumstances. Consequently they then generate a resolve through which they take on just such physical form, height, build, voice, and karmic-retribution circumstance, all of this for the sake of causing those beings to swiftly accept instruction.

---

084 – In the Midst of Evil, Don the Armor and Don't Yield to Either Loathing or Fear

In the midst of all sorts of circumstances rife with evil,
And when among beings prone to guileful flattery and deceit,
One should don one's sturdy armor.
One must not yield to either loathing or fear.

COMMENTARY:

When subjected to scolding or cursing, terror, hatefulness, whippings or beatings, bondage or imprisonment, castigation or vilification, or to other such awful circumstances—where, due to beings' countless forms of guileful flattery and deceit, one verges on the conviction that they are not amenable to instruction—one should not be slow to don one's armor. Additionally, one must not be overcome by loathing for cyclic existence or by fearfulness at the prospect of continuing the quest for bodhi.

Additionally, one should reflect, "It is not for beings disinclined to guileful flattery and deception that I must strap on this armor. It is precisely for just such beings as these that I strap on this armor. I should indeed proceed with the work and raise forth vigor as I do so." It is to cause beings to become swiftly established in circumstances free of guileful flattery and deception that one should don one's sturdy armor.[83]

Question: The cultivation of bodhisattvas with powers has now already been described. How then should the bodhisattva not endowed with the powers proceed with cultivation?

Response: (As below...)

繁體字

具足勝淨意　　不諂亦不幻
發露諸罪惡　　覆藏眾善事

[0534a15]　　具足勝淨意者。謂增上意。又是善增也。意者心也。即彼心具足。名具足勝淨意。不諂亦不幻者。諂謂別心。別心者不質直也。又諂者名為曲心。幻者謂誑也。若心不曲不誑。彼是不諂不幻。發露諸罪惡者。若有罪惡顯說發露彼名發露諸罪惡。覆藏眾善事者。若有善業[3]竟大覆藏。彼名覆藏眾善事。若菩薩欲疾得菩提。應當具足淨意不諂不幻發露罪惡覆藏善事。是故世尊說云。諂非菩提。幻非菩提

简体字

具足胜净意　　不谄亦不幻
发露诸罪恶　　覆藏众善事

[0534a15]　　具足胜净意者。谓增上意。又是善增也。意者心也。即彼心具足。名具足胜净意。不谄亦不幻者。谄谓别心。别心者不质直也。又谄者名为曲心。幻者谓诳也。若心不曲不诳。彼是不谄不幻。发露诸罪恶者。若有罪恶显说发露彼名发露诸罪恶。覆藏众善事者。若有善业[3]竟大覆藏。彼名覆藏众善事。若菩萨欲疾得菩提。应当具足净意不谄不幻发露罪恶覆藏善事。是故世尊说云。谄非菩提。幻非菩提

ESSENTIAL MATTERS REGARDING HONESTY AND PURE INTENTIONALITY

085 – Maintain Pure Intentions, Eschew Guile, Confess Wrongs, Conceal Good Deeds

One equips oneself with supremely pure intentions,
Does not resort to guileful flattery or deception,
Reveals the wrongs of his karmic offenses,
And conceals his many good deeds.

COMMENTARY:

As for "equipping oneself with supremely pure intentions," this is a reference to developing a superior class of motivation and also is an indication of an enhanced degree of goodness. As for "intentions," this is a reference to one's mind. This is just to say that it is one's very mind which is "completely equipped" in these respects. This is what is intended by "one equips oneself with supremely pure intentions."

As for "one does not resort to guileful flattery or deception," "guileful flattery" is a reference to harboring different intentions. "Harboring different intentions" is a reference to a mind which is not straight in its character. Additionally, "guileful flattery" is a reference to a crooked mind. As for "deception," this is a reference to deceitfulness. If the mind is not crooked and is not deceitful, then one does not resort to guileful flattery and does not engage in deception.

As for "one reveals all of the wrongs of his karmic offenses," this means that whenever one has evils which have arisen through the creation of karmic offenses, one confesses them and thus reveals them. That is what is meant by "one reveals all of the wrongs of his karmic offenses."

As for "one conceals his many good deeds," this means that whenever one has done good works, no matter how grand those good works might be, one nonetheless keeps these matters private from others. That is what is meant by "one conceals his many good deeds."

In an instance where a bodhisattva wishes to swiftly gain the realization of bodhi, he should equip himself with pure intentions, should not engage in guileful flattery, should not engage in deception, and should reveal the wrongs of his karmic offenses while also keeping his good works hidden. Thus it was that the Bhagavān stated, "Guileful flattery is incompatible with bodhi and deception is incompatible with bodhi."

清淨身口業　　亦清淨意業
修諸戒學句　　勿令有缺減

[0534a27]　　此諸菩薩欲與修念相應故。先當清淨身口
意業。於中殺生不與取非淨行等三種身惡行。應當
清淨。與此相違三種身善行。應當受之。妄語破壞
語麁惡語雜戲語等四種口惡行。應當清淨。與此相
違四種口善行。應當受之。貪瞋邪見等三種意惡
行。應當清淨。與此相違三種意善行。應當受之。
諸波羅帝摹叉學句。亦當受而隨轉。於彼學句。無
有知而故破。若缺漏戒者。於修念中。心則不定

安住於正念　　攝緣獨靜思
用念為護己　　心得無障心

清净身口业　　亦清净意业
修诸戒学句　　勿令有缺减

[0534a27]　　此诸菩萨欲与修念相应故。先当清净身口
意业。于中杀生不与取非净行等三种身恶行。应当
清净。与此相违三种身善行。应当受之。妄语破坏
语麁恶语杂戏语等四种口恶行。应当清净。与此相
违四种口善行。应当受之。贪瞋邪见等三种意恶
行。应当清净。与此相违三种意善行。应当受之。
诸波罗帝摹叉学句。亦当受而随转。于彼学句。无
有知而故破。若缺漏戒者。于修念中。心则不定

安住于正念　　摄缘独静思
用念为护己　　心得无障心

ESSENTIAL PRIORITIES ESPECIALLY CRUCIAL TO MEDITATION PRACTICE

086 – Purify Three Karmas, Observe Moral Codes, Allow No Omissions or Slackening

One purifies the karma of body and mouth
And also purifies the karma of the mind.
Cultivating observance of all passages in the moral-code training.
One must not allow any omissions or diminishment in this.

COMMENTARY:

Because these bodhisattvas wish to accord with the standards for cultivation and mindfulness, they should first make the karma of the body, mouth, and mind pure. Thus one should observe purity as regards restraint from killing, taking what is not given, impure conduct (sexual misconduct), and other such actions corresponding to the three bad karmic actions of the body. Hence one should accept the three wholesome actions which stand in opposition to these.

One should observe purity as regards lying, speaking in a way ruinous of others, harsh speech, the various sorts of frivolous speech, and other speech corresponding to the four bad karmic actions of the mouth. Hence one should accept the four wholesome actions which stand in opposition to these.

One should observe purity as regards covetousness, hatefulness, wrong views, and other such mental actions corresponding to the three bad karmic behaviors of the mind. Hence one should accept the three good mental behaviors which stand in opposition to these.

One should also accept, accord with, and turn into corresponding actions all of the statements contained within the *pratimokṣa* training discipline. There must not be any instances of being aware of the statements contained in the training and yet deliberately breaking them. If there are deficits in cultivation of the moral precepts, in one's cultivation and mindfulness, the mind will be unable to develop concentration (*samādhi*).

SPECIFIC INSTRUCTIONS ON THE PRACTICE OF MEDITATION

087 – Focus on the Object, Still Thoughts in Solitude, Eliminate Obstructive Thoughts

One establishes himself in right mindfulness,
Focuses on the object condition, and stills his thought in solitude.
Having put mindfulness to use as a guard,[84]
The mind becomes free of any obstructive thoughts.

繁體字

[0534b09]　　如是於戒正清淨已。斷除五蓋。於空閑淨潔離眾之處。少聲少喧少蚊虻蛇虎賊等。不甚寒熱不置臥床。若立若經行若結[4]加坐。或於鼻端或於額分。迴念安住隨於一緣善攝作已。若於境界有躁動心。則用念為守門。如是置守護已。遠離障礙賊心。獨在一處無散亂意。而修習思惟

若起分別時　　當覺善不善
應捨諸不善　　多修諸善分

[0534b18]　　於思惟時若起分別。即於起時覺此分別。若是不善即應捨離勿令復增。若是善分唯當數數多作。不應散亂。如室中燈不閉風道

緣境心若散　　應當專念知
還於彼境中　　隨動即令住

简体字

[0534b09]　　如是于戒正清净已。断除五盖。于空闲净洁离众之处。少声少喧少蚊虻蛇虎贼等。不甚寒热不置卧床。若立若经行若结[4]加坐。或于鼻端或于额分。迴念安住随于一缘善摄作已。若于境界有躁动心。则用念为守门。如是置守护已。远离障碍贼心。独在一处无散乱意。而修习思惟

若起分别时　　当觉善不善
应舍诸不善　　多修诸善分

[0534b18]　　于思惟时若起分别。即于起时觉此分别。若是不善即应舍离勿令复增。若是善分唯当数数多作。不应散乱。如室中灯不闭风道

缘境心若散　　应当专念知
还于彼境中　　随动即令住

COMMENTARY:

Having achieved such purity through observance of moral precepts, one proceeds to cut off the five hindrances,[85] carrying on one's cultivation in an unpopulated, pure location at a distance from the multitude. There should be a minimum of noise, disturbance, mosquitoes, snakes, tigers, thieves, and so forth. It should not be too cold or too hot. One does not set up a sleeping cot, but may stand, may engage in meditative walking, or may sit in the lotus posture.

One may keep returning one's focus of mindful attention to the tip of the nose or to the forehead, establishing it there. After one has skillfully focused on whichever is the single chosen objective condition, if it occurs that there is agitated movement in the mind, one then employs mindfulness to guard the door [of the mind]. When one has established this as a means of protection, one abandons insurgent thoughts which might otherwise obstruct the mind.

Thus it is that one cultivates the practice of contemplative meditation in solitude, [focusing the mind] on a single place, and becoming thereby free of any scattering of the mind.

---

088 – When Discriminating Thoughts Arise, Abandon the Bad, Cultivate the Good

When discriminating thoughts arise,
One should realize which are good and which are unwholesome,
Should forsake any which are not good,
And extensively cultivate those which are good.

COMMENTARY:

When involved in meditation, if one brings up discriminations, one becomes aware of such discriminations immediately upon their generation. If they are not good, one should immediately abandon them and must not allow their increase. As for those which are good, one should course exclusively in those, with repeated and increased emphasis on those. One should not allow any scatteredness of thought. This is analogous to taking care not to obstruct a lantern's air source when lighting it and illuminating a room.

---

089 – When Scattered, Reestablish Focus, Return to the Object, Enforce Stillness

If the mind trained on the object becomes scattered,
One should focus one's mindful awareness,
Return it to that object,
And, whenever movement occurs, immediately cause it to halt.

[0534b23]　於中修定比丘。心思惟時專意莫亂。若心離境即應覺知。乃至不令離境遠去。還攝其心安住境中。如繩繫猿猴繫著於柱。唯得繞柱不能餘去。如是應以念繩繫心猿猴繫著境柱。唯得數數繞於境柱。不能餘去

　　不應緩惡取　　　而修於精進
　　以不能持定　　　是故應[5]常修

[0534c01]　　緩者謂離策勤。惡取者謂非善取（謂太急也）。若欲成就三摩提者。不應緩作及惡取精進。以緩作及惡取精進。不能持三摩提。是故修定行者。應[*]常正修

　　若[6]登聲聞乘　　　及以獨覺乘
　　唯為自利行　　　不捨牢精進

[0534b23]　于中修定比丘。心思惟时专意莫乱。若心离境即应觉知。乃至不令离境远去。还摄其心安住境中。如绳系猿猴系着于柱。唯得绕柱不能馀去。如是应以念绳系心猿猴系着境柱。唯得数数绕于境柱。不能馀去

　　不应缓恶取　　　而修于精进
　　以不能持定　　　是故应[5]常修

[0534c01]　　缓者谓离策勤。恶取者谓非善取（谓太急也）。若欲成就三摩提者。不应缓作及恶取精进。以缓作及恶取精进。不能持三摩提。是故修定行者。应[*]常正修

　　若[6]登声闻乘　　　及以独觉乘
　　唯为自利行　　　不舍牢精进

COMMENTARY:

When the bhikshu cultivating meditative concentration is carrying on contemplative practice, he keeps the mind focused. He must not allow it to become scattered. If the mind departs from the chosen object of focus, he should immediately become aware of it, doing so with whatever intensity is required to prevent it from straying away from the object. He keeps returning the mind to its focus, establishing it directly on the object.

In this, it is like using a rope to tie a monkey so securely to a post that it can only wind itself more closely to the post and cannot wander off elsewhere. In this same manner, one should use the rope of mindfulness to tie the monkey of the mind securely to the post of the object of meditation, doing so in a way that it can only wind itself ever more closely to that post of the meditation object, thus becoming unable to stray off somewhere else.

---

090 – Refrain from Laxity and Wrong Attachment as They Prevent Concentration

One should refrain from laxity and from wrong attachment
Cultivated with intensity,
For they make it impossible to maintain concentration.
One should therefore remain constant in one's cultivation.[86]

COMMENTARY:

As for "laxity," this refers to desisting from goading oneself to maintain diligence. As for "wrong attachment," this refers to a type of grasping which is unwholesome.[87] If one wishes to succeed in developing samādhi, then one should refrain from any relaxation in the stringency of one's endeavors and any wrong attachments pursued with vigor (i.e. with "avid intensity"). This is because relaxation of stringency in one's endeavors and wrong attachments pursued with vigor [are conditions] making it impossible to abide in samādhi. It is for this reason that one cultivating meditative concentration should always accord with what is correct in cultivation.

ON THE IMPORTANCE OF VIGOR TO THESE PRACTICES

---

091 – Even Two-Vehicles' Men Focused on Self-Benefit Insist on Vigor in Meditation

Even were one to take up the vehicle of the Śrāvakas
Or the vehicle of the Pratyekabuddhas,
And hence practice solely for one's own benefit,
One would still not relinquish the enduring practice of vigor.

繁體字

[0534c07] 若欲[*]登聲聞乘及獨覺乘。唯為自利故。
自涅槃故。[7]尚於晝夜不捨牢固精進。策勤修行

何況大丈夫　　自度亦度人
而當不發起　　俱致千倍進

[0534c11]　然此菩薩應於流轉河中度諸眾生。亦應自
度。何得不發起過彼聲聞獨覺乘人。俱致百千倍精
進也。如自度流轉之河度他亦如是

半時或別行　　一時行餘道
修定不應爾　　應緣一境界

[0534c16]　今此一日不應半時修習別定。餘時之中復
行異道。唯於一定應善緣境。心隨一境。勿向餘處

簡体字

[0534c07] 若欲[*]登声闻乘及独觉乘。唯为自利故。
自涅盘故。[7]尚于昼夜不舍牢固精进。策勤修行

何况大丈夫　　自度亦度人
而当不发起　　俱致千倍进

[0534c11]　然此菩萨应于流转河中度诸众生。亦应自
度。何得不发起过彼声闻独觉乘人。俱致百千倍精
进也。如自度流转之河度他亦如是

半时或别行　　一时行馀道
修定不应尔　　应缘一境界

[0534c16]　今此一日不应半时修习别定。馀时之中复
行异道。唯于一定应善缘境。心随一境。勿向馀处

COMMENTARY:

Even if one wished to enter the vehicles of either the Śrāvaka-disciples or the Pratyekabuddhas, those vehicles wherein one strives solely for one's own self-benefit and nirvāṇa, one would still strive both day and night, never relinquishing that enduring and solid implementation of vigor through which one is goaded into diligent cultivation [of meditation].

---

092 – How Much the Less Might a Bodhisattva Fail to Generate Infinite Vigor

How much the less could it be that a great man
Committed to liberate both himself and all others
Might somehow fail to generate
A measure of vigor a thousand *koṭīs* times greater?

COMMENTARY:

Now, this bodhisattva should be engaged in bringing all beings across the river of cyclic existence while also bringing about his own liberation. How could it be then that he might fail to raise forth vigor a hundred thousand *koṭīs* times greater in its measure than that of the followers of the Śrāvaka-disciple and Pratyekabuddha vehicles? [That he would generate such great vigor flows from his vow to devote] as much effort to liberating everyone else from the river of cyclic existence as he devotes to liberating himself.

ON THE NEED TO FOCUS EXCLUSIVELY ON A SINGLE MEDITATION PRACTICE

093 – Don't Pursue Other Practice Half-Time or Conjoint Practice of Other Paths

As for cultivating some other practice half the time
Or simultaneously practicing some other path,
One should not do this when cultivating meditative concentration.
One should rather focus exclusively on a single objective condition.

COMMENTARY:

Now, on any particular day, one should not cultivate the practice of some other type of meditative concentration half the time. Nor should one carry on the practice of some other path at other times. One should rather devote oneself solely to skillfully focusing on a single object as one practices a single type of meditative concentration. The mind then focuses on whichever single objective phenomenon one has chosen. Thus one must refrain from directing it toward any other circumstance.

繁體字

於身莫有貪　　於命亦勿惜
縱令護此身　　終是爛壞法

[0534c21]　　應當生如是心。我此身中。唯有薄皮厚皮肉血筋骨髓等。終歸乾枯。我此壽命亦當終盡。彼丈夫精進丈夫勢力丈夫健行。我亦應得。若其未得。我於精進不應賒緩。雖復百歲護此爛身。必定當是破壞之法

利養恭敬名　　一向勿貪著
當如然頭衣　　勤行成所願

[0534c28]　　今此若在曠野宿住之時。勿貪身命於中遊行。若有利養恭敬名聞起時。不應貪著。為自願成就故。應速勤行。如然頭衣

決即起勝利　　不可待明日
明日太賒遠　　何緣保瞬命

简体字

于身莫有贪　　于命亦勿惜
纵令护此身　　终是烂坏法

[0534c21]　　应当生如是心。我此身中。唯有薄皮厚皮肉血筋骨髓等。终归干枯。我此寿命亦当终尽。彼丈夫精进丈夫势力丈夫健行。我亦应得。若其未得。我于精进不应赊缓。虽复百岁护此烂身。必定当是破坏之法

利养恭敬名　　一向勿贪着
当如然头衣　　勤行成所愿

[0534c28]　　今此若在旷野宿住之时。勿贪身命于中游行。若有利养恭敬名闻起时。不应贪着。为自愿成就故。应速勤行。如然头衣

决即起胜利　　不可待明日
明日太赊远　　何缘保瞬命

094 – Covet Neither Body nor Life as the Body is Bound for Destruction

One must not indulge any covetousness regarding the body
And must not cherish even one's own life.
Even were one to allow any protectiveness toward this body,
It is but a dharma bound in the end to rot away.

COMMENTARY:

One should reflect thus: "This body of mine is only a collection of thin skin, thick skin, flesh, blood, sinews, bones, marrow, and so forth, and is a thing which will finally retreat into a state of desiccation. As for this life of mine, it too is bound in the end to be exhausted. Those things achieved through a man's vigor, a man's strength, and the health-filled actions engaged in by a man—I too should be able to achieve them. So long as they have not been achieved, I must not indulge any laxness in my practice of vigor."

Although one might guard this rot-prone body even for a hundred years, still, it is a dharma definitely bound for destruction.

095 – Never Coveting Offerings, Reverence, or Fame, Strive Urgently to Fulfill Vows

One must never develop a covetous attachment
To offerings, reverence from others, or fame.
Rather one should strive diligently to fulfill one's vows,
Acting with the urgency of one whose turban has caught fire.

COMMENTARY:

In this, one proceeds as when traveling, spending nights in the wilds, intent on progressing, cognizant one must not obsess on incidentals related to one's body or life. If under such circumstances, some offerings were contributed, some reverences demonstrated, or some reputation spread around, it would be unseemly to develop any sort of covetous attachment for those matters. Here, in the same manner, in order to complete what one has vowed to do, one should now devote oneself to swift and diligent action, acting with the same urgency as one whose turban has caught fire.

096 – Resolutely Seize Victory, Not Waiting till Later as Survival Isn't Guaranteed

Acting resolutely and immediately, pull forth the supreme benefit.
In this, one cannot wait for tomorrow.
Tomorrow is too distant a time,
For how can one ensure survival even for the blink of an eye?

[0535a04]　彼於如然頭衣勤行之時。明日賒遠莫待明日。若於我身有勝利者。決即發起。應當生如是心。何緣能保開眼合眼時命。我今即起勝利。明日太遠。莫待明日

安住於[1]正命　　如食愛子肉
於所食噉中　　勿愛亦勿嫌

[0535a10]　如是定行比丘。若村若僧坊中。隨有如法無所譏嫌乞得食已。勿起貪心愛著。亦勿嫌之。應當安住正念。如食所愛子肉。但為身住不壞存於壽命。攝護淨行故。猶如昔云夫妻行曠野時。共食子肉

出家為何義　　我所作竟未
今思為作不　　如十法經說

[0535a04]　彼于如然头衣勤行之时。明日赊远莫待明日。若于我身有胜利者。决即发起。应当生如是心。何缘能保开眼合眼时命。我今即起胜利。明日太远。莫待明日

安住于[1]正命　　如食爱子肉
于所食噉中　　勿爱亦勿嫌

[0535a10]　如是定行比丘。若村若僧坊中。随有如法无所讥嫌乞得食已。勿起贪心爱着。亦勿嫌之。应当安住正念。如食所爱子肉。但为身住不坏存于寿命。摄护净行故。犹如昔云夫妻行旷野时。共食子肉

出家为何义　　我所作竟未
今思为作不　　如十法经说

COMMENTARY:

When engaged in diligent practice pursued with the urgency of one whose turban has caught fire, tomorrow is recognized as too distant a time. Thus one must not wait until tomorrow. If there be some endeavor which will provide for me the most supreme form of benefit, I must resolutely and immediately bring it about.

One should reflect: "On what basis would one be able to ensure that life will continue even for the space of the opening or shutting of the eyes? I shall now immediately pull forth the most supreme form of benefit. Tomorrow is too distant a time. I must not wait until tomorrow to do this."

MORE ON CORRECT PRACTICE AND CULTIVATION OF THE MIND

097 – Established in Right Livelihood, Be Mindful and Free of Preferences in Eating

Having established oneself in right livelihood,
When eating, it is as if consuming the flesh of a cherished son.
One must not indulge in either affection for or disapproval of
Whatever food one has taken for the meal.

COMMENTARY:

Here we have this bhikshu, focused on cultivating meditation, having obtained his alms meal in accordance with Dharma and in a manner invulnerable to criticism. Whether that meal was obtained in the village or within the monastic precincts, he must in any case refrain from developing any craving-laden cherishing attachment for it. He must not generate any disapproval of it, either. Rather, he should establish himself in right mindfulness and, just as if he were being compelled to eat the flesh of a cherished son, he consumes it solely with the aim of allowing the body to survive and stave off deterioration, hence solely for the sake of preserving his life.

He proceeds thus in order to preserve and guard purity in his practice. This is a reference alluding to the story of the husband and wife traveling in the wilderness [forced by circumstance] to eat the flesh of their [just-deceased] son.

098 – Review One's Monastic Deeds and Accordance with the Ten Dharmas Sutra

For what purpose has one left the home life?
Have I finished what is to be done or not?
Reflect now on whether or not one is doing the work,
Doing so as described in the *Ten Dharmas Sutra*.

繁體字

[0535a17] 應當如是觀察。我為何義故而行出家。為畏不活耶。為求沙門耶。若為求沙門者。應作是念。我於沙門之事。為已作為未作為今正作。如其未作及正作者。為成就因緣故。應當精勤。我離家類則名非類。應數思念。我之活命繫在於他。我亦應作別異儀式。我自於戒得無嫌不。有智同淨行者。於我戒所復無嫌不。我已與諸恩愛其相別異。不與共俱。我屬於業。業之所。生受用於業。業是所親依業而行。我所作業。若善若惡我當自受。我於晝夜云何而[2]過。我喜樂空寂不。我有上人法不。能得聖人勝知見不。

簡体字

[0535a17] 应当如是观察。我为何义故而行出家。为畏不活耶。为求沙门耶。若为求沙门者。应作是念。我于沙门之事。为已作为未作为今正作。如其未作及正作者。为成就因缘故。应当精勤。我离家类则名非类。应数思念。我之活命系在于他。我亦应作别异仪式。我自于戒得无嫌不。有智同净行者。于我戒所复无嫌不。我已与诸恩爱其相别异。不与共俱。我属于业。业之所。生受用于业。业是所亲依业而行。我所作业。若善若恶我当自受。我于昼夜云何而[2]过。我喜乐空寂不。我有上人法不。能得圣人胜知见不。

COMMENTARY:

One should carry out an analytic contemplation in the following manner:

1) "For what purpose did I take up the practice of the monastic? Was it only out of a fear of not surviving? Or was it to seek [the fruits of] the śramaṇa?"

2) If it was for the sake of seeking [the fruits of] the śramaṇa, one should reflect in this manner: "As for my relationship with the endeavors of the śramaṇa, have I already accomplished them, not yet begun to accomplish them, or am I right now in the very process of accomplishing them?"

3) "If one has not yet begun to accomplish them or is rather right in the very process of accomplishing them, then one should initiate energetic diligence to perfect the associated causes and conditions for accomplishing them."

4) "Given that I have departed from the householder's life, then I should qualify as not being of that sort." One should repeatedly contemplate this matter, thinking, "I depend for my survival on their [contributions]. Hence I should in fact be duly carrying out this different form [of life]."

5) "Have I succeeded or not succeeded in adhering to the moral precepts in a manner beyond reproach? Were there someone well-versed in the same pure practices, would he approve or disapprove my implementation of the moral precepts?"

6) "I have already taken up a different appearance from those toward whom I have had affectionate relationships and do not any longer share what one takes as the basis of one's life. I am, however, one who still does belong to my own karmic actions. Whatever is produced through karma is undergone and utilized in karmic [retribution]. Karma is that with which one is in fact still abiding in an intimate relationship. One depends upon karma as the very basis of one's practice. This karma which I actually engage in—whether it is good or whether it is bad—it is I myself who is bound to undergo it myself."

7) "How do I pass my days and nights? Do I or do I not delight in [cultivating realization of] emptiness and quiescence?"

8) "Have I or have I not come into the possession of the dharmas of a superior man?"

9) "Have I or have I not been able to succeed in gaining the superior knowledge and vision of the Āryas?"

若當後時同淨行者問我之時說之不慚。應數思念此
等十法。所謂定行比丘。應數思念

　　觀有為無常　　　若無我我所
　　所有諸魔業　　　應覺而捨離

[0535b04]　　有為謂因緣和合生。以因緣和合生故。彼
無我所。以有為故彼是無常。若是無常。彼為他所
逼迫故苦。若苦彼不自在轉故無我。於有為法應如
是觀。所有諸魔業應覺而捨離者。或於菩提心六度
相應經中作不欲樂因緣散亂因緣賒緩因緣障礙因
緣。若[3]從自起若從他起。皆應覺知。於此諸惡魔
業。皆覺知已離之。莫令彼自在行

　　根力與覺分　　　神足正斷道
　　及以四念處　　　為修發[4]精勤

繁體字

若当后时同净行者问我之时说之不惭。应数思念此
等十法。所谓定行比丘。应数思念

　　观有为无常　　　若无我我所
　　所有诸魔业　　　应觉而舍离

[0535b04]　　有为谓因缘和合生。以因缘和合生故。彼
无我所。以有为故彼是无常。若是无常。彼为他所
逼迫故苦。若苦彼不自在转故无我。于有为法应如
是观。所有诸魔业应觉而舍离者。或于菩提心六度
相应经中作不欲乐因缘散乱因缘赊缓因缘障碍因
缘。若[3]从自起若从他起。皆应觉知。于此诸恶魔
业。皆觉知已离之。莫令彼自在行

　　根力与觉分　　　神足正断道
　　及以四念处　　　为修发[4]精勤

简体字

10) "When in the future I am interviewed by another man who has taken up the same pure practices, will I or will I not have reason to be ashamed?"

One should repeatedly reflect on the ten dharmas. This is a matter which should be repeatedly contemplated by the herein-referenced bhikshu who is cultivating meditative concentration.[88]

---

099 – Contemplate Impermanence and Non-self, Abandoning Demonic Karma

Contemplate conditioned phenomena as impermanent,
As devoid of self, and as devoid of anything belonging to a self.
One must become aware of and withdraw from
All forms of demonic karmic activity.[89]

COMMENTARY:

"Conditioned phenomena" is a reference to whatever is produced through the coming together of causes and conditions. Because they exist through the coming together of causes and conditions, they are devoid of anything belonging to a self. Because they are conditioned, they are impermanent. If they are impermanent, then they are forced along by other factors and hence are marked by suffering. If they are characterized by suffering and are not independent in their own transformation, then they are devoid of a self. One should contemplate conditioned dharmas in this manner.

As for "One must become aware of and depart from all forms of demonic karmic actions," this refers to the development of circumstances involving displeasure, scatteredness, confusion, laxity, or obstacles in relation to the resolve to realize bodhi or in relation to the sutras teaching the six perfections.

Whether these circumstances are generated by oneself or generated by some other source, one must become aware of them all. Having become aware of all of these forms of evil demonic karmic activity, one must then withdraw from any involvement in them. Once one has done so, one must not permit those circumstances to carry on independently.

---

100 – Generate Vigor in the Thirty-Seven Wings of Enlightenment

Generate energetic diligence in order to cultivate
The roots, powers, limbs of enlightenment,
Bases of spiritual powers, right severances, the Path,
And the four stations of mindfulness.

繁體字

[0535b14] 信精進念定慧。是為五根。信精進念定慧。是為五力。念擇法精進喜猗定捨。是為七覺分。欲定精進定心定思惟定。是為四神足。未生惡不善法為令不生。已生惡不善法為令其斷。未生善法為令其生。已生善法為令其住。生欲發勤攝心起願。是為四正斷。正見正分別。正語正業。正命正發行。正念正定。是為八分聖道。身受心法。是為四念處。此等三十七助菩提法。為修習故。發起精勤

　　心與利樂善　　　作傳傳生處

　　及諸惡濁根　　　彼當善觀察

[0535b25] 　　　心若調伏守護禁繫。則與諸利益安樂善事。作傳傳生因。若不調伏不守護不修習不禁繫。則與諸無利惡濁為根知已。

简体字

[0535b14] 信精进念定慧。是为五根。信精进念定慧。是为五力。念择法精进喜猗定舍。是为七觉分。欲定精进定心定思惟定。是为四神足。未生恶不善法为令不生。已生恶不善法为令其断。未生善法为令其生。已生善法为令其住。生欲发勤摄心起愿。是为四正断。正见正分别。正语正业。正命正发行。正念正定。是为八分圣道。身受心法。是为四念处。此等三十七助菩提法。为修习故。发起精勤

　　心与利乐善　　　作传传生处

　　及诸恶浊根　　　彼当善观察

[0535b25] 　　　心若调伏守护禁系。则与诸利益安乐善事。作传传生因。若不调伏不守护不修习不禁系。则与诸无利恶浊为根知已。

COMMENTARY:

Faith, vigor, mindfulness, concentration, and wisdom comprise the five roots. [Once developed], faith, vigor, mindfulness, concentration, and wisdom also comprise the five powers.

The seven limbs of enlightenment consist of: mindfulness, dharma-selectivity, vigor, joy, light easefulness, concentration, and equanimity.

The four bases of spiritual power consist of: zeal in meditative concentration, vigor in meditative concentration, [single-] mindedness in meditative concentration, and contemplative thoughtfulness in meditative concentration.

The four bases of right severance involve: not allowing not-yet-arisen evil and unwholesome dharmas to come into existence, cutting off already-arisen evil and unwholesome dharmas, causing not-yet-arisen good dharmas to arise, causing already-arisen good dharmas to continue abiding, developing zeal, generating diligence, focusing the mind, and bringing forth vows.

The eight-fold path of the Āryas consists of: right views, right mental discriminations, right speech, right karmic action, right livelihood, right effort in one's actions, right mindfulness, and right meditative concentration.

The four stations of mindfulness are: the body, the feelings, the thoughts, and dharmas.

One should generate intensely energetic diligence in the cultivation and practice of these thirty-seven factors assisting the realization of bodhi.[90]

---

101 – Focus Analytic Contemplation on the Mind as Source of Good and Root of Evil

The mind may serve as a source for the repeated generation
Of good deeds bestowing benefit and happiness
Or it may instead serve as the root of all sorts of evil and turbidity.
One should make it the focus of skillful analytic contemplation.

COMMENTARY:

If it is subdued, guarded, and restrained, the mind becomes the cause for the continuous creation of all manner of good endeavors which produce benefit and happiness for others. If, however, one fails to subdue it, fails to guard it, fails to cultivate it, and fails to restrain it, it then becomes the root of all manner of evil and turbid actions which benefit no one.

於彼應極觀察。生住異相故。內外兩間不住故。過
去未來現在世不俱故。無處來故。無處去故。剎那
羅婆牟呼利多時中不住故。猶如幻故。為修習故。

應當觀察

　　我於善法中　　　日日何增長

　　復有何損減　　　彼應極觀察

[0535c05]　　若佛世尊所說。施等善法能出生菩提者。
我於彼諸善法。有何增長有何損減。常應如是專精
觀察。日日之中。起而復起

　　見他得增長　　　利養恭敬名

　　微小慳嫉心　　　皆所不應作

[0535c10]　　若見餘同淨行者。或沙門。或婆羅門。增
長利養恭敬名聞之時。

于彼应极观察。生住异相故。内外两间不住故。过
去未来现在世不俱故。无处来故。无处去故。刹那
罗婆牟呼利多时中不住故。犹如幻故。为修习故。

应当观察

　　我于善法中　　　日日何增长

　　复有何损减　　　彼应极观察

[0535c05]　　若佛世尊所说。施等善法能出生菩提者。
我于彼诸善法。有何增长有何损减。常应如是专精
观察。日日之中。起而复起

　　见他得增长　　　利养恭敬名

　　微小悭嫉心　　　皆所不应作

[0535c10]　　若见馀同净行者。或沙门。或婆罗门。增
长利养恭敬名闻之时。

Once one realizes this, one should then make [the mind] the focus of the most ultimate sorts of analytic contemplation, contemplations which are undertaken to fathom that [manifestations of mind] are characterized by production, abiding, and change [culminating in destruction], to fathom that the mind does not actually abide inwardly, outwardly or between the two, to fathom that the mind does not reside in the past, the future, or the present, to fathom that the mind has no place from which it comes and no place to which it goes, to fathom that it does not continue to abide even for a *kṣaṇa-lava-muhūrta* (an infinitesimally short period of time), and to fathom that it is like a magically-conjured illusion.

One should carry out these sorts of analytic contemplations of one's mind, doing this as a means to enhance the quality of one's practice.

---

102 – Contemplate With Great Concern Daily Increase and Decrease of Good Dharmas

"From one day to the next, what increase has occurred
In my cultivation of good dharmas?"
"Also, what diminishment has occurred in this?"
Those should be the contemplations of utmost concern.

COMMENTARY:

In accordance with the Buddha's instruction, one should contemplate in this manner: "Regarding those good dharmas able to give birth to bodhi including giving and the rest [of the perfections], how much increase has occurred and how much decrease?" One should constantly focus detailed analytic contemplation on concerns such as these, bringing them up time and time again in each succeeding day.

---

103 – Never Indulge Thoughts of Stinginess or Jealousy over Others' Good Fortune

Whenever one observes someone else experiencing an increase
In offerings, reverences, or reputation,
Even the most subtle thoughts of stinginess and jealously
Should never be indulged.

COMMENTARY:

Whenever one observes someone else engaged in the same practice of pure conduct experiencing an increase in offerings, reverence, or reputation, whether they be a śramaṇa or a brahman, one

亦不應生微小慳嫉。復應思量生如是心。我亦喜得
眾生利養衣服飲食臥床病緣藥等眾具。我亦喜得在
家出家之所恭敬。我亦喜得具足可讚之法

不羨諸境界　　行癡盲瘖聾
時復師子吼　　怖諸外道鹿

[0535c17]　　若見他人增長利養恭敬名聞之時。於色等
境界中。不應稀羨。於愛不愛色聲香味中。雖非癡
盲瘖聾。而作癡盲瘖聾之行。若有力能莫常瘖住。
應以正法遣[5]惑破繁[6]時到。為怖外道鹿故。及住持
正教故。復當[7]震師子吼。我已解釋修心。今當解
釋修相。所謂

奉迎及將送　　應敬所尊重
於諸法事中　　隨順而佐助

繁體字

亦不应生微小悭嫉。复应思量生如是心。我亦喜得
众生利养衣服饮食卧床病缘药等众具。我亦喜得在
家出家之所恭敬。我亦喜得具足可赞之法

不羡诸境界　　行痴盲瘖聋
时复师子吼　　怖诸外道鹿

[0535c17]　　若见他人增长利养恭敬名闻之时。于色等
境界中。不应稀羡。于爱不爱色声香味中。虽非痴
盲瘖聋。而作痴盲瘖聋之行。若有力能莫常瘖住。
应以正法遣[5]惑破系[6]时到。为怖外道鹿故。及住持
正教故。复当[7]震师子吼。我已解释修心。今当解
释修相。所谓

奉迎及将送　　应敬所尊重
于诸法事中　　随顺而佐助

简体字

should refrain from even the most subtle [thoughts of] stinginess or jealousy. Moreover, one should contemplate the matter thus: "I too could tend to delight in receiving from beings offerings, robes, food-and-drink, bedding, medicines, and various other things. I too could tend to delight in expressions of reverence by laity and monastics. And I too could tend to delight in having perfected dharmas which others find praiseworthy."

---

104 – Ignore Sense Realms as if Dull, Blind, Deaf, and Mute, Yet Roar the Lion's Roar

One should not cherish any aspect of the objective realms,
But rather should act as if dull-witted, blind, mute, and deaf.
Still, when timely, respond by roaring the lion's roar,
Frightening off the non-Buddhist deer.

COMMENTARY:

When one observes others receiving an increase in offerings, reverence, and reputation, one should not hope for or cherish any aspect of the associated objective realms of forms [sounds, smells, tastes, touchables, or dharmas as objects of mind]. Even though one is not in fact dull-witted, blind, mute, or deaf, still, with respect to both desirable and undesirable forms, sounds, smells, and tastes, one carries on a type of practice wherein one acts as if dull-witted, blind, mute, and deaf.

Where one possesses the ability, one must not always abide in a state of muteness, but rather should employ right Dharma to dispel delusions [cherished by others]. When the time comes to break someone's [delusion-based] attachments, for the sake of frightening off the "deer of the non-Buddhist traditions," and for the sake of authoritatively upholding correct teachings, one should thunder forth the lion's roar.

I have now completed the explanation of one's cultivation of the mind. Now, we should explain the cultivation of the marks [of a buddha's body], as described below. [See next eight ślokas.—Trans.]

BODHISATTVA PRACTICES AS CAUSES FOR ACQUIRING A BUDDHA'S 32 MARKS

105 – Welcome, Escort, and Revere the Venerable, Assisting All Dharma Endeavors

In welcoming them on arrival and escorting them off as they go,
One should be reverential toward those worthy of veneration.
In all endeavors associated with the Dharma,
One should follow along, participate, and contribute assistance.

[0535c25]　　於所尊重奉迎將送。於聽法時花鬘供養。
修理支提等法事中恭敬作故。當得手足輪相。彼又
是大眷屬先相

　　救脫被殺者　　　自[8]然增不減
　　善修明巧業　　　自學亦教他

[0536a01]　　　有被殺者救令解脫。護命因緣離於殺生。
受此等業長夜習近故。當得長指相足[1]跟平正相身
直相。彼是長壽先相。自所受善法。受已增長不令
損減故。當得足跌高如貝相毛上向相。彼二是法無
減先相。善修明論工巧等業。自學及教他故。當得
伊尼[跳-兆+專]相。彼是速攝先相

[0535c25]　　　于所尊重奉迎将送。于听法时花鬘供养。
修理支提等法事中恭敬作故。当得手足轮相。彼又
是大眷属先相

　　救脱被杀者　　　自[8]然增不减
　　善修明巧业　　　自学亦教他

[0536a01]　　　有被杀者救令解脱。护命因缘离于杀生。
受此等业长夜习近故。当得长指相足[1]跟平正相身
直相。彼是长寿先相。自所受善法。受已增长不令
损减故。当得足跌高如贝相毛上向相。彼二是法无
减先相。善修明论工巧等业。自学及教他故。当得
伊尼[跳-兆+專]相。彼是速摄先相

COMMENTARY:

One welcomes and sends off those whom one should rightfully revere. It is through acting respectfully by making offerings of flowers or garlands when hearing explanations of Dharma, by repairing *caityas*, and by engaging in other such Dharma endeavors that one is bound in the future to gain a buddha-body's mark of the wheel on the hands and on the feet. That is a sign foretelling that one will gain a large retinue.

---

106 – Liberate Beings and Cultivate Special Skills, Training Self and Teaching Others

One rescues and liberates beings bound to be killed.
One's goodness increases and never decreases.[91]
One well cultivates karmic works involving the sciences and skills,
Training in them oneself while also teaching them to others.

COMMENTARY:

Where there are those bound to be killed, one rescues them, causing them to be liberated. As for the causes and conditions of protecting life and the abandoning of killing beings, it is on account of adopting these sorts of karmic actions and growing close to them in practice throughout the long night of time that one becomes bound to gain the buddha body's mark of having long fingers, its mark of having heels which are level and upright, and its mark of having an erect body. Those are signs foretelling future enjoyment of a long lifespan.

When with respect to good dharmas which one has adopted, one thereafter sees to their subsequent increase and prevents them from decreasing, one becomes bound in the future to gain the buddha-body's mark of having high ankle bones shaped like shells, that together with its mark of having body hairs directed in the superior direction. Both of those are signs foretelling the future possession of undiminishing Dharma.

Well cultivating the treatises treating [both the esoteric and the mundane] sciences while also devoting oneself to karmic deeds involving the skills of the consummate craftsperson, one not only studies such subjects oneself, but also passes these teachings on to others. One thereby becomes bound to gain a buddha-body's mark of having calves like those of an *aiṇeya*, the black antelope. That is a sign foretelling the future ability to swiftly attract others to the Dharma.

於諸勝善法　　牢固而受之
修行四攝事　　施衣及飲食

[0536a10]　　於諸最勝善法。牢固受之。習近多作故。當得善安立足相。彼是能作事業先相。修行四攝布施愛語利行同事。常習近故。當得手足網相。彼亦是[2]速攝先相。以妙飲食衣服布施。常習近故。當得柔軟手足相七處高相。彼二是得上妙飲食甜味。及衣服等先相

不違乞求者　　和合諸親[3]感
眷屬不乖離　　施宅及財物

[0536a18]　　隨所有物。若來求者。即施不違逆故。當得臂[4]髀傭圓相彼是自在調伏先相。和合親眷朋友共住。不令各各乖異。

于诸胜善法　　牢固而受之
修行四摄事　　施衣及饮食

[0536a10]　　于诸最胜善法。牢固受之。习近多作故。当得善安立足相。彼是能作事业先相。修行四摄布施爱语利行同事。常习近故。当得手足网相。彼亦是[2]速摄先相。以妙饮食衣服布施。常习近故。当得柔软手足相七处高相。彼二是得上妙饮食甜味。及衣服等先相

不违乞求者　　和合诸亲[3]戚
眷属不乖离　　施宅及财物

[0536a18]　　随所有物。若来求者。即施不违逆故。当得臂[4]髀佣圆相彼是自在调伏先相。和合亲眷朋友共住。不令各各乖异。

---

107 – Firmly Adopt Good Dharmas and Cultivate the Four Means of Attraction

Adopt all of the supremely good dharmas,
Through persistent and solid practice.
Cultivate the four means of attraction,[92]
Making gifts of robes and food and drink.

COMMENTARY:

One adopts all of the most supreme sorts of good dharmas through persistent and solid practice. By becoming devoted to them and doing them many times, one becomes bound to gain a buddha-body's mark of solidly planted feet, a sign foretelling the future ability to carry out one's chosen work.

One cultivates the four means of attraction: giving, pleasing speech, beneficial actions, and joint endeavors. Through constant devotion to them, one becomes bound to gain a buddha-body's mark of having webbed junctions at the roots of the fingers and toes, another sign foretelling the future ability to swiftly attract others [to the Dharma].

Through constant devotion to making gifts of fine food, drink, and clothing, one becomes bound to gain a buddha-body's mark of soft hands and feet as well as its mark of the seven prominences. Both of those are signs foretelling the future inevitability that one will receive supremely fine and sweetly-flavored food and drink while also gaining clothing matching one's wishes.

---

108 – Be Generous to Almsmen, Unite Kin and Clan, Give Dwellings and Possessions

Do not turn away from those begging for alms.
Facilitate the uniting of close relatives.
Prevent estrangement between those of the same clan.
Make gifts of dwellings and of material possessions as well.

COMMENTARY:

When someone comes seeking something, one does not turn away from them but rather immediately responds by bestowing gifts befitting one's own resources. Through such actions, one becomes bound to gain a buddha-body's mark of straight and round arms and thighs, a sign foretelling the future possession of the ability to freely subdue [those who must be subdued].

Bringing together relatives, retinue, and friends so that they abide together in harmony and are prevented from becoming estranged

繁體字

若乖異者亦使和合故。當得陰密藏相。彼是多子先
相。布施舍宅財物。及施上妙床敷衣服堂殿宮等
故。當得金色相細滑薄皮相。彼二是得上妙床敷衣
服堂殿宮等先相

　父母及親友　　隨所應安置　　所應安置處　　無上自在主
[0536a27]　　憂波弟[5]邪夜([6]隋云近誦舊云和[7]上者略而訛)阿
遮利夜([＊]隋云正行舊云阿闍梨者亦訛)父母兄弟等。所尊
重者。隨所應處安置。為無上自在主故。當得一孔
一毛相白毫[8]印面相。彼二是平等先相

　雖復是奴僕　　善說亦受取　　應生最尊重　　施藥愈諸病
[0536b04]　　　施藥愈諸病者。於病人所。施藥給侍將息
飲食。以給侍將息。病即能起故。

簡体字

若乖异者亦使和合故。当得阴密藏相。彼是多子先
相。布施舍宅财物。及施上妙床敷衣服堂殿宫等
故。当得金色相细滑薄皮相。彼二是得上妙床敷衣
服堂殿宫等先相

　父母及亲友　　随所应安置　　所应安置处　　无上自在主
[0536a27]　　忧波弟[5]邪夜([6]隋云近诵旧云和[7]上者略而讹)阿
遮利夜([＊]隋云正行旧云阿闍梨者亦讹)父母兄弟等。所尊
重者。随所应处安置。为无上自在主故。当得一孔
一毛相白毫[8]印面相。彼二是平等先相

　虽复是奴仆　　善说亦受取　　应生最尊重　　施药愈诸病
[0536b04]　　　施药愈诸病者。于病人所。施药给侍将息
饮食。以给侍将息。病即能起故。

while also causing those already estranged to come together in harmony—these are the bases for gaining a buddha-body's mark of genital ensheathment, a sign foretelling the future possession of many [Dharma] sons.

Through giving dwellings, material possessions, supremely fine bedding, robes, halls, temple buildings and such, one gains a buddha-body's marks of a gold-colored appearance and smooth skin, both of which are signs foretelling future endowment with supremely fine bedding, robes, halls, temple buildings, and such.

---

109 – Provide for Parents, Relatives, and Friends Appropriately and Deferentially

As for one's father, mother, relatives, and friends,
Provide them circumstances befitting their station.
Wherever one has given them such a suitable situation,
Treat them as supreme and independent sovereigns.

COMMENTARY:

In the case of one's *upādhyāyas*, *ācāryas*, father, mother, elder and younger brothers, and other such persons to whom one extends reverential esteem—one provides for them whichever situation suits their particular circumstances. Through treating them as supreme and independent sovereigns of their own domains, one gains a buddha-body's mark of having a single hair in each hair pore along with the mark of having the countenance graced with the white-haired mark between the brows. Both of those are signs foretelling that one is bound in the future to be peerless.

---

110 – Servants Are Addressed with Kindness, Adopted, Esteemed, and Cared For

Although there may be yet others who are servants,
One speaks to them with goodness and, in effect, adopts them.
One should accord them the highest esteem
And provide them with medicines and treatment for all illnesses.

COMMENTARY:

As for "provide them with medicines and treatment for all illnesses," wherever the invalid abides, one gives them medicines, supplies their needs, and looks after them while also seeing that they are afforded rest as well as food and drink. Through supplying their needs, looking after them, and seeing that they are able to rest, treating them in a manner which allows the illness to quickly

當得[9]髀間平滿相味中上[10]味相。彼二是少病先相

　前行善業首　　　細滑美妙言

　　[11]善為正意語　　　前後無不供

[0536b09]　　　前行善業首者。園林會堂義井花池飲食花鬘。於難行處起橋。及造僧坊遊處等中。勸勵他人自為前導。所施過他故。當得尼瞿嚧陀普圓身相頂髻相。彼二是勝主先相。細滑美妙言者。長夜真實細滑語故。當得廣長舌相梵音相。彼二是得五分五分語道具足音先相。五分五分語道具足音者。一者可知。二者易解。三者樂聞。四者不逆。五者深。

当得[9]髀间平满相味中上[10]味相。彼二是少病先相

　前行善业首　　　细滑美妙言

　　[11]善为正意语　　　前后无不供

[0536b09]　　　前行善业首者。园林会堂义井花池饮食花鬘。于难行处起桥。及造僧坊游处等中。劝励他人自为前导。所施过他故。当得尼瞿嚧陀普圆身相顶髻相。彼二是胜主先相。细滑美妙言者。长夜真实细滑语故。当得广长舌相梵音相。彼二是得五分五分语道具足音先相。五分五分语道具足音者。一者可知。二者易解。三者乐闻。四者不逆。五者深。

let up, one gains a buddha-body's marks of having the area of the back between the shoulders even and of having the most superior sense of taste, both of which are signs foretelling a future wherein one encounters but little illness.

---

111 – Be Foremost in Good Karma, Sublime and Right in Speech, and Generous to All

Be the first to act, taking the lead in good karmic deeds,
Speaking with smooth and sublime words,
Being skillful in discourse guided by right intention,
And having no one above or below to whom gifts are not given.

COMMENTARY:

As for "Being the first to act, taking the lead in good karmic deeds," this refers to the giving of gardens, groves, and meeting halls, to the giving of wells, ponds graced by flower blossoms, food and drink, flowers, and garlands. It refers to erecting bridges where travel is difficult, to constructing buildings for the Sangha together with places where they can walk about, and to other such [acts of generosity]. One encourages others in such deeds as one personally pushes on ahead as a leader in these works.

Through giving which goes beyond the contributions of others, one gains a buddha body's marks of being round in one's girth like the *nyagrodha* tree, [the Indian fig], while also having the prominence on the crown of the head. Both of these are signs foretelling the future possession of the station of overlordship.

As for "speaking with smooth and sublime words," it is through employing throughout the long night of time discourse which is truthful and smooth that one gains a buddha body's marks of having a broad and long tongue, while also having a voice imbued with the "brahman sound." Both of these are signs foretelling future possession of the voice perfect in that speech which is graced by the two groups of five qualities.

As for the voice perfect in that speech which is graced by the two groups of five qualities, those qualities are that one's speech is:

1 – Intelligible.
2 – Easily understood.
3 – Delightful to hear.
4 – Non-repugnant.
5 – Deep in its profundity.

六者寬遠。七者無嫌。八者悅耳。九者辯正。十者
不[12]雜（二種五分故有十也）。善為正意語者。長夜
實語正意語故。當得師子牙相。彼是愛語先相。前
後無不供者。他人雖有前後。然皆供養無不供養。
以如法威儀平等威儀故。當得齊平齒相細滑齒相。
彼二是善淨眷屬先相

　　不壞他眷屬　　慈眼觀眾生
　　亦不以嫌心　　皆如善親友

[0536b25]　　於諸眾生。作懷抱慰喻攝受之心。以不貪
不瞋不癡眼觀故。當得青眼相牛王眼睫相。彼二是
愛眼觀先相

[0536b28]　　我已解釋三十二大丈夫相出生之業。別有
種種菩薩之行。今當解釋

六者宽远。七者无嫌。八者悦耳。九者辩正。十者
不[12]杂（二种五分故有十也）。善为正意语者。长夜
实语正意语故。当得师子牙相。彼是爱语先相。前
后无不供者。他人虽有前后。然皆供养无不供养。
以如法威仪平等威仪故。当得齐平齿相细滑齿相。
彼二是善净眷属先相

　　不坏他眷属　　慈眼观众生
　　亦不以嫌心　　皆如善亲友

[0536b25]　　于诸众生。作怀抱慰喻摄受之心。以不贪
不瞋不痴眼观故。当得青眼相牛王眼睫相。彼二是
爱眼观先相

[0536b28]　　我已解释三十二大丈夫相出生之业。别有
种种菩萨之行。今当解释

6 – Broad and far-reaching [in its import].
7 – Free of loathing.
8 – Pleasing.
9 – Eloquent in its correctness.
10 – Free of disconnected complexities.

As for "being skillful in discourse guided by right intention," it is because, throughout the long night of time, one employs discourse which is truthful and guided by right intention that one gains a buddha body's mark of having jaws like those of a lion, a sign foretelling the future inevitability that one will speak with pleasing words.

As for there being "no one above or below to whom gifts are not given," this means that, although there may be those of higher or lower station, he nonetheless makes gifts to all of them and never fails to give gifts to any particular one of them.

It is through comporting oneself in accordance with the Dharma while also comporting oneself in a way which is uniformly equal in the treatment of others that one gains a buddha-body's marks of having teeth which are uniformly even, and having teeth which are smooth, both of which are signs foretelling that in the future one will lead a following of those who are both good and pure.

---

112 – Avoid Harm or Disapproval; Regard Others with Kindness and as Good Friends

Avoid any harm to the retinue of others.
Instead regard beings with the eye of kindness.
Neither may one course in disapproving thoughts.
Instead treat everyone as a good relative or friend.

COMMENTARY:

In relating to all other beings, one maintains a mind that holds them dear, teaches them with kindness, draws them in, and accepts them. Through regarding them with an eye free of covetousness, hatefulness, or delusion, one gains a buddha-body's marks of possessing blue eyes and having eyelashes like the king of bulls. Both of those marks are signs foretelling one's future inclination to regard others with the eye of kindliness.[93]

I've finished explaining the karmic deeds producing the thirty-two marks of the great man. There are, aside from these, all sorts of other practices in which bodhisattvas course. I shall now explain those.

應當如所言　　即隨如是作
如言若即作　　他人則生信

[0536c03]　應當如言即如是作。若如所言即如是作。他則生信。隨有言教。即當信受

應當擁護法　　覺察放逸者
及作金寶網　　羅覆於支提

[0536c07]　於此法中應自擁護。若有背法放逸眾生。於彼亦應方便覺察令其向法。及於如來支提之所。應以種種寶網羅覆。為令相好滿足故

有欲求婇女　　莊嚴以施之
亦與說佛德　　及施雜光瓔

应当如所言　　即随如是作
如言若即作　　他人则生信

[0536c03]　应当如言即如是作。若如所言即如是作。他则生信。随有言教。即当信受

应当拥护法　　觉察放逸者
及作金宝网　　罗覆于支提

[0536c07]　于此法中应自拥护。若有背法放逸众生。于彼亦应方便觉察令其向法。及于如来支提之所。应以种种宝网罗覆。为令相好满足故

有欲求婇女　　庄严以施之
亦与说佛德　　及施杂光璎

ADDITIONAL PRACTICES TO BE ADOPTED AND ERRORS TO BE AVOIDED

113 – Act Straightaway in Conformity with Pronouncements, Thus Inspiring Faith

One should accord with the words he speaks,
Following them straightaway with concordant actions.
If one acts immediately in accordance with his words,
Others will be inclined then to develop faith.

COMMENTARY:

One should immediately follow up one's words with actions that correspond to them. If one immediately follows up one's words with directly concordant actions, then others will be moved to develop faith and will then consequently become inclined to immediately believe in and accept whichever teaching one thereafter chooses to bestow on them.

114 – Be Protective of Dharma, Observant of Neglect, and Inclined to Adorn Stupas

One should support and protect the Dharma,
And should discover any instances of neglect,
Even going so far as to build canopies graced by gold and jewels
Spreading over and covering the *caityas*.[94]

COMMENTARY:

One should be supportive and protective of this Dharma. Where there may be neglectful beings who have turned their backs on the Dharma, one should adopt skillful means for them as well, means whereby one might be made aware of such cases and then influence them to turn back toward the Dharma.

These [supportive and protective actions] should extend as well to those locations occupied by the *caityas* erected in honor of the Tathāgata wherein it would be appropriate to use all sorts of jewels to adorn a net-like canopy spreading out over and covering it. If one engages in such actions, then it will serve to bring about completeness and perfection in one's future buddha body's major marks and minor characteristics.

115 – Facilitate Marriages, Present the Bride, Praise the Buddha, and Give Mālās

For those wishing to obtain a maiden mate,
See to her adornment and assist in her presentation.
Speak to the parties about the qualities of the Buddha
And then give prayer beads gleaming in varying hues.

[0536c12]　　　若有求婇女者。即便莊嚴婇女。而以布施。此諸婇女普皆端正。以此布施。為令自意所求愛事皆滿足故。又以無量異種。說佛功德之法。應在集會之處。高出美妙悅意之聲。而為演說。為得諸聲分清淨故。又以種種光明照曜瓔珞之具。悅彼心眼而以布施。為得諸隨形好滿足故

　　造作佛形像　　　端坐勝蓮花
　　及於六法中　　　修習同喜樂

[0536c21]　　　以金銀真珠貝石等造作佛像。坐勝蓮花。為得化生。及為得佛身故。六種同喜法者。於彼同梵行中。慈身業口業意業。不分受用物。戒具足見具足。此等六種同喜法中。應數習近。為得徒眾。不被諸外論眾所壞故

[0536c12]　　　若有求婇女者。即便庄严婇女。而以布施。此诸婇女普皆端正。以此布施。为令自意所求爱事皆满足故。又以无量异种。说佛功德之法。应在集会之处。高出美妙悦意之声。而为演说。为得诸声分清净故。又以种种光明照曜瓔珞之具。悦彼心眼而以布施。为得诸随形好满足故

　　造作佛形像　　　端坐胜莲花
　　及于六法中　　　修习同喜乐

[0536c21]　　　以金银真珠贝石等造作佛像。坐胜莲花。为得化生。及为得佛身故。六种同喜法者。于彼同梵行中。慈身业口业意业。不分受用物。戒具足见具足。此等六种同喜法中。应数习近。为得徒众。不被诸外论众所坏故

COMMENTARY:

If there be one who seeks a maiden mate, one may facilitate the adornment of the maiden and see to her presentation. Such maidens in all cases are completely upright and proper. Through the giving involved in this, one brings on [the future effect of] complete fulfillment of whatever one dearly seeks.

Additionally, one should draw from the countless variety of ways to describe the fine qualities of the Buddha in proclaiming them to that assembly, holding forth with an elevated voice replete with lovely and sublime phrasings pleasing to the minds of [the couple and their guests]. Through doing this, one gains [in future lives] a voice pure in all its aspects.

Also, one bestows on them prayer beads made from fine stones gleaming with varying light and pleasing the mind's eye. Through this, one brings about the future effect of having [a buddha body] in which all of the fine subsidiary physical characteristics are entirely complete.

---

116 – Create Buddha Images and Cultivate the Six Dharmas of Community Harmony

Create images of the Buddha
Sitting upright atop supremely fine lotus blossoms
And cultivate common delight and happiness
Through adherence to the six dharmas of community harmony.[95]

COMMENTARY:

One uses gold, silver, pearls, alabaster, and other such materials to create images of the Buddha sitting atop supremely fine lotus blossoms. Through this one gains the future ability to generate transformation bodies and to gain the body of a buddha.

With respect to those joined together in the same community observing the brahman conduct (celibacy), one maintains kindness in one's physical karma, verbal karma, and mental karma. One does not maintain some separate [and unequal] share of items accepted for use [by the community at large]. One is completely correct in observance of the moral prohibitions and is completely correct as regards the views one maintains.

One should maintain continual devotion in one's practice to these six dharmas promoting common delight, this for the sake of enabling future acquisition of a retinue invulnerable to ruin by non-Buddhist traditions.

可供無不供　　為命亦不謗

佛之所說法　　及以說法人

[0536c28]　可供無不供者。於中應可供養。所謂[13]和上阿闍梨父母[14]兄等。無不供養者。無不敬畏。雖為活命。終不謗法及此說佛法人。亦不應謗。不應輕欺。為護自善助故

金寶散教師　　及教師支提

若有忘所誦　　與念令不失

[0537a05]　　應以金銀散於教師。亦應以摩尼金寶散教師寶支提。菩薩有三摩提。名現在佛對面。住此等三摩提。於生生中。現前修習為得聞持故。若有眾生忘失所誦引世利樂經書。於彼眾生。與作憶念。為不忘失菩提心故。及為得憶念現知故

可供无不供　　为命亦不谤

佛之所说法　　及以说法人

[0536c28]　可供无不供者。于中应可供养。所谓[13]和上阿闍梨父母[14]兄等。无不供养者。无不敬畏。虽为活命。终不谤法及此说佛法人。亦不应谤。不应轻欺。为护自善助故

金宝散教师　　及教师支提

若有忘所诵　　与念令不失

[0537a05]　　应以金银散于教师。亦应以摩尼金宝散教师宝支提。菩萨有三摩提。名现在佛对面。住此等三摩提。于生生中。现前修习为得闻持故。若有众生忘失所诵引世利乐经书。于彼众生。与作忆念。为不忘失菩提心故。及为得忆念现知故

---

117 – Make Offerings to All and Never Slander the Buddha or Teachers of Dharma

Of those who may be given offerings, none are not given offerings.
Even for the sake of preserving one's life, one still does not slander
The Dharma spoken by the Buddha
Or the person who expounds the Dharma.

COMMENTARY:

As for "among those who may be given offerings, there are none not given offerings," there should be those among them to whom one may make offerings, namely the *upādhyāyas* or the *ācāryas*, the parents, the elder brothers, or others of this sort. As for "there are none not given offerings," there are none before whom one does not feel reverence.

Even though it might be for the sake of preserving one's life, one would never slander the Dharma or this person who expounds the Buddha's Dharma. Nor should one ever slander, slight, or deceive such persons, either. This is on account of the need to preserve one's own bodhi requisites dependent on goodness.[96]

---

118 – Donate to Teaching Masters and Their Stupas, See to Preservation of Scripture

Gold and jewels are distributed among teaching masters
And also among the *caityas* of teaching masters.
If there are those who forget what is to be recited,
One assists their remembrance, enabling them to stay free of error.

COMMENTARY:

One should distribute gold and silver among the teaching masters and should distribute *maṇi* pearls, gold, and jewels among the bejeweled *caityas* of the teaching masters.

The bodhisattva possesses a samādhi known as "manifesting in the direct presence of the Buddhas." When one abides in samādhis of this sort, in life after life, this "direct presence" is cultivated for the sake of being able to hear and retain [the teachings in memory]. In such a case, if there happens to be some other being who has forgotten those scriptures which he recites, those which guide the world and which bestow benefit and happiness, then [such bodhisattvas] function as refreshers of memory for those beings. Through doing this they gain [future endowment with the ability to] not forget the mind resolved on bodhi and the ability to have that power of recall allowing awareness in the present.[97]

未思所作已　　勿躁勿隨他
外道天龍神　　於中皆莫信

[0537a13]　　所作業行。若身口意。於中諸處。若未思所作已。勿為躁急。亦勿隨他。應如是行。若異於此則生熱惱亦是悔因。於遊行出家尼[1]揵等諸外道及於天龍夜叉[*]揵闥婆等中。皆不應信

心應如金剛　　堪能通諸法
心亦應如山　　諸事所不動

[0537a20]　　安置其心應如金剛。有慧力堪能故。於諸世出世法中。如其自性如實通達。於諸事中安置其心。亦應如山。八種世法。所不能動

憙樂出世語　　莫樂依世言
自受諸功德　　亦應令他受

未思所作已　　勿躁勿隨他
外道天龙神　　于中皆莫信

[0537a13]　　所作业行。若身口意。于中诸处。若未思所作已。勿为躁急。亦勿随他。应如是行。若异于此则生热恼亦是悔因。于游行出家尼[1]揵等诸外道及于天龙夜叉[*]揵闼婆等中。皆不应信

心应如金刚　　堪能通诸法
心亦应如山　　诸事所不动

[0537a20]　　安置其心应如金刚。有慧力堪能故。于诸世出世法中。如其自性如实通达。于诸事中安置其心。亦应如山。八种世法。所不能动

憙乐出世语　　莫乐依世言
自受诸功德　　亦应令他受

119 – Let Reflection Precede Action; Have no Faith in Non-Buddhists, Gods, or Spirits

When one has not yet reflected on the right course of action,
One must not be impulsive and must not simply emulate others.
As for the non-Buddhists, gods, dragons, and spirits,
One must not invest one's faith in any of them.

COMMENTARY:

No matter what circumstance one is involved in, so long as one has not yet completely reflected on the right course of physical, verbal and mental karma, one must not act impetuously or become inclined to simply do what others do. One should ensure that one's practice hews to this precaution. If one deviates from this, then one will become involved in actions done in haste which later cause regret.

One should in all cases avoid developing any faith in the teachings of wandering monastics from any of the non-Buddhist traditions including the followers of the Nirgrantha order and such, and including as well the devotees of deities, dragons (*nāgas*), *yakṣas*, *gandharvas* and so forth.[98]

120 – Make the Mind Penetratingly Sharp Like Vajra and as Immovable as a Mountain

One's mind should be like vajra,
Able to penetrate all dharmas.
One's mind should also be like a mountain,
Remaining unmoved in any circumstance.

COMMENTARY:

In stabilizing one's mind it should be made like *vajra*. Because it possesses the power of wisdom, it penetratingly understands all worldly and world-transcending dharmas in accordance with their own nature and in accordance with reality.

In all circumstances, one establishes ones mind so that it is like a mountain. Thus it cannot be moved by any of the eight worldly dharmas.

121 – Delight in Transcendent Words, Abandon Worldly Talk, Inspire Merit in Others

Delight in world-transcending discourse
And do not take pleasure in worldly words.
Personally adopt all manner of meritorious qualities.
One should then influence others to adopt them as well.

繁體字

[0537a25] 或有言說能出世間。若與佛法僧相應。若與六度相應。若與菩薩地相應。若與聲聞獨覺地相應。彼中應作憙樂。或有言說依止世間。增長世間。與貪瞋癡相應。彼中不應喜樂。若有諸受戒學頭多等殊勝功德善人所讚所受取者。於彼等中皆應受取。亦應令他受此功德

　　修五解脫入　　　修十不淨想
　　八大丈夫覺　　　亦應分別修

[0537b05] 於中解脫入者。一者為他說法。二者自說法。三者自誦法。四者於法隨覺隨觀。五者取隨何等三摩提相。此是五解脫入。應當念修。十不淨想者。謂[2]膖脹想。青瘀想。膿爛想。潰出想。噉想。斷解想。

简体字

[0537a25] 或有言说能出世间。若与佛法僧相应。若与六度相应。若与菩萨地相应。若与声闻独觉地相应。彼中应作憙乐。或有言说依止世间。增长世间。与贪瞋痴相应。彼中不应喜乐。若有诸受戒学头多等殊胜功德善人所赞所受取者。于彼等中皆应受取。亦应令他受此功德

　　修五解脱入　　　修十不净想
　　八大丈夫觉　　　亦应分别修

[0537b05] 于中解脱入者。一者为他说法。二者自说法。三者自诵法。四者于法随觉随观。五者取随何等三摩提相。此是五解脱入。应当念修。十不净想者。谓[2]膖胀想。青瘀想。脓烂想。溃出想。噉想。断解想。

COMMENTARY:

There may be discourse conducing to transcending the world such as that relating to the Buddha, the Dharma, and the Sangha, such as that relating to the six perfections, such as that relating to the bodhisattva grounds, or such as that related to the grounds of the Śrāvakas and the Pratyekabuddhas. One *should* delight in that.

There may also be discourse related to the world and tending to increase one's worldliness, words related to desire, hatred, and delusion. One should *not* find delight in that.

Where there are all manner of especially superior meritorious qualities such as taking on the moral precepts and studying the *dhūta* (ascetic) practices, qualities such as are praised and adopted by good people—one should adopt all such qualities while also influencing others to adopt these meritorious qualities.[99]

---

122 – Cultivate Five Liberation Bases, Ten Impurity Reflections, Eight Realizations

Cultivate the five bases of liberation.
Cultivate the ten reflections on impurity.
The eight realizations of great men
Should also be the focus of analytic contemplation and cultivation.

COMMENTARY:

As for the bases of liberation, they are [gaining realization through]:

1 – Listening to Dharma as explained [for oneself] by others.
2 – Explaining Dharma [for others] oneself.
3 – Reciting the Dharma [from memory].
4 – Subjecting dharmas to [analytic contemplation through skillful use of] ideation (*vitarka*) and discursion (*vicāra*).
5 – Grasping specific aspects of a particular samādhi.

These are the five bases of liberation. One should bear them in mind and cultivate them.

As for "the ten reflections on impurity," this refers to:

1 – Reflection on the distended corpse
2 – Reflection on the corpse blue from stagnant blood.
3 – Reflection on the purulent, rotting corpse.
4 – Reflection on the oozing corpse.
5 – Reflection on the gnawed corpse.
6 – Reflection on the dismembered corpse.

繁體字

分散想。血塗想。肉落想。骨想。此是十不淨想。貪若生時應當念修。本為斷除欲貪故。八大丈夫覺亦應分別修者。於中有八大丈夫覺。謂少欲是法多欲非法。是為初覺。知足是法不知足非法。是為第二。遠離是法雜鬧非法。是為第三。發精進是法懈怠非法。是為第四。安住念是法忘失念非法。是為第五。入定是法不入定非法。是為第六。智慧是法無智慧非法。是為第七。不樂戲論是法樂戲論非法。是為第八。此等八大丈夫覺。應當覺之。多欲等八不善助。應當斷除

　　天耳與天眼　　　神足與他心
　　及與宿命住　　　應修淨五通

簡体字

分散想。血涂想。肉落想。骨想。此是十不净想。贪若生时应当念修。本为断除欲贪故。八大丈夫觉亦应分别修者。于中有八大丈夫觉。谓少欲是法多欲非法。是为初觉。知足是法不知足非法。是为第二。远离是法杂闹非法。是为第三。发精进是法懈怠非法。是为第四。安住念是法忘失念非法。是为第五。入定是法不入定非法。是为第六。智慧是法无智慧非法。是为第七。不乐戏论是法乐戏论非法。是为第八。此等八大丈夫觉。应当觉之。多欲等八不善助。应当断除

　　天耳与天眼　　　神足与他心
　　及与宿命住　　　应修净五通

7 – Reflection on the scattered corpse.
8 – Reflection on the blood-smeared corpse.
9 – Reflection on the mangled corpse.
10 – Reflection on the skeletal corpse.

These are the ten contemplations on impurity. When lust arises, one should bear them in mind and cultivate them. This is because they were originally set forth as a means to do away with sensual desire.[100]

As for, "The eight realizations of great men should also be the focus of analytic contemplation and cultivation," the eight realizations of great men refers to the following:

1 – Whereas but little desire is Dharma, an abundance of desire is non-Dharma. This is the first of the realizations.

2 – Whereas being easily satisfied is Dharma, not being easily satisfied is non-Dharma. This is the second.

3 – Whereas abiding at a distance from others is Dharma, miscellaneous bustling about is non-Dharma. This is the third.

4 – Whereas vigor is Dharma, indolence is non-Dharma. This is the fourth.

5 – Whereas abiding in mindfulness is Dharma, forgetting mindfulness is non-Dharma. This is the fifth.

6 – Whereas entry into meditative absorption is Dharma, the failure to enter meditative absorption is non-Dharma. This is the sixth.

7 – Whereas wisdom is Dharma, absence of wisdom is non-Dharma. This is the seventh.

8 – Whereas not finding enjoyment in frivolous discourse is Dharma, enjoying frivolous discourse is non-Dharma. This is the eighth.

These eight realizations of great men are worthy of one's own realization. As for the eight matters promoting what is not good, those involving "an abundance of desire" and the others, one should do away with them entirely.[101]

---

123 – Cultivate Purification in the Five Types of Spiritual Abilities

The heavenly ear, the heavenly eye,
The bases of spiritual powers, the cognition of others' thoughts,
And the cognition of past lives and abodes—
One should cultivate purification of these five spiritual abilities.

繁體字

[0537b22] 　於中天眼天耳憶念宿住知他心神足。此等五種智通。應當修習

[0537c07] 　問云何修習答

四神足為根　　欲進心思惟
四無量住持　　謂慈悲喜捨

[0537c10] 　於此四無量中。習近多作已。得心堪能。得心堪能已。便入初禪那。如是第二。如是第三。如是第四。彼得禪那已得身心輕。彼以身心輕具足故。出生入神通道。出生入神通道具足故。便生神足。謂若欲若精進若心若思惟。於中欲者向法。精進者成就法。心者於法觀察。思惟者於法善巧。彼菩薩於神通若信解若作用。其心自在。隨欲所行。以善成熟故。自根本住持故。諸處順行如風遍空。

简体字

[0537b22] 　于中天眼天耳忆念宿住知他心神足。此等五种智通。应当修习

[0537c07] 　问云何修习答

四神足为根　　欲进心思惟
四无量住持　　谓慈悲喜舍

[0537c10] 　于此四无量中。习近多作已。得心堪能。得心堪能已。便入初禅那。如是第二。如是第三。如是第四。彼得禅那已得身心轻。彼以身心轻具足故。出生入神通道。出生入神通道具足故。便生神足。谓若欲若精进若心若思惟。于中欲者向法。精进者成就法。心者于法观察。思惟者于法善巧。彼菩萨于神通若信解若作用。其心自在。随欲所行。以善成熟故。自根本住持故。诸处顺行如风遍空。

COMMENTARY:

One should cultivate the practice of the five types of penetrative spiritual knowledge gained through the heavenly eye, the heavenly ear, the remembrance of past lives and abodes, awareness of others thoughts, and the bases of spiritual power.[102]

Question: How does one go about cultivating their practice?
Response: (As below...)

---

124 – The Four Bases Are Their Root; the Four Immeasurables Govern Them

The four bases of spiritual powers comprise their root.
They are zeal, vigor, mental focus, and contemplative reflection.
The four immeasurables govern them.
They are kindness, compassion, sympathetic joy, and equanimity.

COMMENTARY:

With deepening and repeated cultivation of the four immeasurables, the mind's abilities are progressively realized. With this progression in realization of the mind's abilities, one enters the first dhyāna. So, too, with the second. So, too, with the third. And so, too, with the fourth dhyāna.[103]

After one has gained those dhyānas, the body and mind develop "lightness" (i.e. "pliancy," prasrabhi). On account of adequately realizing this lightness of body and mind, one develops the capacity to enter the path of the spiritual superknowledges (abhijñā).

Through developing the capacity to enter the path of the spiritual superknowledges, one then generates the bases of spiritual powers (ṛddhi pāda). This refers specifically to "zeal" (chanda), to "vigor" (vīrya), to "[focused] thought" (citta), and to contemplative reflection (mīmāṃsā).

Among these, "zeal" refers to tending toward a particular dharma, "vigor" refers to perfecting a particular dharma, "thought" refers to the probing contemplation of a particular dharma, and "contemplative reflection" refers to implementing skillfulness in a particular dharma.

As regards the spiritual superknowledges, the minds of those bodhisattvas develop sovereign mastery in both the associated faith and understanding and their implementation. This is because they skillfully accomplish whatever they wish to do while remaining fundamentally in control. In all situations, they pursue their activities just as readily as wind blows along through open space.

於中菩薩得四無量及四禪那已。若信解若作用。出生天眼。若諸天龍夜叉乾闥婆等。若學人及聲聞獨覺天眼於中獨有增上之力。清淨勝過光明勝過。上首勝過殊異勝過。其眼無礙世間色相麁細遠近。隨其所欲彼皆能見。如是聞天人畜生等聲。如是念知前世無邊無際。如是知他心與貪欲等俱乃至八萬四千差別。如是得無量神足。以得神足故。諸所應調伏眾生。悉令調伏

> 四界如毒蛇　　六入如空村
> 五眾如殺者　　應作如是觀

[0538a01]　　　長夜以諸樂具受用因緣。雖守護將息長養。此地等四界。而速疾發動。不知恩養。不可依怙。不可委信故。應當觀察猶如毒蛇。

于中菩萨得四无量及四禅那已。若信解若作用。出生天眼。若诸天龙夜叉乾闼婆等。若学人及声闻独觉天眼于中独有增上之力。清净胜过光明胜过。上首胜过殊异胜过。其眼无碍世间色相麁细远近。随其所欲彼皆能见。如是闻天人畜生等声。如是念知前世无边无际。如是知他心与贪欲等俱乃至八万四千差别。如是得无量神足。以得神足故。诸所应调伏众生。悉令调伏

> 四界如毒蛇　　六入如空村
> 五众如杀者　　应作如是观

[0538a01]　　　长夜以诸乐具受用因缘。虽守护将息长养。此地等四界。而速疾发动。不知恩养。不可依怙。不可委信故。应当观察犹如毒蛇。

After those bodhisattvas have realized the four immeasurable minds and the four dhyānas, those bodhisattvas develop the associated faith and understanding and implementation of the heavenly eye to the extent that its power becomes uniquely superior to that possessed by gods, dragons, yakṣas, śrāvaka-trainees, realized śrāvaka-disciples, and pratyekabuddhas. It is superior as regards purity, superior as regards illumination, superior as regards primacy, and superior as regards being especially distinctive in its capabilities. It is unimpeded in its ability to observe the forms and characteristic features of the world, including both the coarse and subtle, far and the near. They are in all cases able to see whatever they wish to see.

In this same manner, they become able, utilizing the heavenly ear, to hear the sounds of the gods, the sounds of the humans, and the sounds of the animals. So too, they become able to bring to mind and know previous existences, doing so in a manner which is limitless and unbounded. So too, they know the thoughts of others, including such motivations as covetousness and so forth, knowing them completely, even to the extent of being able to distinguish eighty-four thousand variations.

In this same manner, they realize an incalculable level of development of the bases of spiritual powers. Through realization of the spiritual powers, they are able to subdue whichever beings must be subdued.

---

125 – Regard Elements as Snakes, Senses as Empty Village, Aggregates as Assassins

The four elements are like poisonous serpents.
The six sense faculties are like an empty village.
The five aggregates are like assassins.
One should contemplate them in this way.

COMMENTARY:

Throughout the long night of time, even though one has guarded, rested, and raised these four elements of "earth" and such as the constituents of those material means through which happiness is enjoyed, they nonetheless remain precipitously hasty in their movements [expressed as disease, aging, and death]. They know no gratitude for one's nurturance of them. They cannot be depended upon and cannot be trusted. Therefore, one should contemplate them as being like poisonous snakes.

繁體字

以無主故。離我我所故。眼等諸入有六賊眾。逼惱
可畏故。應當觀察猶如空村。共和與物破壞打罰不
能遮障故。猶如殺者。於五受眾。應當日日如是觀
察

　重法及法師　　亦捨於法慳
　教師勿捲祕　　聽者勿散亂

[0538a10]　　於此有四種法。能生大智。應當受取。於
法及法師中應當尊重。亦捨法慳。隨所聞法隨所習
誦。為他演說。若有樂欲法者。教師勿為捲手祕
惜。聽者勿散亂。謂莫有異欲

　無慢無希望　　唯以悲愍心
　尊重恭敬意　　為眾而說法

簡体字

以无主故。离我我所故。眼等诸入有六贼众。逼恼
可畏故。应当观察犹如空村。共和与物破坏打罚不
能遮障故。犹如杀者。于五受众。应当日日如是观
察

　重法及法师　　亦舍于法悭
　教师勿卷秘　　听者勿散乱

[0538a10]　　于此有四种法。能生大智。应当受取。于
法及法师中应当尊重。亦舍法悭。随所闻法随所习
诵。为他演说。若有乐欲法者。教师勿为卷手秘
惜。听者勿散乱。谓莫有异欲

　无慢无希望　　唯以悲愍心
　尊重恭敬意　　为众而说法

Because they are devoid of any subjective agent and are unrelated to any self or possessions of a self, the [six] sense faculties consisting of the eye, [ear, nose, tongue, body] and so forth should be contemplated as like an empty village frequented by a band of six tormenting and fearsome insurgents.

Because the five appropriated aggregates manifest as united in phenomena through which one suffers destruction and punishment, it is as if they were assassins.

One should contemplate [the elements, sense faculties, and aggregates] in this very fashion each and every day.[104]

---

126 – Esteem Dharma and Its Teachers, Eschew Stinginess, Listen Closely to Dharma

Esteem the Dharma and the masters of Dharma
And also relinquish any stinginess with the Dharma.
The instructing masters must not be tight-fisted or secretive
And those listening must not be mentally scattered or confused.

COMMENTARY:

There are four types of dharmas herein which are able to generate great wisdom and which one should adopt:

1 – In the presence of the Dharma as well as the masters of Dharma, one should revere them.
2 – One should also relinquish any stinginess with the Dharma.
3 – Whatever Dharma one has heard and whatever Dharma one practices or recites, one should expounds upon it for others. Where there are those who delight in and desire the Dharma, instructors of Dharma must refrain from being tight-fisted or secretively cherishing.
4 – As for those who listen, they must not fall into mental scatteredness or confusion.

This is to say that one must not entertain any motivations at variance from what is right.

---

127 – Speak Dharma, Free of Arrogance or Hopes, Motivated Solely by Compassion

Free of arrogance and free of hopes,
Motivated solely by thoughts of compassion and pity,
With reverent and respectful mind,
Expound the Dharma for the community.

[0538a16] 復有四種法。是大智相。應當受取。所謂遠離自高輕他。無憍慢故。棄捨利養恭敬名聞。無希望心故。於無明闇障眾生中唯悲愍故。尊重恭敬為其說法。以此四種法故。菩薩大智具足。應當受取

> 於聞無厭足　　聞已皆誦持
> 不誑尊福田　　亦令師歡喜

[0538a23] 多聞無厭。聞已持法。持法已順法行法。不誑所尊福田。亦令教師歡喜此法。是菩提心不忘失因

> 不應觀他家　　心懷於敬養
> 勿以論難故　　習誦於世典

[0538a28] 不應為供養恭敬因緣往觀他家。

[0538a16] 复有四种法。是大智相。应当受取。所谓远离自高轻他。无憍慢故。弃舍利养恭敬名闻。无希望心故。于无明暗障众生中唯悲愍故。尊重恭敬为其说法。以此四种法故。菩萨大智具足。应当受取

> 于闻无厌足　　闻已皆诵持
> 不诳尊福田　　亦令师欢喜

[0538a23] 多闻无厌。闻已持法。持法已顺法行法。不诳所尊福田。亦令教师欢喜此法。是菩提心不忘失因

> 不应观他家　　心怀于敬养
> 勿以论难故　　习诵于世典

[0538a28] 不应为供养恭敬因缘往观他家。

COMMENTARY:

There are four additional dharmas here which are signs of great wisdom and which one should adopt. Specifically, these are:

1 – One abandons any tendency to elevate oneself while slighting others, this due to being entirely free of arrogance.
2 – One renounces any concern for offerings, reverence, or reputation, this due to being entirely free of thoughts freighted with yearning.
3 – When in the midst of beings hindered by the darkness of ignorance, one feels only compassion and pity.
4 – Maintaining a reverential and respectful frame of mind, one proceeds to explain the Dharma for their benefit.

Through these four dharmas, the bodhisattva perfects great wisdom. One should adopt them in one's practice.

---

128 – Be Insatiable in Learning, Don't Deceive the Venerables, Please Instructors

Be insatiable in learning
And always recite and retain what has been learned.
Do not deceive any among the venerable fields of merit.
Moreover, cause one's instructors to be delighted.

COMMENTARY:

In pursuit of abundant learning, one remains free of any sense of weariness. Having heard the teachings, retain that dharma. Having retained that dharma, act in accordance with that dharma and integrate that dharma into the practice. Do not deceive those who are the revered "fields of merit."[105] What's more, cause the teaching master to be delighted. These are karmic causes for never forgetting the mind resolved on bodhi.

---

129 – Don't Pay Visits for Gifts or Respect, Don't Study Worldly Texts for Debate

One should not pay visits to the houses of others
With a mind cherishing reverence or offerings.
One must not take up study and recitation of worldly texts
For the sake of debating challenging topics.

COMMENTARY:

One should not pay visits to the homes of others motivated by the wish to receive offerings and reverence, but rather should not

除為安立菩提心因緣。亦不應欲為論難故習誦諸世
論等。除為多聞因緣

　　勿以瞋恚故　　　毀呰諸菩薩
　　未受未聞法　　　亦勿生誹謗

[0538b04]　何以故。為護續生善法因緣

　　斷除於憍慢　　　當住四聖種
　　勿嫌於他人　　　亦勿自高舉

[0538b07]　　斷除憍慢者。於諸眾生中。當下心如狗斷
除我慢。於輕儉衣食臥床藥具四聖種中亦應當住。
於彼聖種知足故。不應嫌他。亦不應自高舉

　　若實不實犯　　　不得發覺他
　　勿求他錯失　　　自錯當覺知

除为安立菩提心因缘。亦不应欲为论难故习诵诸世
论等。除为多闻因缘

　　勿以瞋恚故　　　毁呰诸菩萨
　　未受未闻法　　　亦勿生诽谤

[0538b04]　何以故。为护续生善法因缘

　　断除于憍慢　　　当住四圣种
　　勿嫌于他人　　　亦勿自高举

[0538b07]　　断除憍慢者。于诸众生中。当下心如狗断
除我慢。于轻俭衣食卧床药具四圣种中亦应当住。
于彼圣种知足故。不应嫌他。亦不应自高举

　　若实不实犯　　　不得发觉他
　　勿求他错失　　　自错当觉知

go forth except where it may serve as a cause facilitating someone's generation of the resolve to realize bodhi.

Nor should one indulge in taking up the study and recitation of worldly treatises and such simply out of a desire to debate challenging topics. One should not initiate these sorts of studies except where doing so will be able to serve as a causal basis facilitating extensive learning.

---

130 – Don't Defame Bodhisattvas or Slander Dharmas Not Yet Understood

One must not be provoked by hatefulness or anger
Into defaming any bodhisattva.
As for dharmas not yet received or learned,
One must not initiate slanders in those cases either.

COMMENTARY:

Why not? In order to preserve the continuous production of good dharmas.

---

131 – Sever Arrogance, Abide in the Lineage Bases, Avoid Disapproving, Halt Conceit

In order to cut off arrogance and pride,
One should abide in the four lineage bases of the ārya.
One must not course in disapproval of others
And must not allow oneself to become conceited.

COMMENTARY:

As for "cutting off arrogance and pride," one should abide among beings with the mind "lowered" as one might were one but a dog, this to cut off self pride. One should also abide in the four lineage bases of the ārya wherein one looks lightly on and tends toward frugality in matters having to do with robes, food, bedding and medicines, this because, in the lineage bases of the ārya, one is easily satisfied. One should not be inclined to course in disapproval of others and one should also not allow oneself to become conceited.[106]

---

132 – Don't Expose Others' Offenses or Find Fault, Be Aware of One's Own Errors

Whether or not someone has actually committed a transgression,
One must not reveal his situation to others.
Do not seek out the errors and faults of anyone else.
Rather one should become aware of one's own errors.

[0538b13] 他同梵行者犯罪。若實若不實。皆不應發覺。他有錯失不應求覓。唯於自錯。即應覺知

佛及諸佛法　　不應分別疑
法雖最難信　　於中應信之

[0538b17] 於佛不應分別。以世尊具足未曾有法故。亦於佛法不應疑惑。以於諸眾生是不共法故。及於最難信佛法中。以深心清淨故。應當信之

雖由實語死　　退失轉輪王
及以諸天王　　唯應作實語

[0538b23] 若菩薩由實語故。若奪物若死。雖退失轉輪王及諸天王。唯應實語。何況其餘而不實語

[0538b13] 他同梵行者犯罪。若实若不实。皆不应发觉。他有错失不应求觅。唯于自错。即应觉知

佛及诸佛法　　不应分别疑
法虽最难信　　于中应信之

[0538b17] 于佛不应分别。以世尊具足未曾有法故。亦于佛法不应疑惑。以于诸众生是不共法故。及于最难信佛法中。以深心清净故。应当信之

虽由实语死　　退失转轮王
及以诸天王　　唯应作实语

[0538b23] 若菩萨由实语故。若夺物若死。虽退失转轮王及诸天王。唯应实语。何况其馀而不实语

COMMENTARY:

In instances where someone else also devoted [through monastic vows] to the brahman conduct (celibacy) might have committed a karmic offense, no matter whether or not any sort of offense was actually committed, one must nonetheless never expose these sorts of situations.[107] Where there are others who have erred or have faults, one should not seek them out. One should instead be concerned solely with one's own errors and should immediately become aware of those.

---

133 – Avoid Criticism or Doubt Toward Buddha or Dharma, Keep Faith in the Abstruse

One should refrain from biased judgments and doubting
In fathoming the Buddha and the Dharma of the Buddhas.
Even though a dharma may be extremely difficult to believe,
One should nonetheless maintain faith in it.

COMMENTARY:

One should not indulge discriminating thought as the means to understand the Buddha, this because the Bhagavān is equipped with dharmas unprecedented [in the common man's direct experience]. Additionally, one should not employ doubt-derived delusions as means to fathom the dharmas of the Buddha, this because these are dharmas not held in common with any other beings.[108] Even in the case of the most difficult to believe dharmas of a buddha, one should maintain faith in them purified through a basis in profound thought.

---

134 – Even Though One May Be Put to Death, One Should Still Speak Only the Truth

Even though one might be put to death for speaking the truth,
Or might be forced to abdicate the throne of a universal monarch,
Or even that of a king among the gods,
One should still utter only truthful speech.

COMMENTARY:

If on account of speaking the truth, a bodhisattva is liable to the confiscation of his possessions or to execution—although he might be caused to retreat from the position of a wheel-turning king (cakravarti-rāja) or the position as a king of the gods—he should still speak only the truth. How much the less might he fail to speak the truth in other circumstances.

打罵恐殺縛　　終不怨責他
皆是我自罪　　業報故來現

[0538b27]　　諸有他來打罵恐怖殺縛幽閉。皆是自罪應
當有此。終不瞋他。此是我業前世已作。今時還受
相似不愛之果。彼諸眾生都無有罪。唯是我罪業報
來現。應當有此

應極尊重愛　　供養於父母
亦給侍[1]和上　　恭敬阿闍梨

[0538c04]　　　　於父母所。應當極愛尊重供養。應作天
想。隨父母意令得悅樂。離諂幻心。又應恭敬給侍
和上阿闍梨。隨和上阿闍梨所說法中。無有內祕。
皆為外化

打骂恐杀缚　　终不怨责他
皆是我自罪　　业报故来现

[0538b27]　　诸有他来打骂恐怖杀缚幽闭。皆是自罪应
当有此。终不瞋他。此是我业前世已作。今时还受
相似不爱之果。彼诸众生都无有罪。唯是我罪业报
来现。应当有此

应极尊重爱　　供养于父母
亦给侍[1]和上　　恭敬阿闍梨

[0538c04]　　　　于父母所。应当极爱尊重供养。应作天
想。随父母意令得悦乐。离谄幻心。又应恭敬给侍
和上阿闍梨。随和上阿闍梨所说法中。无有内秘。
皆为外化

繁體字

简体字

135 – Even if Beaten, Cursed, or Terrorized, Don't Hate or Condemn; See It as Karma

Even if beaten, cursed, or terrorized with death threats or captivity,
One must not hate or condemn others, but should instead reflect:
"This is all the product of my own karmic offenses.
This has happened as a result of karmic retribution."

COMMENTARY:

In all instances where others come and beat one up, curse, ter-
rorize one with death threats or tie one up, holding one in captivity,
this is all a result of one's own previous karmic offenses. Hence it
is only fitting that one should have these things occur. One must
not generate hatred for anyone else, [but rather should reflect in
this manner]: "This is just my karma. I already took part in these
actions in earlier lifetimes. Now, in return, I undergo a similarly
undesirable karmic result.

"As for those beings [who are doing this to me], they are all free
of any karmic offense in this. This is simply a case of karmic retribution for my offenses now coming forth. It is only fitting that such
things should happen to me now."

136 – Support Parents Generously, Serve the Needs of Monastic Instructors as Well

One should, with the most ultimate respect and affection,
Provide offerings in support of one's father and mother.
Also supply the needs of and serve the *upādhyāyas*,
While extending reverence to the *ācāryas* as well.

COMMENTARY:

Wherever one's parents abide, one should, with extreme affection and respectfulness, provide offerings to support them. One
should look upon them as deities and, adapting to their wishes,
cause them to be pleased. In this, one must abandon any thoughts
involving flattery or deceptiveness.

One should also revere, supply the needs of, and serve the
upādhyāyas and *ācāryas* as well. One should accord with those
principles in the dharmas taught by those *upādhyāyas* and *ācāryas*
whereby one remains free of any sort of inward secretiveness [lead-
ing one to hold back Dharma from others]. In all circumstances, one
should instead devote all of one's efforts to facilitating the teaching
of others.[109]

為信聲聞乘　　及以獨覺乘
說於最深法　　此是菩薩錯

[0538c10]　　此中菩薩。有四種菩薩錯失。應當捨離。所謂於聲聞獨覺乘諸眾生中。為說最深之法。是菩薩錯

為信深大乘　　眾生而演說
聲聞獨覺乘　　此亦是其錯

[0538c15]　　於信深大乘諸眾生中。為說聲聞獨覺乘。是菩薩錯

大人來求法　　慢緩不為說
而反攝受惡　　委任無信者

[0538c19]　　若有正住大眾生。來有所求時。應即為說善法。而更慢緩破戒惡法。反攝受之。是菩薩錯。

為信声闻乘　　及以独觉乘
说于最深法　　此是菩萨错

[0538c10]　　此中菩萨。有四种菩萨错失。应当舍离。所谓于声闻独觉乘诸众生中。为说最深之法。是菩萨错

为信深大乘　　众生而演说
声闻独觉乘　　此亦是其错

[0538c15]　　于信深大乘诸众生中。为说声闻独觉乘。是菩萨错

大人来求法　　慢缓不为说
而反摄受恶　　委任无信者

[0538c19]　　若有正住大众生。来有所求时。应即为说善法。而更慢缓破戒恶法。反摄受之。是菩萨错。

FOUR-FOLD BODHISATTVA PATH FACTORS
FOUR BODHISATTVA ERRORS

137 – Discoursing on Profound Dharmas for Two-Vehicles Practitioners Is an Error

When, for those who place their faith in the Śrāvaka Vehicle
Or those dedicated to the Pratyekabuddha Vehicle,
One discourses on the most profound of dharmas,
This, for a bodhisattva, is an error.

COMMENTARY:

Starting here, we have four types of bodhisattva practice errors which should be abandoned by the bodhisattva. Specifically, it is a bodhisattva error to discourse on the most profound sorts of dharmas in the midst of beings dedicated to cultivation of either the Śrāvaka Vehicle or Pratyekabuddha Vehicle.[110]

138 – Discoursing on Two-Vehicles Tenets to the Great-Vehicle Faithful is an Error

When, for believers in the profound Great Vehicle teachings,
One discourses to those beings
On the Śrāvaka or Pratyekabuddha vehicles,
This too is an error for him.

COMMENTARY:

When, in the midst of beings believing in the profound Great Vehicle teachings, one discourses for them on the Śrāvaka and Pratyekabuddha vehicles, this is a bodhisattva error.[111]

139 – The Two Other Errors: Failing to Teach the Worthy, Trusting Wrongdoers

So too where some superior person comes seeking the Dharma,
But one delays and fails to provide him with teachings.
So too where, on the contrary, one takes in wrongdoers
Or delegates responsibilities to those who are untrustworthy.

COMMENTARY:

When an upstanding superior person comes requesting instruction, one should immediately discourse on good dharmas for his benefit. In this case, one fails to do so and, beyond that, delays.

When a person comes who is a transgressor against the moral precepts and who courses in evil dharmas and one takes just the opposite course of action by taking them in, this is a bodhisattva practice error.

於大乘中未有信解。未以四攝事成熟者。而信任
之。是菩薩錯。是為四種

　　遠捨所說錯　　　所說頭多德
　　於彼當念知　　　亦皆應習近

[0538c25]　　此中所說四種錯失。應遠捨離。以此去菩
提遠故。若聲聞獨覺乘中所說。頭多等及餘功德。
但知彼等不與菩提作障礙者。於彼彼中。亦應習近

　　等心平等說　　　平等善安立
　　亦令正相應　　　諸眾生無別

[0539a02]　　此四種菩薩道。應當習近。何等為四。所
謂諸眾生中起平等心。諸眾生中平等說法。諸眾生
中平等善安立。諸眾生中令正相應。

于大乘中未有信解。未以四摄事成熟者。而信任
之。是菩萨错。是为四种

　　远舍所说错　　　所说头多德
　　于彼当念知　　　亦皆应习近

[0538c25]　　此中所说四种错失。应远舍离。以此去菩
提远故。若声闻独觉乘中所说。头多等及馀功德。
但知彼等不与菩提作障碍者。于彼彼中。亦应习近

　　等心平等说　　　平等善安立
　　亦令正相应　　　诸众生无别

[0539a02]　　此四种菩萨道。应当习近。何等为四。所
谓诸众生中起平等心。诸众生中平等说法。诸众生
中平等善安立。诸众生中令正相应。

In this latter case, we speak of a person who has not yet developed faith in or understanding of the Great Vehicle. He has not yet been spiritually matured through skillful use of the four means of attraction (giving, pleasing words, beneficial actions, joint endeavors). Nonetheless, one trusts him and even goes so far as to delegate responsibilities to him. This is a bodhisattva practice error.

These [errors brought up in these three *ślokas*] are four types of bodhisattva practice errors.[112]

---

140 – Abandon These Errors While Also Studying and Adopting the *Dhūta* Practices

One must abandon the errors mentioned above.
As for such herein-described meritorious practices as the *dhūtas*,
One ought to become knowledgeable about them
And then incorporate them into one's own practice.

COMMENTARY:

The four kinds of errors and faults described herein are such as one should abandon, this because they diverge far from bodhi. As for the previously-mentioned practices from within the Śrāvaka and Pratyekabuddha vehicles, including the *dhūta* practices and other such meritorious practices, one should at least realize that practices of those sorts present no obstacle to bodhi. One should also incorporate each one of them into one's own practice.[113]

FOUR TYPES OF BODHISATTVA PATH PRACTICES

---

141 – Maintain Four Types of Uniformly Equal Bodhisattva Path Practices

Regard all equally in one's thoughts, speak equally for all,
Be uniformly equal in establishing all others in goodness,
And influence them all equally to accord with what is right.
Thus one refrains from making distinctions between any beings.

COMMENTARY:

These four types of bodhisattva path practices should be closely cultivated. What are the four? They are:

1 – Uniform equality in thought raised toward all other beings.
2 – Uniform equality in discoursing on Dharma for all beings.
3 – Uniform equality in establishing all beings in goodness.
4 – [Uniform equality] in influencing all beings to act in accordance with what is right.

此等皆無差別。是為四種

　為法不為利　　為德不為名

　欲脫眾生[1]苦　　不欲自身樂

[0539a08]　　此四種真實菩薩。應當覺知。何等為四。所謂但為於法不為財利。但為功德不為名稱。但欲脫眾生苦。不欲自身安樂

　密意求業果　　所作福事生

　亦為成熟眾　　捨離於自事

[0539a13]　　若於業果密意欲求。作三福事。生此福時。唯為菩提利樂眾生。亦唯為菩提成熟於眾。為利眾故捨離自事。此是四種真實菩薩

此等皆无差别。是为四种

　为法不为利　　为德不为名

　欲脱众生[1]苦　　不欲自身乐

[0539a08]　　此四种真实菩萨。应当觉知。何等为四。所谓但为于法不为财利。但为功德不为名称。但欲脱众生苦。不欲自身安乐

　密意求业果　　所作福事生

　亦为成熟众　　舍离于自事

[0539a13]　　若于业果密意欲求。作三福事。生此福时。唯为菩提利乐众生。亦唯为菩提成熟于众。为利众故舍离自事。此是四种真实菩萨

In all such matters, one avoids making discriminating distinctions [between beings]. These are the four types [of bodhisattva path practices].[114]

FOUR TYPES OF GENUINE BODHISATTVAS

142 – One Works for Dharma Over Benefit, Good Over Fame, Beings Over Happiness

One works for the sake of Dharma and not for self-benefit.
One works to develop meritorious qualities, not for renown.
One wishes to liberate beings from suffering
And does not wish merely to ensure his own happiness.

COMMENTARY:

These [two *ślokas*] deal with these four types of genuine bodhisattvas about which one should be aware. What are those four? This refers to:

1) Those who work only for Dharma and do not concern themselves with material benefit.

2) Those who work only for the sake of developing meritorious qualities and not for the sake of gaining a reputation.

3) Those who work only out of a wish to liberate beings from suffering and not simply to achieve happiness for themselves.

143 – One Works in Secret for the Many and so Relinquishes Personal Concerns

With purposes kept secret, one seeks fruition in one's works.
When the results of one's merit-generating endeavors come forth,
Even then, one applies them to the ripening of the many
While abandoning preoccupation with one's own concerns.

COMMENTARY:

4) This refers to a case where, keeping one's intentions to oneself, one strives to bring about the fruition of one's karmic works. Thus one courses in the three types of merit-generating circumstances.[115] Then, once the merit associated with this begins to manifest, it is applied solely to the goal of realizing bodhi and its ability to bring about the benefit and happiness of beings. And it is also applied solely to the goal of realizing bodhi with its ability to bring about the ripening of the community as a whole. Because it is devoted to the benefit of the community as a whole, one abandons any preoccupation with one's own concerns. These are the four types of genuine bodhisattvas.[116]

繁體字

親近善知識　　所謂法師佛
勸勵出家者　　及以乞求輩

[0539a18] 此四種菩薩善知識。應當親近。何等為四。
所謂法師是菩薩善知識。為助持聞慧故。佛世尊是
菩薩善知識。為助持諸佛法故。勸出家者是菩薩善
知識。為助持諸善根故。乞求者是菩薩善知識。為
助持菩提心故。此四種菩薩善知識。應當親近

依止世論者　　專求世財者
信解獨覺乘　　及以聲聞乘

[0539a26] 　　此四種菩薩惡知識。應當知之。何等為
四。

简体字

亲近善知识　　所谓法师佛
劝励出家者　　及以乞求辈

[0539a18] 此四种菩萨善知识。应当亲近。何等为四。
所谓法师是菩萨善知识。为助持闻慧故。佛世尊是
菩萨善知识。为助持诸佛法故。劝出家者是菩萨善
知识。为助持诸善根故。乞求者是菩萨善知识。为
助持菩提心故。此四种菩萨善知识。应当亲近

依止世论者　　专求世财者
信解独觉乘　　及以声闻乘

[0539a26] 　　此四种菩萨恶知识。应当知之。何等为
四。

FOUR TYPES OF GOOD SPIRITUAL FRIENDS FOR A BODHISATTVA

144 – Grow Close to the Four Types of Good Spiritual Friends

Grow close to good spiritual friends,
Specifically, to the masters of Dharma, to the Buddhas,
To those who encourage one to leave the home life,
And to those who are seekers of alms.

COMMENTARY:

These are four categories of individuals who serve as "good spiritual friends" (kalyāṇamitra) for the bodhisattva. One should grow close to them. What are the four categories? This refers to:

1 – The Dharma masters (i.e. learned monks who teach Dharma). They are good spiritual friends for the bodhisattva because they provide assistance with developing the wisdom which comes from learning [about the Dharma].

2 – The Buddhas, the Bhagavāns. They are good spiritual friends for the bodhisattva because they are the ones providing the assistance of preserving the Dharma of all buddhas.

3 – Those who encourage one to abandon the home life serve as good spiritual friends for the bodhisattva because they provide assistance with maintaining one's roots of goodness.

4 – Those who seek alms. They are good spiritual friends for the bodhisattva because they provide assistance with maintaining the [altruistic] mind resolved on realizing bodhi.

These four kinds of good spiritual friends of the bodhisattva are those to whom one should draw near.[117]

FOUR TYPES OF UNSUITABLE SPIRITUAL FRIENDS FOR A BODHISATTVA

145 – Lokāyatas, Wealth Obsessives, Pratyekabuddha and Śrāvaka Vehicles Advocates

Those who ground themselves in worldly treatises,
Those who exclusively seek worldly wealth,
Those with Pratyekabuddha Vehicle faith and understanding,
And those devoted to the Śrāvaka Vehicle—

COMMENTARY:

These are four categories of individuals who would function as unwholesome spiritual friends for a bodhisattva. One should be aware of them as such. What are these four specific categories? This refers to:

所謂世論者。習近種種雜辯才故。攝世財物者。不攝法故。獨覺乘者。少義利少作事故。聲聞乘者。自利行故

　　此四惡知識　　菩薩應當知

　　復有應求者　　所謂四大藏

[0539b03]　　如前所說四種知識。是惡知識知已應離。復有應求得者。所謂四大藏

　　佛出聞諸度　　及於法師所

　　見之心無礙　　樂住空閑處

[0539b07]　　此四種菩薩大藏。應當得之。何等為四。所謂奉事出世諸佛聽聞六波羅蜜。以無礙心見於法師。以不放逸樂住空閑之處。

所谓世论者。习近种种杂辩才故。摄世财物者。不摄法故。独觉乘者。少义利少作事故。声闻乘者。自利行故

　　此四恶知识　　菩萨应当知

　　复有应求者　　所谓四大藏

[0539b03]　　如前所说四种知识。是恶知识知已应离。复有应求得者。所谓四大藏

　　佛出闻诸度　　及于法师所

　　见之心无碍　　乐住空闲处

[0539b07]　　此四种菩萨大藏。应当得之。何等为四。所谓奉事出世诸佛听闻六波罗蜜。以无碍心见于法师。以不放逸乐住空闲之处。

1 – Those whose associations are with worldly treatises (the Lokāyatas), this because their practice involves all kinds of clever rhetoric on miscellaneous topics.

2 – Those who focus on accumulating worldly wealth and possessions, this because they do not focus on Dharma.

3 – Those of the Pratyekabuddha Vehicle this because they bestow but little in the way of meaning-based benefit on others and because they do but little in the way of [good] works.

4 – Those of the Śrāvaka Vehicle this because their practice is devoted to self-benefit.[118]

---

146 – Be Aware of Them As Unfit Spiritual Friends, Seek Out the Four Vast Treasuries

As for these four types of bad spiritual friends,
The bodhisattva should be aware of them as such.
There are, however, other circumstances one should seek out.
This refers specifically to the four vast treasuries:

COMMENTARY:

Those belonging to the four types of spiritual friends described above would function as bad spiritual friends [for a bodhisattva practitioner]. Once one has realized this, one should withdraw [from taking them on as spiritual friends].

There are additional circumstances which one should aspire to bring about, namely the "four vast treasuries." (See next *śloka.*)[119]

FOUR VAST TREASURIES

147 – Meeting Buddhas, Perfections Teachings, Dharma Masters, Solitary Practice

The emergence of buddhas; hearing the perfections explained;
Being able in the presence of a master of Dharma
To behold him with unobstructed mind;
And happily pursuing cultivation in a place of solitude.

COMMENTARY:

One should strive to obtain these four types of vast bodhisattva treasuries. What are the four? They are:

1 – Serving the Buddhas when they come forth into the world.

2 – Listening to explanations of the six pāramitās.

3 – Beholding a master of Dharma with unobstructed mind.

4 – Abiding happily in a place of solitude while remaining free of neglectfulness.

此是四種菩薩大藏。應當得之

　　地水火風空　　　悉與其相似
　　一切處平等　　　利益諸眾生

[0539b13]　　　與地水火風虛空等。有二因緣相似菩薩。應當攝受。所謂平等故。利益故。如地等大及虛空五種。於有心無心中一切處平等。無有異相。諸眾生等[2]常所資用。而無變異不求報恩。我亦如是。乃至覺場究竟。為諸眾生之所資用。而無變異不求報恩

　　當善思惟義　　　勤生陀羅尼
　　勿於聽法者　　　為作於障礙

[0539b21]　　　義者。佛所說義。於彼當善思惟。若共談若獨住。應如是作。又安住禁戒清淨心意。

此是四种菩萨大藏。应当得之

　　地水火风空　　　悉与其相似
　　一切处平等　　　利益诸众生

[0539b13]　　　与地水火风虚空等。有二因缘相似菩萨。应当摄受。所谓平等故。利益故。如地等大及虚空五种。于有心无心中一切处平等。无有异相。诸众生等[2]常所资用。而无变异不求报恩。我亦如是。乃至觉场究竟。为诸众生之所资用。而无变异不求报恩

　　当善思惟义　　　勤生陀罗尼
　　勿于听法者　　　为作于障碍

[0539b21]　　　义者。佛所说义。于彼当善思惟。若共谈若独住。应如是作。又安住禁戒清净心意。

These are the four kinds of vast bodhisattva treasuries. One should strive to obtain them.[120]

ADDITIONAL BODHISATTVA PRACTICE ESSENTIALS

148 – Abide Like the Elements, Uniformly Equal in Benefiting All

Abide in a manner comparable to
Earth, water, fire, wind, and space,
Remaining thus uniformly equal under all circumstances
In providing benefit to all beings.

COMMENTARY:

There are two respects in which one may be like earth, water, fire, wind, and space. The bodhisattva should integrate them. Specifically, they are as regards their being uniformly equally available and also as regards their being beneficial.

For example, the five elemental entities comprised by earth, the other great elements, and space—these are all uniformly equal and free of any aspect whereby they manifest differently among all things, whether those things be possessed of mind or devoid of mind. Thus all beings always remain able to put them to use. In this, those elements still do not undergo any fundamental change, nor do they seek any reward in return for their kindnesses.

One reflects, "I too should be just like this even up to that point when I finally reach the site of the enlightenment, remaining all the while available for the use of all beings, not changing in response to that and not seeking any reward for any kindnesses bestowed."

149 – Reflect on Meanings, Progress in Uses of *Dhāraṇīs*, Don't Block Dharma Study

One should skillfully reflect upon the meanings
And diligently progress in the uses of the *dhāraṇīs*.
One must never create any sort of obstruction
To those seeking to hear the Dharma.

COMMENTARY:

As for "the meanings," this refers to the meanings of what was taught by the Buddha. One should skillfully reflect upon them, whether it be through joint discussion or whether it be while abiding in solitude. One should proceed in this manner.

Additionally, one should abide with stability in the purity of mind instilled by the restrictive prohibitions. Remaining intensely

精勤鮮潔當生及聞銀主海主等陀羅尼。又於聽法者
所。勿以微少因緣而作障礙。為離法災生業故

　惱中能調伏　小事捨無餘　八種懈怠事　皆亦應除斷

[0539b28] 惱中能調伏者。於中有九種惱事。所謂於我
作無利益。已作今作當作。是為三種。於我親愛作
無利益。已作今作當作。復為三種。於我憎嫌與作
利益。已作今作當作。復為三種。此等皆作惱事。
於此九種惱事之中。當自調伏。小事捨無餘者。於
中有二十種小事。所謂不信(一)無慚(二)諂幻(三)掉(
四)亂(五)放逸(六)害(七)無愧(八)懈怠(九)憂(十)昏(十一舊
睡)睡(十二舊眠)恨(十三)覆(十四)嫉(十五)慳(十六)高(十七)忿
(十八)悔(十九)悶(二十)。此等二十種小事。皆捨無餘。
八種懈怠事皆亦應除斷者。於中有八種懈怠事。

精勤鮮洁当生及闻银主海主等陀罗尼。又于听法者
所。勿以微少因缘而作障碍。为离法灾生业故

　恼中能调伏　小事舍无馀　八种懈怠事　皆亦应除断

[0539b28] 恼中能调伏者。于中有九种恼事。所谓于我
作无利益。已作今作当作。是为三种。于我亲爱作
无利益。已作今作当作。复为三种。于我憎嫌与作
利益。已作今作当作。复为三种。此等皆作恼事。
于此九种恼事之中。当自调伏。小事舍无馀者。于
中有二十种小事。所谓不信(一)无惭(二)诌幻(三)掉(
四)乱(五)放逸(六)害(七)无愧(八)懈怠(九)忧(十)昏(十一旧
睡)睡(十二旧眠)恨(十三)覆(十四)嫉(十五)悭(十六)高(十七)忿
(十八)悔(十九)闷(二十)。此等二十种小事。皆舍无馀。
八种懈怠事皆亦应除断者。于中有八种懈怠事。

diligent and immaculate in this, one should progress in one's use of the *dhāraṇīs* and should listen to and learn such *dhāraṇīs* as the "Silver Lord" and "Ocean Lord" *dhāraṇīs*.[121]

Also, one must never create even the most subtle obstructive circumstance in a place where people listen to the teaching of Dharma, this in order to avoid karma conducing to dharmically disastrous rebirth circumstances.

---

150 – Overcome Major Afflictions, Banish Subsidiary Afflictions, Cast off Indolence

When embroiled in the afflictions, be able to overcome them.
Relinquish the lesser instances, retaining not a trace.
Regarding the eight cases involving indolence,
One should cut all of those off as well.

COMMENTARY:

Regarding "When embroiled in the afflictions, be able to overcome them," this is an allusion to the nine different categories of circumstances involving the [six primary] afflictions,[122] namely:

[1-3] Past, present, and future circumstances "not beneficial to me" comprise three categories.

[4-6] Past, present, and future circumstances "not beneficial to those I hold dear" comprise three categories.

[7-9] Past, present, and future circumstances "beneficial to those I detest" comprise an additional three categories.

All of these are situations involving afflictions. One should be able to exercise self-control in these nine affliction-prone circumstances.

Regarding "Relinquish the lesser instances, retaining not a trace," this alludes to the twenty lesser circumstances [involving the twenty subsidiary afflictions], namely: absence of faith; absence of a sense of shame, flattery, deceptiveness, agitation, mental scatteredness, negligence, harming, absence of a dread of blame, indolence, worry, drowsiness, enmity, concealment, jealously, miserliness, elevating oneself, anger, regretfulness, and depression. One relinquishes all of these twenty lesser instances, retaining not so much as a trace of them.

As for "Regarding the eight cases involving indolence, one should cut all of those off as well," there are therein eight circumstances characterized by indolence. Specifically, this refers to [rationalizations for desisting from effort as listed below]:

所謂我欲作務即便安臥。不發精進（一）。我作務已（二）。我於行路（三）。我行路已（四）。我身疲乏。不能修業（五）。我身沈重。不能修業（六）。我已生病（七）。我病得起不久即便安臥。不發精進（八）。由此等故。應得不得應到不到應證不證。此等八種懈怠事中。為除斷故。應發精進

莫作非分貪　　　橫貪不稱意
離者皆令合　　　無問親非親

[0539c18]　　若見具足利養名聞安樂稱譽福德眾生。於彼具足福中。莫作非分貪心。以作非分貪心則不稱意。是故所不應作。又於各各共靜離壞眾生中。無問親與非親。皆令和合。同心相愛

所谓我欲作务即便安卧。不发精进（一）。我作务已（二）。我于行路（三）。我行路已（四）。我身疲乏。不能修业（五）。我身沈重。不能修业（六）。我已生病（七）。我病得起不久即便安卧。不发精进（八）。由此等故。应得不得应到不到应证不证。此等八种懈怠事中。为除断故。应发精进

莫作非分贪　　　横贪不称意
离者皆令合　　　无问亲非亲

[0539c18]　　若见具足利养名闻安乐称誉福德众生。于彼具足福中。莫作非分贪心。以作非分贪心则不称意。是故所不应作。又于各各共静离坏众生中。无问亲与非亲。皆令和合。同心相爱

[1] One thinks, "I'm about to take up [such-and-such] a task," and then immediately lies down peacefully [to take a preparatory nap] and thus does not generate any vigor.

[2] One thinks, "I've now completed that task," or [3] "I've been walking along," or [4] "I've finished with walking along," or [5] "My body is so weary," and hence one concludes he cannot do his cultivation work.

[6] Or else one thinks, "My body feels so heavy" [from eating too much] and hence one concludes that therefore he cannot do his cultivation work.

Or else one thinks, [7] "I've fallen ill," or [8] "My sickness has not yet subsided for very long," and then one immediately lies down peacefully and thus does not generate any vigor.

Due to circumstances such as these, one does not achieve what one should achieve, does not arrive at the point at which one should arrive, and does not bring to realization what one should bring to realization.

In situations such as found in these eight circumstances involving indolence, one should generate vigor to cut it off.[123]

---

151 – Don't Covet What Is Not One's Lot, Reconcile the Estranged

Do not covet what is not one's lot,
For unprincipled covetousness will not bring satisfaction.
Influence all who have become estranged to reconcile,
Whether or not they are one's own relations.

COMMENTARY:

This refers to a case where one observes others who have gained abundant offerings, fame, happiness, esteem, and bounteous merit. As for their plentiful karmic rewards, one must not indulge any covetous thoughts focused on what is not one's own lot. If one generates covetous thoughts for what is not one's own lot, then one will fail to develop a satisfied mind. Hence one should refrain from such behavior.

Additionally, regarding anyone involved in mutual disputation, estrangement, and destructiveness, ignoring the question of whether or not they are one's own relatives, all such individuals should be influenced to achieve that harmonious unity wherein their thoughts are in agreement and they treat each other with kindness.

於空而得空　　智者莫依行
若當得於空　　彼惡過身見

[0539c25]　　　依空拔除大無智聚故。智者莫依得空而
行。若依得空而行。則於有身見人。難治過之惡亦
過之。以諸見行由空出離。若著空見彼不可治。以
更無令出離故

掃塗與莊嚴　　　及多種鼓樂
香鬘等供具　　　供養於支提

[0540a02]　　　於如來支提及形像所。掃地塗地香鬘燒香
末香華蓋幢幡等。莊嚴供養之具。當作供養。為得
端正戒香自在故。貝笛箜篌腰鼓大鼓雷鼓拍手等。
種種鼓樂供養。為得天耳故

于空而得空　　智者莫依行
若当得于空　　彼恶过身见

[0539c25]　　　依空拔除大无智聚故。智者莫依得空而
行。若依得空而行。则于有身见人。难治过之恶亦
过之。以诸见行由空出离。若着空见彼不可治。以
更无令出离故

扫涂与庄严　　　及多种鼓乐
香鬘等供具　　　供养于支提

[0540a02]　　　于如来支提及形像所。扫地涂地香鬘烧香
末香华盖幢幡等。庄严供养之具。当作供养。为得
端正戒香自在故。贝笛箜篌腰鼓大鼓雷鼓拍手等。
种种鼓乐供养。为得天耳故

152 – Seeking to Get at Emptiness Itself Is Worse Than Viewing Body As Self

The wise must not base their practice
On getting at the "emptiness" in what is intrinsically empty.
In the case of one determined to get at that emptiness itself,
That wrong is even more extreme than viewing the body as a self.

COMMENTARY:

One relies upon realization of emptiness to eliminate the accumulation [of conceptions] associated with deficient wisdom. The wise must not rely on getting at emptiness itself as the goal of practice. If one sees getting at emptiness itself as the goal of practice, then that error goes beyond even the difficult-to-cure misconception of those who maintain the view which seizes on the body as constituting a self.

The reason for this is that it is by resort to emptiness that one is able to escape from all view-based practices. In a case where, beyond that, one has developed another view which attempts to grasp at that emptiness itself, this is a circumstance for which there is no cure, this because, there is nothing over and above that through which one can escape [from such a view].[124]

153 – Maintain Stupas, Provide Adornments, and Make Offerings at the Stupas

By sweeping and finishing floors, by providing adornments,
By furnishing many varieties of drums and music,
And by offering fragrances, flower garlands, and other gifts,
Contribute offerings to the *caityas*.

COMMENTARY:

At the *caityas* of the Tathāgata and at the places where there are images, one should keep the floors swept and coated (lit. "smeared") while also providing fragrant garlands, burnable incense, powder incense, floral canopies, banners, and other such articles used as adornments and as offerings. One should make such offerings to gain [in future rebirths] a fine and upright physical form, the fragrance of moral virtue, and sovereign freedoms.

Offerings of all different sorts of drums and music—wind instruments made from shells, stringed instruments, the waist-mounted drums, the large drums, the thundering drums, the clapping of hands [along with the rhythm], and so forth—this is done for the sake of gaining the heavenly ear.

繁體字

作種種燈輪　　供養支提舍
施蓋及革屣　　騎乘車輿等

[0540a08]　　支提舍中。應以種種香油酥燈鬘等善作供養。為得佛眼故。布施傘蓋皮鞋象馬車輿乘等。為得菩薩無上神通乘不難故

專應喜樂去　　樂知信佛得
喜樂給侍僧　　亦樂聞正法

[0540a13]　　於中菩薩。常應如是喜樂於法。莫喜五欲福樂。當知信佛所得之利。莫唯信樂見於色身。當於僧中以諸樂具常憙給侍。莫唯憙[1]詣問訊而已。常憙聞法無有厭足。莫唯憙樂暫聞其語

簡体字

作种种灯轮　　供养支提舍
施盖及革屣　　骑乘车舆等

[0540a08]　　支提舍中。应以种种香油酥灯鬘等善作供养。为得佛眼故。布施伞盖皮鞋象马车舆乘等。为得菩萨无上神通乘不难故

专应喜乐去　　乐知信佛得
喜乐给侍僧　　亦乐闻正法

[0540a13]　　于中菩萨。常应如是喜乐于法。莫喜五欲福乐。当知信佛所得之利。莫唯信乐见于色身。当于僧中以诸乐具常憙给侍。莫唯憙[1]诣问讯而已。常憙闻法无有厌足。莫唯憙乐暂闻其语

---

154 – Provide Lantern Wheels, Stupa Canopies, Sandals, Carriages, Sedan Chairs

Create all sorts of lantern wheels
As offerings to the *caityas* and their buildings.[125]
Provide canopies as well as sandals,
Horse-drawn carriages, sedan chairs, and the like.

COMMENTARY:

In the buildings surrounding the *caityas*, one should assemble all sorts of lanterns fueled by fragrant oils and ghee, garlands, and so forth, using them to make as offerings. This is done for the sake of gaining the buddha eye.

One makes gifts of parasols, canopies, sandals, carriages drawn by elephants and horses, sedan chairs, and so forth. This is done for the sake of gaining the bodhisattva's unsurpassed spiritual penetrations and for experiencing no difficulties in taking up that vehicle.

---

155 – Find Happiness in Listening to Dharma, in Faith in Buddha, in Serving Sangha

One should especially find delight in the Dharma[126]
And be happy knowing what is gained through faith in Buddha.
Delight in providing for and serving the monastic Sangha,
While also finding happiness through listening to right Dharma.

COMMENTARY:

In the midst of all this, the bodhisattva should constantly find in these ways delight and happiness in the Dharma. One must not find one's delight in the karmic blessings and pleasures linked to the five sorts of desire.

One should realize what benefits are gained through faith in the Buddha. One must not look solely to the physical form body as the basis of one's trust and happiness.

One should find constant delight in supplying and serving the Sangha order with those articles which ensure their happiness. One must not find delight solely in obtaining audiences with them and observing the protocols of greeting.

One should experience delight in listening to the Dharma and never become self-satisfied that one has had enough of that. One must not find one's delight and happiness solely through listening briefly to their words.

前世中不生　　現在中不住
後際中不到　　如是觀諸法

[0540a20]　　因緣和合力故。及無所從來故。前世中不生念念破滅故。及不住故。現在中不住滅無餘故。及無所至去故。後際中不到。應當如是觀察諸法

好事與眾生　　不求彼好報
當為獨忍苦　　不自偏受樂

[0540a26]　　菩薩於諸眾生。當以好事而利樂之。自不希望彼等眾生利樂好事。及諸眾生有[2]無量苦相。我獨為其忍受。我有樂具。與諸眾生。受用為樂

雖足[3]大福[4]報　　心不舉不喜
雖貧如餓鬼　　亦不下不憂

前世中不生　　現在中不住
后际中不到　　如是观诸法

[0540a20]　　因缘和合力故。及无所从来故。前世中不生念念破灭故。及不住故。现在中不住灭无馀故。及无所至去故。后际中不到。应当如是观察诸法

好事与众生　　不求彼好报
当为独忍苦　　不自偏受乐

[0540a26]　　菩萨于诸众生。当以好事而利乐之。自不希望彼等众生利乐好事。及诸众生有[2]无量苦相。我独为其忍受。我有乐具。与诸众生。受用为乐

虽足[3]大福[4]报　　心不举不喜
虽贫如饿鬼　　亦不下不忧

156 – Dharmas Don't Arise in the Past, Abide in the Present, or Extend into the Future

They do not arise in the past.
They do not abide in the present.
They do not go forward into the future.
Contemplate all dharmas in this manner.

COMMENTARY:

Because their "existence" is based solely on the strength of component causes and conditions, and because they have no place from whence they come, dharmas are not produced in the past.

Because they undergo continuous [and complete] destruction in each successive micro-moment (kṣaṇa), and also because they do not abide at all, dharmas do not dwell in the present.

Because they are completely destroyed, leaving no trace, and also because there is no place to which they go, dharmas do not proceed on into the future.

One should direct such analytic contemplation to all dharmas.

157 – Bestow What Is Best, Seek No Reward, Take on Sufferings, Do Not Covet Bliss

Give to beings whatsoever is fine
And do not wish that they bestow anything fine in return.
One should prefer it be solely oneself who endures suffering
While not favoring oneself in the enjoyment of happiness.

COMMENTARY:

In his interactions with beings, the bodhisattva should use whatever is fine to provide them benefit and happiness while cherishing no hope that those beings use fine things to provide him any benefit or happiness in return.

This extends even to the point that, wherever beings are beset with countless sufferings, he thinks, "I alone should endure those sufferings on their behalf. I should bestow on beings whatever happiness-facilitating things I possess that they might use them to enjoy some happiness."

158 – Don't Be Overjoyed at Karmic Rewards Nor Downcast at Karmic Misfortune

Although replete with karmic rewards from immense merit,
The mind should not become lofty or overwhelmed with delight.
Although one may be as poverty-stricken as a hungry ghost,
One should still not become downcast or overcome with distress.

[0540b03] 雖住大具足福報天中。其心不作喜之與舉。
雖為餓鬼貧窮破散逼惱此最難活。不應生下心。亦
復不應憂。何況人道貧窮破散

　　若有已學者　　　應極尊重之
　　未學令入學　　　不應生輕蔑

[0540b08] 　　若有已學眾生。於彼應作至極尊重。若未
學者應令彼等入學。亦不應輕蔑之

　　戒具者恭敬　　　破戒令入戒
　　智具者親近　　　愚者令住智

[0540b12] 　　戒具足人應當問訊。合掌向禮等而恭敬
之。亦應為彼說持戒福。若破戒者應令入戒。亦應
為彼說破戒罪。智具足者。應當親近。

[0540b03] 虽住大具足福报天中。其心不作喜之与举。
虽为饿鬼贫穷破散逼恼此最难活。不应生下心。亦
复不应忧。何况人道贫穷破散

　　若有已学者　　　应极尊重之
　　未学令入学　　　不应生轻蔑

[0540b08] 　　若有已学众生。于彼应作至极尊重。若未
学者应令彼等入学。亦不应轻蔑之

　　戒具者恭敬　　　破戒令入戒
　　智具者亲近　　　愚者令住智

[0540b12] 　　戒具足人应当问讯。合掌向礼等而恭敬
之。亦应为彼说持戒福。若破戒者应令入戒。亦应
为彼说破戒罪。智具足者。应当亲近。

COMMENTARY:

Even if one ascends to the heavens of those karmic rewards generated by immensely replete merit, one's mind should not become delighted or raised aloft by that. Even though one might have fallen into this most extremely difficult life of the hungry ghost afflicted with extreme poverty, disastrous misfortune, and torment, one should still not adopt a downcast mind and should not become overcome with anguish. How much the less should one allow this to occur when, still abiding in the human realm, one falls into poverty and experiences disastrous misfortune.

---

159 – Esteem the Learned, Inspire the Untrained to Study Without Belittling Them

Accord the most ultimate degree of esteem
To those already accomplished in learning.
Inspire those as yet unlearned to devote themselves to study.
One should not behave in a manner belittling them.

COMMENTARY:

On encountering those already accomplished in their studies, one should express the most ultimate degree of esteem for them. As for those who have not yet become learned, one should influence them to course in learning. One should refrain from acting toward them in a manner which slights or belittles them.[127]

---

160 – Revere Virtue, Inspire Purity, Draw Close to the Wise, Promote Wisdom in Fools

Revere those perfect in observance of the moral precepts
And influence those who break precepts to take on the precepts.
Draw close to those perfect in wisdom
And influence those who act foolishly to abide in wisdom.

COMMENTARY:

On encountering those perfect in observance of the moral precepts, one should press palms together and observe the protocols of reverence. One should also speak to them about the karmic merit generated by observing the moral precepts.

On encountering those who break the precepts, one should influence them to take on the moral prohibitions. One should also speak to them about the karmic punishments resulting from breaking precepts.

One should draw close to those possessed of well-developed

亦應為彼顯智慧德。愚者應令住智。亦應為彼演愚癡過

　　流轉苦多種　　　生老死惡趣
　　不怖此等畏　　　當降魔惡智

[0540b19]　　菩薩於流轉中。流轉多種。生老死憂悲苦惱等。地獄畜生餓鬼阿修羅惡趣等。不應怖畏。唯當降伏惡魔惡智

　　所有諸佛土　　　搏聚諸功德
　　為皆得彼故　　　發願及精進

[0540b24]　　十方無量諸佛國土。若佛土具足。若佛土莊嚴。若從諸佛菩薩聞。若自見之。彼皆搏聚殊勝功德。皆令彼等入到自佛土中。應當作如是願。隨所願即隨成就。亦應如是精勤修行

亦应为彼显智慧德。愚者应令住智。亦应为彼演愚痴过

　　流转苦多种　　　生老死恶趣
　　不怖此等畏　　　当降魔恶智

[0540b19]　　菩萨于流转中。流转多种。生老死忧悲苦恼等。地狱畜生饿鬼阿修罗恶趣等。不应怖畏。唯当降伏恶魔恶智

　　所有诸佛土　　　抟聚诸功德
　　为皆得彼故　　　发愿及精进

[0540b24]　　十方无量诸佛国土。若佛土具足。若佛土庄严。若从诸佛菩萨闻。若自见之。彼皆抟聚殊胜功德。皆令彼等入到自佛土中。应当作如是愿。随所愿即随成就。亦应如是精勤修行

wisdom, and should also speaking to them in a manner revealing the fine qualities accruing to those coursing in wisdom.

One should also influence those who act foolishly to abide in wisdom and should also discourse for them on the karmic transgressions inherent in foolish actions.

FINAL SECTION
CONCLUDING INSTRUCTIONS

161 – Don't Be Terrorized by Saṃsāra, Rather Subdue Demons and Evil Knowledge

The sufferings of cyclic existence are of many kinds,
Involving birth, aging, death, and the wretched destinies.
One should not be frightened by the fearsomeness of these.
One must instead subdue demons and knowledge rooted in evil.

COMMENTARY:

In the midst of cyclic births and deaths, the bodhisattva undergoes many kinds of sufferings such as birth, aging, death, lamentation, suffering-inducing afflictions, and the wretched destinies of the hells, animals, hungry ghosts, and *asuras* (demi-gods). One should not fear those things, but rather should especially focus on subduing evil demons and types of knowledge rooted in evil.[128]

162 – Amass Merit in All Buddhalands, Make Vows That Others Will Reach Them Too

Amass every form of merit
In the lands of all the Buddhas.
Bring forth vows and proceed with vigor
So that everyone may succeed in reaching them.

COMMENTARY:

In all of the lands of the innumerable buddhas throughout the ten directions, whether it be from bringing a buddhaland to perfection, whether it be from adorning a buddhaland, whether it be from listening to the teachings of all buddhas and bodhisattvas, or whether it be from being able to see them personally, one amasses in all such cases especially superior forms of merit.

All of this is dedicated to causing those beings to be able to reach their own buddhaland. One should make vows concordant with this intent. Whatever one vows to do, one proceeds immediately to accomplish that. In this too, one should proceed accordingly, availing oneself of intense diligence as one proceeds with cultivation.

恒於諸法中　　　不取而行捨

此為諸眾生　　　受擔欲荷負

[0540c01]　　以取故苦不取故樂。作是念已。恒於諸法
不取而捨。雖不取而捨。若此先時為趣菩提故。作
願受擔眾生。未度者我當度。未脫者我當脫。未寂
滅者我當寂滅。此應荷負為諸眾生故

正觀於諸法　　　無我無我所

亦勿捨大悲　　　及以於大慈

[0540c08]　　說諸法無所有。如夢如幻故。諸法無我。
其無我所者觀無相故。如是以最勝義法。觀此相
時。然於眾生亦不捨大悲及以大慈。如是應當

恒于诸法中　　　不取而行舍

此为诸众生　　　受担欲荷负

[0540c01]　　以取故苦不取故乐。作是念已。恒于诸法
不取而舍。虽不取而舍。若此先时为趣菩提故。作
愿受担众生。未度者我当度。未脱者我当脱。未寂
灭者我当寂灭。此应荷负为诸众生故

正观于诸法　　　无我无我所

亦勿舍大悲　　　及以于大慈

[0540c08]　　说诸法无所有。如梦如幻故。诸法无我。
其无我所者观无相故。如是以最胜义法。观此相
时。然于众生亦不舍大悲及以大慈。如是应当

On Right-View Equanimity and Preserving Kindness and Compassion

163 – Never Seize on Dharmas, Abide in Equanimity, Take Up the Burden for Beings

Even in the midst of all dharmas, one is constant
In not seizing on them, thus coursing along in equanimity.
One takes on the burden, wishing to bear it on forth,
Proceeding in this manner for the sake of all beings.

COMMENTARY:

It is on account of grasping that one suffers and on account of refraining from grasping that one enjoys happiness. Once one has reflected in this manner, even in the midst of all dharmas, one constantly refrains from seizing on them and so abides in equanimity.

Although one refrains from seizing on them and thus abides in equanimity, still, in an earlier time, for the sake of their being able to go on forth to bodhi, one made vows to take on their burden, vowing that, "I shall escort across to enlightenment those who have not yet gone across, shall liberate those who have not yet gained liberation, and shall bring to cessation those who have not yet arrived at cessation."

It is on account of this that one should bear such a burden for the sake of all beings.

164 – Contemplate Dharmas as Non-Self, Don't Relinquish Compassion or Kindness

Abide in the right contemplation of all dharmas
As devoid of self and as devoid of anything belonging to a self.
Even so, one must not relinquish the great compassion
Or one's reliance on the great kindness.

COMMENTARY:

As for the declaration that all dharmas are devoid of any [inherent] existence, it is because they are like a dream and like a magical conjuration that dharmas are devoid of self.

As for their being devoid of anything belonging to a self, this is based on the contemplation of their signlessness. Pronouncements of this sort correspond to the dharma of the supreme meaning (paramārtha).

Even when one undertakes the contemplation of these signs [from the standpoint of the supreme meaning], one still refrains from relinquishing the great compassion or the great kindness employed in relation to beings. This being so, one should gauge the

繁體字

倍復稱量歎言奇哉。彼諸眾生癡闇所覆。著我我所。於此最勝義道法中。而不覺知。我當何時。令彼眾生於此最勝義道法中而得覺知。是為於眾生中不捨大悲及以大慈

　勝過諸供養　　　以供佛世尊
　彼作何者是　　　所謂法供養

[0540c17]　　若有以諸供具。供養諸聲聞獨覺菩薩及佛世尊。所謂或以諸華香鬘末香燈輪供養。或以諸蓋幢幡供養。或以諸音樂等供養。或以諸藥美飲食等布施供養。若欲勝過彼諸供養以供養佛。復何者是。答言所謂法供養。彼法供養復有何相

　若持菩薩藏　　　及得陀羅尼
　入深法源底　　　是為法供養

[0540c25]　於中若與菩薩藏相應。

簡体字

倍复称量叹言奇哉。彼诸众生痴暗所覆。着我我所。于此最胜义道法中。而不觉知。我当何时。令彼众生于此最胜义道法中而得觉知。是为于众生中不舍大悲及以大慈

　胜过诸供养　　　以供佛世尊
　彼作何者是　　　所谓法供养

[0540c17]　　若有以诸供具。供养诸声闻独觉菩萨及佛世尊。所谓或以诸华香鬘末香灯轮供养。或以诸盖幢幡供养。或以诸音乐等供养。或以诸药美饮食等布施供养。若欲胜过彼诸供养以供养佛。复何者是。答言所谓法供养。彼法供养复有何相

　若持菩萨藏　　　及得陀罗尼
　入深法源底　　　是为法供养

[0540c25]　于中若与菩萨藏相应。

situation yet again and be moved to utter the sighing exclamation, "Strange indeed! All of those beings are blanketed by the darkness of delusions, are attached to 'I' and 'mine,' and are incognizant of this dharma of the supreme meaning path. Just how long will it be before I am finally able to instigate those beings to realize this dharma of the supreme meaning path?"

This is what is meant by not relinquishing the great compassion or the great kindness toward beings.

On the Giving of Dharma

165 – Making Offerings of Dharma Is Superior to Giving Every Gift to the Buddha

As for that which is superior even to using every sort of gift
In making offerings to the Buddha, the Bhagavān,
What sort of action might that be?
This refers specifically to making offerings of Dharma.

COMMENTARY:

In a case where one takes all manner of gifts and makes offerings of them to all of the Śrāvaka-disciples, the Pratyekabuddhas, the Bodhisattvas, and the Buddhas, the Bhagavāns—these may include offerings of all manner of flowers, fragrances, garlands, powdered incenses, and lantern wheels, may include offerings of all sorts of canopies, banners, and pennants, may include offerings of all sorts of music, or may include giving as offerings all manner of medicines, fine foods and beverages, and other such things.

If one wishes to perform an act of offering superior to taking all of those gifts and offering them to the Buddhas, what additional sort of thing might that be? The reply states that it refers specifically to making an offering of Dharma. Now what additional characteristic features would such an offering of Dharma possess?

166 – Upholding the Bodhisattva Canon Is the Foremost Dharma Offering

If one upholds the Bodhisattva Canon,
Even to the point of gaining realization of the *dhāraṇīs*—
If one enters into and reaches the bottom of Dharma's source—
This is what constitutes the offering of Dharma.

COMMENTARY:

If one is to conform in this to the Bodhisattva canon, [one should contemplate the following ideas from the *Vimalakīrti Sutra*]:

如來所說經等甚深明相背諸世間難得其底。難見微細無著了義。以總持經王印印之。不退轉因從六度生。善攝所攝順入助菩提法合正覺性。入諸大悲說於大慈。離眾魔見善說緣生。入無眾生無命無長養無人。與空無相無願無作相應。坐於覺場轉於法輪。為天龍夜叉乾闥婆之所讚歎。度在家泥攝諸聖人。演說諸菩薩行。入法義辭樂說之辯。震於無常苦無我等音聲之雷。怖諸外論見得之執。諸佛所歎對治流轉示涅槃樂。如是等經若說若持觀察攝取。是名法供養。又法供養者。得不退墮順行總持故。

如来所说经等甚深明相背诸世间难得其底。难见微细无着了义。以总持经王印印之。不退转因从六度生。善摄所摄顺入助菩提法合正觉性。入诸大悲说于大慈。离众魔见善说缘生。入无众生无命无长养无人。与空无相无愿无作相应。坐于觉场转于法轮。为天龙夜叉乾闼婆之所赞叹。度在家泥摄诸圣人。演说诸菩萨行。入法义辞乐说之辩。震于无常苦无我等音声之雷。怖诸外论见得之执。诸佛所叹对治流转示涅盘乐。如是等经若说若持观察摄取。是名法供养。又法供养者。得不退堕顺行总持故。

"The sutras spoken by the Tathāgata and the other scriptures are extremely profound in their clarification of the characteristics of dharmas. They are diametrically opposed to the ways of the world. It is difficult to succeed in reaching to the very bottom of them. It is difficult to perceive the subtleties involved in the ultimate meaning of being free of attachment.

"[That which is included in the Bodhisattva Canon] is such as receives the seal of certification of the seal described in the *King of Dhāraṇīs Sutra*. It explains that the causes for realizing irreversibility are born from the six perfections. [The Bodhisattva Canon] skillfully subsumes what should be subsumed. It complies with and enters into the dharmas which equip one for bodhi. It brings one into unity with the nature of the right enlightenment. It enters into all forms of the great compassion and discourses on the great loving kindness.

"It abandons the many demonic views, skillfully explains conditioned arising, and enters into the sphere of the nonexistence of beings, the nonexistence of a life, the nonexistence of any developing entity, and the nonexistence of persons. It accords with emptiness, signlessness, wishlessness, and non-production.

"It leads one to sit at the site where bodhi is realized and set in motion the wheel of Dharma whereupon one is praised by the gods, dragons, *yakṣas*, and *gandharvas*. It delivers one from the mire of the householder's life and draws one in among the Āryas. It expounds on all of the bodhisattva practices and enters into the eloquence consisting of [being unobstructed in understanding] dharmas, in realizing their meanings, in formulating articulate phrasing, and in speaking about them with delight.

"It shakes the world with the thunder of that sound which proclaims impermanence, suffering, absence of self, and other such dharmas. It strikes terror into all who subscribe to the attachments to views and attainments characteristic of the non-Buddhist treatises. It is praised by all buddhas. It counteracts one's coursing in cyclic existence and reveals the bliss of nirvāṇa. If one explains, if one upholds, if one analytically investigates, and if one adopts sutras such as these, it is this which qualifies as the offering of Dharma."

Additionally, those who give offerings of Dharma succeed in achieving irreversibility and thus do not fall, this on account of the dhāraṇīs which follow along with them [from life to life, guarding them] in their practice. In those profound dharmas corresponding

於空無相無願無作相應深法中。入至其底無動無疑。是名最勝義中法之供養

應當依於義　　莫唯愛雜味

於深法道中　　善入莫放逸

[0541a12]　　又法供養者。若於法中思法行法。隨順緣生離諸邊取之見。得無出無生忍入於無我。於因緣中無違無鬪無諍離我我所。應當依義。莫愛馳逐雜飾句味。應當依智莫依於識。依了義經莫著不了義世俗言說。應當依法莫取人見。應當隨順如實法行入無住處。善觀無名行識明色六入觸受愛取有生老死憂悲苦惱困極。皆悉寂滅。如是觀緣生已引出

于空无相无愿无作相应深法中。入至其底无动无疑。是名最胜义中法之供养

应当依于义　　莫唯爱杂味

于深法道中　　善入莫放逸

[0541a12]　　又法供养者。若于法中思法行法。随顺缘生离诸边取之见。得无出无生忍入于无我。于因缘中无违无鬪无诤离我我所。应当依义。莫爱驰逐杂饰句味。应当依智莫依于识。依了义经莫着不了义世俗言说。应当依法莫取人见。应当随顺如实法行入无住处。善观无名行识明色六入触受爱取有生老死忧悲苦恼困极。皆悉寂灭。如是观缘生已引出

to emptiness, signlessness, wishlessness, and non-production, one enters and reaches to their very bottom where one remains unmoving and free of doubts. It is this which qualifies as the offering of the dharma of the most supreme meaning.[129]

---

167 – Rely on Meaning, Not Flavors; Enter the Profound Path, Avoiding Negligence

One should rely upon the meaning.
One must not cherish only the various flavors.
In the Path of the profound Dharma
One enters with skill and must not fall prey to negligence.

COMMENTARY:

Additionally, as for this making of offerings of Dharma, whether it be in the meditative reflection on dharmas or in the implementation of dharmas in one's practice, whether it be in acting in accord with conditioned arising, whether it be in the abandonment of views seizing on extremes, whether it be in the realization whereby one never leaves the unproduced-dharmas patience, whether it be in gaining entry to the nonexistence of the self, whether it be in remaining free of any opposing, struggling, or disputation in the midst of the circumstances formed by causes and conditions, or whether it be in the abandonment of the self and anything belonging to a self—in all such circumstances, one should rely upon the meaning. One must not be motivated by an affection which chases after the flavor of the various forms of decorous phrasing.

One should rely upon wisdom and must not merely rely upon impressions gained through one's consciousnesses. One should rely upon ultimate-meaning scriptures and must not become attached to worldly and common discourses which do not reflect the ultimate meaning. One should rely upon Dharma and must not seize upon the views which people hold. In one's practice, one should accord with and follow those dharmas which correspond to reality, thus entering into that place wherein there is no abiding.

One should skillfully contemplate the cycle of ignorance, karmic compositional factors, consciousness, name-and-form, the six sense faculties, contact, feeling, craving, grasping, becoming, birth, aging, death, sorrow, lamentation, suffering-laden afflictions, and the very extremes of difficulty—perceiving them all as abiding in a state of complete cessation. After one has contemplated the circumstances of conditioned arising in this manner, one may draw upon

無盡。以愍念眾生故。不著諸見不作放逸。若常如
此。乃名無上法之供養

　　如是此資糧　　　恒沙等大劫
　　出家及在家　　　當得滿正覺

[0541a24] 　　如前所說資糧於[1]恒伽沙等量大劫中出家
眾及在家眾菩薩乘者。多時滿願得成正覺

　　繫彼資糧頌　　　為菩提思惟
　　資糧義無闕　　　能[2]如在彼頌
　　我今[3]擇彼頌　　　於義或增減
　　善解頌義等　　　賢智當[4]忍之
　　釋彼資糧頌　　　我所作福善
　　為流轉眾生　　　當得正遍覺

聖者龍樹所作菩提資糧論竟。我比丘自在解釋竟

無盡。以愍念眾生故。不着諸見不作放逸。若常如
此。乃名无上法之供养

　　如是此资粮　　　恒沙等大劫
　　出家及在家　　　当得满正觉

[0541a24] 　　如前所说资粮于[1]恒伽沙等量大劫中出家
众及在家众菩萨乘者。多时满愿得成正觉

　　系彼资粮颂　　　为菩提思惟
　　资粮义无阙　　　能[2]如在彼颂
　　我今[3]择彼颂　　　于义或增减
　　善解颂义等　　　贤智当[4]忍之
　　释彼资粮颂　　　我所作福善
　　为流转众生　　　当得正遍觉

圣者龙树所作菩提资粮论竟。我比丘自在解释竟

it endlessly and, on account of remaining sympathetically mindful of beings, one refrains from becoming attached to any views and refrains from falling into negligence.

If one is able to constantly act in this manner, then and only then does this qualify as an offering of the unsurpassed Dharma.[130]

FINAL SUMMARIZING STATEMENT

168 – Buddhahood is Gained by Cultivating the Provisions in Countless Future Lives

One cultivates these provisions in this manner
For kalpas as numerous as the Ganges' sands,
Doing so sometimes as a monastic, sometimes as a householder.
Thus one will succeed in perfecting the right enlightenment.

COMMENTARY:

One cultivates the provisions in accordance with the preceding explanations, doing so for a Ganges' sands number of great kalpas. One does so within the monastic communities and householder communities of the Bodhisattva Vehicle. It is over a long period of time that one fulfills one's vows and then finally succeeds in realizing the right enlightenment.

I present this based on those stanzas about the provisions
To stimulate contemplative reflections about bodhi.
As their portrayal of the provisions' meaning is already flawless.
The aim here was merely to be able to accord with those verses.

My present analysis of those stanzas
May have either enhanced or detracted from their meanings.
Where the explanation has well matched the verses' meanings,
I pray the wisdom of the Worthies will acquiesce in it.

May any meritorious goodness I might have created
Through explaining those verses devoted to the provisions
Be dedicated to the beings coursing on in cyclic existence
That they may gain the right and universal awakening.

The End of Ārya Nāgārjuna's *Treatise on the Provisions for Enlightenment*.
The End of the Explanation Set Forth by Me, Bhikshu Vaśitva.

ENDNOTES

1. I have noticed one dictionary-translation effort which, by the author's own admission, was aimed only at paraphrasing the general meaning of the treatise stanzas. See Christian Lindtner's *Master of Wisdom: Writings of the Buddhist Master Nāgārjuna* (Berkeley: Dharma Press, rev. ed. 1986, 1997), pages 125–151.

2. The "three realms" (proceeding from coarsest to most refined) are: the desire realm, the form realm, and the formless realm. They correspond to the thirty-one planes of cyclic existence, as follows:

   The "desire realm" is comprised of the five lowest levels of rebirth consisting of the hells, animals, ghost realms (the *pretas*), humans, the demi-gods or "titans" (the *asuras*); and the six coarsest levels of celestial rebirth known as "the six desire heavens." (The lowest three desire realm rebirth destinies consisting of hells, animals, and ghost realms comprise what are referred to as "the three wretched destinies" [*durgati*].)

   The "form realm" is comprised of sixteen levels of intermediate celestial rebirth corresponding to the meditation states encountered in the four dhyānas.

   The "formless realm" is comprised of the four most refined levels of celestial rebirth corresponding to the four formless meditation states.

3. One may notice, beginning here, Bhikshu Vaśitva's repeated use of a clever transitioning device to wed his commentary to the root text, that of finishing his commentary on one of Nāgārjuna's *ślokas* with a question nicely answered in brief by the text of Nāgārjuna's very next *śloka* and *in extenso* by the commentary following on that. He uses this same device some seventy times throughout his commentary.

4. Implicit in Bhikshu Vaśitva's raising of the topic of "the boundless meritorious qualities of a buddha's body" is a reference to a buddha body's 32 marks and 80 subsidiary characteristics which are collectively emblematic of vast previous-life causal practices perfected by a buddha and which are also representative of present-moment possession of the fully-developed qualities linked to the six perfections. Although it might seem obvious that the reference here is to a buddha's physical body, Bhikshu Vaśitva makes the distinction to clarify that there is no intended reference to either a buddha's Dharma body or reward body.

5. Dharmagupta then relays a brief and obscure transliteration of the commentary author's evidence for a Sanskrit etymological

relationship between the term for "motherhood" and the term for "placement": "This is comparable to when one says, '*ming-bo-luo-ni-bo-di.*' In this, '*ming*' is a reference to 'nature.' '*bo-luo-ni-bo-di*' is a reference to "recitation." It is by virtue of the marks associated with this nature that this constitutes '*mo-do*' (*mātṛ*?)." Additionally, there has been a note added in the Chinese text which may or may not originate with Dharmagupta's editorial assistants: "When *mo-do* is translated, it means 'mother.' It says in the *Treatise on the Sounds of Words* that '*mo-do*' derives from the phrase '*ming-bo-luo-ni-bo-di*' and that '*ming*' is the essential nature of '*mo-do*' and that '*bo-luo-ni-bo-di*' has the meanings of 'to recite' and '*mo-do.*' Because '*bo-luo-ni-bo-di*' translates as 'to place,' one then allows that 'placement' has the meaning of 'motherhood.'"

6. Dharmagupta then relays another brief and obscure transliteration of the commentary author's evidence for a Sanskrit etymological relationship between the term for "motherhood" and the term for "to measure": "This is comparable to when one says, '*mang-mo-ni.*' '*Mang*' constitutes the 'nature,' whereas '*mo-ni*' constitutes the 'recitation.' It is by virtue of the marks associated with this nature that this constitutes '*mo-do.*'" Additionally, there is another note added in the Chinese text which again may or may not originate with Dharmagupta's editorial assistants: "It says in the *Treatise on the Sounds of Words* that '*mo-do*' also derives from the phrase '*mang-mo-ni.*' '*Mang*' is also the 'essential nature,' whereas '*mo-ni*' refers to the 'recitation' of the meaning. Because '*mo-ni*' translates as 'to measure,' one allows that 'to measure' shares the meaning of 'motherhood.'"

7. Dharmagupta produces here transliterations of Sanskrit terms for Indian units of measure: "the '*bo la sa ta,*' the '*e zhai jia,*' the '*tu lu na,*' and the '*que li di,*' and other such things." There is an accompanying Chinese editorial note which gives Chinese terms for Chinese units of measure.

8. Dharmagupta has inexplicably left his simple Sanskrit term for "come forth," or "appear" (*āgama*) transliterated into Chinese (as *e-han*) rather than translated into Chinese. Hence I go ahead and translate it.

9. Examples of bestowing fearlessness categorized as "material" would be giving food to the cold in fear of freezing, giving food to the hungry in fear of starving, and giving shelter to the homeless in fear of the suffering and dangers of homelessness.

10. The giving of "well-adorned maidens" refers to the facilitating of marriage wherein one bestows dowry, wedding attire, and prayer-bead *mālas*, while also speaking Dharma as appropriate to those attending the marriage ceremony. This bodhisattva practice is detailed elsewhere in the commentary, specifically in the treatment of *śloka* 115.

11. The last line of the stanza means literally: "This is what qualifies as giving gone to the far shore." In interpreting this stanza, it may help to know that the Sanskrit word for "perfection" (*pāramitā*) was interpreted to the sino-Buddhist audience as etymologically meaning "reaching the far shore," i.e. having gone from "the near shore" of imperfection all the way on across to "the far shore" of perfection.

12. "The three factors": benefactor, recipient, gift. "Purified" refers to elimination of any delusion-based imputations such as the idea that there is any inherently existent "self," "other," or "gift."

13. Bhikshu Vaśitva is probably "rounding off" here. He is almost certainly referring to the sixty-seven aspects of bodhisattva moral-precept cultivation in which the bodhisattva develops inexhaustible purity. These are set forth by Akṣayamati Bodhisattva in the "Akṣayamati Chapter" of the *Mahā-vaipulya-mahā-saṃnipāta-sūtra*, this in fascicle twenty-seven (大方等大集經 / T13.397.189c24–190b10).

14. My translation of this passage is tentative, this because Bhikshu Vaśitva's explanation of these two types of precepts and Dharmagupta's Chinese translation of it are both mildly cryptic. It appears here that Bhikshu Vaśitva is referring to the issue of life-to-life continuity versus discontinuity of moral codes, one's accomplishment in moral virtue, and the karmic effects of particular levels of moral virtue, all as a reflection of the momentum of associated karmic propensities.

    Regarding the directly related issue of continuity versus discontinuity of obligations to particular groups of moral precepts such as the five precepts, the bhikshu precepts, or the bodhisattva precepts, the standard Mahāyāna doctrine on that holds that the five precepts and monastic precepts are discontinuous and, as such, must be taken anew in each life to continue to remain in force as regards one's obligations to them and as regards the availability of Dharma-protecting precept spirits and so forth.

    The bodhisattva precepts are held to be uniquely different in this respect, for they are vows taken not for a single lifetime only, but rather are vows taken with the intention that they apply for the span of all one's future lifetimes. As such, although it would be ideal to be able to take them anew in every lifetime, in the absence of that opportunity, they are still held to carry forward their force in subsequent lifetimes in a manner whereby they are "the same when transplanted." Bhikshu Vaśitva alludes to this issue later in this discussion.

15. As I understand it, only the Āryas have reached that level of moral virtue entirely transcending any need to rely on intentionality to abide effortlessly in constant moral perfection.

16. The context, language, and tailoring of content apparent in these verses indicate that they originate with Bhikshu Vaśitva, the commentator.

17. The second of the ten bodhisattva grounds is called *vimala*, meaning "stainless."

18. This verse lists in standard order the "four means of attraction" (*catuḥ-saṃgraha vastu*) used by bodhisattvas to draw beings into the path toward enlightenment: giving, pleasing words, beneficial actions, joint endeavors.

19. "Drying up the great sea" may be intended as a metaphor for "drying up the sea of suffering."

20. Regarding "When this world ends and the fires increase and spread...," it may be helpful to realize that a standard feature of Buddhist cosmology is the teaching that worlds and eons are created and destroyed endlessly (as with the newest model of astronomy and physics which sets aside the "single big-bang theory" in favor of the "multiple big-bang theory"). In Buddhism, however, it is taught that the destruction of worlds is attended by all-consuming fires so intense that they vaporize worlds, incinerating even the lowest levels of beings residing in the celestial realms.

21. Lest "defilement-induced turbidity" seem obscure, it refers to any roiling of the mind by afflictions (attachment, anger, confusion, arrogance, etc.) kicked up by either negative or positive experiences (success, failure, praise, blame, esteem, disesteem, happiness, anguish, etc.). The point here is that simply restraining oneself from throttling an assailant does not qualify as "the perfection of patience." As we shall see from Bhikshu Vaśitva's ensuing discussion, it also requires the maintenance of such complete mental coolness that one's mind does not move at all, even in the midst of the most viciously painful experiences.

22. "As interpreted by Vaśitva" is a third-person self-reference by the commentator.

23. "Inward" in these contexts is a literal but misleading translation of the standard sino-Buddhist rendering of the Sanskrit *adhyātma*. The term really means "belonging to the self" or "subject-related." Hence it refers not just to one's "inward" private mental life, but also to anything typically construed by conventional perception as constituting a "self," including the body. Here we will notice here that Bhikshu Vaśitva accordingly directs his recommended "inwardly-focused" or "subject-related" contemplation to all five aggregates (*skandha*): form, feelings, perceptions, karmic formative factors, and consciousness.

24. The four immeasurable minds (kindness, compassion, sympathetic joy, and equanimity) are referenced here under an often-encountered, but less-common list name.

25. Adopting here 己 in place of 已 to correct an obvious scribal error.

26. "Reviving those not yet revived" likely refers to awakening to the Path all beings so overpowered by the oppressiveness and sufferings of uncontrolled cyclic existence that they simply course along in it so unconsciously that they retain no awareness of karma and its alternately marvelous and disastrous effects.

27. This specific form of "bliss" (*sukha*) is associated with the particular form of "light easefulness" (*praśrabdhi*) that is connected to the karmic-formative-factor (*saṃskāra*) aggregate.

28. This "bliss" (*sukha*) too is associated with "light easefulness" (*praśrabdhi*). Both of these first two manifestations of bliss differ from that which follows in the third dhyāna (see below).

29. This "blissful sensation" (*sukha-vedanā*) is distinctly different from the "bliss" associated with the first and second dhyānas, this because it is associated with the "feeling aggregate" (*vedanā skandha*).

30. As Taisho notes, Bhikshu Vaśitva's commentary does not expand on the meaning of the sixteenth type of dhyāna, perhaps because the rationale for its cultivation seems obvious from its name.

31. Bhikshu Vaśitva is likely referring here to expansive wisdom comprehending all aspects of the mind of the buddha and all aspects of the Path to the utmost, right, and perfect enlightenment.

32. Taisho records what seems fairly clearly to be an erroneous editorial note which claims that the text is missing two of the supposed thirty-two types of purity, this due to a failure on the part of some editor to read the text correctly and recognize that numbers sixteen through eighteen (by my enumeration) reference three different sorts of emptiness of inherent existence, not just the one assumed by that editor.

33. Bhikshu Vaśitva's restatement here of the earlier verse (at least as translated into Chinese by Dharmagupta) varies slightly from the previously-discussed version which reads as follows:

> Giving, moral virtue, patience, vigor, and meditative discipline
> As well as that which extends beyond these five—
> In every case, because they arise from the perfection of wisdom,
> They are subsumed within this pāramitā.

34. Nāgārjuna's treatise on the ten grounds condenses this vow down to the essential issue of "influencing all beings to perfect the bodhi of the Buddhas, including where they incline toward the Śrāvaka-disciple or Pratyekabuddha paths."

35. Nāgārjuna's treatise on the ten grounds condenses this vow down to its essentials, that of "realizing the uniform equality of all dharmas," doing so "through faith and understanding." He then lists an encyclopedic range of dual dharmas, concluding by saying of "all of the other incalculably many millions of dharmas": "In every case, one causes

them to enter into the gates of emptiness, signlessness, and wishlessness such that they are [realized to be] of a single uniform equality transcendent of duality."

36. Nāgārjuna's treatise on the ten grounds makes it clear that the main topic here is the extinguishing of all forms of evil, this in order to successfully carry forth the work of purifying buddhalands.

37. Bhikshu Vaśitva's wording here is highly euphemistic. All other iterations of the vow in the canon make it reasonably clear that the issue here is the scrupulous avoidance of disharmony, enmity, or struggling with others engaged in the same altruistic works of the bodhisattva.

38. These ten vows are standard, with minor variations, in the *Avataṃsaka* tradition. They are found in that sutra (大方廣佛華嚴經 / T10.279.181c–182b) and in the *Ten Grounds Sutra* (十住經 / T10.286.501a13–502a03). They are treated extensively in Nāgārjuna's *Ten Grounds Vibhāṣā*, this in the "Vows" chapter (at T26.1521.30b14–34c11). They are also given a complete discussion in Vasubandhu's commentary on the *Ten Grounds Sutra* (十地經論 / T26.1522.138b3–141b17).

The version represented here in Bhikshu Vaśitva's commentary reflects the uncondensed presentation found in the *Avataṃsaka Sutra* itself. To facilitate easy understanding, one may care to compare my translation of Nāgārjuna's distillation of these vows as found in his *Ten Grounds Vibhāṣā*:

[1] One vows to make offerings to, supply the needs of,
And extend reverence to all buddhas.
[2] One vows that in all cases one will protect and uphold
The Dharma of all buddhas.

[3] From that time when all Buddhas depart the Tuṣita Heaven
And come back to abide in the world,
On forward to the end of their teaching and transforming
And their eternal entry into the realm of [nirvāṇa] without residue,

Including when they abide in the womb, on up to their birth,
On to their leaving lay life, proceeding to the site of enlightenment,
Their conquering the demons, realizing the path to buddhahood,
And their first turning of the wheel of the sublime Dharma—

I will respectfully welcome all Tathāgatas,
And throughout that entire time—
I vow that in all cases I shall
Be entirely devoted to making offerings to them.

[4] I vow to teach and transform beings,
Causing them all to enter the paths.
[5] I vow to influence all beings
To perfect the bodhi of the Buddhas,

[Including] where they incline toward the Śrāvaka-disciple
Or Pratyekabuddha paths.
[6] I vow that, through faith and understanding,
I shall realize the uniform equality of all dharmas.

[7] I vow that, in order to purify the buddhalands,
I shall extinguish all of the various forms of evil.
[8] Where all are engaged in the practice of a single endeavor,
One vows that there will be no enmity or struggling.

[9] One vows to practice the Bodhisattva Path
And to set to turning that irreversible wheel,
Thus causing the removal of all afflictions
And facilitating success in entering the state of purified faith.

[10] One vows that, in all worlds,
One shall manifest the realization of bodhi.
All such bodhisattvas as these
Take the ten great vows as foremost.

In their immense vastness, they are comparable to empty space
And exhaust even the bounds of the future.
They entirely include all of the other incalculably many vows
And exhaust as well one's ability to describe them all in detail.

39. The Taisho text records this reduced-font interlinear Chinese note: "This refers to the winds, bile, viscous disease fluids, thin disease fluids, and other things of this nature."

40. The Taisho text records this reduced-font interlinear Chinese note: "This refers to treatises devoted to medical prescriptions."

41. Lest Bhikshu Vaśitva's intent be misunderstood: The purpose behind skill in humor and satire is not simply to inspire delight in and of itself, but rather to spur an audience to more readily enjoy associated teachings on Dharma. Limitations on the acceptable domain of humor and satire are still governed by the proscriptions in the path of the ten good karmic deeds. These forbid lying, harsh speech, divisive speech (including slander), and frivolous / useless / lewd speech.

42. The Taisho text records this reduced-font interlinear Chinese note: "A stone as white as a seashell."

43. It may be worth noting that what translators often render as "the four elements" of "earth, water, wind, and fire" are really not "elements" at all, but rather are four different phase manifestations in which physical-world "elements" may be encountered: solidity, liquidity, vaporization, and ignition.

44. The four "bases" or "foundations" (adhiṣṭhāna) consist of "truth" (satya), "relinquishment" (tyāga), "cessation" (upaśama), and "wisdom (prajñā). They are encountered in the Pali canon, for example

in the *Dhātuvibhanga Sutta* within the *Majjhima Nikāya* and are also found in Mahāyāna works, for example in Harivarman's *Satyasiddhi Śāstra* (T32.1646.250c) as "the four bases of meritorious qualities," in Nāgārjuna's *Ten Grounds Vibhāṣā* (T26.1521) in at least thirteen different locations as "the four bases of merit / meritorious qualities," in Nāgārjuna's *Ratnāvalī* in Chapter Two (verses thirty-four through thirty-nine) where Nāgārjuna recommends them as crucial points of spiritual practice for the monarch, and also in Nāgārjuna's *Mahāprajñāpāramitā Upadeśa* (T25.1509.222c) as "the four stations," the abiding in which will result in being "adorned with meritorious qualities."

45. This *śloka* is the first of three treating "the four immeasurable minds" (kindness, compassion, sympathetic joy, equanimity).

46. When Bhikshu Vaśitva speaks of "the four abodes of Brahmā," (*brahma-vihāra*) consisting of kindness, compassion, sympathetic joy, and equanimity, one should note per Nāgārjuna's explanation in his *Exegesis on the Great Perfection of Wisdom Sutra*, that lesser-level practice of these contemplations (as distinct from their use in Mahāyāna practice) is as contemplations pure and simple, for they do not genuinely involve or even aspire to involve practices devoted to liberating other beings. This is equally true of Śrāvaka-vehicle practice and the practice of worldlings aspiring to achieve rebirth in celestial realms. In Śrāvaka-vehicle practice, these contemplations are undertaken solely to condition the mind in a way whereby it is not prone to generate the bad karma arising from afflictions felt for other beings.

The Mahāyāna approach to these four practices differs completely. They are known in the Great Vehicle context as "the four immeasurable minds" (*apramāṇa-citta*). Therein, the bodhisattva practitioner definitely does aspire to liberate beings through cultivation of these four immeasurables and in fact relies upon them as foundational contemplations enabling his endless efforts on behalf of other beings.

Bhikshu Vaśitva's recommendation of these practices here arises from the knowledge that beings who take them on will generate less bad karma and will therefore be less likely to plunge so efficiently into the lower realms as those beings who do not adopt such salutary states of mind. Hence we see in that a certain kinship with the Śrāvaka-vehicle cultivation rationale. Additionally, since many worldlings do in fact aspire to the bliss of the heavens, this stratagem may be more readily adopted by those viewing practices directed at liberation as too difficult or beyond their powers of faith.

As for "the three merit-generating circumstances," this is most likely a reference to the "three bases of meritorious activity" (*puṇya-kriyā-vastu*), namely giving, moral virtue, and meditation (*dāna, śīla, bhāvanā*) which Nāgārjuna references directly in *śloka* number 53.

47. The standard list of "the four means of attraction" (*catuḥ-saṃgraha-vastu*) consists of: 1) Giving (*dāna*); 2) Pleasing words (*priyavacana*); 3) Beneficial action (*arthakṛtya*); and 4) Joint endeavors (*samānārthatā*). Here Nāgārjuna frames the second solely in terms of the speaking of Dharma while collapsing the third and the fourth into "endeavors beneficial to them."

48. When Bhikshu Vaśitva mentions "realization of nirvāṇa" here, he is not referring to that nirvāṇa realized when a fourth-stage arhat or a buddha leaves behind his last physical body. He is instead referring to the inherent nirvāṇa-like nature of all phenomena, that state constantly perceptible to the highly evolved bodhisattva as he directly perceives the non-arising of all dharmas even in every moment and even in the midst of day-to-day phenomena.

49. These four agreeable and disagreeable states comprise what are commonly known as "the eight winds" or as "the eight worldly dharmas."

50. Adopting the variant reading found in four other editions, this because it clarifies ambiguous enumeration in the *Taisho* edition.

51. Adopting the variant reading found in four other editions, this because it clarifies ambiguous enumeration in the *Taisho* edition.

52. Adopting the variant reading found in four other editions, this because it clarifies ambiguous enumeration in the *Taisho* edition.

53. There are two issues deserving amplification here: 1) "Patiences"; 2) "Irreversibility. (See below.)

   1) On "patiences": The whole topic of the various types of "patiences" realized in Buddhist cultivation is not nearly so simple as one might suspect, this because there are multiple types of patience associated with the sixteen mental states of comprehension involved in developing the Path of Seeing. (See Chapter Six of Vasubandhu's *Abhidharma-kośa-bhāṣyam* for a tour of the topic.)

   Additionally, in explaining the bodhisattva practices, Nāgārjuna speaks in place after place and at great length on two types of patience: 1) patience with respect to beings; and 2) patience with respect to dharmas. (See Chapter Three of my translation: *Nāgārjuna on the Six Perfections*.)

   Moreover, Bhikshu Vaśitva himself speaks of three basic kinds of patience, this based on three bases of patience found in the body, in the mind, and in the Dharma.

   That said, Bhikshu Vaśitva indicates that, in this context, "patiences" refers specifically to the "unproduced dharmas patience" (*anutpattika-dharma-kṣānti*). As an aid to making sense of the topic, "patience" of this sort may be provisionally understood as that type of deeply patient "acquiescence" which one may develop toward coursing in cyclic existence. This can only really come about once one has gained the direct perception of the emptiness of all dharmas. This cognition of emptiness has the ability to engender a continuous perception that all dharmas are essentially identical to nirvāṇa and hence neither produced nor destroyed. It is this level of cognition and acquiescence which, when linked to the great compassion, figures most strongly in the bodhisattva's ability to continue on endlessly and selflessly, working for the liberation of other beings.

2) On "irreversibility": It has so far remained unclear in the Bhikshu Vasitva commentary that, although this "irreversibility" associated with the first four causal circumstances does constitute a virtual guarantee that enlightenment will be gained sooner or later, still, that particular "enlightenment" which awaits the practitioner might not in fact be the enlightenment of a buddha. It could end up being the individual-liberation result gained by those who do not cultivate the altruistic path of the bodhisattva.

How could this occur? If the bodhisattva falls into negligence, he risks a precipitous plunge back down into the Śrāvaka or Pratyekabuddha practice modes where the population of beings liberated may be but very few. Hence the reference to the terminal nature of such a downfall, one by which it is metaphorically compared to a tragic death. Certainly not all deaths are "tragic," but those involving being cut off in the flower of a promising youth may justifiably be seen as such. Here we have the prospect of a beginning bodhisattva full of promise and great aspirations losing his grip and plummeting to his death while still only "young" in the practices, thus leaving countless beings bereft of the benefits of his unrealized buddhahood. Hence the appropriateness of the metaphor.

54. Adopting here the variant (諸) present in four other editions in lieu of the obvious scribal error (說) preserved in *Taisho*.

55. Adopting here the additional "seizing" character (取) found in four other editions.

56. There are two points to note here:

1) Although the longer (seven-character per foot) Chinese line length in this *śloka* sets it apart from the rest of the treatise (five characters per foot), it is clear from the flow of the text as well as from the way this *śloka* is treated in the Bhikshu Vasitva commentary that it definitely *is* a part of Nāgārjuna's root text and is not simply an exogenous verse cited by Bhikshu Vasitva for enhancement purposes. This line-length variation is probably simply a case of surrendering to the need to more adequately encompass the meaning of the Sanskrit text. This is not particularly unusual in Chinese translations of Indian Buddhist texts, for consistent line-length *per se* was not considered

to be canonically sacred nor was it considered worthy of preservation at the expense of meaning. For example, the great translator, Yi-jing, employed varying line lengths repeatedly in translating the *Suhṛllekha*.

2) The text reads literally: "This stage alone is designated as 'irreversible.'" That is literally true in the sense that only this stage is singled out to specifically receive that designation. The real meaning here, though, is: "It is only at this point that the designation 'definitely irreversible' begins to apply to the bodhisattva stages." In short, it is not solely this ground, but also the ninth and tenth grounds which are "definitely irreversible." The first seven grounds still involve a "relative" level of reversibility making those practitioners continue to be vulnerable to being diverted off to the individual liberation paths of the arhats and pratyekabuddhas.

57. "Faith and the rest" is referring to "the five root-faculties" (*pañca-indriya*) which, when fully-developed, change in name to "the five powers" (*pañca-bala*). Both of these lists are included in the thirty-seven wings of enlightenment. The five root-faculties are: faith, vigor, mindfulness, concentration, and wisdom. That this five-component list is what Bhikshu Vaśitva intends becomes obvious enough when one notes that he is using the *śloka*-phrase "irreversible wisdom" as the take-off point for this comment referencing "faith and the rest." (This "irreversible wisdom" is subsumed under the fifth root-faculty, namely, "wisdom" [*prajñā-indriya*]). Bhikshu Vaśitva's intentionality on this account becomes doubly obvious when, a few paragraphs later, we encounter the very specific reference to "the five world-transcending roots of goodness," this midway through the commentary on this *śloka*.

58. There appears to be a textual corruption here. There is no valid rationale for a seventh-ground bodhisattva having any motivation to obstruct an eighth-ground bodhisattva. The original text more likely read: "Śrāvaka-disciples and pratyekabuddhas are able to obstruct bodhisattvas on up through the seventh ground, causing them to turn back in retreat. However, they are unable to obstruct these [eighth-stage] bodhisattvas and cause them to turn back in retreat."

59. Emending the text here to correct an obvious scribal error wherein the graphically-similar glyph "ten" (十) was at some point erroneously substituted for the originally-intended "seven" (七), perhaps through the very common mechanism of a chipped woodblock. If not emended, the text would state that "the other ten levels of bodhisattvas are not "irreversible." It is obvious however that only the first seven levels of bodhisattvas (referred to two sentences prior) are not irreversible, this because only they are subject to being obstructed

and caused to turn back in retreat.

60. The "eight difficulties" refers to eight terribly unfortunate rebirth circumstances wherein one has little hope of being able to cultivate the Path. This refers to the following types of unfortunate rebirth: in the hell realms; in the hungry-ghost realms; in the animal realms; on the most blissful continent; in the long-life heavens; in the condition of being deaf, mute, or blind; in the condition of possessing eloquence and intelligence obsessed solely with worldly priorities; at a time either before or after a buddha's Dharma reign.

61. The ground of "direct presence" (*abhimukha-bhūmi*) is the sixth of the ten bodhisattva grounds.

62. "Mental transformation of form-related or Dharma-related objective conditions" may seem very obscure. The principle, however is simple. In the case of the former, one might use a meditation visualization to alter the appearance in the mind's eye of a visualized object, as of the image of Buddha, changing it from very small to very large. In the case of the latter, one might mentally envision a feeling of great compassion, great kindness, great sympathetic joy, or equanimity being generated in one's mind-stream, taking all beings in the westerly direction as the objects, then change that to envision the feeling extending to all beings of the ten directions, whether they be former adversaries or intimates.

63. Adopting the variant present in four other editions which drops the text-corrupting *wu* (無), the retention of which would make the sentence senseless.

64. The "three types of suffering" are:

    1) The suffering of suffering (*duḥkha-duḥkhatā*).

    2) The suffering inherent in conditioned existence, i.e. that associated with the karmic formative factors (*saṃskāra-duḥkhatā*).

    3) The suffering wrought by change, i.e. through deterioration of states not seen as suffering (*pariṇāma-duḥkhatā*).

65. This *śloka* and the next collectively describe all six perfections as they occur in fully-developed bodhisattva practice.

66. It is fairly clear from the word order and syntax of the *śloka* phrases I translate as "...through *giving, moral virtue,* / And so forth, including through cultivation of *meditation*—" that Nāgārjuna is referring to the "three bases of meritorious activity" (*puṇya-kriyā-vastu; dāna, śīla, bhāvanā*) encountered in both the Pali and Mahāyāna canons. They are discussed at the end of Chapter Four of Vasubandhu's *Abhidharma-kośa-bhāṣyam*.

67. The Sanskrit for "rejoicing in other's merit" is *puṇya-anumodana*.

68. Nāgārjuna's rationale for focusing on beginning bodhisattvas as the

primary object of concern in this *śloka* probably has to do with the fact that it would be easiest for another novice bodhisattva's critical eye to find fault with them, thus most easily stumbling into an unwitting, but nonetheless "fatal" karmic mistake.

69. Adopting here the graphically similar variant (妄 for 妾) found in four other editions, this to correct an obvious scribal error.

70. One may read the whole story in its sutra context in the *Mahāyāna-vaipulya-dhāraṇī-sūtra* (大乘方廣總持經 / T09.275.380a–b).

71. On the matter of precisely which "two offenses" are intended by Nāgārjuna's *śloka* text, Nāgārjuna himself seems to be quite clear, as follows:

a) "Although a bodhisattva may have committed transgressions, one should still not speak about them, how much the less so where there is no truth to the matter." (per *śloka* 61).

b) "Where one hasn't yet understood extremely profound scriptures, one must not claim they were not spoken by a buddha." (per *śloka* 63).

That said, we might be led into some consternation by Bhikshu Vaśitva's sutra citation and what appears to be his own slightly variant view flowing therefrom that the offense not related to sutra authorship is "Causing someone already resolved on bodhi to retreat from that resolve."

When we peruse the text, we do indeed notice that "causing someone already resolved on bodhi to retreat from that resolve" is more-or-less "implicit" in each of Nāgārjuna's immediately preceding four *ślokas*, this because, were we to fail at the concerns in any of the four *ślokas*, it could very likely cause someone formerly resolved on buddhahood to abandon the entire endeavor. The logic is as follows:

1) Where one fails to be kind and respectful toward a newly-resolved bodhisattva, we may discourage him, thus causing him to retreat from his resolve (*śloka* 60).

2) Where we broadcast the karmic errors or falsely claim the virtues of followers of the Bodhisattva Path, this may cause one formerly resolved on buddhahood to retreat from his resolve (*śloka* 61).

3) Where we fail to assist discouraged practitioners with inspiring teachings about the nature of the Bodhisattva Path and the unique qualities of buddhas, this may cause one formerly resolved on buddhahood to retreat from his resolve (*śloka* 62).

4) Where we claim the profound sutras describing the Bodhisattva Path weren't spoken by buddhas, this too may cause one formerly resolved on buddhahood to retreat from his resolve (*śloka* 63).

Although one easily appreciates the validity of Bhikshu Vaśitva's interpretation and the inherent identity of the principles discussed in both texts, I suspect Nāgārjuna deliberately stressed the two offenses so clearly articulated in his own treatise text and that these two were the ones he intended to reference in *śloka* 63.

72. The "five non-intermittent retributions" associated with the most extremely grave karmic offenses are:

1) No intervening rebirths prior to direct descent into the hells.

2) Non-intermittent continuity of hell punishments.

3) Non-intermittency of that period of time wherein punishments are undergone.

4) Non-intermittency of lifespan during karmic punishments (i.e. no temporary "escapes" via death).

5) Non-intermittency of the space occupied by one's body as it undergoes karmic punishments. (i.e., whatever the size of the particular hell, one's body is of commensurate size, undergoing excruciating tortures on every square inch of its entire expanse.

73. See 佛說廣博嚴淨不退轉輪經 T09.268.283c–4a.

74. The stock translation "wishlessness" (*apraṇihita*) may seem mildly confusing at first glance. It simply means that, once one realizes the true character of any and all phenomena, i.e. that they are devoid of any genuine intrinsic nature of their own, one realizes that they are devoid of any genuine means through which to provoke the mind into aspirations on their behalf. In short, "emptiness" and "signlessness" provoke the question to which one immediately realizes there is no sensible answer: "If there's no "there" there, why would you want to go there?"

Understanding of emptiness, signlessness, and wishlessness may be facilitated by contemplating dharmas from several standpoints:

a) As mere temporary conjunctions of subsidiary conditions (per Bhikshu Vaśitva);

b) As involving only "names" with no genuinely-existent substrates;

c) As merely micro-momentary products of a process of serial chronological production, this last standpoint being best aided through meditation on "the twelve links of conditioned co-production" (*pratītya-samutpāda*).

75. The point in this śloka is that, in cultivating the three gates to liberation, if one fails to remain focused on the Mahāyāna quest for the utmost, right, and perfect enlightenment of a buddha, one will proceed on through these three gates right into the nirvāṇa realized by the arhat or pratyekabuddha with the tragic result that one forever loses the Bodhisattva Path.

One can only become a buddha through completing the cultivation of the bodhisattva's six perfections and myriad practices. It is because there is absolutely no room for deviation in aiming one's determination accordingly that Nāgārjuna finishes the *śloka* with two imperative negative warnings, lest we lose the Bodhisattva Path:

1) "Do not bear in mind anything not resulting in a buddha's body."

2) "And, in that matter, one must not allow any negligence."

76. As for "the right and definite position" (*samyaktva-niyāma*), for the bodhisattva, this is typically held to coincide with the eighth bodhisattva ground, "the ground of unshakability" (*acala bhūmi*) wherein the bodhisattva has reached the stage of definite irreversibility in his path to buddhahood.

For a *śrāvaka* or pratyekabuddha, this "right and definite position" coincides with the Path of Seeing wherein the emptiness of all phenomena is perceived directly. From the standpoint of this treatise, once this position is reached, a *śrāvaka* practitioner is definitely bound for final nirvāṇa as an arhat and will definitely not be able to switch over to the Bodhisattva Path.

The rationale for Nāgārjuna's strong and repeated emphasis in this treatise on avoiding the nirvāṇa of the Śrāvaka Vehicle arhat is that, were the bodhisattva to allow himself to enter it through failing to maintain the skillful means and altruistic vow which would ordinarily prevent him from doing so, this would bring about an irreversible fall from the Bodhisattva Path from which someone aspiring to buddhahood cannot ever under any circumstances recover. Even in spite of the teachings offered in the *Lotus Sutra* (which Nāgārjuna will discuss later), that is the position of this treatise. This entire issue is dealt with at much greater length in the ensuing *ślokas* of this treatise wherein Nāgārjuna offers the view that the *Lotus Sutra* circumstance was a special one specific to certain individuals which cannot be generalized to the general population of Buddhist practitioners who might otherwise feel that, even after arhatship, buddhahood might somehow be possible.

77. The thirty-two dharmas serving to define a bodhisattva are listed in multiple places in the Buddhist canon. Two of note are the *Mahāratnakūṭa Sūtra* (大寶積經 T11.310.633a) and Nāgārjuna's treatise on the ten bodhisattva grounds, the *Daśabhūmika Vibhāṣā* (十住毘婆沙論 / T26.1521.93c–4a).

My translation of Nāgārjuna's *Daśabhūmika Vibhāṣā* passage containing his list of the thirty-two bodhisattva dharmas (and seven additional subsidiary dharmas) is as follows:

If a person generates the aspiration to seek the Buddha Path and says of himself that he is a bodhisattva, but only in a way empty of meaning takes on the name, this while failing to put into practice the meritorious qualities such as the lovingly-kind mind, the compassionate mind, and the pāramitās, this is not one who qualifies as a bodhisattva. He is like a city made of dirt (adobe?; stamped-earth?) being called a "bejeweled city." This amounts only to cheating himself, cheating the Buddhas, and also cheating the beings in the world. If a person possesses thirty-two sublime dharmas while also being able to generate the vows, it is this which qualifies him as a genuine bodhisattva. What are the thirty-two? [They are]:

1) With a profound mind, he seeks every form of happiness for all beings;

2) He is able to enter into the wisdom of the Buddhas;

3) Through his own investigations, he knows whether or not he is capable of becoming a buddha;

4) He does not course in detestation of others;

5) His mind intent on pursuing the Path is solid;

6) He does not resort to and rely on the feigning of close affections;

7) He constantly serves as a close friend to beings even up to the point of entering nirvāṇa;

8) Whether personally close or at a distance, his mind remains the same;

9) He does not retreat from good endeavors he has assented to;

10) He does not cut off his kindness for all beings;

11) He does not cut off his compassion for all beings;

12) In his constant pursuit of right Dharma, his mind remains unwearied and does not shrink away from it;

13) He is diligent and never sated in his generation of the mind of vigor;

14) He is possessed of extensive learning and is comprehending of concepts;

15) He is constantly aware of his own faults;

16) He does not deride others for their shortcomings;

17) In all matters he observes or hears, he remains constant in his cultivation of the bodhi mind;

18) In giving, he seeks no reward;

19) His observance of the moral-virtue precepts is not done with a motivation to achieve rebirth in any particular place at all (i.e. he does not do so for the sake of celestial rebirth);

20) He exercises patience toward all beings, remaining free of

hatefulness or obstructiveness;

21) He is able to diligently and vigorously cultivate the practice of all roots of goodness;

22) He does not allow himself to take a [celestial] rebirth corresponding to the formless samādhis;

23) His wisdom is inclusive of skillful means;

24) His skillful means are inclusive of the four means of attraction (giving; pleasing words; beneficial actions; joint endeavors);

25) He does not have two different capacities for kindness and sympathy for those who observe moral precepts and those who break moral precepts;

26) He is single-minded in his listening to Dharma;

27) He is single-minded when dwelling in an *araṇya* (a secluded meditation retreat);

28) He does not find pleasure in any of the many different and varying sorts of worldly circumstances;

29) He does not covet or retain any attachment for the Small Vehicle;

30) He perceives that the benefit brought about by the Great Vehicle is in fact great;

31) He departs far from bad [spiritual] friends (i.e. bad gurus);

32) He draws close to good [spiritual] friends (i.e. good gurus).

As the bodhisattva abides in these thirty-two dharmas, he is able to perfect seven [additional] dharmas. Specifically, they are:

[1] The four immeasurable minds (kindness; compassion; sympathetic joy; equanimity);

[2] [The ability to] roam about happily in the exercise of the five spiritual powers;

[3] Constancy in reliance upon wisdom;

[4] Constancy in not forsaking either good or evil beings;

[5] Decisiveness in all pronouncements;

[6] Definite truthfulness in all statements;

[7] Non-satiety in the accumulation of every sort of good dharma.

These constitute the thirty-two dharmas and the seven dharmas. A bodhisattva who perfects these qualifies is a genuine bodhisattva.

78. But this inability to stop short of buddhahood only becomes true once the "right and definite position" is reached. Up until that event has occurred coincident with the eighth bodhisattva ground, the bodhisattva is still vulnerable to being turned back to the individual-

liberation nirvāṇa.

79. "Three types of blazing vigor" is probably intended as reference to those exercised in physical, verbal, and mental karma.

80. "The perfection of skillful means" is one of the "ten perfections" standard in the Mahāyāna. Instead of simply translating the term "perfection," Dharmagupta has apparently chosen to use the more-or-less standard Chinese explanation of the etymology of its Sanskrit antecedent *"pāramitā,"* namely "reaching the far shore," this apparently to place extra emphasis on the fact that these *Lotus Sutra* predictions represented the most extreme expression of skillful means as implemented by the Buddha. The opacity of Dharmagupta's rendering forced me to in essence translate *"pāramitā"* twice in the fourth foot of the *śloka,* once as "perfection" in the phrase "the perfection of skillful means," and once as "taking... to the far shore."

81. This *śloka* is referring to the predictions of eventual buddhahood bestowed on arhats in the *Lotus Sutra.* The reason for mentioning these in this treatise is because, with the exception of such special cases, it is generally held that, once a practitioner on the individual-liberation arhat-vehicle path reaches that vehicle's "right and definite position," (正位 a.k.a. 正定位 = *samyaktva niyāma*), he thereby passes beyond any further ability to turn away from arhatship and proceed toward buddhahood on the Bodhisattva Path. Absent this explanation, one might think that no difficulties are posed for the realization of buddhahood by coursing in the mind-states of the Śrāvaka-vehicle and Pratyekabuddha-vehicle paths.

   The reader may find it useful at this point to refer back to Bhikshu Vaśitva's commentary on *śloka* number thirty-two (Those bodhisattvas already dwelling at "the stage of immovability"...) where the issue of predictions is considered in some detail. It includes comments on just this very sort of prediction, which is one of five types. Of the five types, this one is referred to as a "secretly-intentioned and specially-spoken prediction."

82. Nāgārjuna's treatise assumes one is already familiar with the sutras in which these comparisons are made. Hence the *śloka* he provides here is an extremely terse mnemonic intended primarily to remind the reader of the standard sutra-based analogies involved. Since such prior knowledge cannot be assumed for modern-day Dharma students (either East or West), I go ahead and write out the meaning of the *śloka* in full as follows:

> The ability of an irreversible *śrāvaka*-disciple or pratyekabuddha
>   to nourish the seed of buddhahood in their unconditioned state
>   would be like trying to plant seeds in empty space or like trying
>   to grow lotuses on the high plains.

For the bodhisattva, to fall into the paths of *śrāvaka*-disciples or pratyekabuddhas would be like falling over a precipitous cliff to one's death. For the irreversible *śrāvaka*-disciple or pratyekabuddha to aspire to coursing in the Bodhisattva Path would be like someone not trained in mountain climbing to think they could enter and leave deep mountain crevasses or abysses at will rather than be bound to die therein as would certainly be the case.

The realms coursed in by irreversible *śrāvaka*-disciples or pratyekabuddhas, by their very nature, bar any possibility of begetting the dharmas of buddhahood just as an impotent man would be altogether incapable of gaining satisfaction or begetting a child in the sphere of the five desires and just as nobody can possibly transform common quartz into *vaiḍūrya* gems,

Another analogy compares such a prospect to that of being able to cause a burnt seed to germinate and produce growth.

Nāgārjuna's intent here is not to disparage Two-Vehicles practitioners or the paths they have chosen. Rather it is an attempt to warn those contemplating or already confirmed in the Bodhisattva Path that cultivation of the Two-Vehicles path will lead to a point of no return making it impossible to proceed with the Bodhisattva Path, hence the importance of using skillful means when cultivating techniques such as the three gates to liberation lest one fall away from the Bodhisattva Path.

83. "Armor" may be understood to refer to all of those bodhisattva practices protecting one from generating mental afflictions or bad karmic deeds, in particular: patience (*kṣānti*), so as not to become hateful; moral virtue (*śīla*), so as not to fall into the error of reacting negatively; meditative discipline (*dhyāna*), so as to remain entirely unmoved; equanimity (*upekṣā*), so as to have no special affection for the virtuous or enmity for the evil; wisdom (*prajñā*), so as to realize others' evil is just recompense for one's countless bad karmic deeds in the past, so as to realize that there are ultimately no inherently-existent beings or evil deeds to which one might react, and so as to realize that there is no inherently-existent self which might be the victim of others' evil actions; compassion (*karuṇa*), so as to implement the antidote to hatefulness recommended by the Buddha; and vigor (*vīrya*), so as to not grow weary of the length and difficulty of the Bodhisattva Path.

84. Substituting here the graphically similar glyph (已) in place of the obvious scribal error (己), a correction supported by a very specific reference in the commentary as well as by common sense.

85. The "five hindrances" (*nīvaraṇa* or *āvaraṇa*) to which Bhikshu Vaśitva refers are: "desire" (*kāma-chanda*); "ill will" (*vyāpāda*); "lethargy and sleepiness" (*styāna-middha*); "excitedness and regretfulness" (*auddhatya-kaukṛtya*); and "[afflicted] doubt" (*vicikitsā*).

On the question of why "lethargy-and-sleepiness" is a dual-component hindrance, Vasubandhu indicates (in Chapter Five of his *Abhidharma-kośa Bhāṣyam*) that it is because both "lethargy" and "sleepiness" are nourished by the same five factors (bad omens seen in dreams [*tandrī*]; unhappiness [*arati*]; physical exhaustion [*vijṛmbhikā*]; uneven consumption of food [*bhakte'samatā*]; mental depression [*cetaso līnatva*]), are starved by the same single factor (illuminated perception [*āloka-saṃjñā*]), and are productive of the same result of mental languor. (See Pruden, *Abhidharma-kośa Bhāṣyam* [851–2]).

On the question of why "excitedness-and-regretfulness" is a dual-component hindrance, Vasubandhu indicates that it is because both "excitedness" and "regretfulness" are nourished by the same four factors (ideation regarding relatives, land, immortals, previous pleasures and the associated companions), are starved by the same single factor (calmness), and are productive of the same result of mental agitation. (See Pruden, *Abhidharma-kośa-bhāṣyam* [852]).

86. Other editions of the text recommend an initially-attractive emendation referencing a graphically-similar glyph (perhaps a scribal error) in place of the *chang* (常) glyph. I decline it because it suggests an import-neutralizing binome for "should" (應當) directly robbing the stanza of the dual connotations of the *chang* (常) glyph describing the recommended character of one's cultivation: "always, constant"; and b) "faithful, normal." These dual senses are crucial to preserving the essential message: "One must *always* hew to what is *right* while cultivating meditation." Bhikshu Vaśitva's commentary explicitly supports this interpretation. (See next note.)

87. We find here preserved in *Taisho* a four-character parenthetical Chinese editorial note of unknown origin attempting to clarify Bhikshu Vaśitva's comment on Nāgārjuna's use of the term "wrong attachment." That anonymous note says: "This refers to 'extreme urgency.'" (謂太急也) So we have here a comment referencing a standard mental-adjustment issue addressed in most traditional Buddhist meditation texts, that of the need to hew to the middle way in one's mental intensity, taking care to avoid the extremes of "laxity" versus "urgency."

But that little four-character note over-simplifies and in effect ignores the problem being addressed by Nāgārjuna and explained by Bhikshu Vaśitva who are, after all, not discussing "urgency" *per se*, but rather are discussing a common sort of attachment in meditation which has a negative character. When Bhikshu Vaśitva says, "As for 'wrong attachment,' this refers to a type of grasping which is unwholesome," he is referring to a type of metaphysically-erroneous attachment (probably *durgṛhīta*, glossed by Conze as "seize badly"). In abstract discussions on doctrine, this applies for instance to seizing on emptiness so unskillfully that one engages in antonomian denial of the efficacy of cause-and-effect, the classic case of "seizing the snake of emptiness by the tail, thus incurring a morally-fatal snake bite."

Here, however, Nāgārjuna and Bhikshu Vaśitva are discussing meditation wherein the issues, though involving the same negative attachment mechanism, are not precisely the same. They are really referring to grasping at unwholesome states in meditation and then pursuing them with a degree of avid intensity.

This is actually an especially important issue crucial to success in meditation practice. Many unwholesome meditation mind states may arise when cultivating meditative discipline, some arising from karmic propensities rooted in the past, some having to do with unskillfulness in the present, and some having to do with exogenous factors. (See my translation of the Sui Dynasty Dhyāna Master Zhiyi's *Essentials of Buddhist Meditation* for a comprehensive discussion of these issues.)

If one indulges involvement in these mind states, one may experience proliferation and intensification of afflictions. Examples include attachment to powerful psychic phenomena and attachment to intensely blissful sensual pleasures arising in meditation as subtle *prāṇa* energies manifest in meditation. The nature of these "unwholesome attachments" is such that, because they engender such intense bliss, one may be hard pressed to avoid actively pursuing them by "cultivating them with intensity." Lending any supportive attention at all to these phenomena tends to magnify the afflicted-attachment and distraction-invoking aspects and tends to make them more chronically present. This inevitably kills concentration, thereby straight-away defeating the right-Dharma rationale behind one's taking up the cultivation of meditation in the first place.

It is for this reason that the 25,000-line *Great Perfection of Wisdom Sutra* and Nāgārjuna himself state, "It is on account of remaining unattached to the delectable flavor of meditative states that one becomes able to achieve the perfection of dhyāna meditation." (See my translation *Nāgārjuna on the Six Perfections*, at the very beginning of the chapters devoted to the perfection of dhyāna meditation.)

88. Dharmagupta's Chinese is vague here and has required minor interpretive interpolations in the sixth of the ten points. The meaning is clear enough, however, and in the absence of countervailing evidence, the text should be taken at the face value available in this English rendition. There are two related sutras in the Chinese canon, one which is Mahāyāna in character (T11.0314.764a–70b) and the other of which appears not to be so. Bhikshu Vaśitva's list does not conform

closely to either one, though in tenor, it is more attuned to the latter (T24.1480.956c–57b).

89. Dhyāna Master Zhiyi devotes an entire chapter to the issue of demons, demonic karma, how they manifest, and how their influences may be countered in his *Essentials for Practicing Calming-and-Insight and Dhyāna Meditation.* I have translated that entire work and am publishing it separately under the title *The Essentials of Buddhist Meditation.*

90. In his listing here of the thirty-seven wings of enlightenment, one may notice that Bhikshu Vaśitva lists not thirty-seven, but rather a total of forty-one components. However, this is merely because "the four bases of right severance" has developed in Buddhist doctrine as an alternative list to "the four right efforts." Bhikshu Vaśitva simply lists all eight of these list components, but places them all here under the "four bases of right severance."

It is interesting to note that such a confirmed Mahāyānist as Nāgārjuna points to the thirty-seven wings of bodhi as fundamental and essential components of Buddhist practice. Although this should be obvious, some latter-day advocates of the Great-Vehicle path have tended at times to diminish their importance, championing the various iterations of the perfections in their stead, almost as if the perfections and the thirty-seven wings were mutually exclusive practice modes.

Nāgārjuna comments on this issue in his commentary on the 25,000-line *Great Perfection of Wisdom Sutra,* pointing out that, absent competence in the thirty-seven wings of bodhi, there is no way that a bodhisattva would be able to endure on the Mahāyāna path for countless lifetimes without falling away, back into the karma-bound sufferings of cyclic existence.

See my translation of this extensive discussion entitled *Nāgārjuna on the Thirty-Seven Wings of Enlightenment.* Here is a brief selection from that text:

> Furthermore, where is it said that the thirty-seven wings are only dharmas of the Śrāvaka-disciples and the Pratyekabuddhas and are not the path of the Bodhisattvas? Within this very *Prajñāpāramitā [Sutra],* in the chapter entitled "The Mahāyāna," the Buddha discussed the four stations of mindfulness and so forth until we come to the eight-fold path of the Āryas. Nor is it stated anywhere within the three repositories of the Mahāyāna canon that the thirty-seven wings are solely dharmas of the Small Vehicle.
>
> It was on account of his great compassion that the Buddha proclaimed the thirty-seven-winged path to nirvāṇa. It is in correspondence to the vows of beings and the causes and conditions of beings that each of them then takes up his [own

particular] path. Those persons who seek that of the Śrāvaka-disciples gain the path of the Śrāvaka-disciples. Those persons who plant the good roots of the Pratyekabuddha gain the path of the Pratyekabuddha. Those who seek the path of the Buddha gain the path of the Buddha. This corresponds to one's original vows, to the acuity or dullness of one's faculties, and to the possession or non-possession of the great compassion.

91. Adopting here the variant found in four other editions, thus substituting *shan* (善) for *ran* (然). This produces a sense more consistent with the context of the *śloka* and the explanation provided by Bhikshu Vaśitva's commentary.

92. As noted in Bhikshu Vaśitva, the four means of attraction (*catvāri-saṃgraha-vastūni*) are: giving (*dāna-saṃgraha*), pleasing discourse (*priya-vādita-saṃgraha*), beneficial actions (*artha-caryā-saṃgraha*), and accompaniment of others in joint endeavors (*samānārthatā-saṃgraha*). These are four essential altruistic stratagems through which the bodhisattva successfully influences beings to more readily accept and cultivate Dharma where they might not otherwise be well-disposed to do so.

93. Bhikshu Vaśitva makes no comment on Nāgārjuna's instruction to "avoid any harm to the retinue of others." This may well refer to attempting to draw into one's own following the disciples of some other teacher of Dharma, perhaps based on jealousy, perhaps based on arrogance, or perhaps based on either well-founded or baseless disapproval of some aspect of that Dharma teacher's abilities. In any case, chipping away at the respect others hold for some other ethically pure teacher of Dharma would not represent the highest expression of the Bodhisattva Path. Hence the warning to avoid it.

94. A *caitya* is a memorial monument, mound, or stupa commemorating a holy place or person. Sometimes they are located where the remains of a realized being were cremated (as with the cremation stupa close to Kusinigar) and sometimes they are located where the relics and ashes are currently preserved and made the focus of commemorative reverence.

When he mentions "neglectful beings who have turned their back on the Dharma," Bhikshu Vaśitva is perhaps referring to monastics occupying temple or stupa facilities, but not seeing to their maintenance in a manner appropriately respectful to and protective of Dharma. Under such a circumstance, a follower of the Bodhisattva Path might look into the matter and see what if anything might be done to offer support in restoration of the facilities and perhaps even, through the fourth of the four means of attraction ("joint endeavors"), he might simultaneously buoy renewed enthusiasm for more attentive cultivation of the Path.

95. "The six dharmas of harmony and respectfulness" pertain to six identities in the monastic community already united through common observance of *brahmacarya* (strict celibacy):

1) Kindness in physical karma.

2) Kindness in verbal karma.

3) Kindness in mental karma.

4) Common and equal sharing of offerings contributed to the monastic community by the laity.

5) Common and identical monastic moral-code adherence as defined by the Buddha.

6) Common and identical adherence to right view as defined by the Buddha.

Although the Buddha clearly formulated this set of bases for harmony and mutual respect with the monastic community in mind, there is no reason that an analogue version of the same six dharmas could not serve as a useful community-unity reference for lay Buddhists, this by simply stipulating the five lay precepts or the ten good karmic deeds as the operative standard for what is agreed to constitute basic moral excellence.

(The five precepts proscribe killing, stealing, sexual misconduct, lying, and intoxicants, whereas the ten good karmic deeds involve abstention from killing, stealing, sexual misconduct, lying, harsh speech, divisive speech, frivolous / lewd speech, covetousness, hatefulness, and wrong views.)

96. The phrase "those who may be given offerings" may seem confusing if we assume that this option is open to anyone. However, in a community of monks observing the strictest traditions, none will personally even touch money or other valuables (such as gold or silver). In such a situation, an offering to the community at large might only properly be accepted on its behalf by the lay attendant of a senior monastic holding a position of responsibility in the community (such as attendants of the *upādhyāyas* or *ācāryas* mentioned by Bhikshu Vaśitva).

In the case of an offering intended to benefit an individual monk not living in community, but rather living in a hermitage or other solitary situation, the offering might have to be made to a trusted lay attendant, or in the absence of same, might have to be made to close relatives such as parents or an elder brother who could be trusted to use it in benefiting the monastic recipient.

As for the extreme scrupulousness regarding avoiding slander of the Dharma or one who expounds Dharma (as recommended by

Nāgārjuna), and regarding avoiding merely slighting or deceiving one who speaks Dharma (as warned against by Bhikshu Vaśitva), one should realize that such karma not only threatens the goodness imbuing one's own requisites for bodhi, it also establishes causes for future-life difficulty in ever being able to encounter either the monastic community or the Dharma again.

97. There is no inherent implication in either Nāgārjuna's *śloka* or Bhikshu Vaśitva's commentary that those specializing in teaching Dharma would have any personal interest or need to possess "gold and jewels." On the contrary, they are most likely to be most well aware of the karmic dangers involved in their misuse and most likely to understand their correct use in serving the interests of the Three Jewels (the Buddha, the Dharma, and the Monastic Sangha).

As for the passage devoted to faithful remembrance of scriptures, it may be helpful to remember that important scriptures were traditionally committed to memory by monastics, especially by those who specialized in teaching the Dharma. This was done perhaps primarily because the teachings were most effectively internalized in this way, but also because palm-leaf copies were comparatively rare, fragile, and prone to rapid destruction by white ants.

Bhikshu Vaśitva is likely referring here to the samādhis of the sixth bodhisattva ground, the ground known as "the ground of present manifestation" (*abhimukha-bhūmi*).

98. Nāgārjuna is not insisting here that one should fail to believe in the existence of "gods, nāgas (rendered in the Chinese as "dragons"), and spirits." On the contrary, those classes of entities do exist and often enough do have enough in the way of low-grade powers to seriously interfere with a practitioner's mental clarity, especially in cases where one has voluntarily entered into some sort of psycho-spiritual relationship with them.

What all of these entities have in common is a complete inability to extricate their followers from the endless karma-bound sufferings of cyclic existence. Hence Nāgārjuna's admonition: "One must not invest one's faith in any of them."

As regards Bhikshu Vaśitva's advice to avoid nominally "spiritual" activities not preceded by careful reflection and not clearly based directly on the Buddha's teaching, the Buddha admonished the monastic community to avoid not only those actions which he had specifically forbidden in the moral codes, but also to avoid those actions which were semblances of what was specifically forbidden. Where we find no clear basis in classic Southern Tradition or Mahāyāna teachings for certain practices which may have become popular after the first one thousand years post-nirvāṇa, a certain amount of circumspection is well justified lest one fall into practices which are essentially non-Buddhist and hence not really conducive to liberation at all. An obvious example would be propitiation of ghosts, wrathful deities, and so forth. There are of course many other examples of which the serious Dharma student will already be well aware.

99. Bhikshu Vaśitva mentions the *dhūta* practices. These are relatively ascetic forms of Dharma practice, practices which require considerable dedication to uphold in practice. Examples include: abiding in a charnel field; living in solitude in a hermitage; living out in the open; living beneath a tree, usually only for a fixed amount of time after one must move to another tree; eating but one meal each day, consuming it before noon; eating that one meal at a single sitting; eating a fixed amount in that one meal; having eaten the single meal before noon, not drinking beverages other than water after noon; wearing only robes made of cast-off rags; only wearing the three robes; only consuming food obtained on the alms round; and only sitting, never lying down.

The difference between the Buddhist set of twelve *dhūta* practices and the asceticism of the non-Buddhists is that the *dhūta* practices all actually benefit some aspect or another of one's spiritual practice, bringing about more rapid progress in the development of essential spiritual qualities. This sets them apart from useless forms of asceticism found in non-Buddhist traditions, practices such as: abiding on a bed of nails; wandering around naked, covered with ashes; standing on one leg; never cutting one's hair; and attempting to wash away one's evil karma simply by washing in the Ganges River.

100. Bhikshu Vaśitva's list of the ten reflections on the impure records an only slightly different list from the commonly-encountered Northern-School list of nine reflections deriving from the *Mahāprajñāpāramitā Sūtra* (upon which Nāgārjuna comments at great length in his exegesis on that sutra). Bhikshu Vaśitva's list does not include the "burned" corpse of the list of nine, and adds the "oozing" corpse and "dismembered" corpse not in the list of nine. For more on this from Nāgārjuna himself, see my translation of his discussion of this practice entitled *Nāgārjuna on the Nine Reflections*.

101. Bhikshu Vaśitva's list of the eight realizations of great men is standard, but somewhat different from the Mahāyāna sutra of that name translated in the middle of the second century by Tripiṭaka Master An Shigao (T17.0779.715b). Bhikshu Vaśitva's list accords with the version recorded by Nāgārjuna in his treatise on the ten bodhisattva grounds (T26.1521.92c) and with the Āgamas (T01.0001.55c).

The scripture translated by An Shigao describing eight realizations of great men is somewhat more profound in terms of the breadth and depth of topics mentioned and in its descriptiveness of the Path. Topics it mentions upon which the *Āgama* list is silent are: impermanence, suffering, emptiness, and non-self; the practice of giving; equal regard for friends and adversaries; absence of grudge-bearing thought; non-hatred of evil-doers; renunciation of cyclic existence; and generation of the altruistic Mahāyāna mind to realize buddhahood, relieve the sufferings of beings, take on the sufferings of beings, and establish beings in happiness. This sutra is so extremely short, I simply translate it here as the easiest way to illustrate the ways in which it is different:

The Sutra on the Eight Realizations of Great Men
(T17.0779.715b)
Translated by the Parthian Tripiṭaka Master An Shigao (100?–170 CE)
Of the Latter Han Dynasty

This was spoken for the sake of the disciples of the Buddha. They were constant in their ultimately sincere recitation and remembrance, both day and night, of the eight realizations of great men.

First, one realizes:

That the world is impermanent;

That one's country is a fragile entity;

That the four great elements are freighted with suffering and are themselves empty;

That the five aggregates are devoid of self, that they are subject to change and transformation through production and destruction, and that they are empty, false, and devoid of any [inherently-existent subjective] agent.

That the mind is a source of evil and that one's physical form is like a thicket in which karmic offenses are created.

One carries on analytic contemplation in accordance with these factors and gradually abandons cyclic births and deaths.

Second, one realizes that an abundance of desire is the basis of suffering, that the laboriousness and weariness arising in the sphere of cyclic births and deaths arises from desire, and that it is in less desire and realization of the unconditioned that the body and mind experience sovereign independence.

Third, one realizes that the mind is insatiable and prone to ever greater seeking and to the proliferation of the evils associated with karmic offenses. The bodhisattva is not this way. He is constantly mindful in knowing when enough is enough. He establishes himself in circumstances akin to poverty, and guards [the practices which accord with] the Path, realizing that it is wisdom alone which constitutes the Path.

Fourth, one realizes that indolence is associated with falling [into unfortunate circumstances]. Thus one is constant in the practice of vigor and the destruction of the evils associated with the afflictions. One conquers the four demons [of the four great elements] and escapes from the prison of the aggregates and sense realms.

Fifth, one realizes the nature of delusion and cyclic births and deaths. The bodhisattva remains constantly mindful of this and, being broad-ranging in his studies, possesses much learning. He increases his wisdom, perfects eloquence, provides transformative teaching to everyone, and thereby brings great happiness to all.

Sixth, one realizes that poverty, suffering, and an abundance of adversaries makes for the sudden and tragic development of conditions associated with evil. Thus the bodhisattva practices giving and is equally mindful of both adversaries and close relations. He does not hold in mind evils from long ago, and does not detest people who are evil.

Seventh, one realizes the faults and disastrousness associated with the five desires. Even though one may still be a layperson, he does not allow himself to become defiled by worldly pleasures. He bears in mind those "vessels of Dharma" possessing the three robes and the bowl. He becomes determined to leave behind the home life and to guard [the practice of] the Path in pristine purity. Thus he becomes lofty and far-reaching in the brahman conduct (celibacy, etc.) and acts out of kindness and compassion for everyone.

Eighth, one realizes that cyclic births and deaths are as if ablaze and are connected with countless sufferings and afflictions. Thus one generates the mind associated with the Mahāyāna resolved to rescue everyone. He vows to substitute for beings in the taking on of their incalculably many sufferings and vows to cause all beings to develop the most ultimate form of great happiness.

Eight matters such as these are realized by all buddhas and bodhisattvas, those who are great men. They are vigorous in the practice of the Path and are imbued with kindness and compassion as they cultivate wisdom. They go aboard the ship of the Dharma body and thereby arrive at the shore of nirvāṇa. They then repeatedly return to the sphere of cyclic birth and death to bring about the liberation of beings.

They resort to the above eight matters in their instruction and guidance of everyone. Thus they influence beings to awaken to the sufferings of cyclic birth and death, influence them to abandon the five desires, and influence them to cultivate the mind's path of the Āryas.

If a disciple of the Buddha recites these eight topics, he thereby extinguishes countless karmic transgressions and advances along toward bodhi. He will swiftly ascend to the right enlightenment, thus eternally cutting off cyclic births and deaths and abiding forever in happiness.

End of The Sutra on the Eight Realizations of Great Men

102. These powers may be realized as a consequence of past-life spiritual cultivation or as a consequence of present-life path practices such as dhyāna meditation. Such "powers" are not, in and of themselves, particularly desirable or useful unless counterbalanced by wisdom, this because of the inherent karmic hazards to both self and others in their misuse.

These dangers make cultivation and realization of Mahāyāna altruistic motivation (bodhicitta) and the four immeasurables more urgent. Why? They help insure the constant presence of that correct motivation which always bears in mind the spiritual welfare of others. If one does gain adequately counter-balancing wisdom together with well-developed integration of the four immeasurables, one may then skillfully use such powers in teaching. This is why Nāgārjuna makes the four immeasurables a primary topic in the very next śloka.

The cognition of another's thoughts, and the cognition of another's past lives are probably the two most useful of these spiritual "skills" in teaching others. This is because the knowledge which they allow one to access is especially helpful in the clear diagnosis of another's karmic circumstances. With the ability to clearly observe past lives and present thought-streams, one becomes better able to select the precisely appropriate teachings well tailored to the karmic needs of any given Dharma student.

103. Although Bhikshu Vaśitva implicitly describes how the generation of powers through cultivation of the four bases of spiritual powers flows forth from the four immeasurables, he does not really comment directly on Nāgārjuna's declaration that the four immeasurables (apramāṇacitta) "govern" the practices and spiritual powers mentioned immediately above. Nāgārjuna's intent in making the statement is worthy of our curiosity and warrants further exploration.

The rationale for Nāgārjuna's statement regarding the "governance" function of the four immeasurables may be in large measure deduced simply through recalling the uses of the four immeasurables (see my translation of Nāgārjuna on the Four Immeasurable Minds):

Kindness (*maitrī*) nurtures an affectionate mindfulness of beings, counters the development of hatred toward particularly unsavory classes of beings, and has as its motivation the desire to provide beings with happiness and security.

Compassion (*karuṇā*) causes one to bear in mind the physical and mental sufferings of beings, counters the development of any tendency to want to harm beings coursing in evil, and has as its motivation the wish to relieve suffering.

Sympathetic joy (*muditā*) nurtures a concordant celebration in the successes of beings, counters any tendency toward petty jealousies, and has as its motivation to cause beings to graduate from the mere experience of happiness to the ability to experience joyfulness.

Equanimity (*upekṣā*) allows one to relinquish any attachment to the goals involved in the first three of the four immeasurables even as one refuses to forsake the welfare of beings. The consequence of cultivating equanimity is an ability to abide in a state devoid of either aversion or affection. This is to a certain degree essential to a bodhisattva's ability to course on in the infinitely long practice of the Bodhisattva Path without succumbing to disappointment over the seeming futility of wishing to bestow happiness on all beings, to relieve the suffering of all beings, and to bring them all to a state of abundant joyfulness.

Finally, given the above, it should be obvious how the four immeasurables would counter any tendency toward arrogant misapplication of powers. It is in these senses then that one can understand Nāgārjuna's statement that the four immeasurables "govern" the spiritual powers.

104. Nāgārjuna relates this scripture-based analogy more fully in his commentary on the *Great Perfection of Wisdom Sutra* (大智度論 / T25.1509.145b9–26). It is quoted here from my translation of *Nāgārjuna on the Six Perfections*:

> In the *Buddha Speaks the Analogy of the Poisonous Snakes Sutra*, there once was a man who had offended the King. The King ordered that he be required to carry around a basket and look after it. Inside the basket there were four poisonous snakes. The King ordered the criminal to look after them and raise them.
>
> This man thought to himself, "It is a difficult thing to have to draw close to four snakes. If one grows close to them, they bring harm to a person. I could not raise even one of them, how much the less could I do that for four of them." And so he cast aside the basket and ran away.
>
> The King ordered five men carrying knives to chase after him. There was yet another man who tried to persuade him to

obey. [This other man] had it in mind to bring him harm and so said to him, "Just raise them in a sensible fashion. There will be no suffering in that." But the man became wise to this and so ran off, fleeing for his life. When he came to an empty village there was a good man who assisted him by telling him, "Although this village is empty, it is a place that is frequented by thieves. If you now take up residence here you will certainly be harmed by the thieves. Be careful. Don't dwell here."

At this point he took off again and next arrived at a great river. On the other side of the river there was a different country. That country was a peaceful, blissful, and easeful place. It was a pure place devoid of any form of calamity or adversity. Then he gathered together a mass of reeds and branches and bound them into the form of a raft. He moved it along with his hands and feet. He exerted all of his strength in seeking to make a crossing. When he had reached the other shore, he was at peace, happy, and free of distress.

The King represents the demon king. The basket represents the human body. The four poisonous snakes represent the four great elements. The five knife-wielding assassins represent the five aggregates. The man of fine speech but evil mind represents defiled attachment. The empty village represents the six sense faculties. The thieves represent the six sense objects. The one man who took pity on him and instructed him represents the good [spiritual] teacher.

The great river represents love. The raft represents the eightfold right path. The hands and feet earnestly applied to making a crossing represent vigor. This shore represents this world. The far shore represents nirvāṇa. The man who crossed over represents the arhat who has put an end to outflow impurities. This is just the same in the dharma of the bodhisattva.

Those unfamiliar with the idea of "the four elements" of earth, water, fire, and air may find them conceptually confusing when they are stood alongside the western scientific "elements" most of us know from studying chemistry and physics. In fact, the concept is quite simple and easy to understand in scientific terms, as follows: The "four elements" of Indian Buddhist thought simply refer to the four elemental phases within which all manifest phenomena may be subsumed.

The four elements are not actually inherently-existent "fixed" categories reflecting an irreducible chemical nature as per the western scientific concept of "elements." In fact, it is common for the elements of western science to manifest, depending upon their temperature, as any of these four elemental phases referred to by Buddhists: as "earth" (i.e. "solidity," when at lower relative temperatures), as "water" (i.e. "liquidity," when heated to a relatively higher temperature), as "fire" (during combustion), and as "air" (i.e. "vaporousness," when forced by heat to enter a gaseous state).

Understanding this relationship between the two concepts of "elements" should make the nature of the Buddha's "four elements" obvious and conceptually agreeable, both as valid categories of epistemological observation and as important didactic concepts assisting understanding of the Path.

Now, having made the concept of the four primary elements more intellectually accessible, it is worth noting that Nāgārjuna makes a point of utterly demolishing the idea that they might enjoy any degree of ultimate reality. An exemplary case may be found in the first chapter (*ślokas* 83–90) of the *Ratnāvalī*. See under separate cover my complete translation of that treatise's earliest extant version (approximately 550 CE, via Tripiṭaka Master Paramārtha).

It is precisely the mutability of the four elemental phases described by the Buddha which make them every bit as dangerous as carrying around a basket of venomous snakes which may bite and kill one at any time.

105. "Field of merit," is a specific reference to recipients of generosity which, through that act of giving, produce karmic merit for the benefactor. The Buddha, the Dharma, and the Ārya Sangha are the most obvious examples. In this context, the reference is specifically to monastic sangha members serving as teachers of Dharma.

The Buddha sought to illustrate this concept by ordering that the robes of monks and nuns be sewn in a patchwork pattern resembling the patch-work appearance of plots of cultivated farmland, this to illustrate that deeds done in support of monastics are karmically meritorious and are bound to bring definite karmic rewards. When done, such deeds plant karmic "seeds" which sprout forth as positive karmic circumstances in the benefactor's future.

106. In fascicle twenty-seven of his commentary on the *Great Perfection of Wisdom Sutra*, Nāgārjuna lists the four lineage bases of the ārya (*āryavaṃśa*) as: "refraining from selective discrimination regarding robes, food, bedding, and medicines, while delighting in cutting off suffering and cultivating meditative absorption." (大智度論 / T25.1509.258a)

107. "Brahman conduct" (*brahmacarya*) refers primarily to the absolute celibacy vow of a monk, nun, novice, or female probationer, but also refers less directly to the other major monastic vows.

It may be worth noting here that neither Nāgārjuna or Bhikshu

Vaśitva are recommending either tolerating or covering up ethics violations in the Buddhist community. The Buddha laid down very clear methods for dealing with all such problems. Traditional Buddhist communities adhering to those protocols deal with these sorts of issues very efficiently and effectively.

108. When Bhikshu Vaśitva mentions "dharmas not held in common with any other beings," he is directly referencing "the eighteen dharmas exclusive to the Buddhas" and indirectly referencing the ten powers, the four fearlessnesses, and the four unimpeded knowledges which, although shared to a greater or lesser degree by exalted beings such as arhats, pratyekabuddhas, and bodhisattvas, are unfamiliar territory for the common man. I list these thirty-six dharmas below, as short selections from much larger discussions in Nāgārjuna's commentary on the *Great Perfection of Wisdom Sutra*, this to make it obvious why Nāgārjuna would warn us: "One should refrain from using the discriminating mind and doubt in fathoming the Buddha and the Dharma of the Buddhas."

The Eighteen Dharmas Exclusive to Buddhas:

1) They are free of physical errors.

2) They are free of verbal errors.

3) They are free of errors in mindfulness.

4) They are free of thoughts tethered to distinctions.

5) They are free of unconcentrated thoughts.

6) They are free of equanimity deriving from incomplete awareness.

7) Their zeal is free of any diminishment (i.e. always complete).

8) Their vigor is free of any diminishment (i.e. always complete).

9) Their mindfulness is free of any diminishment (i.e. always complete).

10) Their wisdom is free of any diminishment (i.e. always complete).

11) Their liberations are free of any diminishment (i.e. always complete).

12) Their knowledge and vision associated with the liberations are free of any diminishment (i.e. always complete).

13) All of their physical actions accord with their prior cognition.

14) All of their verbal actions accord with their prior cognition.

15) All of their mental actions accord with their prior cognition.

16) They are unimpeded in their knowledge of the past.

17) They are unimpeded in their knowledge of the future.

18) They are unimpeded in their knowledge of the present.

The Ten Powers:

The first power is that he knows in accordance with actual truth what can be as what can be and what cannot be as what cannot be.

The second power is that he knows all of the karmic activity and all of the experiences of beings throughout past time, throughout future time, and in the present time, knows the location at which they created the karmic action, knows its associated causes and conditions, and knows the associated retribution.

The third power is that he knows all of the dhyānas, liberations, samādhis, and absorptions and knows in accordance with actual truth the distinctive characteristics defining their relative defilement and purity.

The fourth power is that he knows all of the faculties possessed by other beings and knows in accordance with actual truth the characteristics by which they (the faculties) qualify as superior or inferior.

The fifth power is that he knows all of the different sorts of desires possessed by other beings.

The sixth power is that he knows all of the world's countless categories of different natures.

The seventh power is that he knows the characteristic features of the end point of all paths.

The eighth power is that he knows the various sorts of previous lifetimes together with their commonly-held characteristics and their commonly-held causes and conditions, knows them for a single lifetime, for two lifetimes, and so forth until we come to a hundred thousand lifetimes, knows them from the very beginning of the kalpa on through to the very end of the kalpa, and knows, "I possessed this surname and this given name as I abided among those particular beings, consumed such-and-such drink and food, and experienced such-and-such sufferings and happinesses, and possessed a lifespan of such-and-such a length. Having died among those beings, I was then reborn in this place. Having died in this place, I returned to birth in this place. And when I was born in this place, precisely this was my surname, given name, the sorts of drink and food consumed, the sufferings and happinesses experienced, and the length of lifespan lived out."

The ninth power is that the Buddha's heavenly eye is purified beyond that of the heavenly eye possessed by the gods. He sees with that eye the time of beings' death, the time of their births, the fineness and ugliness of their physical features, whether they are great or small, whether they fall into the wretched destinies, and whether they fall in among the wholesome destinies.

He sees that they undergo karmic retribution on account of the causes and conditions associated with such-and-such karmic activity, sees that the evil physical karmic activity of these beings ripens completely, sees that their evil verbal karmic activity ripens completely, and sees that their evil mental karmic activity ripens completely.

He sees the erroneous views leading them to slander the Āryas, sees that the karmic activity associated with those erroneous views ripens completely, and sees that, on account of these causes and conditions, when their physical body comes to ruin and dies, they then enter the wretched destinies wherein they are reborn in the hells.

He sees that the wholesome physical karmic activity of these beings ripens completely, sees that their wholesome verbal karmic activity ripens completely, sees that their wholesome mental karmic activity ripens completely, and sees that their refraining from slandering the Āryas, their correct views, and their karmic actions arising from correct views—these all ripen completely as well. He sees that, on account of these causes and conditions, when their physical body comes to ruin and dies, they then enter into the wholesome destinies and are reborn in the heavens.

The tenth power is that, because the Buddha has brought all outflow impurities to an end, he has achieved the liberation associated with the mind free of outflow impurities, has achieved the wisdom associated with the mind free of outflow impurities, and knows and recognizes for himself, in accordance with actual truth, that, with respect to the dharmas of the present, "My births are already ended, my observance of the prohibitions has already been accomplished, and all subsequent existence has been brought to an end."

The Four Fearlessnesses (a.k.a. "grounds of self-confidence"):

The first fearlessness: The Buddha set forth the honest statement in which he claimed, "I am a person possessing right knowledge of all things. I do not see even the slightest sign that I should fear that any śramaṇa, brahman, god, *māra*, Brahmā, or member of any other group could rightfully state that I do not know these dharmas. Based on this, I have realized the security and fearlessness of one established in the position of the leader among the Āryas [and abide there] like the king of bulls. In the midst of the Great Assembly, I roar the lion's roar and set rolling the brahman wheel which no śramaṇa, brahman, god, *māra*, Brahmā, or member of any other group can rightfully set rolling. This is the first of the fearlessnesses.

The second fearlessness: The Buddha set forth the honest statement in which he claimed, "I have put an end to all outflow impurities. I do not see even the slightest sign that I should fear that any śramaṇa, brahman, god, māra, Brahmā, or member of any other group could rightfully state that I have not brought these outflow impurities to an end. Based on this, I have realized the security and fearlessness of one established in the position of the leader among the Āryas [and abide there] like the king of bulls. In the midst of the Great Assembly, I roar the lion's roar and set rolling the brahman wheel which no śramaṇa, brahman, god, māra, Brahmā, or member of any other group can rightfully set rolling. This is the second of the fearlessnesses.

The third fearlessness: The Buddha set forth the honest statement in which he claimed, "I have described the dharmas which constitute obstacles. I do not see even the slightest sign that I should fear that any śramaṇa, brahman, god, māra, Brahmā, or member of any other group could rightfully state that one may take on these obstructive dharmas and yet not find that they obstruct the Path. Based on this, I have realized the security and fearlessness of one established in the position of the leader among the Āryas [and abide there] like the king of bulls. In the midst of the Great Assembly, I roar the lion's roar and set rolling the brahman wheel which no śramaṇa, brahman, god, māra, Brahmā, or member of any other group can rightfully set rolling. This is the third of the fearlessnesses.

The fourth fearlessness: The Buddha set forth the honest statement in which he claimed, "The path of the Ārya which I have proclaimed is able to take one beyond the world. If one follows this path, one becomes able to put an end to all suffering. I do not see even the slightest sign that I should fear that any śramaṇa, brahman, god, māra, Brahmā, or member of any other group could rightfully state that, coursing in this path, one remains unable to go beyond the world and unable to put an end to suffering. Based on this, I have realized the security and fearlessness of one established in the position of the leader among the Āryas [and abide there] like the king of bulls. In the midst of the Great Assembly, I roar the lion's roar and set rolling the brahman wheel which no śramaṇa, brahman, god, māra, Brahmā, or member of any other group can rightfully set rolling. This is the fourth of the fearlessnesses.

The Four Unimpeded Knowledges: Unimpeded knowledge in the ability to bring forth meanings, dharmas, language, and eloquence.

109. *Upādhyāyas* are monastic preceptors and instructors of slightly lesser station, whereas the *ācāryas* are those who discharge the highest monastic teaching and precept-transmittal responsibilities.

110. By "the most profound of dharmas," Nāgārjuna would likely include any of the Great Vehicle teachings which would not be readily understood and believed by an audience dedicated to rapid acquisition of the individual-liberation paths culminating in arhatship or pratyeka-buddhahood. For example, we have:

1) Not just "the emptiness of persons" which is already available in those traditions (but potentially problematic for a lay audience), but rather also: "the emptiness of dharmas" (and its implications for understanding and practice).

2) The identity of nirvāṇa and *saṃsāra* (cyclic existence).

3) The identity of afflictions (*kleśas*) and bodhi (the danger being here that a shocked audience might misconstrue this to imply endorsement of affliction-ridden karma).

4) The great kindness and compassion of the bodhisattva (as distinct from the mere mind-conditioning contemplation of kindness and compassion as affliction-countering stances, this latter being what is typical in Two-Vehicles' *brahma-vihāra* practice).

5) The three great *asaṃkhyeya* eons of practice required to perfect the causes of buddhahood, including the willingness to enter even the hells to pursue the Bodhisattva Path.

Teaching such dharmas to a Two-Vehicles audience poses two obvious dangers:

1) They might well be moved to slander Great-Vehicle teachings, thus doing themselves unnecessary but very serious karmic harm.

2) They could well find that their faith in the Śrāvaka Vehicle is undermined while they are as yet unable to develop deep faith in the Great Vehicle. This then could result in their falling away from all Buddhist paths to liberation.

For an audience of this sort, it is probably best to stick to discussing any of the marvelous concepts and practices involved in the four truths of the Ārya, the eight-fold path, the thirty-seven wings of enlightenment, the twelve links of conditioned arising, or correct practice of calming-and-contemplation (*śamatha-vipaśyanā*) meditation.

111. The problem with discoursing on Śrāvaka-Vehicle doctrine to a

Mahāyāna audience is that those who have nominally dedicated themselves to the Bodhisattva Path but have not yet gained irreversible advancement in it may be moved to turn back to the individual-liberation path of the Śrāvaka Vehicle. In effect, they could thereby cheat themselves out of buddhahood while also cheating countless beings out of liberation whom they would otherwise have been able to bring across to liberation as they coursed along on the Bodhisattva Path.

When people come [to stay at a temple or monastery] as seekers, one must offer them instruction. If one delays this, refrains from imparting instruction, and then acquiesces in that person's falling into precept-breaking behavior, this is a bodhisattva practice error.

Where someone not yet ripe in faith and understanding is entrusted with important responsibilities, this too is an error.

112. This same list of "four bodhisattva errors" is also found in Nāgārjuna's treatise on the ten bodhisattva stages (*Daśabhūmika Vibhāṣā*). There, briefly commenting on his *śloka* line, "The bodhisattva should abandon the four types of bodhisattva errors," Nāgārjuna explains them as follows:

> "What are 'the four types of [bodhisattva] errors'? They are:
>
> 1) Where one discourses on extremely recondite dharmas for beings who are not vessels [appropriate for such teaching], this is an error.
>
> 2) Where one discourses on the Small Vehicle for those who delight in recondite, vast-scope dharmas, this is an error.
>
> 3) Where one is slightingly arrogant and disrespectful toward someone who engages in correct practice of the Path, is a holder of precepts, and who has a wholesome mind, this is an error.
>
> 4) Where we have someone who has not yet developed and has not yet become trustworthy, and yet one places trust in him—where one takes in an evil man who is a breaker of precepts, taking him to be a friend and someone who is good, this is an error."
>
> (十住毘婆沙論 / T26.1521.66b–c)

113. So long as one maintains strong resolve focused on highest bodhi, those fundamental doctrines and practice methods often more directly associated with the arhat or pratyekabuddha path may be viewed and *should* be viewed as essential foundational training for the bodhisattva practitioner. This is why Nāgārjuna makes a point of bringing up this matter repeatedly in this and other treatises.

114. Although the order of presentation differs in the commentary (numbers two and three are switched), this same list of four bodhisattva path practices is also found in Nāgārjuna's treatise on the ten bodhisattva stages (*Daśabhūmika Vibhāṣā*). Because Dharmagupta's rendering

is ambiguous, I present a translation of Nāgārjuna himself to corroborate the validity of this English rendering of Dharmagupta. Briefly commenting on his *śloka* line "The bodhisattva should cultivate the four types of bodhisattva path practices," Nāgārjuna explains them as follows:

"What are 'the four types of bodhisattva path practices'? They are:

1) One courses in uniform equality of thought toward all beings.

2) One instructs them all in the dharmas of goodness.

3) One discourses on Dharma equally for all beings.

4) One adopts the practice of right conduct [as a teaching] for all beings." (十住毘婆沙論 / T26.1521.66b–c)

For those who might find it useful, I briefly discuss and distinguish these ideas below:

1) "Uniform equality of thought" would require, for instance, that one consider a being coursing in evil no less worthy of kindness and compassionate concern than a person coursing in goodness.

2) "Uniform equality in discoursing on Dharma for all beings" would require, for instance, that, though the dharmas chosen in teaching would necessarily differ for the morally dissolute and those with refined spiritual sensibilities, they would both be deemed equally worthy of instruction in Dharma.

3) As for "establishing all beings in goodness," what comprises "goodness" in this context is defined by the path of the ten good karmic deeds (restraint from killing, stealing, sexual misconduct, lying, harsh speech, divisive speech, frivolous or lewd speech, covetousness, hatefulness, wrong views).

4) As for "influencing all beings to act in accordance with what is right," what is right in this context is defined by the degree to which any given act of body, mouth, or mind aligns itself with wisdom.

115. "The three types of merit-generating circumstances" (*puṇya-kriyā-vastu*)) were encountered before in both treatise (*śloka* 53) and commentary (to *śloka* 15). They are giving, moral virtue, and meditation.

116. These two *ślokas* constitute another case where Nāgārjuna is directly referencing a section from his treatise on the ten bodhisattva stages, this time speaking of "four kinds of genuine bodhisattvas" which are the opposite of "the four kinds of counterfeit bodhisattvas" treated in that other treatise. Here is the passage from the treatise on the ten bodhisattva stages where he comments on his *śloka* line which says, "In the Dharma of the Bodhisattvas, there are four kinds of counterfeit bodhisattvas":

"What are 'the four [kinds of counterfeit bodhisattvas]'? They are:

1) He covets offerings and does not esteem the Dharma.

2) He devotes his efforts solely to gaining a reputation and does not seek to develop meritorious qualities.

3) He seeks to ensure his own happiness and so pays no mind to the plight of other beings.

4) He covets and finds pleasure in a personal retinue and so finds no happiness in renunciative solitude." (十住毘婆沙論 / T26.1521.66c)

It is easy to see how this list of "four types of genuine bodhisattvas" is simply the opposite of Nāgārjuna's "four types of counterfeit bodhisattvas" described in the *Daśabhūmika Vibhāṣā*. Perhaps the least obvious case is the fourth wherein the genuine bodhisattva, rather than cultivating a retinue, renounces all of that in favor of working secretly at perfecting the karma of the Bodhisattva Path, dedicating all of that merit to the welfare of other beings.

117. In the traditional context "masters of Dharma" is a specific reference to learned monks discoursing on Dharma.

In his treatise on the ten bodhisattva stages, Nāgārjuna, commenting on this very list, adds:

"The bodhisattva who cherishes *anuttara-samyak-saṃbodhi* (the utmost, right, and perfect enlightenment) should draw close to, revere, and make offerings to four kinds of good spiritual friends and should withdraw far from four kinds of bad spiritual friends." (十住毘婆沙論 / T26.1521.66c)

118. There is no intention on the part of either Nāgārjuna or Bhikshu Vaśitva to cast any sort of aspersion on the refined moral qualities of these last two profiles. Although they advocate valid Buddhist individual-liberation paths taught by the Buddha himself, they would still be unsuitable as close companions for a bodhisattva because the inadequately-altruistic nature of their practice could exert a corrosive effect upon the determination of the bodhisattva practitioner.

Nāgārjuna's treatment of this list in his treatise on the ten grounds specifically refers to "the non-Buddhist Lokāyatas," whereas Dharmagupta translated it more generically as "those who are grounded in worldly treatises." (十住毘婆沙論 / T26.1521.67a)

119. Nāgārjuna comments on this in his treatise on the ten grounds:

"Therefore the bodhisattva should draw near to the four kinds of good spiritual friends and withdraw from the four kinds of bad spiritual friends. If the bodhisattva is able to withdraw from the four kinds of bad spiritual friends and draw near to the four kinds of good spiritual friends, then he will be able to gain four vast treasuries and will be able to step beyond all dharmas linked to demon-related matters. He will be able to generate an immeasurable amount of merit and will be able to exhaustively accumulate all good dharmas." (十住毘婆沙論 / T26.1521.67a)

120. In Nāgārjuna's comments on this list in his treatise on the ten bodhisattva grounds, one discovers a few clarifying details:

"Bodhisattvas have four vast treasuries of sublime Dharma....
The third is that one's mind remains free of the obstacle of anger felt toward one who teaches the Dharma.
The fourth is that one's mind does not become neglectful as one happily abides in an *araṇya* (i.e. in an isolated meditation hermitage)." (十住毘婆沙論 / T26.1521.67a)

120. The deep quietude of mind required for meditation practice or *dhāraṇī* practice is impossible to develop or maintain in the absence of the mental purity instilled by observance of moral precepts, hence Bhikshu Vaśitva's emphasis on the issue here.

The "Silver Lord" *dhāraṇī* mentioned by Bhikshu Vaśitva is still extant approximately 1500 years after its Sui Dynasty translation as the main topic of Chapter Eleven of the "Composite Edition" *Golden Light Sutra* (T16.664.386b5–11). I've so far been unable to locate the "Ocean Lord" *dhāraṇī*. Because *dhāraṇīs* often have several alternate names, it too could still be extant, just unrecognized for the time being.

Nāgārjuna discourses at length on *dhāraṇīs* in his commentary on the *Great Perfection of Wisdom Sutra*, most specifically in fascicle six and fascicle eight. Although I have translated all of that material, it is too long for inclusion here. Hence I simply present a detailed synopsis of the nature and uses of *dhāraṇīs* immediately below:

Dhāraṇīs are dharmas developed through spiritual cultivation by which one: a) retains good dharmas; b) blocks the arising of bad dharmas, and c) protects oneself from interference from negative spiritual forces which would otherwise destroy progress on the path of liberation.

In the popular imagination, *dhāraṇīs* are most usually associated with mantras (spiritually potent incantatory formulae), but that is not an entirely accurate perception, this because *dhāraṇīs* may in many instances be more closely identified with samādhis (deep meditative absorption states having very specific qualities and uses) or in come cases may not be particularly strongly associated with either mantras or samādhis.

I cite here a few examples of the "preservation," "suppression," and "protection" functions of dhāraṇīs:

a) Examples of good dharmas preserved by *dhāraṇīs* not just across

the course of years, but also across the course of many lifetimes: karmic merit; moral precepts; specific well-developed meditation abilities; vows to continually pursue particular bodhisattva deeds.

b) Examples of bad dharmas, the arising of which may be sponta-
neously suppressed through well-matured practice of *dhāraṇīs*: negative karmic propensities originating with patterned negativity in the
past; the arising of lust, hatred, delusion, or arrogance in response to
objective circumstances in the present; the ability to formulate and
carry through misguided or evil ideas such as hunting, drug-use,
hate-speech, elective office for fame-and-profit, and so forth.

c) Examples of "negative spiritual forces" which may be countered
through well-matured practice of *dhāraṇīs*: predatory criminals; char-
ismatic cult leaders motivated by avarice for power, money or sex;
powerfully negative mantras used by others for evil purposes; ghosts;
demons; physical attackers.

Finally, a note of caution: Use of *dhāraṇīs* for other than the highest
spiritual purposes is bound to be karmically disastrous. It is to be
avoided at all costs.

122. The six primary afflictions are covetousness, hatred, delusion, arrogance, doubtfulness, and wrong views.

123. A somewhat more full and hence clearer description of the eight indo-
lence-related circumstances may be found in the *Āgamas* (長阿含經;
T01.0001.55b–c).

124. "Emptiness" is not a thing in itself. It is simply an absence of something. And of precisely what is it an absence? It is an absence of any
inherent existence of some supposedly real entity over and above the
mere assemblage of conditions composing any given phenomenon.
That conception of some supposedly existent entity is really just an
idea associated with a mere name, period.

For instance: A "car" doesn't have any inherent existence of its own
above and beyond being just a simple temporary collection of metal,
rubber, glass, paint, and so forth upon which we have psychically
stamped the label "car" in an act of deluded imputation. Realizing the
emptiness of inherent existence of some supposedly real entity we
associate with the name "car" is simply recognizing this fact. There
isn't actually any "emptiness" above and beyond that.

Hence there is no "entity" called "emptiness" which one might
somehow be able to lay hold of through some yet more refined act of
enlightened perception. The inference of the text is that to imagine
such a thing and then tenaciously cling to such a concept is really a
type of metaphysical pathology worse even than thinking of the body
as constituting a "self."

125. One might well wonder what is meant by a "lantern wheel," a type

of offering seemingly not much present in modern Buddhist practice. Apparently it is a circular arrangement of lanterns set up and lit as an offering. There is a description in the Tripiṭaka of an offering of a "lantern wheel" inspired by a monk from India, this occurring in China during the Tang Dynasty and witnessed by the emperor from atop a city gate.

The lamp reached to a height of some two hundred feet (lit. "twenty *zhang*") and involved the lighting of five hundred lanterns made from gold and silver. Its appearance is described has having been "like a flowering tree."

This occurred at the very dawn of the eighth century, during the height of Buddhism's flourishing in China, by coincidence in the year Bodhiruci completed the new translation of the *Accumulation of Jewels Sutra* and in the same year that the famous *Avataṃsaka Sutra* patriarch, Fazang, passed away (712 CE).

Although the precise shape is not described, the name suggests that the pattern of lantern arrangement may well have been in the design of the eight-spoked wheel of Dharma emblematic of the eight-fold path. (佛祖統紀 / T49.2035.373a)

126. Emending the text to restore the water radical in the fifth character of the *śloka* (法), thus eliminating the nonsensical scribal error (去). The correctness of the emendation is corroborated by the Bhikshu Vaśitva commentary and common sense.

127. By "those already accomplished in learning," Nāgārjuna probably means not so much those in command of a sea of Dharma "facts" as those whose practice of the Path and wisdom have become well developed through wide-ranging study and integration of Dharma teachings.

Slighting beginning students of Dharma tends to beget future-life negative karmic consequences such as: dull-wittedness, inability to encounter right Dharma, inability to find a genuinely good guru, low social station, and being constantly mocked by others.

128. "Demons" are of many sorts. They include:

  1) The demons of one's own mind (path-eroding thought patterns, etc.).

  2) The demons of afflictions (desire, hatred, delusion, arrogance, doubt, wrong views, etc.).

  3) Mischievous ghosts.

  4) Sixth desire heaven deities.

  5) Also, figuratively speaking, unwholesome acquaintances devoid of ethics or spiritual interests who, intentionally or not, subtly undermine one's faith and practice.

"Knowledge rooted in evil" is a reference to whichever forms of either esoteric or mundane knowledge may influence one to deviate from right-Dharma Path practice in favor of pursuing objects of the desires (wealth, sex, fame, power, etc.).

As for "subduing demons," helpful prophylactic and counteractive stratagems in dealing with demons include:

1) Deeply sincere daily repentance purifications, even if only as brief reflections at the altar.

2) Daily refreshing of the three refuges and at least the four basic bodhisattva vows, even if only as brief reflections at the altar.

3) Prayers to buddhas and bodhisattvas for their assistance.

4) Mantras invoking the protective assistance of Dharma-protecting spirits.

5) Constant purity in upholding the moral precepts.

6) Intensely diligent dedication to meritorious works.

7) Avoidance of involvement in worldly entertainments and pastimes.

As noted earlier in these notes, Dhyāna Master Zhiyi devotes an entire chapter to the issue of demons, demonic karma, how they manifest, and how their influences may be countered in his *Essentials for Practicing Calming-and-Insight and Dhyāna Meditation* (修習止觀坐禪法要 / T46.1915.462a–473c). See Chapter Eight: "Recognizing the Work of Demons" (470b02–471b01). I have translated that entire work and am publishing it separately under the title *The Essentials of Buddhist Meditation*.

129. Bhikshu Vaśitva's long passage which I have enclosed in quotes (all but the last paragraph) is his free paraphrase quoting Medicine King Buddha in the "Dharma Offerings" chapter of the *Vimalakīrti Sutra*. (See T14.475.556b–c and T14.476.586b–c for the Kumārajīva and Xuanzang translations.)

130. Bhikshu Vaśitva continues here his paraphrasing of ideas from the Vimalakīrti Sutra. One will note here his encouragement to hew to the dictates of the four reliances with respect to Dharma together with his counsel on transcendence-based contemplation of the twelve links of conditioned co-production. It is through such an elevated perspective and perception that one is able to draw forth endless compassion as one works for the liberation of countless beings trapped in karma-bound suffering. It is through deep realization of this contemplation that one directly perceives the emptiness and intrinsically nirvāṇa-like nature of all that exists. It by resort to contemplations of this sort that the Great Vehicle is able to proclaim the possibility of "sublime existence" even as one works ceaselessly in the arena of cyclic births and deaths.

SOURCE TEXT VARIANT READINGS

Fasc.1 Variant Readings:

[0517006] 大隋南印度＝隋天竺【宋】【元】【明】【宮】＊

[0517007] 磨＝摩【宋】【元】【明】【宮】＊

[0517008] 〔覺〕－【宋】【元】【明】【宮】

[0517009] 是＝見【宋】【元】【明】

[0518001] 能無＝無能【宋】【元】【明】

[0518002] 住＝往【明】

[0519001] 囉＝邏【宋】＊【元】＊【明】＊

[0519002] 挐＝拏【宋】【元】【明】【宮】

[0519003] 亦＝示【宮】

[0519004] 險＝際【宋】【元】【明】【宮】

[0519005] 猗＝倚【宋】【元】【明】

繁
體
字

Fasc.1 Variant Readings:

[0517006] 大隋南印度＝隋天竺【宋】【元】【明】【宮】＊

[0517007] 磨＝摩【宋】【元】【明】【宮】＊

[0517008] 〔觉〕－【宋】【元】【明】【宮】

[0517009] 是＝见【宋】【元】【明】

[0518001] 能无＝无能【宋】【元】【明】

[0518002] 住＝往【明】

[0519001] 罗＝逻【宋】＊【元】＊【明】＊

[0519002] 挐＝拏【宋】【元】【明】【宮】

[0519003] 亦＝示【宮】

[0519004] 险＝际【宋】【元】【明】【宮】

[0519005] 猗＝倚【宋】【元】【明】

简
体
字

繁
體
字

［0520001］等＝知【宋】

［0520002］諸＝謂【宋】【元】【明】【宮】

［0520003］迦＋（偈）【宋】【元】【明】【宮】

［0520004］善＝若【宮】

［0521001］痰癊＝淡飲【宮】

［0521002］無＝起【宋】【元】【明】

Fasc.2 Variant Readings:

［0521003］覺＝坐菩提【宋】【元】【明】【宮】

［0522001］著＝者【元】

［0522002］於＝此【宋】【元】【明】【宮】

［0522003］曠＝廣【宋】【元】【明】

［0523001］（已）＋說【宋】【元】【明】【宮】

［0523002］（善）＋巧【宋】【元】【明】【宮】＊［＊ 1］

［0523003］思＋（惟）【宋】【元】【明】【宮】＊［＊ 1］

［0523004］趣＋（於）【宋】【元】【明】【宮】

简
体
字

［0520001］等＝知【宋】

［0520002］诸＝谓【宋】【元】【明】【宮】

［0520003］迦＋（偈）【宋】【元】【明】【宮】

［0520004］善＝若【宮】

［0521001］痰癊＝淡饮【宮】

［0521002］无＝起【宋】【元】【明】

Fasc.2 Variant Readings:

［0521003］觉＝坐菩提【宋】【元】【明】【宮】

［0522001］着＝者【元】

［0522002］于＝此【宋】【元】【明】【宮】

［0522003］旷＝广【宋】【元】【明】

［0523001］（已）＋说【宋】【元】【明】【宮】

［0523002］（善）＋巧【宋】【元】【明】【宮】＊［＊ 1］

［0523003］思＋（惟）【宋】【元】【明】【宮】＊［＊ 1］

［0523004］趣＋（于）【宋】【元】【明】【宮】

[0523005] 多＝滋【宋】【元】【明】【宮】

[0523006] 劣＝芳【宮】

[0523007] 在＝有【宮】

[0523008] 行＋（其）【宮】

[0523009] 魔＝應【宮】

[0523010] 六＝於【宮】

[0523011] 慜＝門【宮】

[0523012] 退墮＝下降【宋】【元】【明】【宮】

[0524001] 雜＝離【宋】【元】【明】【宮】

[0524002] （十）＋地【宋】【元】【明】【宮】

[0524003] 論＝輪【宋】【元】【明】【宮】

[0524004] 〔即〕－【宋】【元】【明】【宮】

[0524005] （即）＋令【宋】【元】【明】【宮】

[0524006] 悉＝慧【明】

[0524007] 〔一〕－【宋】【元】【明】【宮】

繁體字

[0523005] 多＝滋【宋】【元】【明】【宮】

[0523006] 劣＝芳【宮】

[0523007] 在＝有【宮】

[0523008] 行＋（其）【宮】

[0523009] 魔＝应【宮】

[0523010] 六＝于【宮】

[0523011] 慜＝门【宮】

[0523012] 退墮＝下降【宋】【元】【明】【宮】

[0524001] 杂＝离【宋】【元】【明】【宮】

[0524002] （十）＋地【宋】【元】【明】【宮】

[0524003] 论＝轮【宋】【元】【明】【宮】

[0524004] 〔即〕－【宋】【元】【明】【宮】

[0524005] （即）＋令【宋】【元】【明】【宮】

[0524006] 悉＝慧【明】

[0524007] 〔一〕－【宋】【元】【明】【宮】

简体字

繁體字

[0525001] 界＋（性）【宋】【元】【明】【宮】

[0525002] 瘶＝飲【宮】

[0525003] 顛＝癲【宋】【元】【明】【宮】

[0525004] 〔石白如貝〕－【宋】【元】【明】【宮】

[0525005] （石）＋玉【宋】【元】【明】【宮】

[0525006] 出＋（世）【宋】【元】【明】【宮】＊［＊ 1］

[0525007] 〔等諸資糧〕－【明】

Fasc.3 Variant Readings:

[0525008] （如）＋是【宋】【元】【明】【宮】

[0525009] 陀＝檀【宋】【元】【明】【宮】

[0525010] 濁＋（處）【宋】

[0525011] 處＋（攝）【宋】【元】【明】【宮】

[0526001] 魔＝癡【宋】【元】【明】【宮】

[0526002] 思＋（議）【宋】【元】【明】【宮】

[0526003] 功德＋（聞諸佛神變者於中諸佛

简体字

[0525001] 界＋（性）【宋】【元】【明】【宫】

[0525002] 瘶＝饮【宫】

[0525003] 颠＝癫【宋】【元】【明】【宫】

[0525004] 〔石白如贝〕－【宋】【元】【明】【宫】

[0525005] （石）＋玉【宋】【元】【明】【宫】

[0525006] 出＋（世）【宋】【元】【明】【宫】＊［＊ 1］

[0525007] 〔等诸资粮〕－【明】

Fasc.3 Variant Readings:

[0525008] （如）＋是【宋】【元】【明】【宫】

[0525009] 陀＝檀【宋】【元】【明】【宫】

[0525010] 浊＋（处）【宋】

[0525011] 处＋（摄）【宋】【元】【明】【宫】

[0526001] 魔＝痴【宋】【元】【明】【宫】

[0526002] 思＋（议）【宋】【元】【明】【宫】

[0526003] 功德＋（闻诸佛神变者于中诸佛

世尊為教）【宋】【元】【明】【宮】

　[0526004] 心勇＝若心勇悅【宋】【元】【明】【宮】

　[0526005] 共＋(彼)【宋】【元】【明】【宮】

　[0526006] 登＝行【宋】【元】【明】【宮】

　[0526007] 〔答〕－【宋】【元】【宮】

　[0527001] (是)＋念【宋】【元】【明】【宮】

　[0527002] 說＝脫【元】

　[0527003] 性＝住【宋】【元】【明】【宮】

　[0527004] (心)＋得【宋】【元】【明】【宮】

　[0527005] 復＝大【宋】【元】【明】【宮】

　[0527006] 心無分別心＝無復分別【宋】【元】【明】【宮】

　[0527007] 所＝有【宋】【元】【明】【宮】

　[0527008] (呰)＋毀【宋】【元】【明】【宮】

　[0527009] 說＝謂【宋】【元】【明】【宮】

　[0527010] 故＋(是為第一因緣)【宋】【元】【明】【宮】

繁
體
字

世尊为教）【宋】【元】【明】【宫】

　[0526004] 心勇＝若心勇悦【宋】【元】【明】【宫】

　[0526005] 共＋(彼)【宋】【元】【明】【宫】

　[0526006] 登＝行【宋】【元】【明】【宫】

　[0526007] 〔答〕－【宋】【元】【宫】

　[0527001] (是)＋念【宋】【元】【明】【宫】

　[0527002] 说＝脱【元】

　[0527003] 性＝住【宋】【元】【明】【宫】

　[0527004] (心)＋得【宋】【元】【明】【宫】

　[0527005] 复＝大【宋】【元】【明】【宫】

　[0527006] 心无分别心＝无复分别【宋】【元】【明】【宫】

　[0527007] 所＝有【宋】【元】【明】【宫】

　[0527008] (呰)＋毁【宋】【元】【明】【宫】

　[0527009] 说＝谓【宋】【元】【明】【宫】

　[0527010] 故＋(是为第一因缘)【宋】【元】【明】【宫】

简
体
字

繁體字

[0527011] （第）＋二【宋】【元】【明】【宮】

[0527012] 轉＋（是為第五因緣）【宋】【元】【明】【宮】

[0527013] （於）＋彼【宋】【元】【明】【宮】

[0527014] （於其）＋中間【宋】【元】【明】【宮】

[0527015] 說＝諸【宋】【元】【明】【宮】

[0528001] 〔生〕－【宋】【元】【明】【宮】

[0528002] 斷＋（取）【宋】【元】【明】【宮】

[0528003] 記＋（故）【宋】【元】【明】【宮】

[0528004] 名＝是【明】

[0529001] 〔無〕－【宋】【元】【明】【宮】

[0529002] 〔百〕－【明】

Fasc.4 Variant Readings:

[0529003] 與＝於【明】

[0529004] 常＝帝【元】

[0529005] 善＝菩【宮】

简体字

[0527011] （第）＋二【宋】【元】【明】【宮】

[0527012] 转＋（是为第五因缘）【宋】【元】【明】【宮】

[0527013] （于）＋彼【宋】【元】【明】【宮】

[0527014] （于其）＋中间【宋】【元】【明】【宮】

[0527015] 说＝诸【宋】【元】【明】【宮】

[0528001] 〔生〕－【宋】【元】【明】【宮】

[0528002] 断＋（取）【宋】【元】【明】【宮】

[0528003] 记＋（故）【宋】【元】【明】【宮】

[0528004] 名＝是【明】

[0529001] 〔无〕－【宋】【元】【明】【宮】

[0529002] 〔百〕－【明】

Fasc.4 Variant Readings:

[0529003] 与＝于【明】

[0529004] 常＝帝【元】

[0529005] 善＝菩【宮】

[0529006] 穌＝甦【明】

[0530001] 若＝共【元】【明】

[0530002] 囉＝羅【明】

[0530003] 為＋（耶）【宮】

[0530004] 田＝由【宋】【元】【宮】

[0530005] 田＝由【宋】【元】【明】【宮】

[0530006] 於＝佛【宋】【元】【明】

[0531001] 異＝界【宋】

[0531002] 最＝是【明】

[0531003] 證＝正【明】

[0531004] 髆＝膊【宋】【元】【明】【宮】＊

[0531005] 各＝若【明】

[0531006] 恒＝[口*恒]【宋】【元】【宮】＊　[＊　1]

[0531007] 摩＝磨【宋】【元】【明】【宮】

[0531008] 姜＝妾【宋】【元】【明】【宮】

繁體字

[0529006] 稣＝苏【明】

[0530001] 若＝共【元】【明】

[0530002] 罗＝罗【明】

[0530003] 为＋（耶）【宫】

[0530004] 田＝由【宋】【元】【宫】

[0530005] 田＝由【宋】【元】【明】【宫】

[0530006] 于＝佛【宋】【元】【明】

[0531001] 异＝界【宋】

[0531002] 最＝是【明】

[0531003] 证＝正【明】

[0531004] 髆＝膊【宋】【元】【明】【宫】＊

[0531005] 各＝若【明】

[0531006] 恒＝[口*恒]【宋】【元】【宫】＊　[＊　1]

[0531007] 摩＝磨【宋】【元】【明】【宫】

[0531008] 姜＝妾【宋】【元】【明】【宫】

简体字

繁
體
字

[0531009] 癩＝癘【宋】【元】【宮】

[0531010] 菩＝善【宋】

[0532001] 佛體＝方便【明】

[0532002] 位＝住【宋】【元】【明】【宮】

[0533001] 是涅槃性＝斷是涅槃【宋】【元】【明】【宮】

[0533002] 成就＝成熟【宋】【元】【明】【宮】

[0533003] 暖＝煖【明】

Fasc.5 Variant Readings:

[0533004] 及＝亦【明】

[0534001] 錍＝甲【明】＊

[0534002] 罾＝言【元】

[0534003] 竟＝寬【宋】【元】【明】【宮】

[0534004] 加＝跏【宋】【元】【明】【宮】

[0534005] 常＝當【宋】【元】【明】【宮】＊ ［＊ 1］

[0534006] 登＝證【宋】＊【元】＊【明】＊ ［＊ 1］

简
体
字

[0531009] 癩＝疬【宋】【元】【宫】

[0531010] 菩＝善【宋】

[0532001] 佛体＝方便【明】

[0532002] 位＝住【宋】【元】【明】【宫】

[0533001] 是涅盘性＝断是涅盘【宋】【元】【明】【宫】

[0533002] 成就＝成熟【宋】【元】【明】【宫】

[0533003] 暖＝煖【明】

Fasc.5 Variant Readings:

[0533004] 及＝亦【明】

[0534001] 钾＝甲【明】＊

[0534002] 罾＝言【元】

[0534003] 竟＝宽【宋】【元】【明】【宫】

[0534004] 加＝跏【宋】【元】【明】【宫】

[0534005] 常＝当【宋】【元】【明】【宫】＊ ［＊ 1］

[0534006] 登＝证【宋】＊【元】＊【明】＊ ［＊ 1］

[0534007] 尚＝常【宋】【元】【明】【宮】

[0535001] 正命＝正念【宋】【元】【明】【宮】

[0535002] 過＝造【宋】【元】【明】【宮】

[0535003] 從＝欲【明】

[0535004] 精勤＝精進【宋】【元】【明】【宮】

[0535005] 惑＝或【宋】【元】【明】【宮】

[0535006] 時到＝持倒【宋】【元】【明】【宮】

[0535007] 震＝振【宋】【元】【明】【宮】

[0535008] 然＝善【宋】【元】【明】【宮】

[0536001] 跟＝根【明】

[0536002] 速＝迷【宮】

[0536003] 慼＝戚【宋】【元】【明】【宮】

[0536004] 髀＝[跳-兆+坒]【宋】【宮】

[0536005] 邪＝耶【宋】【元】【明】【宮】

[0536006] 隋＝此【明】＊ [＊ 1]

繁體字

[0534007] 尚＝常【宋】【元】【明】【宮】

[0535001] 正命＝正念【宋】【元】【明】【宮】

[0535002] 过＝造【宋】【元】【明】【宮】

[0535003] 从＝欲【明】

[0535004] 精勤＝精进【宋】【元】【明】【宮】

[0535005] 惑＝或【宋】【元】【明】【宮】

[0535006] 时到＝持倒【宋】【元】【明】【宮】

[0535007] 震＝振【宋】【元】【明】【宮】

[0535008] 然＝善【宋】【元】【明】【宮】

[0536001] 跟＝根【明】

[0536002] 速＝迷【宮】

[0536003] 戚＝戚【宋】【元】【明】【宮】

[0536004] 髀＝[跳-兆+坒]【宋】【宮】

[0536005] 邪＝耶【宋】【元】【明】【宮】

[0536006] 隋＝此【明】＊ [＊ 1]

简体字

繁體字

[0536007] 上＝尚【宋】【元】【明】【宮】

[0536008] 印＝仰【宋】【元】【明】【宮】

[0536009] 髆＝膊【宋】【元】【明】【宮】

[0536010] 味＝朱【宋】

[0536011] 善＝言【宮】

[0536012] 雜＝離【宋】【元】【明】【宮】

[0536013] 和上＝和尚【宋】【元】【明】【宮】

[0536014] 兄＋（弟）【宋】【元】【明】【宮】

[0537001] 捷＝犍【元】【明】＊〔＊ 1〕

[0537002] 〔膁〕－【宋】【元】【明】【宮】

Fasc.6 Variant Readings:

[0538001] 和上＝和尚【宋】【元】【明】【宮】下同

[0539001] 苦＝若【元】

[0539002] 常＝當【明】

[0540001] 詣＝[(彥-文+(立--一))*(友-又+日)]【宮】

简体字

[0536007] 上＝尚【宋】【元】【明】【宫】

[0536008] 印＝仰【宋】【元】【明】【宫】

[0536009] 髆＝膊【宋】【元】【明】【宫】

[0536010] 味＝朱【宋】

[0536011] 善＝言【宫】

[0536012] 杂＝离【宋】【元】【明】【宫】

[0536013] 和上＝和尚【宋】【元】【明】【宫】

[0536014] 兄＋（弟）【宋】【元】【明】【宫】

[0537001] 捷＝犍【元】【明】＊〔＊ 1〕

[0537002] 〔膁〕－【宋】【元】【明】【宫】

Fasc.6 Variant Readings:

[0538001] 和上＝和尚【宋】【元】【明】【宫】下同

[0539001] 苦＝若【元】

[0539002] 常＝当【明】

[0540001] 诣＝[(彦-文+(立--一))*(友-又+日)]【宫】

［0540002］無量＋（種種）【宋】【元】【明】【宮】

［0540003］大＝天【宋】【元】【明】【宮】

［0540004］報＝樂【宋】【元】【明】【宮】

［0541001］恒＝[口*怛]【宋】【元】【明】【宮】

［0541002］如＝知【宋】【元】【明】【宮】

［0541003］擇＝釋【宮】

［0541004］忍＝思【宋】【元】【明】

繁體字

［0540002］无量＋（种种）【宋】【元】【明】【宮】

［0540003］大＝天【宋】【元】【明】【宮】

［0540004］报＝乐【宋】【元】【明】【宮】

［0541001］恒＝[口*怛]【宋】【元】【明】【宮】

［0541002］如＝知【宋】【元】【明】【宮】

［0541003］择＝释【宮】

［0541004］忍＝思【宋】【元】【明】

简体字

About the Translator

Bhikshu Dharmamitra (ordination name "Heng Shou" – 釋恆授) is a Chinese-tradition translator-monk and one of the early American disciples (since 1968) of the late Weiyang Ch'an patriarch, Dharma teacher, and exegete, the Venerable Master Hsuan Hua (宣化上人). He has a total of 23 years in robes during two periods as a monastic (1969–1975; 1991 to present).

Dharmamitra's principal educational foundations as a translator lie in four years of intensive monastic training and Chinese-language study of classic Mahāyāna texts in a small-group setting under Master Hua from 1968–1972, undergraduate Chinese language study at Portland State University, a year of intensive one-on-one Classical Chinese study at the Fu Jen University Language Center near Taipei, and two years at the University of Washington's School of Asian Languages and Literature (1988–90).

Since taking robes again under Master Hua in 1991, Dharmamitra has devoted his energies primarily to study and translation of classic Mahāyāna texts with a special interest in works by Ārya Nāgārjuna and related authors. To date, he has translated a dozen important texts, most of which are slated for publication by Kalavinka Press.

Kalavinka Buddhist Classics Title List

Meditation Instruction Texts

The Essentials of Buddhist Meditation
A marvelously complete classic *śamathā-vipaśyanā* (calming-and-insight) meditation manual. By Tiantai Śramaṇa Zhiyi (538–597 CE).

Six Gates to the Sublime
The earliest Indian Buddhist meditation method explaining th essentials of breath and calming-and-insight meditation. By Śramaṇa Zhiyi.

Bodhisattva Path Texts

Nāgārjuna on the Six Perfections
Chapters 17–30 of Ārya Nāgārjuna's *Mahāprājñāpāramitā Upadeśa*.

Marvelous Stories from the Perfection of Wisdom
130 stories from Ārya Nāgārjuna's *Mahāprājñāpāramitā Upadeśa*.

A Strand of Dharma Jewels (Ārya Nāgārjuna's *Ratnāvalī*)
The earliest extant edition, translated by Paramārtha: *ca* 550 CE

Nāgārjuna's Guide to the Bodhisattva Path
The *Bodhisaṃbhāra Treatise* with abridged Vaśitva commentary.

The Bodhisaṃbhāra Treatise Commentary
The complete exegesis by the Indian Bhikshu Vaśitva (*ca* 300–500 CE).

Letter from a Friend - The Three Earliest Editions
The earliest extant editions of Ārya Nāgārjuna's *Suhṛlekkha*:
Translated by Tripiṭaka Master Guṇavarman   (*ca* 425 CE)
Translated by Tripiṭaka Master Saṅghavarman   (*ca* 450 CE)
Translated by Tripiṭaka Master Yijing   (*ca* 675 CE)

Resolve-for-Enlightenment Texts

On Generating the Resolve to Become a Buddha
On the Resolve to Become a Buddha by Ārya Nāgārjuna
Exhortation to Resolve on Buddhahood by Patriarch Sheng'an Shixian
Exhortation to Resolve on Buddhahood by the Tang Literatus, Peixiu

Vasubandhu's Treatise on the Bodhisattva Vow
By Vasubandhu Bodhisattva (*ca* 300 CE)

*All Kalavinka Press translations include facing-page source text.